MW01258492

THE
REVIVALIST'S
DEVOTIONAL

OTHER BOOKS BY JENNIFER LECLAIRE

The Prophet's Devotional

The Making of a Watchman

The End Times Watchman

The Intercessor's Devotional

The Next Great Move of God

Mornings with the Holy Spirit

Victory Decrees

Walking in Your Prophetic Destiny

JENNIFER LECLAIRE

THE
REVIVALIST'S
DEVOTIONAL

365 DAILY IGNITIONS
THAT EQUIP YOU TO CARRY
REVIVAL FIRE IN THE NATIONS

© Copyright 2023 Jennifer LeClaire

All rights reserved. This book is protected by the copyright laws of the United States of America. This book may not be copied or reprinted for commercial gain or profit. The use of short quotations or occasional page copying for personal or group study is permitted and encouraged. Permission will be granted upon request. Unless otherwise identified, Scripture quotations are taken from the Holy Bible, New Living Translation, copyright 1996, 2004, 2015. Used by permission of Tyndale House Publishers., Wheaton, Illinois 60189. All rights reserved. Scripture quotations marked NKJV are taken from the New King James Version. Copyright © 1982 by Thomas Nelson, Inc. Used by permission. All rights reserved. Scripture quotations marked NIV are taken from the HOLY BIBLE, NEW INTERNATIONAL VERSION®, Copyright © 1973, 1978, 1984, 2011 International Bible Society. Used by permission of Zondervan. All rights reserved. Scripture quotations marked TPT are taken from *The Passion Translation*, Copyright © 2017, 2018, 2020 by Passion & Fire Ministries, Inc., www.thepassiontranslation.com. Used by permission of BroadStreet Publishing Group, LLC, Racine, Wisconsin, USA. All rights reserved. Scripture quotations marked AMPC are taken from the Amplified® Bible, Classic Edition, Copyright © 1954, 1958, 1962, 1964, 1965, 1987 by The Lockman Foundation. All rights reserved. Used by permission. Scripture quotations marked AMP are taken from the Amplified® Bible, Copyright © 2015 by The Lockman Foundation, La Habra, CA 90631. All rights reserved. Used by permission. Scripture quotations marked KJV are taken from the King James Version. Scripture quotations marked ESV are taken from The Holy Bible, English Standard Version® (ESV®), copyright © 2001 by Crossway, a publishing ministry of Good News Publishers. Used by permission. All rights reserved. Scripture quotations marked MEV are taken from *The Holy Bible, Modern English Version*. Copyright © 2014 by Military Bible Association. Published and distributed by Charisma House. All rights reserved. Used by permission. Scripture quotations marked MSG are taken from *The Message*. Copyright © 1993, 1994, 1995, 1996, 2000, 2001, 2002. Used by permission of NavPress Publishing Group. Scripture quotations marked NASB are taken from the NEW AMERICAN STANDARD BIBLE®, Copyright © 1960,1962,1963,1968,1971,1972,1973,1975,1977,1995 by The Lockman Foundation. Used by permission. Scripture quotations marked CEV are taken from the Contemporary English Version Copyright © 1995 by the American Bible Society, New York, NY. All rights reserved. Scripture quotations marked GW are taken from

AWAKENING MEDIA, INC.

P.O. Box 30563, Ft. Lauderdale, FL 33303

Awakening Your Spirit

This book and all other Awakening Media and Jennifer LeClaire books are available at www.jenniferleclaire.org and online book sellers.

Cover design by: Ina Neeleman

For more information on foreign distributors, message jenniferleclaire.org/contact. Reach us on the Internet: www.jenniferleclaire.org

ISBN: 9781949465136

For Worldwide Distribution, Printed in the U.S.A.

DEDICATION

The Revivalist's Devotional is dedicated to modern-day revivalists who are burning to see a Great Awakening in their nation, remaining undaunted by the doom and gloom and ready to stand and pray, preach, teach, decree and declare God's will done in the earth. I applaud every well-digger who refuses to give up and give in though revival tarries. I stand with every revival-minded apostle, prophet, evangelist, pastor and teacher who is equipping the saints to contend for revival. You are champions in this hour.

CONTENTS

INTRODUCTION

I'll always remember the night I stepped into a Florida Panhandle church that was experiencing full-blown revival. A pastor from the region invited me to visit during what was known in 2014 as the Gulf Stream Revival. I didn't waste any time making my way up the Sunshine State.

Being a journalist by trade, I stood back and watched as the preacher emphatically declared, "If you need a healing, run circles around the sanctuary." I watched, trying to discern what was going on. Was it hype? Was it the Holy Spirit? I had never been in an atmosphere like that. Indeed, I had never seen anything like it. The hunger in the room had reached a boiling point.

After one lady passed me a second time, the Holy Spirit spoke these attention-getting words to my heart, "I've called you to be a participant in revival, not just an observer of it." Those words forced doubt to flee from me. And at the sound of His voice, I started running circles round the sanctuary with the rest of them—even though I didn't need a healing.

That night awakened in me a newfound hunger for transforming revival. Not long after that night, I had a dream in which Dutch Sheets shared advice with me about the next step in my journey—and weeks later, I heard Dutch's appeal-to-heaven message for the first time.

I've been contending for revival in every way, shape and form I can employ for many years now. I've met plenty of hungry believers along the way who are also waging war with the prophecies over their cities, states and nations, fasting, and crying out day and night.

I'm sober. My eyes are wide open. I see the conditions in nations. I hear the cries of legitimate prophetic voices warning us of the destruction they see in the days ahead—some of which has already occurred since 2014. But I believe there is evidence of a Great Awakening on the horizon.

Yes, I do believe God is disciplining America—and other nations. Yes, I do believe that we're reaping what we've sown—the abortion, the immorality, the idolatry, the racism and more. Yes, I do believe things are going to get worse before they get better as of the time of this writing in 2023. But I absolutely, positively refuse to buy into the notion that God is not going to pour out His Spirit once again. I reject the idea that widespread transforming revival that sees a great harvest of souls is impossible in the nations.

Yes, I believe God sends warnings through prophets and watchmen. I, too, have received many such warnings from His Spirit. I pray over them and trumpet them with clarity, humility and weeping—but always with hope that God can relent if we stand in the gap and continue to walk in 2 Chronicles 7:14, even when it looks like nothing is happening.

I believe we need to lift up our voices and speak the hard truths so that we don't end up with the blood of lost souls on our hands. But I refuse to lose hope for a Third Great Awakening. Even Isaiah, who offered plenty of prophetic words about judgment, goes down in Bible history as the prophet of hope.

I see rising as part of the great end times intercessory army to prepare the way of the Lord. They are decreeing and declaring revival—and making an appeal to heaven for awakening. I see hope rising in communities where believers are allowed to express what they sense the Lord is saying and doing. God is a God of hope even in the midst of what appears to be dark clouds all around us.

I pray this book stirs your heart, challenges your soul, and inspires your mouth to pray without ceasing until God rends the heavens, pours out His Spirit and brings a history-making revival in your city. If you have a heart for prayer, join my prayer family, Awakening Prayer Hubs. You can find out more about our vision online at www.awakeningprayerhubs.com.

JANUARY

"Have you noticed how much praying for revival has been going on of late—and how little revival has resulted? I believe the problem is that we have been trying to substitute praying for obeying, and it simply will not work." —A.W. Tozer

JANUARY 1

Our Covenant-Keeping God

"My covenant I will not break, nor alter the word that has gone out of My lips" (Psalm 89:34).

On April 21, 2007, the Lord woke me up at midnight to share His heart with me about my nation. This prophecy has shaped my entire ministry. I hope it will touch your heart, as I believe the Holy Spirit wants to bring an awakening to your nation as well as mine. I heard the Lord say:

"There is a Great Awakening coming to this nation. For I have heard your cries and I long to heal your land. I am a covenant God, and I will not forget the covenant I made with your founding forefathers. Yes, there will be a shaking, but the foundations will not crack, and they will not crumble. Only those things which can be shaken will be shaken that the sin in the land may be laid bare.

"Repentance. I require repentance from My people who have through the generations allowed the enemy to take ground in this nation. I require repentance for the abortions and for the prayerlessness. I require repentance for the apathy and for the idolatry. You shall have no other gods before me. I am indeed the God of America."

God is a God of covenant. Perhaps your nation didn't cut covenant with Him. Perhaps you are in a nation where Christians are the minority. Don't let that move you. God has a covenant with you, and He hears and answers your prayers for His will to be done in your city and nation. Stand in the gap and pray for revival and awakening. Your city is worth the fight.

As I write these words, many nations around the world are in natural and spiritual crises. Indeed, it will take an intervention from God to avoid disaster. Although "man" can't solve the problems in my nation or yours, God can move in the midst of the darkest nations and among the hardest hearts to bring revival and awakening. He is, after all, Almighty.

As Jeremiah the prophet said "Ah, Lord God! Behold, You have made the heavens and the earth by Your great power and outstretched arm. There is nothing too hard for You" (Jer. 32:17). Believe that and pray on.

— *Prayer* —

Father, in the name of Jesus, I put my hope in our covenant. Help me to stand in the gap for my city and nation, knowing that You hear and answer prayers. Remind me when I get weary that my prayers are not in vain.

Great Faith for a Great Awakening

"I have not found such great faith, not even in Israel" (Matthew 8:10).

God wants you to build your faith for a Great Awakening in your nation. I am believing for my nation, and I encourage you to believe for yours. Continuing on from the prophetic word in yesterday's devotion, I heard the Lord say:

"Yes, there is a Great Awakening coming to this nation. I am the Author of it, and I will bring it to pass. Just turn from your wicked ways and humble yourselves. Stand in the gap and make up the hedge. I am the Lord, and I am a Warrior. I will not leave or forsake this country. I will fight through you and with you to regain what has been lost.

"Be encouraged now because as you go forth boldly with My Word and My Spirit there will be the sound of truth and it will prevail in the land. Speak boldly and clearly and watch as the mighty men arise to take their positions on the wall and in the churches and in the marketplaces. For I am raising up deliverers and reformers in this generation who will not shrink back at the challenge that is coming in the days ahead.

"Yes, it will grow darker before My light shines brightly from this nation again. But the light has not been extinguished and will not be extinguished. The time to rise up is now. I am calling you to war. I am calling you to repentance. I am calling you to My side. I am the Captain of the hosts. I am calling you to victory. I am calling you to destiny. Will you answer?"

Our answer needs to be a resounding "yes, Lord!" Our heart posture needs to be, "Here I am, Lord. Send me!" (see Is. 6:8). We need to go into realms of prayer and break down strongholds that hold back revival and awakening. We need to go into hard territories and prayer walk without ceasing. We need to go where God sends us and preach Jesus. Are you willing?

— *Prayer* —

Father, in the name of Jesus, I am willing. Here I am. Send me. Use me as an agent of awakening in my city and in my nation. Send me into deep intercession, even travail, for the lost souls in my region. Help me to share Jesus with the conviction that He is alive, and He saves. Use me as an agent of awakening.

JANUARY 3

Waking Up the Sleeping Giant

"Awake, you who sleep, arise from the dead, and Christ will give you light" (Ephesians 5:14).

The church—AKA the sleeping giant—needs to wake up. If the church were being the church, perhaps we wouldn't face as many societal problems. Perhaps our churches wouldn't be half-empty on Sunday mornings. We need to wake up personally so we can be agents of corporate awakening in our city.

What if we all lived the Sermon on the Mount lifestyle? The Sermon on the Mount speaks against murder, which is what abortion really is. The Sermon on the Mount speaks against sexual immorality. The Sermon on the Mount speaks against divorce. But many in the church are ignoring the Sermon on the Mount's Christianity 101 lessons. Many in the church look, think, and act too much like the world.

Christians are having abortions. Christians are committing adultery. Christians are fornicating. Christians are getting divorced. Lord, help us!

At the same time, the Sermon on the Mount speaks to giving to the needy, prayer and fasting. I can't prove it with hard numbers, but I submit to you it's likely that most Christians aren't giving to the poor. It's probable that most Christians aren't praying for their nation. I'm sure most Christians aren't fasting. Many Christians are not serving as salt and the light. And that's one reason why it's getting darker.

Adding insult to this injurious lifestyle, some Christians declare prayer rallies and solemn assemblies are useless. I believe the greatest sin of the church is prayerlessness. The government of the world happens in the prayer rooms. Yet some are too busy feeding their souls on worldly entertainment to meet God at the altar.

Nations are in crisis. Nations will continue growing darker until people turn to God. The good news is when we do, we'll see a Great Awakening and many souls will come into the Kingdom. I'm blowing the trumpet. I'm sounding the alarm. There is hope for the nations and that hope lies in the Body of Christ responding to Christ's commanded to pray and "Occupy until I come" (see Luke 19:13).

— *Prayer* —

Father, in the name of Jesus, would You wake up the sleeping giant? Would You shake the church free from complacency? Would You set Your bride on fire for souls? Would You help me live the Sermon on the Mount Lifestyle? Help me be the salt and the light that makes people thirsty for Jesus.

Revival Strategists Rising

"The plans of the diligent lead surely to abundance and advantage"
(Proverbs 2:15).

God is looking for a new breed of revival strategists in this hour. See, yesterday's revival doesn't look like tomorrow's revival and the strategy that worked in the past may not work in the future. While prayer is the baseline for any and every revival, the strategy for revival in one church may be different than in another church, city, region, or nation.

I heard the Lord say, "I am giving my red-hot revivalists strategies to see revival in churches, cities, and territories. I am pouring our prayer strategies and offering blueprints to build revival centers in the nations. I am looking for those who will set aside the old wineskin and adopt new treasures from My heart. I am looking for those who are willing to look foolish in the eyes of the church in order to win many souls into My Kingdom."

Are you a revival strategist? A strategist is a person skilled in strategy. Strategy is a careful plan toward a goal. For example, God's strategy for salvation is Jesus Christ. What is God's strategy for revival in your life or your city or your church? Before you pray for revival, pray for a strategy for revival, which may include a prayer strategy, a spiritual warfare strategy, a worship strategy, a teaching strategy and so on.

Why do you need a strategy? Because God's strategy outlines God's best path to revival—and around enemy resistance. Every goal needs a strategy. With revival as our goal, our strategy defines and clarifies the mission, helps others pull in the same direction, and offers insight into how to overcome the obstacles of revival, including the world, the flesh and the devil.

Proverbs 24:6 (*The Message*) tells us "Strategic planning is the key to warfare." Make no mistake, a war will rise up against the revival—and even after revival manifests the enemy will try to pour water on the fire. What's your revival strategy?

— *Prayer* —

Father, in the name of Jesus, would You make me a revival strategist? Help me receive Your specific instructions for bringing revival to my city—and stewarding the revival You bring. Help me see the pathway to revival clearly and the strategy for spreading the revival fire.

Is This Why Revival Tarries?

"Now I urge you, brethren, note those who cause divisions and offenses, contrary to the doctrine which you learned, and avoid them" (Romans 16:17).

Year after year I hear the same prayers rising to heaven from many denominations, flows and camps across the body of Christ: "God, pour out your Spirit. Send revival!"

Yet, that fervent prayer seems to be largely ineffective. Those prayers seem to go unanswered most of the time. What gives? Doesn't God want to send revival? Doesn't God want to see the church wake up and rise up? Doesn't God want to see the flood of souls come into the Kingdom that results from an awakening?

Why won't God answer our intercessory prayers? Doesn't James 5:16 (AMP) say, "The earnest (heartfelt, continued) prayer of a righteous man makes tremendous power available [dynamic in its working]?"

Are our prayers not heartfelt enough? The prayers for revival I hear sound heartfelt to me. Do we lack persistence? Not so that I can tell. Do we lack righteousness? Not in Christ. Does God lack the power to bring revival to our nation? Of course not! So, what gives?

I believe the culprit is division, a lack of unity—the absence of harmony. I've long noticed a lack of unity in the Body of Christ, especially in my region of South Florida. It has long grieved me. But the Holy Spirit has recently given me a keen awareness of the gravity of this lack of harmony. It troubles me deep in my spirit—and if it troubles me, I can only imagine how it troubles the Spirit of God.

Many, if not most, believe other denominations are flowing in some sort of error, whether that's speaking in tongues, baptizing in the name of Jesus only rather than in the name of the Father, Son and Holy Ghost, how to receive salvation or the path to heaven, whether or not women can preach or some other doctrine. You know me. If there's major delusions going on, I call it out. But there are some issues over which it's not worth making a mountain out of a molehill. There are open-handed differences and closed-handed differences. Let's unify around Jesus!

— *Prayer* —

Father, in the name of Jesus, would You forgive me for engaging in petty, frivolous arguments that have no eternal value, but rather skew my effectiveness in prayer? Help me walk in peace with people who have minor differences. Help me to embrace the diversity in the true Body of Christ.

What Revival Isn't...

"But seek first the kingdom of God and His righteousness, and all these things shall be added to you" (Matthew 6:33).

Before we look at what revival is, let's look at the other side of the question: What revival isn't. Many people have wrong perspectives and paradigms of revival. To be sure, the word "revival" is overused to the point that many believers are skeptics and even critics of true outpourings.

Revival isn't a series of tent meetings, even though we've seen revivals in history under massive tents. Revival it not a simple outpouring or a visitation, even though revival often starts with an outpouring or visitation. Revival isn't a mere increase in church attendance, even though revival often results in increased church attendance. Indeed, the word "revival" is overused.

Revival isn't simply signs, wonders and miracles, even though signs, wonders and miracles often manifest during revivals. Revival isn't an evangelistic crusade, although evangelistic crusades can be a catalyst for revival. Revival isn't emotionalism, even though revivals can come with great emotion. The word "revival" is overused.

Revival isn't a feeling, a goosebump, or a meeting with exuberant worship or bold preaching, though revival can include all of these. Charles Finney, a key figure in the Second Great Awakening once said, "There can be no revival when Mr. Amen and Mr. Wet-Eyes are not found in the audience." Still, the word "revival" is overused.

Revival isn't a prayerless endeavor. By contrast, prayer has preceded every revival known to mankind. Leonard Ravenhill, author of *Why Revival Tarries*, wrote, "The man who can get believers to praying would, under God, usher in the greatest revival that the world has ever known." No, all of these are welcomed in the four walls of the church, but these markers alone don't make revival.

Revival is an overused term and an underseen reality. When you see true revival, you will know it. Let's not settle for what some call revival. Let's press in for the authentic move of God that brings true and lasting change.

— *Prayer* —

Father, in the name of Jesus, help me not to get caught up in revival hype. Help me not to mislabel revival or settle for less than what You have planned. Help me to be a revival-carrier in the earth, urging people to pray, pressing into Your presence, and surrendering my heart as a willing vessel.

What Is Revival, Really?

"Let my prayer be set before You as incense, the lifting up of my hands as the evening sacrifice" (Psalm 141:2).

If you ask ten people what revival is, you might get ten different answers. Scripture doesn't actually use the word "revival"—but it does speak of reviving. Revival is more than a series of summer meetings.

In *The Sword and the Trowel*, Charles H. Spurgeon wrote this about revival: "We are constantly speaking about and praying for a 'revival;' would it not be as well to know what we mean by it? Of the Samaritans our Lord said, 'Ye worship ye know not what,' let him not have to say to us, 'Ye know not what ye ask.'

"The word 'revive' wears its meaning upon its forehead; it is from the Latin, and may be interpreted thus—to live again, to receive again a life which has almost expired; to rekindle into a flame the vital spark which was nearly extinguished ... When Christians are revived they live more consistently, they make their homes more holy and more happy, and this leads the ungodly to envy them, and to enquire after their secret."

Charles Finney, a leader in the Second Great Awakening, said, "A revival is nothing else than a new beginning of obedience to God. Just as in the case of a converted sinner, the first step is a deep repentance, a breaking down of heart, a getting down into the dust before God, with deep humility, and forsaking of sin."

"In the history of the church, the term revival in its most biblical sense has meant a sovereign work of God in which the whole region of many churches, many Christians has been lifted out of spiritual indifference and worldliness into conviction of sin, earnest desires for more of Christ and his word, boldness in witness, purity of life, lots of conversions, joyful worship, renewed commitment to missions," says New Testament scholar John Piper. "You feel God has moved here."

— *Prayer* —

Father, in the name of Jesus, would You help me understand the dimensions and purposes of prayer by Your Spirit, which are vaster than I can comprehend with my finite mind alone? Would You share with me Your definition of prayer? Let a revelation of prayer power inspire me to pray more and more.

When We Need Revival

"You, who have shown me great and severe troubles, shall revive me again, and bring me up again from the depths of the earth" (Psalm 71:20).

When do we need revival? We need revival when we've strayed from our first love. Jesus told the church at Ephesus, "Nevertheless I have this against you, that you have left your first love. Remember therefore from where you have fallen; repent and do the first works, or else I will come to you quickly and remove your lampstand from its place—unless you repent" (Rev. 2:4-5).

When do we need revival? We need revival when we're more concerned with what people think than what God thinks. When we love the things of the world more than the things of the Spirit. When we would rather earn money at work than sow into the Kingdom. When we are stingy toward God instead of extravagant toward Him.

When do we need revival? We need revival when we'd rather binge-watch TV than read the Bible and pray. When we talk more about entertainment than the Word of God. When we know the Word but don't do the Word. When church fellowships are bigger than our prayer meetings. When we don't pray fervently.

When do we need revival? We need revival when we don't have the joy of the Lord. When we don't share our faith with the lost or have a burden for the lost. When we don't have the fear of the Lord. When we don't weep over our sin and wage war against it. When we don't want to go to church. When we don't engage in worship. When we're content with Christianity as usual.

When do we need revival? We need revival when we've let the fire on the altar of our heart go out. Oh, Lord, may the fire on Your altar never go out, but burn and shine for the glory of God.

— *Prayer* —

Father, in the name of Jesus, would You help me discern when I need personal revival, when my church needs revival, and when my denomination needs revival so I can respond appropriately? I know revival starts with me, so help me stay in a self-examining heart posture.

A Revival of the Fear of the Lord

"Therefore you shall keep the commandments of the Lord your God, to walk in His ways and to fear Him" (Deuteronomy 8:6).

Every revivalist needs to cultivate a healthy fear of the Lord. Let's define the fear of the Lord by looking at some Greek and Hebrew words before we pray.

One definition of the Hebrew word *yare* means "to fear, to respect, to reverence." The Greek word *phobos* can be translated "reverential fear." *Vine's Complete Expository Dictionary* defines it as "not a mere 'fear' of His power and righteous retribution, but a wholesome dread of displeasing Him."

The fear of the Lord is to hate evil (see Prov. 8:13). The fear of the Lord is the beginning of wisdom (see Prov. 9:10). The fear of the Lord is the beginning of knowledge (see Prov. 1:7). The secret of the Lord is with those who fear Him (see Ps. 25:14). There is no want for them who fear Him (see Ps. 34:9). In the fear of the Lord, there is strong confidence and a fountain of life (see Prov. 14:26-27). By the fear of the Lord are riches, honor and life (see Prov. 22:4).

The fear of the Lord marked the early church in revival. Acts 9:31 tells us that "the churches throughout all Judea and Galilee and Samaria had peace and were built up. And walking in the fear of the Lord and in the comfort of the Holy Spirit, they were multiplied."

We yearn to see signs, wonders and miracles manifest today as they did in the Book of Acts, don't we? But are we willing to pay the price the early church paid? Are we willing to die to self? Are we willing to relinquish control to the Holy Spirit so He can move like He wants to move? Are we willing to repent for the character flaws that hold us back? Are we willing to walk in love and unity with true believers who don't believe exactly the same as we do?

When we do, we're on our way to revival.

— Prayer —

Father, in the name of Jesus, would You give me the spirit of the fear of the Lord? Help me never to take Your presence or Your commands for granted. Help me to model what walking in the fear of the Lord looks like in daily life. Help me to be quick to repent when I stumble.

Evan Robert's Personal Revival Methods

"For it is God who works in you both to will and to do for His good pleasure" (Philippians 2:13).

What's your revival method? In other words, how do you go about seeking revival? A young Evan Roberts had a way about him—and that way led to revival. These are the words of Roberts, the leader of the Welsh Revival in 1904-1905:

"I have been asked concerning my methods. I have none. I never prepare the words I shall speak. I leave all that to Him. I am not the source of this revival. I am only one agent in what is growing to be a multitude. I am not moving men's hearts and changing men's lives; not I, but 'God worketh in me.'

"I have found what is, in my belief, the highest kind of Christianity. I desire to give my life, which is all I have to give, to helping others to find it also. Many have already found it, thank God, and many more are finding it through them.

"This is my work as He has pointed it out to me. His Spirit came to me one night, when upon my knees I asked Him for guidance, and five months later I was baptized with the Spirit. He has led me as He will lead all those who, conscious of their human weakness, lean upon Him as children upon a father.

"I know that the work which has been done through me is not due to any human ability that I possess. It is His work and to His Glory. 'I was not ever thus, nor prayed that Thou should'st lead me on. I loved to choose and see my path, but now lead Thou me on.'

"I desire nothing but to be allowed to continue this work that has begun. 'The Lord is my Shepherd. I fear no want.' All things necessary He has provided, and will provide. I wish no personal following, only the world for Christ."

— *Prayer* —

Father, in the name of Jesus, would You work in me to will and to do Your good pleasure? Point out to me the revival works I should pursue for Your glory. Lead me on the revival path You have purposed for me. I want to be effective in stirring hearts to pursue You.

JANUARY 11

Making Your Revival Mark

"She opens her mouth with wisdom, and on her tongue is the law of kindness" (Proverbs 31:26).

Evan Roberts is widely known as the leader of the Welsh Revival. His prayer meeting in Loughor, South Wales in which he cried out, "Bend me!" has been well documented. But fewer know about the nineteen-year-old girl whose testimony served as the fire starter—the ignition of revival.

Roberts himself testifies: "The story of the very first outbreak of the revival traces it to the trembling utterance of a poor Welsh girl, who, at a meeting in a Cardigan village, was the first to rise and testify, 'If no one else will, then I must say that I love the Lord Jesus Christ with all my heart.'"

Florrie Evan's declaration was in response to a question posed after a church service at a Calvinistic Methodist Chapel to a group of teenagers and young adults: "What does the Lord Jesus Christ mean to you?" Her sincere answer set hearts ablaze. That poor Welsh girl then became part of Roberts' team of traveling evangelists.

Florrie was known for her uncompromising faith. She preached, prayed and prophesied boldly. She shared her testimony passionately. She co-labored with Christ through tears to help people see their need for a Savior. As a result, Holy Spirit's conviction fell, and many turned to Christ.

Florrie challenged the status quo of revivalists in her day. In other words, we didn't see many women out on the revival circuits. But that didn't stop her. As a matter of fact, after the Welsh revival waned, she continued her work in other parts of the world.

When Florrie heard about a revival in India's Khasi Hills, she applied to serve the Foreign Mission of the Calvinistic Methodists there. She headed to Karachi and served as a nurse until she was too sick to continue. Few know what happened to her between that time and the day she passed away in 1967. But she left her mark on revival history. You can, too!

— *Prayer* —

Father, in the name of Jesus, help me cultivate a heartfelt love for You that burns in my soul and compels me to share about Your saving grace with others. Give me an anointing to preach, pray and prophesy—and lay down my life for the cause of true revival that wins souls.

Seven Signs You Need Personal Revival

"No one can serve two masters...." (Matthew 6:24).

The late A.W. Tozer, a pastor, author, magazine editor, and spiritual mentor to many, encouraged believers to consider seven points of self-discovery that speak to our spiritual health.

1. What we want most: What do you want more than anything? In Psalm 27:4. David said, "One thing I have desired of the Lord, that will I seek: That I may dwell in the house of the Lord all the days of my life, to behold the beauty of the Lord, and to inquire in His temple."

2. What we think about most: What we think about the most says a lot about our spiritual condition. Proverbs 23:7 gives us the key, "For as he thinks in his heart, so is he."

3. How we use our money: Jesus said in Matthew 6:24, "No one can serve two masters; for either he will hate the one and love the other, or else he will be loyal to the one and despise the other. You cannot serve God and mammon."

4. What we do with our leisure time: Tozer said, "Most people waste [leisure time] staring at the television, listening to the radio, reading the cheap output of the press, or engaging in idle chatter. What I do with mine reveals the kind of man I am."

5. The company we enjoy: Do you have friends that call to pray but just want to gossip? Do you have friends who tempt you into sin? Proverbs 13:20, "He who walks with wise men will be wise, But the companion of fools will be destroyed."

6. Who and what we admire: Tozer once said, "I have long suspected that the great majority of evangelical Christians ... have a boundless, if perforce secret, admiration for the world,"

7. What we laugh at: Yes, laughter is good medicine but what we laugh at can be toxic. So I ask you, How's your heart? How's your spiritual health? Do you need a personal revival?

— Prayer —

Father, in the name of Jesus, would You help me take Tozer's words to heart? It's easy to stray away from Your purposes and into my purposes. It's too easy to walk in my will instead of Your will. Help me reassess my activities, my thoughts, and my words. Help me examine my heart.

The First Revival in Human History

"While Peter was still speaking these words, the Holy Spirit fell upon all those who heard the word" (Acts 10:44).

God created Adam and Eve and they lived in paradise. Can you imagine walking with God in the cool of the day, never having to toil or labor, and being in perfect peace? Such was the state of mankind in the creation.

But soon man's need for revival would emerge. The serpent crept into the divine oasis we call the Garden of Eden. Genesis 3:1 tells us the serpent was more cunning than any beast of the field which the Lord God had made.

Suddenly, the enemy introduced a vain imagination into Eve's mind that led her into rebellion. She ate of the only tree in the garden that contained forbidden fruit, and she tempted her husband to do the same. Now, sin was in the bloodline, and it didn't take long to multiply.

By Genesis 4, we see jealousy manifesting—probably also incited by the serpent. Cain was jealous of Abel and killed his twin brother in cold blood. Think about the track record of mankind. Out of the first four human beings on the earth, three of them fell into sin and the other was murdered. Adam and Eve later had a child named Seth—and revival was on the horizon.

"'For God has appointed another seed for me instead of Abel, whom Cain killed' and as for Seth, to him also a son was born; and he named him Enosh. Then men began to call on the name of the Lord" (Gen. 4:25). Mankind was still a relative newcomer to the earth God created and needed a revival in the second generation.

In his book, *The Distinguishing Mark of a Work of the Spirit of God*, Jonathan Edwards, an American revivalist, wrote of Genesis 4: "This seems to have been the effect of a remarkable outpouring of the Spirit of God—the first remarkable outpouring that ever was." Revival is always a result of a remarkable outpouring of the Spirit.

— *Prayer* —

Father, in the name of Jesus, You tell me in Your Word the heart is evil above all things. Would You purify my heart? I don't want to fall to temptation. I don't want to murder people with my mouth. I want to walk in Your presence in the cool of the day. I want to walk in Your Spirit.

Repenting for Prayerlessness

"Watch therefore, and pray always that you may be counted worthy to escape all these things that will come to pass, and to stand before the Son of Man" (Luke 21:36).

We don't see more revival because we don't have more prayer. Paul said, "Pray without ceasing" (Thess. 5:17). Every revivalist should take that command seriously in this hour as the enemy is roaming and violence is raging in the nations. Prayer to the God of hope—the God of revival—is our only path forward.

If Scripture had commanded us to pray once, that would have been adequate. But the admonitions are repetitive. Make no mistake. Prayerlessness is absolute rebellion. Indeed, I believe prayerlessness is among the greatest sins in the church—and unfortunately some leaders are propagating this sin and discouraging those with true prayer burdens from cooperating with the Spirit of God to bring His will to the earth. It grieves the Holy Spirit.

I've seen for years how prayer is lacking in many churches. Even churches that do have prayer meetings often relegate intercessors to the back rooms, lest their effectual fervent prayer offend the lukewarm saints. Thankfully, I'm seeing more church leaders repent of prayerlessness in this hour.

E.M. Bounds, a 19th Century Methodist who wrote nine important volumes on prayer, said this: "Prayerless praying has no burden, because no sense of need; no ardency, because none of the vision, strength, or glow of faith. No mighty pressure to prayer, no holding on to God with the deathless, despairing grasp, 'I will not let Thee go except Thou bless me.' No utter self-abandon, lost in the throes of a desperate, pertinacious, and consuming plea: 'Yet now if Thou wilt forgive their sin—if not, blot me, I pray Thee, out of Thy book.'"

Revivalists, cast the vision of the necessity of prayer to your Christian friends and family. Don't condemn your church or any other church for prayerlessness. Pray for them and help them see the value of constant prayer. When they see prayer results, they will realign with this heavenly principle and fewer will fall into temptation.

— *Prayer* —

Father, in the name of Jesus, help me to steer clear of prayerlessness. I don't want to live in spiritual dryness. Help me be part of the solution to inspire other Christians to engage in fervent intercession for revival in their cities, knowing You delight in the prayers of the righteous.

JANUARY 15

The Abel Clary Revivalist Anointing

"And whatever you do, do it heartily, as to the Lord and not to men" (Col. 3:23).

Abel Clary was just as able with intercession as his counterpart Daniel Nash. Clary traveled with Charles Finney, the most famed preacher of America's Second Great Awakening, everywhere the revivalist went.

Finney himself wrote of Clary, "Mr. Clary continued as long as I did, and he did not leave until after I had left. He never appeared in public, but he gave himself wholly to prayer. [Clary] had been licensed to preach; but his spirit of prayer was such, he was so burdened with the souls of men, that he was not able to preach much, his whole time and strength being given to prayer.

"The burden of his soul would frequently be so great that he was unable to stand, and he would writhe in agony. I was well acquainted with him, and knew something of the wonderful spirit of prayer that rested upon him. He was a very silent man, as almost all are who have that powerful spirit of prayer."

As history tells it, Finney found Clary's prayer journal after Clary went on to glory. Recorded within its pages were the chronicles of the prayer burdens the Lord put on his heart. It's no accident or coincidence that those prayer burdens aligned, one by one, with the order of the blessings poured out on Finney's ministry and the people who came to his meetings.

Leonard Ravenhill once wrote: "I met an old lady who told me a story about Charles Finney that has challenged me over the years. Finney went to Bolton to minister, but before he began, two men knocked on the door of her humble cottage, wanting lodging. The poor woman looked amazed, for she had no extra accommodations.

"Finally, for about twenty-five cents a week, the two men, none other than Fathers Nash and Clary, rented a dark and damp cellar for the period of the Finney meetings (at least two weeks), and there in that self-chosen cell, those prayer partners battled the forces of darkness."

— *Prayer* —

Father, in the name of Jesus, give me Your prayer burdens and a humility to stay behind the scenes even though I am qualified to preach in front of masses. Burden my soul with what burdens Your Spirit and help me to stay steady in intercession for revival and revivalists of my generation.

JANUARY 16

The Spiritual State of the Nations

"Why do the nations rage, and the people plot a vain thing?" (Psalm 2:1)

Every year the President of the United States gives the State of the Union address. If King Jesus presided over such an address to the Body of Christ, we would surely fall to our knees in repentance. And we should.

Christianity is declining in the West. According to the 2022 Ligonier Ministries State of Theology survey conducted by LifeWay Research to take "the theological temperature of the United States to help Christians better understand today's culture and to equip the church with better insights for discipleship" there are profound misunderstandings about Scripture and its Author.

Only 73 percent agree with the claim that Jesus is the "first and greatest being created by God." More than half (58 percent) believe that God accepts the worship of all religions, including Christianity, Judaism, and Islam. More than half (56 percent) agree that worshiping alone or with one's family is a valid replacement for regularly attending church. Almost half (44 percent) say that Jesus was a great teacher, but He was not God.

More than half (55 percent) believe the Holy Spirit is a force but is not a personal being. More than half (55 percent) agree that "everyone sins a little, but most people are good by nature." More than half (53 percent) disagree with the claim that even the smallest sin deserves eternal damnation. More than one in four (46 percent) disagree that every Christian has an obligation to join a local church. Almost one-third (29 percent) agreed with the statement that God learns and adapts to different circumstances, while only forty-three percent disagreed.

These statistics are shocking—and it's not just America. While some nations in the earth are seeing growth in Christianity, many are backsliding. There's never been a more critical time to see revival—transforming revival—in the nations.

— *Prayer* —

Father, in the name of Jesus, would You help me see how critical it is to pray without ceasing for revival? Even though I am on fire, help me not to be content until I see the Body of Christ catch Your fire. Teach me to pray with Your heart for the nations. Help me to be a prayer solutionist.

JANUARY 17

Training Young Revivalists

"Out of the mouth of babes and nursing infants You have ordained strength…" (Psalm 8:2).

I see the eyes of children opening. Parents with children between five- and ten-years-old—and children's ministry workers—should begin to train young ones up in the principles of seeing in the spirit through the door of Jesus, because they are going to begin to prophesy through dreams and visions.

This is going to start with dreams, but as you nurture them in the realm of dreams and teach them, show them and encourage them, they'll begin to see visions. I heard the Lord say:

"Don't be concerned when some of your children start falling into trances. Don't take them to the doctor, because it's Me, and they will come out of that trance, and they will have prophetic insight, wisdom and knowledge on things to come because I'm showing them things that eye has not seen nor ear heard.

"Encourage the young ones. Encourage the children. Encourage them. Don't push them away. Don't tell them, 'Later on I'll talk to you,' but take the time even now, because in this season, I'm pouring out My Spirit on all flesh, but I have a special eye on the young ones who have not yet been corrupted and polluted by the ways of the world. And I want to use them as pure voices and pure visionaries in their generation.

"So, encourage them, teach them, show them the way. I am the way, and you will see and know that I will activate even the very young ones in these gifts and the gifts of My Spirit, and they will see with clarity and know and understand even be able to articulate things that their human capacity could not possible comprehend."

— *Prayer* —

Father, in the name of Jesus, give me a heart for the next generation. Help me be mindful of any opportunity to impact them with Your Word and by the outpouring of Your Spirit. Use me to demonstrate Your love, Your kindness, and Your Spirit's power to save, heal and deliver.

Redigging the Wells of Revival

"Spring up, O well! All of you sing to it" (Numbers 21:17).

James Goll prophesied over me that Awakening House of Prayer—my church and house of prayer in South Florida—would redig the wells of revival that Derek Prince dug in the region years ago. We've been digging for a decade and won't stop digging. Lou Engle offers keen insight in his book, *Digging the Wells of Revival.* He writes:

"First, a revival well provides water that refreshes and revives dying people who are spiritually thirsty. When Hagar fled into the desert of Beersheba, she cried out to God for water to give to her son Ishmael, who was all but dead. God mercifully responded by opening her eyes so that she could see a well of fresh water (see Gen. 21:14-20). That drink in the desert saved her life and the life of her son. How many thousands, or millions, are dying in our cities—just looking for a well of revival?

"Second, revival wells are communal in nature. All are free to come and receive of the well's refreshing. This is part of the beauty of revival. Believers from every race and denomination come together and stand side by side at the same pool. Maintaining this communal nature requires a soft spirit of all who would drink the well's refreshing waters.

"Third, the water from a true revival well is transferable. That is, it can be taken home, thereby impacting many people who may not have the opportunity to go to the well and get a drink. The water from Toronto and Pensacola, for example, has touched the lives of multitudes of people who have never traveled to either city. There is a tangible presence of God that goes with it that can be shared with others.

"Fourth, wonderful ministries that bless thousands of people begin to form around a revival well. Bible schools and training centers are established, ministries to the poor are released, and missionary vision explodes." Amen

— *Prayer* —

Father, in the name of Jesus, give me the grit to dig and keep on digging the wells of revival—and to redig the wells of revival You lead me to. Give me the strength I need and help me not to grow weary in digging knowing that in due season I will reap a harvest of revival if I don't give up.

Holy, Holy, Holy

"Therefore, having these promises, beloved, let us cleanse ourselves from all filthiness of the flesh and spirit, perfecting holiness in the fear of God" (2 Corinthians 7:1).

The first Pentecostals in modern history came out of a Topeka, Kansas Bible school under the leadership of Charles Fox Parham, a holiness teacher. William Joseph Seymour, the central figure in the Azusa Street Revival in Los Angeles was a student. Holiness was the emphasis.

According to Church of God historian David G. Roebuck, the evangelists preached a new doctrine for the Camp Creek community where revival broke out. They proclaimed the necessity of holiness and called for their hearers to seek sanctification. They were "given to much prayer and fasting," preached earnestly, and throngs of people responded.

Church of God Historian Charles W. Conn wrote, "Almost from the start of the meeting, the altars were filled with repentant sinners and seekers for the experience of sanctification. Many skeptics of holiness were convinced, and many more rough-living sinners were converted."

We need a revival of holiness. Hebrews 12:14 tells us, "Strive for peace with everyone, and for the holiness without which no one will see the Lord." If we want revival, we must seek peace. We must forgive. We must strive for holiness.

In 2 Corinthians 7:1, Paul wrote, "Since we have these promises, beloved, let us cleanse ourselves from every defilement of body and spirit, bringing holiness to completion in the fear of God." We need to cleanse ourselves. We need to consecrate ourselves.

1 Thessalonians 4:7 makes it plain: "For God has not called us for impurity, but in holiness." Paul didn't mean holier-than-though, self-righteous or religious. He meant holiness. It's time to pursue holiness again.

Our society is full of Jezebel's immorality and idolatry, and this spirit has seduced many in the church. We see pastors falling into adultery and committing suicide. We see entire denominations embracing all manners of perversion. Christians are watching pornography and movies that glorify violence—and behaving in ways that are not Christ-like. Without holiness, no one will see the Lord.

— *Prayer* —

Father, in the name of Jesus, would You help me to walk away from everything that defiles my soul? Cleanse me from all unrighteousness and make me holy even as You are holy. Convict me of sin and lead me into repentance and righteous living. Sanctify me in Your truth.

Time-Tested Advice for Revival Pastors

"Where there is no counsel, the people fall; But in the multitude of counselors there is safety"
(Proverbs 11:14).

"I preached, as never sure to preach again, and as a dying many to dying men." Such were the emphatic words of Richard Baxter. You might his words the secret to success for pastors in revival.

Baxter saw an awakening that lasted for thirty-one years—from 1660-1691. As a result, most of the town of Kidderminster, Worcestershire in England got saved.

"When I came thither first, there was about one family in a street that worshipped God and called on His name, and when I came away there were some streets where there was not past one family in the side of a street that did not so; and that did not, by professing serious godliness, give us hopes of their sincerity."

Richard Baxter is considered a moderate in an age of extremes. Indeed, the nonconformist was at the center of every English controversy of his time. A Puritan, he suffered persecution, imprisonment, and sickness throughout his ministry, which spanned The English Civil war that ousted the monarchy. Baxter offers advice to revivalists today:

"Make sure saving grace has regenerated your own soul. Don't be content just existing in a state of grace. Make sure your graces are vigorously exercised, preaching your sermons to yourself before preaching them to others. Make sure your example doesn't contradict your doctrine. Make sure you don't live in those sins that you preach against. Make sure you're not lacking the qualifications necessary for pastoral work."

Baxter also offered seven primary duties of biblical pastoring: Labor for the conversion of the unconverted. Give answers to seekers who are under conviction of sin. Study so you can build up those already in the faith. Exercise careful oversight of families. Be diligent in visiting the sick. Be faithful in correcting and admonishing offenders. Be careful in exercising church discipline.

Nearly four hundred years after it was written, Baxter's book, *The Reformed Pastor,* is leaving wisdom nuggets for pastors of revival and awakening.

— *Prayer* —

Father, in the name of Jesus, would You help me to walk with the heart of a pastor? Help me labor for the lost in prayer. Give me boldness to offer an answer for the hope of my salvation. Grace me to step into the gifts and calling You have given me with integrity.

Revival Begins with You

"Arise, for this matter is your responsibility. We also are with you. Be of good courage, and do it" (Ezra 10:4).

Revival begins with you—and me. What do you want most? What do you want more than anything? Many people will say they want to be a millionaire, or they want to have a big family or a successful ministry. It's not wrong to have godly ambition, but what do you want most?

We find the answer in Psalm 27:4. David said, "One thing I have desired of the Lord, that will I seek: That I may dwell in the house of the Lord all the days of my life, to behold the beauty of the Lord, and to inquire in His temple." Revival begins with you—and me.

What we think about the most says a lot about our spiritual condition. Many Christians think more about how to pay their bills than how to fund the Kingdom. Many think more about what the enemy is doing than what God has done, is doing and has promised to do. Many think more about the party on the weekend than how they can serve in church on Sunday.

Proverbs 23:7 gives us the key, "For as he thinks in his heart, so is he." We become what we think about. We need to think about Jesus and advancing His Kingdom. Revival begins with you—and me.

When you have a day off is it also a day off from God or is it a day to spend more time with God? A.W. Tozer said, "Most people waste [leisure time] staring at the television, listening to the radio, reading the cheap output of the press, or engaging in idle chatter. What I do with mine reveals the kind of man I am." Revival begins with you—and me.

Do you have friends that call to pray but just want to gossip? Do you have friends who tempt you into sin? What if your friends were holding you back from revival? Proverbs 13:20, "He who walks with wise men will be wise, but the companion of fools will be destroyed." Revival begins with you—and me.

— *Prayer* —

Father, in the name of Jesus, would You help me remember that I am responsible for my own revival—and that when I enter revival, I can be a contagion for awakening among those around me? Help me remember that revival starts with me. Teach me how to walk in revival that stirs the faith of others.

Beware the Spirit of Error

"We are of God. He who knows God hears us; he who is not of God does not hear us. By this we know the spirit of truth and the spirit of error" (1 John 4:6).

In the middle of the Twentieth Century, America saw an outpouring that many compared to the Azusa Street Revival. The movement finds its origins in a tiny Pentecostal school in Saskatchewan, Canada. Revival broke out in the middle of a Bible study at the Sharon Orphanage on Feb. 12, 1948. The school was part of the Church of the Foursquare Gospel under Aimee Semple-McPherson.

Here's what happened: One student laid hands on another student and began to prophesy. According to George Hawtin, the school's leader, two days later, "all heaven broke loose upon our soul and heaven came down to greet us." The movement was marked by the laying on of hands and gifts of the Spirit. It goes down in church history as the Latter Rain movement, but there was leaven in the lump.

Indeed, some Pentecostal denominations fervently rejected the movement and even stripped these preachers of their ministry credentials. In question was the "Manifest Sons of God" theology that suggested a restoration of the five-fold ministry—including the offices of the apostle and prophet. We've seen this bear out.

However, other aspects of the theology included the notion that some believers would become manifested as the sons of God, perfected and immortalized, with the ability to change their physical appearance and speak any language as they were used to usher in the Millennial Reign of Christ. There was also the Joel's Army doctrine that espoused Christians would conquer and dominate the world before Christ's return. Both of these doctrines are, of course, errors.

Despite these revival errors, that didn't stop the move of God. Healings and other miracles marked the movement. Ultimately, the Latter Rain Movement was a forerunner to the Charismatic movement. But this shines a light on a serious issue. Many great revivalists, including William Branham, had scandals in their ministries due to giving heed to a spirit of error. That doesn't mean the outpouring is false, but that people stray from the Holy Spirit's original intent. Beware revival error by rightly dividing the Word.

— *Prayer* —

Father, in the name of Jesus, would You help me get so rooted and grounded in Your Word that I never allow the spirit of error access to my soul? I declare I hear Your voice and the voice of a stranger I will not follow. Lead me and guide me into all truth and help me walk in the truth that keeps me free.

JANUARY 23

Revival Resolutions

"Commit your works to the Lord, and your thoughts will be established" (Proverbs 16:3).

American revivalist preacher Jonathan Edwards penned a long list of revival resolutions—seventy of them over the years—because, "Being sensible that I am unable to do anything without God's help, I do humbly entreat him by his grace to enable me to keep these Resolutions, so far as they are agreeable to his will, for Christ's sake." Space does not permit me to reproduce them all here. But I'll give you a taste of how the revivalist committed to live.

"Resolved, that I will do whatsoever I think to be most to God's glory, and my own good, profit and pleasure, in the whole of my duration, without any consideration of the time, whether now, or never so many myriads of ages hence," he wrote. "Resolved to do whatever I think to be my duty and most for the good and advantage of mankind in general. Resolved to do this, whatever difficulties I meet with, how many soever, and how great soever."

Edwards resolved to repent if he fell short of his resolutions. He resolved to never lose a moment of time, to live with all his might, to think of the pains of martyrdom and of hell when he felt physical pain, to never do anything out of revenge, to never speak evil of anyone, and to be temperate in eating and drinking.

"Resolved, whenever I do any conspicuously evil action, to trace it back, till I come to the original cause; and then, both carefully endeavor to do so no more, and to fight and pray with all my might against the original of it," he wrote. "Resolved, to examine carefully, and constantly, what that one thing in me is, which causes me in the least to doubt of the love of God; and to direct all my forces against it."

Edwards resolved to study, to pray, and to live in peace with people. His resolutions serve as revelations to us about living a revival lifestyle. Edwards held himself to high spiritual standards. What are your revival resolutions?

— *Prayer* —

Father, in the name of Jesus, help me to pen my own revival resolutions—
guidelines of mindsets and behaviors that help me stay on the course You have set
for my life. Help me to erect standards of heart and mind that serve as guardrails
and help me avoid all appearances of evil.

Calling All Remnant Revivalists

"Even so then, at this present time there is a remnant according to the election of grace"
(Romans 11:5).

God always has a remnant. What is a remnant? The remnant is a small number of people among a large crowd. It's a group of survivors with boldness to do and say what the Lord wants done and said despite the personal cost. The remnant, you might say, is the church within the church.

While on my *Mornings with the Holy Spirit* prayer broadcast, I heard the Lord say: "I am calling forth My remnant, those who will cooperate with My Spirit and with truth; those who will speak forth the words that I put in their mouth no matter who likes it and no matter who doesn't like it.

"For I have called you to gather together and to band together in small groups and even large groups. But unified groups are what I am after. I am after groups of unified believers who are crying out in my name so I can hear their voice and heal their land.

"Who will gather? Who will be part of the remnant that I am calling together in this hour? The praying church.... the on-fire believers ... the ones who will not take no for an answer when the enemy is standing in the way between what I've called you to and the reality of the promise.

"I am rising. I am rising. My Spirit is rising, and I am looking for the remnant to rise with Me. Who will ascend to the holy hill, to the mountain of the Most High? Those with clean hands and a pure heart. The remnant.

"I am calling the remnant. I am calling the remnant. I am calling the remnant. I am calling you out of your caves and out of your closets. I'm calling some of you out of your churches. I'm calling some of you out of the business world and into ministry. I am calling the remnant. I am calling the remnant to prayer. I want to hear the prayers of the remnant, unified, unified, unified, unified, unified, unified together, touching and agreeing together."

— Prayer —

Father, in the name of Jesus, I choose to be part of the remnant. I choose to set myself apart for Your revival works. I choose to ascend to the holy hill and hear Your words of life to share with others. I choose to stand in intercession for the Bride. Please, help me.

A Righteous Revolution

"And do this, knowing the time, that now it is high time to awake out of sleep; for now our salvation is nearer than when we first believed" (Romans 13:11).

J. Edwin Orr, an Oxford-educated church historian, shared his heart on prayer, spiritual awakening, and the connection between the two. He couldn't have made the picture any clearer in his 1976 speech.

Orr began his talk with a quote from Dr. A.T. Pierson, "There has been never been a spiritual awakening in any country or locality that did not begin in united prayer." He then went on the recount what God has done through concerted, united, sustained prayer.

"Not many people realize that in the wake of the American Revolution there was a moral slump.... Crime, drunkenness, profanity rose to alarming levels. Churches stopped growing and began to shrink. Christians were so few on the campuses of Ivy League colleges in the 1790s that they met in secret, like a communist cell, and kept their minutes in code so that no one would know," he said.

"The Chief of Justice of the United States, John Marshall, wrote to the Bishop of Virginia, James Madison, that the Church 'was too far gone ever to be redeemed.' Voltaire averred, and Tom Paine echoed, 'Christianity will be forgotten in thirty years.'"

Does this scenario sound familiar in your nation? Whatever nation in which you live, what's needed is a spiritual awakening. Orr went on in his speech to ask and answer a question: "How did the situation change? It came through a concert of prayer."

While Christian Gospel music concerts have their place, if we're not careful we will pursue music concerts and forsake prayer concerts. If we're not careful, we'll put entertainment above intercession. If we're not careful, we'll fall asleep in the prayer room in a soaking session when we should be warring for awakening.

There is prayer that drives spiritual awakening, and it's not complacent. It's not half-hearted. It's not an add-on or an afterthought. Prayer that drives spiritual awakening is launched in desperation for the state of the church and for the salvation of souls. Are you ready to enter into it?

— *Prayer* —

Father, in the name of Jesus, would You give me a passion to see a spiritual awakening in my generation that sees churches revived, marriages restored, souls saved, bodies healed, and people set free by Your mighty power?

Worshipping Your Way Into Revival

"Oh come, let us worship and bow down; Let us kneel before the Lord our Maker"
(Psalm 95:6).

While prayer is a prerequisite for revival, worship and prayer—harp and bowl—offers what in some ways is a fast track to revival. That's because God enthrones the praises of His people (see Psalm 22:3). I learned that a Japanese translation of that verse actually reads, "When God's people praise Him, He brings a chair and sits there." Imagine that!

What is worship? A.W. Tozer, an American pastor and writer, defines it this way: "Worship is to feel in the heart and express in an appropriate manner, a humbling but delightful sense of admiring awe. Worship humbles you. The proud man can't worship God, any more than the proud devil can worship God. There must be humility in the heart, before there can be worship."

God is looking for those who worship Him in spirit and in truth (see John 4:24). He is also looking for those who will pray without ceasing. Worship makes prayer more enjoyable. Worship is agreeing with who God is and one way we express our worship is through declaring the truth of His beauty and character. Intercession is coming into agreement with what God has promised to do.

"Without doubt the emphasis in Christian teaching today should be on worship. There is little danger that we shall become merely worshipers and neglect the practical implications of the Gospel. No one can long worship God in spirit and in truth before the obligation to holy service becomes too strong to resist. Fellowship with God leads straight to obedience and good works. That is the divine order, and it can never be reversed," Tozer said.

"A cultivation of high thoughts of God through prayer, humble soul-searching and avid feasting upon the Scriptures—would go far to awaken the church. Some people mistake enrapt feeling, for worship. It's entirely possible to have a religious experience—and not be a Christian and not be converted, and be on our way to eternal hell."

— *Prayer* —

Father, in the name of Jesus, teach me to worship You in spirit and in truth. Give
me a revelation of how worship changes my mind and prepares me to pray
effectively and fervently for revival in my generation. Show me how to worship my
way into revival.

A Book of Acts Prayer Movement

"And they continued steadfastly in the apostles' doctrine and fellowship, in the breaking of bread, and in prayers" (Acts 2:42).

We often look to the Book of Acts as a measuring point for revival, or a rod stick for signs and wonders. We look at the Book of Acts and we long to see the Holy Spirit move like that again——and sometimes we do.

But I submit to you that if we are going to see a revival like the one in Ephesus or signs, wonders, miracles, deliverances and dead raisings like we saw in the early church, we need a Book of Acts Prayer movement. Everything worth doing is undergirded by prayer.

Johnathan Edwards, the founder of the Methodist church and a key figure in the First Great Awakening, said this: "It is God's will through His wonderful grace, that the prayers of His saints should be one of the great principal means of carrying on the designs of Christ's kingdom in the world.

"When God has something very great to accomplish for His church, it is His will that there should precede it the extraordinary prayers of His people; as is manifest by Ezekiel 36:37, 'And it is revealed that, when God is about to accomplish great things for His church, He will begin by remarkably pouring out the spirit of grace and supplication.'"

When we study the Book of Acts we see the words "pray," "prayer" and "praying" mentioned thirty-three times. The number thirty-three is connected to a promise or the promises of God. Thirty-three is also the numeric equivalent of the word "amen."

Book of Acts Prayer movements gather the remnant. Jesus invited five hundred people to the Upper Room to wait on the promise of the Holy Spirit. Only one hundred twenty showed up. The Upper Room in Acts 2 wasn't like a modern mega church. These hungry believers forsook everything else they needed to accomplish in the natural to go wait in a crowded room for the Spirit. This was the remnant.

Join a Book of Acts Prayer movement at www.awakeningprayerhubs.com.

— *Prayer* —

Father, in the name of Jesus, inspire my heart to read the Book of Acts, studying and gaining revelation on how prayer undergirded everything the early apostles and church did for your glory. Teach me to pray like the apostles prayed so I can walk in revival as they walked.

Living for Revival

"And those who are Christ's have crucified the flesh with its passions and desires"
(Galatians 5:24).

Surrender is one thing, but there's another level altogether: crucifying the flesh. When I say "crucify" you think of hanging on a cross. But crucify the flesh means to destroy its power over your soul. Living for revival means dying to self.

The secret to Paul's power was a crucified life. He wrote in Galatians 2:20 (AMP), "I have been crucified with Christ [in Him I have shared His crucifixion]; it is no longer I who live, but Christ (the Messiah) lives in me; and the life I now live in the body I live by faith in (by adherence to and reliance on and complete trust in) the Son of God, Who loved me and gave Himself up for me."

Jesus crucified His flesh for you, now He wants you to crucify your flesh for Him. Jesus put it this way in John 12:24-25 (AMP), "I assure you, most solemnly I tell you, unless a grain of wheat falls into the earth and dies, it remains [just one grain; it never becomes more but lives] by itself alone.

"But if it dies, it produces many others and yields a rich harvest. Anyone who loves his life loses it, but anyone who hates his life in this world will keep it to life eternal. [Whoever has no love for, no concern for, no regard for his life here on earth, but despises it, preserves his life forever and ever."

See, the world tells you not to waste your life on Christ. But the world is upside down. The Kingdom way is to lose your life in Christ, to die to self. Our old self was crucified with Christ, but it keeps trying to get back up again.

Benny Hinn once said, "God only trusts the dead." Paul put it this way: "I die daily." And Kathryn Kuhlman said, "I've died a thousand deaths." That was probably an understatement.

— *Prayer* —

Father, in the name of Jesus, would You help me see the need to crucify my flesh in order to live for revival? Would You grace me to put my flesh down so Your Spirit can rise within me and flow through me unrestrained? Help me to choose, like Paul, to die daily to the ways of the world.

JANUARY 29

An Apostle of Revival

"And He Himself gave some to be apostles, some prophets, some evangelists, and some pastors and teachers, for the equipping of the saints for the work of ministry, for the edifying of the body of Christ" (Ephesians 4:11).

John Sung goes down in Christian history as an apostle of revival. He was an apostolic evangelist in the truest sense of the word. Like Paul the apostle, Sung saw signs and wonders following him.

Sung, who lived from 1901 to 1944 had many names, including the Ice-Braker, the Apostle of Revival, and the John Wesley of China. Unfortunately, most of the Western church has never heard the name of the man who stewarded a revival in China from 1927 to 1937.

Born in China, Sung studied at Wesleyan University of Ohio. He earned three degrees. Sadly, he his lost his spiritual fervor during his time in the States. But in February 1927, Sung returned to Christ with his whole heart and set out to preach the Gospel. The sudden change in heart led seminary authorities to believe he was mentally ill, and they committed him to an insane asylum.

Can you imagine being so on fire for God that people thought you were crazy? He was held for about six months but took advantage of the time to read through the entire Bible forty times.

Once released, Sung returned set off for Shanghai to preach the Gospel. Although highly educated with accolades he, like Paul, counted it all rubbish. History tells how he threw all his diplomas and awards into the vast ocean. Although reserved in daily life, he was fervent in spirit when he preached Christ and Him crucified.

"For a servant of God to have authority in every sentence he utters, he must first suffer for the message he is to deliver. Without great tribulation, there is no great illumination," he said. "Man's works do not even come close to the works of the Holy Spirit. If the Holy Spirit does not work, all the efforts of man will come to naught."

— *Prayer* —

Father, in the name of Jesus, give me an apostolic thrust like Sun. Give me a heart that's willing to suffer for the sake of revival. Give me a persevering spirit to press past the suffering and into revival glory. Help me to be a role model to others of a modern-day revivalist.

The Edward Payson Revivalist Anointing

"For I have heard a voice as of a woman in labor, the anguish as of her who brings forth her first child" (Jeremiah 4:31).

"Prayer is the first thing, the second thing, and the third thing necessary for a minister, especially if he have revivals. Pray, then, my dear brother, pray, pray, pray." These were the words of Edward Payson, an American prayer hero and preacher from the 19th Century.

Payson saw revivals sparked and souls saved in his ministry. E.M. Bounds, a mighty man of prayer himself, wrote of Payson, "He prayed without ceasing and felt safe nowhere but at the throne of grace. He may be said to have studied theology on his knees."

Indeed, Payson goes down in church history as a mighty man of prayer. It's well known that the success of his ministry was his deep prayer life. An examination of his bedroom reveals deep grooves in the hardwood floor from the long hours he spent on his needs in intense intercession.

"As in poetry, so in prayer, the whole subject matter should be furnished by the heart, and the understanding should be allowed only to shape and arrange the effusions of the heart in the manner best adapted to answer the end designed," he wrote.

"From the fullness of a heart overflowing with holy affections, as from a copious fountain, we should pour forth a torrent of pious, humble, and ardently affectionate feelings; while our understandings only shape the channel and teach the gushing streams of devotion where to flow, and when to stop."

Payson's diary is especially revealing. On January 4, 1807, he penned these words: "I was favored with a spirit of prayer beyond all my former experience. I was in great agony and wrestled both for myself and others with great power. God seemed to bow the heavens and come down and open all His treasures, bidding me, take what I would."

Oh, that intercessors like Payson would flood the earth with prayer for God's Kingdom and will to be done in the earth again.

— *Prayer* —

Father, in the name of Jesus, would You favor me with a spirit of prayer beyond all my former experience? Would You grace me with a heart overflowing with holy affections, as from a copious fountain? Would You help me flood the earth with prayer until the knowledge of Your glory covers the earth?

JANUARY 31

Angels of Awakening

"Suddenly an angel shook him awake and said, 'Get up and eat!'" (1 Kings 19:5, *Message*).

Angels are appearing, intervening, and delivering messages around the world—and there is a running theme: awakening and the harvest.

"Angels are communicating strategies for the greatest campaign in church history," says Tim Sheets, author of *Angel Armies*. "The theme is 'harvest, harvest, harvest.' This includes awakening and revival. Holy Spirit is releasing angels in unprecedented numbers to do as on the Day of Pentecost in Acts 2—fire up the Remnant to be His witness."

James Goll, author of *Angelic Encounters: Engaging Help from Heaven*, rattled off a list of things the heavenly host of angels is declaring in this hour: breakthrough, prepare, be on the alert, go forth, the time to shift from reformation to transformation, a call for the shields of the earth to arise to protect Israel, and a time of great harvest upon us.

"I actually had an angel come and appear at the end of my bed, wake me up and declare, 'Be on the alert!' My senses were heightened and I knew that sudden change was coming across the face of the earth," Goll says. "Prophetic evangelists are being selected and empowered and the heavenly host are engaged in this process."

Matt Sorger, author and founder of Matt Sorger Ministries, agrees but hears angels at the same time heralding consecration and purity. Consecration and purity prepare the hearts of God's people to move in signs, wonders and miracles that will cause the lost to see that Jesus is alive.

"As angels are fighting on behalf of God's people they are helping many overcome temptation and sin and live in a deeper level of consecration," he says. "A new greater authority will be displayed in and through the church. I know Christ is coming again, but I also know it's for a glorious bride without spot or wrinkle. I believe God is calling many to a fresh consecration, to remove any landing place the enemy could have in their lives."

— Prayer —

Father, in the name of Jesus, help me to cooperate with the angels of awakening. Help me stay ready, consecrated and in faith to believe for signs and wonders that prove Jesus is alive. Put Your Word in my mouth so angels can execute your will through my decrees

FEBRUARY

"You never have to advertise a fire. Everyone comes running when there's a fire. Likewise, if your church is on fire, you will not have to advertise it. The community will already know it"
—Leonard Ravenhill

How the Church Fell Fast Asleep

"You are all sons of light and sons of the day. We are not of the night nor of darkness. Therefore let us not sleep, as others do, but let us watch and be sober" (1 Thessalonians 5:5-6).

Where was the church when prayer was taken out of schools in 1962? Or when abortion was legalized in 1973? Or when same-sex marriage started to gain momentum to the point that Christian businesses are persecuted for refusing to bake a wedding cake for a gay couple? Or when it was legalized?

I'm referring to America right now. But your nation probably has similar or worse issues. Some nations stray away from God. Some were never submitted to Him in the first place.

When did the church fall asleep? What caused the church to fall asleep? And how can we wake up the so-called sleeping giant? I don't have all the answers, but what I do know is the church didn't fall asleep overnight. It's like the proverb of the slowly boiled frog.

Speaking of China, Napoleon once said, "There lies a sleeping giant. If it ever wakes up, it will be unstoppable." The same holds true of the church. There are nearly three billion Christians in the world as of this writing. That's about one third of the earth. If we wake up, there's no stopping the Gospel from reaching the ends of the earth as every joint supplies.

"You don't know you were asleep until you wake up. We've all done this—to lie down for a moment to relax—only to find out we slept for a while!" said R.T. Kendall, former pastor of Westminster Chapel in England.

"You do things in your sleep you would not do if you were awake. Our dreams prove this. Whether such dreams are unexpressed fears or wishes, as Sigmund Freud might say, we do things when asleep we would not do if awake. We hate the sound of an alarm. How would you like to be awakened at 2 am? We resent being woken up. We want to sleep on."

— *Prayer* —

Father, in the name of Jesus, would You wake up the sleeping giant that is the church? Would You help Your bride find her identity and her voice so she can trumpet Your goodness and mercy to the nations? Wake me up, God. I want to be part of the solution. I want to see the Great Awakening.

Shaken to Awaken

"Now this, 'Yet once more,' indicates the removal of those things that are being shaken, as of things that are made, that the things which cannot be shaken may remain" (Hebrews 12:27).

The shaking is undeniable. Natural disasters are claiming lives. Economic disasters are driving poverty. Agronomists are predicting famines. Politicians are being shot. Protesters are taking to the streets. Some nations are on the verge of civil war.

It will continue growing darker until we turn back to God. The good news is when we do, we'll see a Great Awakening and many souls will come into the Kingdom. There will be a great harvest.

I'm blowing the trumpet. I'm sounding the alarm. There is hope for the nations, and that hope lies in the body of Christ rising up to do as Jesus commanded. "Occupy till I come" (Luke 19:13, KJV).

We must stand during the shaking just like the Israelites stood while Egypt was being shaken with plagues. We must not bow to fear. We must stay confident in the God of awakening, knowing that when we wake up and pray He will answer. Yes, He will answer. When we seek Him, we will find Him.

Isaiah 54:10 can encourage our hearts in these perilous times: "'For the mountains shall depart and the hills be removed, But My kindness shall not depart from you, nor shall My covenant of peace be removed,' says the Lord, who has mercy on you."

Don't fear the shaking. Everything that can be shaken will be shaken but you don't have to let current affairs shake you. You were called for such a time as this! Rise up and pray for unbelievers from your position of authority in Christ. Stand on Hebrews 12:28-29, "Therefore, since we are receiving a kingdom which cannot be shaken, let us have grace, by which we may serve God acceptably with reverence and godly fear."

— *Prayer* —

Father, in the name of Jesus, would You help me to stay steady in the shaking? Help me remember that I am a citizen of the Kingdom of heaven—a Kingdom that cannot be shaken. Help me to become a stabilizing force through prayer and evangelism as unbelievers are shaken to the core.

FEBRUARY 3

How Much Shaking Do We Need?

"Now this, 'Yet once more,' indicates the removal of those things that are being shaken, as of things that are made, that the things which cannot be shaken may remain" (Hebrews 12:27).

Make no mistake. The war that was raging in the heavens has, at least in some measure, manifested in the natural realm. The only way we can turn this around is to get desperate enough in our own hearts to see the salvation of the souls the enemy has taken captive—in the world and in the church—and enter intercession from a place of victory, recognizing we are seated in heavenly places with Christ Jesus.

I hope it doesn't have to get much worse in our nations to make us desperate enough to fall on our faces in prayer, but I am concerned it will.

Even still, desperation alone is not enough. True desperation demands something from us. As a church, we must deny ourselves, pick up our cross and follow Christ day in and day out (see Luke 9:23). We must choose to die to our own desires daily (see 1 Cor. 15:31). We must crucify our flesh and the lusts thereof with fervency (see Gal. 5:24). We must stand for the truth even in the face of persecution continually.

Famine is rising, horrific violence in the Middle East is spilling over into our other nations. Souls are dying and going to hell every day while we play patty cake in church and argue over who gets to lead prayer.

I pray the Lord will stir a desperation in your heart to make intercession—to pray even while no one is watching. I pray the Lord will continually stir your heart with a desperation that will drive you to put away anything that gets in the way of pursuing His perfect will for your life.

If we all just did what the Holy Spirit told us to do, we could turn our cities and nations upside down for Jesus. We could see a Third Great Awakening that ushers in salvation and reformation unto transformation in the name of Jesus.

— *Prayer* —

Father, in the name of Jesus, would You give me a deeper revelation of the correlation between the spiritual realm and the natural real so I can interrupt enemy's plans? I am standing for awakening. Give me Your desire for the nations. Show me how to turn my city upside down for Jesus.

The War for Awakening

"Be watchful, and strengthen the things which remain, that are ready to die, for I have not found your works perfect before God" (Revelation 3:2).

You've heard it said the enemy doesn't fight fair. Well, that's a spiritual warfare understatement if I've ever heard one. The devil is a dirty fighter—and he's just as subtle as he is dirty. He never sleeps or slumbers, but he works to put us to sleep through apathy, complacency, and waves of weariness.

Indeed, the enemy has lulled many in the church to sleep—and we've allowed it. Paul clearly warned us not to be ignorant of the devil's devices (see 2 Cor. 2:11), which implies the Lord will reveal the enemy's devices, schemes, plots and plans if we walk in connection with His heart. And that's where many of us miss it. If we are living in compromise, we're likely to become spiritually drowsy—but we won't fall right to sleep any more than we enter deep sleep the second our head hits the pillow.

Make no mistake: Satan has been working since the Second Great Awakening to put the church back into a deep sleep. He had some stops and starts. The Azusa Street Revival, the birthplace of the modern Pentecostal Movement, revived the saints at the beginning of the 20th century. But that slumbering spirit crept back in unawares.

Although Pentecostals and charismatics are the fastest-growing segment of the church in the 21st century, the enemy effectively lulled much of the church to sleep a long time ago—even Pentecostals and charismatics. Some segments of the church are waking up and fighting in the culture wars, but too many are listening to the enemy's lullabies (see Judges 16:19).

We're like modern-day Samsons, seduced and lulled to sleep by devilish Delilahs and losing our power to combat the enemy's onslaught. Of course, we haven't really lost our power. But by compromising with the spirit of the world, much of the church has effectively and willfully taken off its armor and laid down its weapons because that makes it more comfortable to sleep through the noise of sin that's erupting all around us. We need to pray!

— *Prayer* —

Father, in the name of Jesus, help me fight the good fight of faith against the war for my personal awakening so that I can stand in the gap more effectively for a sleeping church to wake up. Give me the grace to stand, with eyes wide open, and withstand the war against awakening.

FEBRUARY 5

Discerning High Time

"Now it is high time to awake out of sleep; for now our salvation is nearer than when we first believed" (Romans 13:11).

The church needs to wake up, open her eyes wide, pray and take acts of courage to ignite revival, awakening, reformation and transformation for the glory of God in the nations. We cannot be like the disciples who fell asleep at critical times—even while the Son of Man was being betrayed into the hands of sinners (see Matt. 26:45).

Antichrist spirits are rising, persecuting Christ and His church while we hit the snooze button. Some may be sleeping from sorrow (see Luke 22:45). Others may be slumbering after devilish Delilahs that found a way to lull them to sleep through a compromised lifestyle. Still others may be sleeping because the devil has brought weariness to their souls and they failed to respond to Christ's invitation to come to Him for rest (see Matt. 11:28).

No matter whether you are in a deep sleep or just dozing off, I offer you this admonishment: "Now it is high time to awake out of sleep; for now our salvation is nearer than when we first believed" (Rom. 13:11). And for those of you—the remnant within the remnant—who are wide awake, sounding the alarm, and interceding for the slumbering masses, take heart in these words from revivalist Leonard Ravenhill:

"Some Christians have already hung their harps on the willows, and yet others seem to delight in speaking of the Church's present lapse as a proof of divine inspiration. But I myself believe that if the Church will only obey the conditions, she can have a revival any time she wants it.

"The problem of the Church is the problem in the garden of Gethsemane—sleep! For while men sleep, the enemy sows his seed through his cults. Lest men sleep the sleep of eternal death, Oh arm of the Lord, Oh Church of the living God, awake!"

— *Prayer* —

Father, in the name of Jesus, give me the determination never to hang my harps on the willows. Help me obey the conditions of revival. Help me to discern the enemy who wants to sow seeds of slumber in my heart. Help me stay wide awake so I can hear Your voice and do Your will. Help me discern high time.

Revival Will Sprout Again

"For there is hope for a tree, if it is cut down, that it will sprout again, and that its tender shoots will not cease" (Job 14:1-9).

It is impossible to revive something that has never been alive. The word "revival" in its ordinary sense, means the coming of life and renewal to something that has already possessed life. These are the words of revival historian Edward Orr.

As an example, Orr uses a garden in the winter. The old oak tree is leafless, standing as a sorry sight and, to all outward appearances it is dead. But, he said, if you come back a month later the little buds of beautiful, delicate green push their way towards the light.

"Soon the tree is in the glory of its leafy splendour. It is a seasonal marvel, this renewal of spring, when all that seemed dead becomes alive before our wondering eyes," Orr writes. "What has happened? There has come about a revival of the old tree."

Indeed, his insight reminds me of Job's words in Job 14:1-9, "For there is hope for a tree, if it is cut down, that it will sprout again, and that its tender shoots will not cease. Though its root may grow old in the earth, and its stump may die in the ground, yet at the scent of water it will bud and bring forth branches like a plant."

It is the same, Orr, says, in the spiritual realm. Again, revival, primarily, is the renewal of life in something that has already possessed life. But there is one important difference—the dying of the summer life of the tree is due to natural causes, and the same causes bring about the springtime awakening.

Spiritual death, on the other hand, is due to the disease of sin. Perhaps the best definition of "revival," then, is the phrase "Times of refreshing from the presence of the Lord.'"

— *Prayer* —

Father, in the name of Jesus, I am grateful there is still a root of awakening in my land. Help me to water that root with my prayers until it sprouts again—and flourishes. Help me to hold out hope to see revival bud in my city. Help me to step into my own times of refreshing.

Revival That Sets the Captives Free

"He has sent Me to heal the brokenhearted, to proclaim liberty to the captives and recovery of sight to the blind, to set at liberty those who are oppressed" (Luke 4:18).

When Paul and Silas were imprisoned in Thyatira, they were singing praises and praying despite the blood and bruises on their bodies. The result: a revival broke out in the prison. Do it again, Lord!

Ultimately, if we had mass salvations, great awakenings and transforming revival in the earth—and in the prisons—we'd see fewer less crime. And we'd see fewer prisoners released only to return to prison for yet another term. Prayer moves the hand that moves the world. Prayer changes things.

I believe jails and prisons are a great harvest field for souls—one of the greatest. I believe prayers can reach through the walls of the prison to drive salvation, undergirding the work of prison ministries who visit inmates behind bars, agreeing with the families of inmates, and setting the stage for supernatural manifestations of God's presence in the prisons.

Pray for spontaneous prayer and worship to break out in the prisons so others may see the goodness of God in the land of the living and worship the one and true living God (see Acts 16). Pray for revival to break out in prisons and jails, from the inmates to the prison guards and administrators (see Acts 2:1-4).

Pray for a revival of faith in God and for the miracle of salvation to break out in jail and prisons (see Acts 16). Pray for signs and wonders to abound in jails and prisons and for the testimony of Jesus to be heard through every ward and cell (see Mark 16:17-18).

Pray for broken-hearted prisoners and their families to receive deliverance and healing through the ministry of chaplains and prison ministries (see Luke 4:18). Pray for deliverance ministry—casting out of demons—to be commonplace in the prisons and for deliverance ministers have open doors in the prisons (see Mark 16:17-18).

— *Prayer* —

Father, in the name of Jesus, I am asking You to pour out Your Spirit in jails and prisons all over the world. I am asking You to bring conviction of sin unto deep repentance and salvation to inmates. Do what You want to do and set the spiritual captives free for Your glory.

Great Awakening Prophets

"The Sovereign Lord has given me his words of wisdom, so that I know how to comfort the weary. Morning by morning he wakens me and opens my understanding to his will" (Isaiah 50:4).

God woke me up at midnight in April 2007 and told me He was bringing a Great Awakening to America. He later told me that awakening would spill out beyond the borders of my nation and sweep through other nations. I've been prophesying those words ever since. By some measure, I'm an awakening prophet. And I'm not alone.

At a time when some prophets are releasing curses on their nations, a new breed of prophetic people—some younger, some older—are declaring and decreeing the greatest-ever great awakening. It's an awakening that will touch the nations of the earth with great signs, wonders, and miracles—and mass salvations and deliverances—that demonstrate Jesus is alive.

As you've discerned, I call these awakening prophets. Awakening prophets are equipping a generation of prophetic people who see, hear, and say what the Lord is doing in their cities and regions—and have the persistence to contend to the end for more than a summer revival. They have the wherewithal to intercede for transformation and reformation that only comes from a spiritual awakening.

These awakening prophets trumpet a call for repentance mixed with hope for God's mercy that triumphs over judgment (see James 2:13). They are prophetic messengers who recall nation-shaking revivals like the First and Second Great Awakening, Azusa Street, the Voice of Healing Movement, and the Toronto Blessing and fervently cry out, "Do it again, Lord!"

Despite all the talk of awakening, some prophets are holding to words of judgment—and even cursing America with foretelling of tsunamis that put Florida under water, a massive asteroid that hits Puerto Rico, "new Madrid" earthquakes that split America down the middle, and other fearful prophecies.

So which is it? Judgment or revival? Shaking or awakening? The awakening prophet acknowledges judgment when it comes but stands on the promise of the coming awakening because of God's mercy. What kind of prophet are you?

— *Prayer* —

Father, in the name of Jesus, wake me up! Help me see what You want to do in my city, my state, and my nation—and the nations of the earth. Help me agree with Your glory covering the earth like the water covers the sea. Amid judgment, help me remember grace and mercy.

FEBRUARY 9

Unified Faith

"Behold, how good and how pleasant it is for brethren to dwell together in unity! It is like the precious oil upon the head, running down on the beard, the beard of Aaron, running down on the edge of his garments. It is like the dew of Hermon, descending upon the mountains of Zion; for there the Lord commanded the blessing—life forevermore" (Psalm 133).

When I read Ephesians 4:11-13 about apostles, prophets, evangelists, pastors and teachers equipping the Body, I agree with Paul's Spirit-inspired words. But we should pay special attention to the "come to the unity of the faith" aspect of this revelation.

See, we usually stop after the "equipping the saints for the work of the ministry" portion of the verses. But we can equip the saints for the work of the ministry all day long and that won't necessarily bring revival. You can't build, prophesy or teach your way into revival. The anointing will flow in our churches when we come to the unity of the faith.

Sure, we may disagree on whether gifts of the Spirit have ceased or whether women can preach but we can still unite under the Apostle's Creed. And if we want revival—not just powerful meetings but sustained revival that brings true and lasting reformation—we must.

I am convinced this disunity in the body of Christ is causing more problems than we can see, even with a discerning eye. I am convinced people are dying and going to hell because the church isn't walking in unity.

I don't want this blood on my hands so I am challenging you—and challenging myself—to be on one accord and of one mind (see Phil. 2:2) with our fellow Christians; to put on love that binds us together in perfect harmony (see Col. 3:14); and to strive side by side for the faith of the Gospel even with those who have small differences in how they interpret the rapture, spiritual gifts and other issues that aren't central to the Gospel of Christ (see Phil. 1:27).

With so much strife in the church—when we are biting and devouring each other—can we expect God's blessing of revival? Does He even hear our prayers when we're in discord? Think about it.

— *Prayer* —

Father, in the name of Jesus, equip me for unity. Equip me to be a peacemaker in Your church. Help me to walk in peace with all men as far as it depends on me. Help me be a bridge builder and not a bridge burner. Help me to never engage in strife at any level.

Praying in the Spirit of Revival

"But you, beloved, building yourselves up on your most holy faith, praying in the Holy Spirit"
(Jude 20).

I heard the Lord say, "Pray in My Spirit and I will do a work on the inside of you that will birth miracles in you and miracles through you. Pray in the Spirit. That is the master key that so many of My children are missing.

"For they read the Word, read the Word, read the Word, read the Word—which does so much good in their soul. But when they begin to pray in the Spirit in conjunction with reading the Word a revival begins to break out in their heart that spills over into their words, into their cities and churches, and the lost begin to take notice.

"I'm supercharging you even now as you pray in the Spirit. So do not delay by putting off this vital aspect of your life in Christ any longer. But begin to walk like He walked as you talk like He talked and think like He thinks and pray like He prayed, going off to secret places early in the morning, waiting on Me for direction, only doing what He saw Me do.

"Do it my way. I won't do it your way, but I'll help you do it My way. I have a life of power, of prophetic wonder for you. So stand firm in My promises and do not budge from the place that I've called you to stand, and pray in the Spirit and speak the Word only and watch what happens when you combine this with that, the Word with the Spirit.

"Watch the revival that breaks out in your heart and in your mind, in your soul, in your emotions, every bit of you. You will begin to burn and shine for Me and the world will stand up and take notice."

If you want to learn more about the benefits of praying in tongues, check out my book *Tongues of Fire: 101 Supernatural Benefits to Praying in the Holy Spirit.*

— Prayer —

Father, in the name of Jesus, would You baptize me afresh in the Holy Spirit?
Would You baptize me in fire? Would You compel me to pray in the spirit—to
pray in my heavenly language—as often as possible? You pray the perfect prayer
for revival through me.

FEBRUARY 11

Revival-Killing Leaven

"A little leaven leavens the whole lump" (Galatians 5:9).

After Delilah got what she wanted from Samson—just a little compromise—she was able to lull him to sleep on her knees. He was sleeping so deeply that a man came in and shaved off seven locks of his hair without him noticing.

When the Philistines broke in, Samson thought he could break free as in times past—but he was deceived. "Then the Philistines took him and put out his eyes, and brought him down to Gaza. They bound him with bronze fetters, and he became a grinder in the prison" (Judges 16:21-22).

Samson compromised. Samson was lulled to sleep by his enemy. Samson was left completely blind. That's the condition much of the church is in today. But there is good news. We can pray for another Great Awakening. We can pray that God will wake us up and give us another chance. We can pray like Samson did:

"O Lord God, remember me, I pray! Strengthen me, I pray, just this once, O God, that I may with one blow take vengeance on the Philistines for my two eyes!" (Judges 16:28). Samson repented. Samson defeated the enemy of his people. Samson died doing the will of God. If Samson can do it, so can we. It starts on our knees, making an appeal to heaven for a compromising nation that needs to turn back to God. It starts with me and it starts with you—no compromise believers.

We must develop a no compromise mindset. Remember, a little leaven leavens the whole lump (see Gal. 5:9). The Amplified Bible puts it this way: "A little leaven [a slight inclination to error, or a few false teachers] leavens the whole batch [it perverts the concept of faith and misleads the church]." Don't listen to the enemy's false promises and false teachings. He's a liar and the Father of lies (see John 8:44).

— *Prayer* —

Father, in the name of Jesus, help me avoid the leaven of compromise so it doesn't contaminate my resolve. I don't want to give the enemy an inch—not a single opportunity to lull me to sleep through my sin. Help me evict the little foxes that spoil the vine.

An End Times Awakening

"Then I saw another angel flying in the midst of heaven, having the everlasting gospel to preach to those who dwell on the earth—to every nation, tribe, tongue, and people" (Revelation 14:6).

Could God use angels to usher in another Great Awakening before the return of Christ? And if so, how? Dutch Sheets, best-selling author of *Intercessory Prayer*, sees five distinct divisions of angels that Holy Spirit is releasing to assist the New Testament Church.

First, he says, are angels helping minister a fresh Pentecost—a new outpouring of the Holy Spirit. Second, he sees angels ministering to build Kingdom government, a ruling and reigning ecclesia. Sheets says God's government will increase, greatly assisted by these powerful angels.

"Third, angels of healing and miracles are being released. Dramatic and visual healings and miracles will now go to new levels. Holy Spirit is opening healing wells and angels are assisting that movement," Sheets says. "Fourth, angels of evangelism are now being released. They have three areas they are primarily targeting: Prodigals—millions of prodigals will return to Christ, new converts are being drawn in and true five-fold ministry evangelists are being connected to apostolic hubs to fuel regional revival. These angels will help usher in a Great Awakening."

Prophetic healing minister Matt Sorger believes angels are sent on assignment as we prophecy, decree and declare God's Word and take authority over the works of darkness. Regions that have been hindered by principalities and powers, he says, will experience great breakthrough. He expects a resurgence of God's manifest presence where before it has been "hard" in the spirit.

James Goll, author of *The Seer*, reports seeing these words written in large amber glowing letters before his eyes, "The Beginning of the third Great Awakening!" "When I move into the 'seer realm,' it often comes with angelic assistance. This is something I have learned over my many years of prophetic ministry," he explains. "When that realm opens up to me in eternal visions and the manifested presence becomes every so thick, it is in part due to angels on assignment."

— *Prayer* —

Father, in the name of Jesus, would You help me discern, activate, and cooperate with end times angels of awakening? Help me not to grieve the angels or worship the angels but to work with them to see Your will come to pass. Teach me how to cooperate with the angelic ministry.

FEBRUARY 13

Find Your Gap

"He saw that there was no man, and wondered that there was no intercessor; Therefore His own arm brought salvation for Him; And His own righteousness, it sustained Him" (Isaiah 59:16).

There's never been a more critical time to stand in the revival gap. What does that really mean? Standing in the gap is a selfless posture, a Christ-like posture. Standing in the gap is making a defense against an enemy attack. Standing in the gap is exposing oneself to enemy fire to protect something or someone else.

That may sound somewhat daunting, but when you understand the plan and will of God it's exhilarating. When you stand in the gap God assigns you to, you are standing in His will and nothing by any means shall harm you. When you stand in the Gap God assigns you to, God is fighting for you and with you and you cannot lose. When you stand in the gap God assigns you to, you are surrounded with favor like a shield (see Ps. 5:12). He is your rear guard (see Is. 52:12).

As I've said many times, God is not a one-issue God. There are many issues on God's heart, and He will place certain issues on our hearts at certain times. He will call us to stand in the gap—a specific gap. Indeed, I believe God is always looking for someone to stand in the gap, just like He did in Ezekiel's day.

"I looked for someone who might rebuild the wall of righteousness that guards the land. I searched for someone to stand in the gap in the wall so I wouldn't have to destroy the land, but I found no one" (Ez. 22:30).

If you are an intercessor, there's a revival gap for you to stand in. When you find that gap, you'll be the most effective in your intercessory prayer efforts. Remember, though, that although God may give you specific assignments for specific seasons, He's not a one-issue God. Find your revival gap.

— *Prayer* —

Father, in the name of Jesus, as a revivalist I know I must also be an intercessor. Would You give me the grace to pray without ceasing? Would You show me the revival gap to stand in? Would You help me to stand and withstand in the evil day?

A Love Revival

"And now abide faith, hope, love, these three; but the greatest of these is love"
(1 Corinthians 13:13).

In the prayer room at Awakening House of Prayer, I had a vision of a banner that read, "Love Revival." God wants a revival of love and, like all revivals, it starts with us. What does a love revival look like? We get a hint in 1 Corinthians 13:1-8:

"Though I speak with the tongues of men and of angels, but have not love, I have become sounding brass or a clanging cymbal. And though I have the gift of prophecy, and understand all mysteries and all knowledge, and though I have all faith, so that I could remove mountains, but have not love, I am nothing. And though I bestow all my goods to feed the poor, and though I give my body to be burned, but have not love, it profits me nothing.

"Love suffers long and is kind; love does not envy; love does not parade itself, is not puffed up; does not behave rudely, does not seek its own, is not provoked, thinks no evil; does not rejoice in iniquity, but rejoices in the truth; bears all things, believes all things, hopes all things, endures all things. Love never fails. But whether there are prophecies, they will fail; whether there are tongues, they will cease; whether there is knowledge, it will vanish away."

What does a love revival look like?

God is love. Jesus said all men would know we are His disciples by the love that we have for one another (see John 13:35). John made it clear: "We know that we have passed from death to life, because we love our brothers. The one who does not love remains in death" (1 John 3:14).

If we can't love our brothers and sisters in Christ, we need a personal revival. God wants to start the love revival with you—and me—and spread His love throughout the world.

— Prayer —

Father, in the name of Jesus, reduce me to love. Burn away anything in me that keeps me from loving You, loving myself and loving my neighbors as myself. I want to walk in love, talk in love, work in love and pray in love. I am in love with You. Help me show Your love to others.

FEBRUARY 15

The Steve Hill Revivalist Anointing

"Therefore I say to you, her sins, which are many, are forgiven, for she loved much. But to whom little is forgiven, the same loves little" (Luke 7:47).

Steve Hill dedicated his life to spreading the Gospel. He was a missionary, church planter in Argentina, Spain and Russia, organizer of evangelistic crusades—and a revivalist.

But he didn't start out that way. Hill came to the Lord through a dramatic deliverance from drugs, alcohol, and crime. He found Jesus in 1975 and was immediately sold out and on fire. David Wilkerson's Teen Challenge ministry school shaped him. His story is one of "the one who has been forgiven much, loves much" (see Luke 7:47).

God's hand was on Steve Hill. From 1995 to 2000, Hill stood as a key figure in the Brownsville Revival in Pensacola, Florida, which drew over four million people through the doors of the Brownsville Assemblies of God church. His messages had titles such as: *How to Miss God, The Devil in Your Head,* and *The Seduction of Satan.*

Dr. Michael L. Brown, another figure at Brownsville, says, "I remember another service when Steve planned to preach from Luke 13, the parable of the fig tree owner who was about to chop the tree down because it had not born any fruit and its allotted time was running out. To illustrate his message, Steve was carrying an ax on his shoulder."

Speaking of Brownsville, Hill said, "We're seeing miraculous healings, cancerous tumors disappear, and drug addicts immediately delivered." Leonard Ravenhill, author of *Why Revival Tarries,* was Hill's mentor. And Hill was one of my mentors for the last few years of his life.

I could go on and on about Steve Hill. He was a man of conviction, a man of courage, a man who refused to compromise the Gospel. He was more than an inspiration to me; he was a general of the faith whom the Lord used to strengthen my stand against anything that would come between God's love and His creation.

Steve imparted to me a heart for evangelism, a determination to see revival and so much more before he went home to be with the Lord after his battle with cancer in 2014. We need his revivalist anointing today.

— *Prayer* —

Father, in the name of Jesus, would You give me a heart for revival like Steve Hill carried? Would You help me sell out to You completely, to die to self, and to crucify my flesh continually? Give me an anointing for revival and holiness like You poured out on Steve Hill.

The Brownsville Revival

"Will You not revive us again, that Your people may rejoice in You?" (Psalm 85:6)

The Brownsville Revival—also known as the Pensacola Outpouring—broke out on Father's Day, June 18, 1995, at the Brownsville Assembly of God in Pensacola, Florida. Evangelist Steve Hill was a guest speaker in the pulpit when the fire started. The revival finally ended in 2000.

With the meetings drawing more than four million people, the secular media covered the Pentecostal revival extensively. The revival went viral as news spread about supernatural encounters. As described in Steve Hill's biography:

"During those five years, the devout, the cynical, and the curious came from all walks of life, traveling from as many as one hundred fifty different nations around the globe. Hundreds of thousands wept at the altars, repented of sinful lifestyles, and gave their lives to Jesus. Lives were dramatically changed, marriages were restored, and addictions were broken as the Gospel of Jesus Christ was presented with clarity."

What sparked the Brownsville Revival?

In 1993, John Kilpatrick, pastor of the church, started fervently praying with his congregation for revival. Indeed, revival was a consistent prayer focus, especially given a prophecy Dr. David Yonggi Cho, the late pastor of the Yoido Full Gospel Church in South Korea, had released. Cho said God told him He was "going to send revival to the seaside city of Pensacola, and it will spread like a fire until all of America has been consumed by it."

The Brownsville Assembly of God was open Tuesday through Sunday for people to experience the revival. Some even camped in the parking lot over night for the opportunity to get into the building. The revival was marked by singing, dancing, salvation and supernatural healings, repentance and a call for holiness.

During the Brownsville Revival about two hundred thousand people found salvation. Thousands of pastors took revival fire back to their congregations, which drove smaller revivals across the Assemblies of God denomination in the late 1990s.

— *Prayer* —

Father, in the name of Jesus, thank You for the work of repentance and the call to holiness at the Pensacola Outpouring. Put in me a hunger and thirst for righteousness, holiness, and purity. Help me to clean my hands and purify my heart. Let your revival fire consume me.

Do You Hold the Key to Revival?

"For thus says the High and Lofty One Who inhabits eternity, whose name is Holy: "I dwell in the high and holy place, with him who has a contrite and humble spirit, to revive the spirit of the humble, and to revive the heart of the contrite ones" (Isaiah 57:15).

David Yonggi Cho, a pastor in South Korea who built one of the largest prayer movements in the world, once said this: "A new outpouring of the Holy Spirit is desperately needed. At no time in the history of the modern world has there been such an outpouring of satanic influence as there is today.

"The bottom of the pit of hell is belching out its filth in murder, rape, pornography, lawlessness, and violence. Just as the preaching of the Wesleys kept Britain from following France in revolution in the eighteenth century, so too a new outbreak of revival can bring about the social and political changes necessary to keep us from international destruction and calamity. What will bring about the revival that can lead the world away from the brink of total destruction and annihilation? The answer is a new call to prayer!"

Do you hold the key to revival in your city?

We can't manufacture revival, but we can ask for it. Prayer has preceded every revival in church history. Even in the Old Testament, we see prayer preceded revival. The key to revival is found in desperate prayer—like the prayer you would pray for someone you love who is about to die. That's because revival is only necessary when something is unconscious. It's not moving. It's asleep or sick. It's incapacitated.

Samuel Chadwick, a 20th Century, Wesleyan Methodist minister, once said this: "Prayer turns ordinary mortals into men of power. It brings power. It brings fire. It brings rain. It brings life. It brings God."

Ask the Lord to give you a heart for revival. If you already have a heart for revival, ask Him to help you understand your critical role in calling forth power, fire, rain, life and God.

— *Prayer* —

Father, in the name of Jesus, I want to see revival in my life, my family, my city and my nation—and in the nations of the world. Would You use me as an agent of revival? Would You help me not to grow weary in calling down your power, fire, rain, life and presence?

Intercessors of Revival

"Therefore I exhort first of all that supplications, prayers, intercessions, and giving of thanks be made for all men, for kings and all who are in authority, that we may lead a quiet and peaceable life in all godliness and reverence" (1 Timothy 2:1-2).

I heard the Lord say, "I've called you to rise up. I've called you to contend in this hour. I've called you to stand in the gap. I've called you to occupy until I come. You will do it through prayer. So pray. Pray as hard as you've ever prayed before. Pray long and pray strong.

"For the enemy will resist you, but he cannot resist your prayer in the name of Jesus. He cannot resist your Holy Spirit-inspired utterance. He cannot resist your fervency in this hour. So keep standing for I Am with you. I am hearing your prayers. I am answering your prayers. I am ready to pour and pour and pour some more.

"Continue to stand. Continue to press. Continue to fight the good fight of faith. for much is at stake. Do not allow the fire on the altar to go out. But put more wood on the fire. Put yourself on the altar. Be living sacrifices—intercessors of sacrifice. Lay down your life in this hour because souls depend upon your prayers.

"So do not neglect this moment because then you will regret this moment, but press into it and you will see a great reward. For there are great rewards in this hour for the intercessors who will stop what they're doing—who will set aside the things of the world and press into the things of the Spirit."

This is a word that every intercessor of revival should use as a sword in the spirit! Fight the devil and your flesh with this word! When you feel too weary to continue standing in prayer for revival, know that God is standing with You as you stand for His will. Don't give up. Though revival tarries, wait for it in faith.

— *Prayer* —

Father, in the name of Jesus, help me step into revival prayer at a deeper level. Help me to press into intercession for souls, lukewarm churches, and wayward nations so that You can hear and answer my cries. Give me an enduring heart to press into revival for Your glory.

Revival at Rock Bottom

"Then God said to Jacob, 'Arise, go up to Bethel and dwell there; and make an altar there to God, who appeared to you when you fled from the face of Esau your brother'" (Genesis 5:1).

Before we see widespread revival, we need a personal revival. In his early years, Jacob was a deceiver and a liar. He was selfish and self-centered. He stole the birthright from his brother Esau.

God would later change Jacob's name to Israel, and he would birth twelve sons that would become the twelve tribes of Israel as we know them. What a transformation! This is transforming personal revival.

Jacob was the first person we see in Scripture experiencing revival in his heart. We see the account in Genesis 35. God gave Jacob instructions to go to Bethel and make an altar to Him at a place He appeared to him long ago.

With that, Jacob called his household to repentance: "Put away the foreign gods that are among you, purify yourselves, and change your garments" (Gen. 35:2). Verse four tells us they gave Jacob all the foreign gods that were in their hands, and the earrings. They turned wholly back to the Holy God. This is the revival. Notice it started with Jacob, but it touched his entire family.

Then look what happens next. Genesis 35:5 reveals, "And they journeyed, and the terror of God was upon the cities that were all around them, and they did not pursue the sons of Jacob." Since they were walking with a revived heart—and walking in the fear of the Lord—Jehovah caused their enemies to fear them. No one dared to rise up against them. This is a fulfillment of the Proverbs 16:7, "When a man's ways please the Lord, He makes even his enemies to be at peace with him."

Notice in this instance how God took the initiative with Jacob. This was after a time when his daughter was raped, and his sons committed mass murder. Jacob and his family were at a low point, but God remembered the covenant He made with Abraham. We have a covenant with God. Believe this: God can revive us at our lowest point.

— *Prayer* —

Father, in the name of Jesus, would You encounter my heart with Your kindness? It's Your kindness that leads me to repentance. Just as You showed Jacob kindness for Abraham's sake, would You show me kindness for Your Son's sake? Revive me and I will be revived.

An Outpouring is Not a Revival

"Rain down, you heavens, from above, and let the skies pour down righteousness; Let the earth open, let them bring forth salvation, and let righteousness spring up together. I, the Lord, have created it" (Isaiah 45:8).

Scripture speaks of outpourings over and again. God prophesied through Isaiah, "For I will pour water on him who is thirsty, and floods on the dry ground; I will pour My Spirit on your descendants, and My blessing on your offspring" (Is. 44:3).

And Isaiah 32:15 speaks of time when "the Spirit is poured upon us from on high, and the wilderness becomes a fruitful field, and the fruitful field is counted as a forest." While we celebrate everything the Holy Spirit does, some confuse an outpouring with a revival. What is an outpouring?

As I wrote in *Revival Hubs Rising*, "An outpouring is a supernatural move of the Holy Spirit that emphasizes a particular gift or ministry. Over the generations, there have been healing outpourings, fire outpourings, charismatic gift outpourings, glory outpourings, and so on. An outpouring typically has a destined beginning and end. It is seasonal—even if the season is many years—and has a specific purpose in the earth. The Holy Spirit pours out what is needed in the hour or in a generation."

In his book *Revival*, Richard Owen Roberts offered definitions of various revival terms, such as awakening, fire, fullness, glory, judgment, and outpouring. With regard to an outpouring, he wrote:

"Isaiah pled with God to rend the heavens and to come down (Isa. 64:1). Our current scene is readily depicted by a vast layer of heavy clouds between heaven and earth. The idea of God taking His mighty hand and parting these clouds and then tipping the heavenly vats of divine mercy and pouring fresh graces upon the land is very attractive."

How to you discern an outpouring? An outpouring brings fire and wind. An outpouring exalts Jesus. An outpouring changes us from the inside out as His presence encounters us in a fresh way. An outpouring may spark healings, signs, wonders and other gifts of the spirit in manifestation. An outpouring may drive people to repentance and salvation.

— Prayer —

Father, in the name of Jesus, would You help me to be accurate in the spirit with my language around revival? I don't want to mislabel what You are doing. I want to see clearly what is happening in the spirit so I can respond rightly and steward it well. Help me discern Your movements in my midst.

What is an Outpouring?

"I will cause showers to come down in their season; there shall be showers of blessing" (Ezekiel 34:26).

An outpouring is different than a revival—but a genuine outpouring can spark a full-blown revival. So, what is an outpouring? An outpouring is a supernatural move of the Holy Spirit that emphasizes a particular gift or ministry.

An outpouring is often the response to prayers based on Scriptures such as, "Until the Spirit is poured upon us from on high, and the wilderness becomes a fruitful field, and the fruitful field is counted as a forest" (see Is. 32:15).

Think of Joel 2:28, a familiar revival verse: "And it shall come to pass afterward That I will pour out My Spirit on all flesh; Your sons and your daughters shall prophesy, your old men shall dream dreams, your young men shall see visions." Solomon penned these words regarding pursuing wisdom: "Turn at my rebuke; Surely I will pour out my spirit on you; I will make my words known to you" (Prov. 1:23).

As I wrote in *Revival Hubs Rising*, over the generations, there have been healing outpourings, fire outpourings, charismatic gift outpourings, glory outpourings, and so on. An outpouring typically has a destined beginning and end. It is seasonal—even if the season is many years—and has a specific purpose in the earth. The Holy Spirit pours out what is needed in the hour or in a generation.

While we like to talk about redigging the wells of revival, an outpouring doesn't come from a well. It comes from above. A well issues water from the earth. You don't dig for an outpouring. You receive it freely. A well must be dug before it will bring forth water or oil. An outpouring is sovereign. It's God responding to the contrite heart. It's God responding to those who hunger and thirst after righteousness (see Matt. 5:6).

Do you want more? If there is a "more, Lord" in your heart, ask God to pour the more. He is the God of more than enough and He wants to pour His Spirit out upon you.

— *Prayer* —

Father, in the name of Jesus, help me discern even the smallest idols in my life that distract me from Your heart. I don't want to serve an idol who cannot see and cannot hear and cannot speak. I pledge my allegiance to the one true living God who loves me and gave Himself for me.

A Call to the Valley of Shechem

"I beseech you therefore, brethren, by the mercies of God, that you present your bodies a living sacrifice, holy, acceptable to God, which is your reasonable service" (Romans 12:1).

If you are reading these words, then you've probably already chosen this day whom you will serve. But could it be possible there are yet things you need to put away in order to truly worship the Lord in spirit and in truth and love Him with all your heart, soul, strength and mind?

Today, the Lord is calling you to the Valley of Shechem. The Valley of Shechem is where Joshua called together all the tribes of Israel and delivered a powerful prophetic word to the nation. Joshua prophesied about Abraham, a prophet who once worshipped other gods, about the plagues on Egypt, and the parting of the Red Sea.

God was going somewhere with this prophetic history lesson. Indeed, He was methodically working to drive a point home. See, God had given Israel a land for which she did not labor and cities she did not build. Israel was dwelling safely in the Promised Land, eating of the vineyards and the olive groves. In other words, God followed His miraculous deliverance with His abundant grace.

Much the same, God has blessed us with every spiritual blessing in heavenly places in Christ, and predestined us to adoption as sons, according to the good pleasure of His will (see Eph. 1:3-6). With this spiritual truth in mind, come with me to the Valley of Shechem. The crux of his message was calling a nation to choose who they would serve.

This is my challenge to you: Choose this day whom you will serve: self or Spirit. I urge you by the Spirit of God not to be conformed to this world, but to be transformed by the renewing of your mind, that you may prove what is that good and acceptable and perfect will of God to a lost and dying world. Choose God. Choose revival.

— *Prayer* —

Father, in the name of Jesus, would You show me anything in my soul that resists You? I don't want to serve myself. I want to serve Your purposes and plans in the earth. I want to serve You. I want to serve the Kingdom agenda of revival and awakening in my generation.

FEBRUARY 23

Casting Down Your Idols

"Those who make them are like them; So is everyone who trusts in them" (Psalm 115:8).

The question is simple: Will you serve Jehovah whole-heartedly or will you serve an idol? The simplest definition of "idol" is a false god. The revivalist must cast down his idols before he calls others to cast down theirs. But idols are sneaky.

Merriam-Webster defines idol as a "representation or symbol of an object of worship; a false god." Another definition is "pretender, impostor." Yet another definition is "an object of extreme devotion" or "a false conception."

In ancient times, people created idols to worship. They gave these wooden, silver, and golden idols names that represented gods. Today, we are a little more sophisticated and the enemy is a little more subtle. We would never dream of worshipping a golden calf. But we may be tempted to worship our favorite sport, our career, our children or even our ministry.

In other words, we may set up people, places, and things as idols in our lives that draw our attention away from God. Anything that draws our attention away from Jesus is a pretender and an imposter. Any object of extreme devotion apart from God is a false god.

The Bible clearly says, "You shall have no other gods before me" (Ex. 20:3). In case you didn't hear it loud and clear in Exodus, the Holy Spirit repeats Himself in Deuteronomy 5:7: "You shall have no other gods before me." And once more, "For thou shalt worship no other god: for the Lord, whose name is Jealous, is a jealous God" (Ex. 34:14).

Maybe you have "idols" in your life, like your kids or your car. But this is what the Lord is saying in this hour: More often than not the idol in our lives is self. It's time to lay everything on the altar and let the Lord give back only that which agrees with His plans and purposes for our lives.

— *Prayer* —

Father, in the name of Jesus, help me discern even the smallest idols in my life that distract me from Your heart. I don't want to serve an idol who cannot see and cannot hear and cannot speak. I pledge my allegiance to the one true living God who loves me and gave Himself for me.

A Revival of the Word of God

"Man shall not live by bread alone, but by every word that proceeds from the mouth of God"
(Matthew 4:4).

"The time is surely coming,' says the Sovereign Lord, 'when I will send a famine on the land—not a famine of bread or water but of hearing the words of the Lord" (Amos 8:11, NLT). This wasn't the first time in Israel's history where a word famine made the pages of Scripture.

In Samuel's day, the word of the Lord was rare, and visions were scarce (see 1 Sam. 3:1). For many years, Israel was without the law (see 2 Chron. 15:3). The written Word and the prophetic word are vital in any generation but in the 16th Century the Bible had not been translated into many languages and the prophetic restoration was centuries away.

That set the stage for a revival of the Word of God. There was a strong emphasis on Scripture, as well as societal reforms that set the stage for moves of God in centuries to come.

Take Desiderius Erasmus, for example. You've probably never heard his name, but he published the Scriptures in Greek in 1516 and was an influence on the life of the famed Martin Luther. Luther published the first Bible in German in 1522.

Following Luther was William Tyndale. He was an early English reformer that published the Bible in English, although incomplete, in 1525. He followed with a full translation in 1526.

Today, the Bible has been translated into nearly seven hundred different languages, according to Wycliffe Bible Translators. This is critical since when people have the Bible in their own languages they can learn of Christ, share the Gospel, and plant churches.

John 1:1 tells us, "In the beginning was the Word, and the Word was with God, and the Word was God." Jesus is the Word made flesh (see John 1:4). The Word of God is alive and sharper than any two-edged sword (see Heb. 4:12). Thank God for these pioneers who ended the Word famine.

— *Prayer* —

Father, in the name of Jesus, would You stir my heart to pursue the depths of Your Word? Help me store Your Word in my heart so that it comes out of my mouth when I pray. Give me a deep love and hunger for Your Word so that the revival I'm standing for is on a firm foundation.

Revival Martyrs

"I saw the woman, drunk with the blood of the saints and with the blood of the martyrs of Jesus. And when I saw her, I marveled with great amazement" (Revelation 17:6).

We often talk about a revival that leads to reformation—and we should. That's the hope. If revival doesn't breed reformation—societal changes—then it hasn't accomplished the fullness of its work.

That's what so interesting about the 16th Century, a period that wasn't marked by revival as we know it today. It was marked by reforming voices that demanded change for the sake of the Gospel.

While many point to Martin Luther, Jan Hus (or John Hus as some write it) preceded him in pressing toward what we now call Protestantism. Huss was a Czech theologian and philosopher who came on the scene after John Wycliff but before John Calvin in Christian history's timeline.

Hus made a name for himself in the Bohemian Reformation—also known as the Czech Reformation or Hussite Reformation—that became one of the most critical religious, intellectual, societal, and political movements in the early modern period. The Bohemian Reformation, for example, drove the first national church that was separate from Roman Catholic authority. Huss birthed what some call the first pacifist Protestant church.

Because of the times in Czechoslovakia, the Hussites crossed religious boundaries to become a political and military faction that fought Catholic forces. He even confronted the Pope, saying, "As for antichrist occupying the papal chair, it is evident that a pope living contrary to Christ, like any other perverted person, is called, by common consent, antichrist."

Like Paul the apostle, Hus ended up in prison but still wrote words that impacted the generations after him: "I, Master John Hus, in chains and in prison, now standing on the shore of this present life and expecting on the morrow a dreadful death, which will, I hope, purge away my sins, find no heresy in myself, and accept with all my heart any truth whatsoever that is worthy of belief."

He was burned at the stake for his beliefs. Would you be willing to suffer the same fate? What makes men like Hus different? Selah.

— *Prayer* —

Father, in the name of Jesus, would You give me a revelation of the importance of reformation. Revival is a gift, but reformation is the real prize. Help me war in the spirit for the same of reformation that seeks Your Word run swiftly in cities and nations for the sake of the lost.

Quaking and Awaking

"Be angry, and do not sin. Meditate within your heart on your bed, and be still. Selah. Offer the sacrifices of righteousness, and put your trust in the Lord" (Psalm 4:4-5).

You have heard of the Quakers, but have you heard of the man behind the movement? His name is George Fox. Fox's sensitivity to the Holy Spirit marked his life even from childhood. He came from a godly heritage and recalls an encounter with God at an early age.

In his journal Fox wrote, "When I came to eleven years of age, I knew pureness and righteousness; for, while I was a child, I was taught how to walk to be kept pure. The Lord taught me to be faithful, in all things, and to act faithfully two ways; viz., inwardly to God, and outwardly to man."

Unfortunately, Fox grew up in an age of political violence and church hypocrisy. Once a frustrated seeker of Christ who was critical of his culture in 1647 England, Fox turned to the Scriptures and prayer. He kept pursuing Jesus until he had a spiritual epiphany in 1652 and discovered the Holy Spirit would interpret the Word of God and bring joy to his heart.

Fox wrote, "And when all my hopes in them and in all men were gone, so that I had nothing outwardly to help me, nor could tell what to do, then, oh, then, I heard a voice which said, 'There is one, even Christ Jesus, that can speak to thy condition'; and when I heard it my heart did leap for joy."

Fox had a personal awakening that led to a ministry that awakened vast numbers of people to Christ our King. Despite being thrown down church steps, beaten with sticks even spending time in jail for his faith, Fox kept pressing into holiness.

By 1660, Fox had fifty thousand followers who called themselves Quakers. The Quaker movement is still alive today, marked by direct experience with God and the inspiration of the life and teachings of Jesus. In a sense, we should all be Quakers like Fox.

— *Prayer* —

Father, in the name of Jesus, I admit I'm frustrated by what I see in the church today. I am frustrated with the apathy and the falsity. But help me to use that frustration as fuel to see change. Let it drive me to my knees in prayer until an awakening of holiness comes.

FEBRUARY 27

When Awakening Spans a Generation

"But His word was in my heart like a burning fire shut up in my bones; I was weary of holding it back, and I could not" (Jeremiah 20:9).

What if the next awakening lasted thirty-one years? God has done it before, so we must cry, "Do it again, Lord!" Richard Baxter's ministry saw a thirty-one-year awakening in Kidderminster, Worcestershire in England. The remarkable revival spanned from 1660-1691.

Baxter was known as the prince of Puritan pastors. Indeed, he had the heart of a pastor but the fiery zeal of a prophet. His Kidderminster church sparked the revival among heathens in a town of three thousand. By the time the Holy Spirit was done moving in their midst, most of the town turned to saving faith in Jesus Christ.

Baxter's ministry saw miracles, including tumors dissolved, epilepsy healed, and sinners turn to Christ through fervent prayer and fasting. A prayer warrior himself, Baxter was known to take on demonic strongholds and speak bold words that brought politicians to tears. But he was also practical, once sharing:

"Make careful choice of the books which you read: let the holy Scriptures ever have the preeminence. Let Scripture be first and most in your hearts and hands and other books be used as subservient to it.

"While reading ask yourself: 1. Could I spend this time no better? 2. Are there better books that would edify me more? 3. Are the lovers of such a book as this the greatest lovers of the Book of God and of a holy life? 4. Does this book increase my love to the Word of God, kill my sin, and prepare me for the life to come?

"The words of the wise are like goads, their collected sayings like firmly embedded nails—given by one Shepherd. Be warned, my son, of anything in addition to them. Of making many books there is no end, and much study wearies the body. Ecclesiastes 12:11-12." Baxter's blend of prayer, fasting, fiery preaching and practical teaching lit up a city for Jesus.

— *Prayer* —

Father, in the name of Jesus, give me the heart of a pastor and the fire of a prophet like Richard Baxter. I want to see cities turned upside down for Jesus. Give me the wisdom to tackle demonic strongholds, to speak boldly and to love fervently. Help me be like Jesus.

Sowing Seeds of Revival

"What shall we say then? Shall we continue in sin that grace may abound? Certainly not! How shall we who died to sin live any longer in it?" (Romans 6:1-2).

Everything starts with a seed—and that seed must die in the ground before it blossoms and flourishes. This is the story of the First and Second Great Awakenings. Modern-day revivalists can learn a lesson from the Pietists.

Pietism was birthed among German Lutherans in the 17th Century. Philipp Jakob Spener (1635-1705), a German theologian and author, is considered the "Father of Pietism." The movement focused on personal faith and individual holiness in Christian living and is still alive and well today. But it also centered on prayer and purity unto power. Spener wrote:

"How many there are who live such a manifestly unchristian life that they themselves cannot deny that the law is broken at every point, who have no intention of mending their ways in the future, and yet who pretend to be firmly convinced that they will be saved in spite of all this!"

Spener was a prophetic voice in his day, with insight into the ails of the 18th Century church and how to work with the Spirit of God to heal them. In some ways, he picked up where reformer Martin Luther left off. While many turned to Christ in Luther's day, understanding the just shall live by faith (see Rom. 1:17), there was still something lacking.

Spener saw the lack of the reverential fear of the Lord and tendency for some to take the grace of God for granted (see Rom. 6:1-2). In 1670 Spener started gathering those of like precious faith who were fed up with religion as it was handed to them. They came together to study the Bible, pray, and enter healthy accountability. He once wrote:

"Let us…be diligent in investigating ever more deeply our own shortcomings and those of the rest of the church in order that we may learn to know our sicknesses, and then with a fervent invocation of God for the light of his Spirit let us also search for and ponder over the remedies."

Spener's boldness sowed seeds that sprouted up in great awakenings. What seeds can you sow today that could impact the spiritual destiny of nations?

— *Prayer* —

Father, in the name of Jesus, forgive me for any seeds I have sown that caused trouble instead of triumph in Your church. Help me to sow seeds of righteousness and holiness with my thoughts, words, deeds—and prayers. Help me look inward and upward before I look outward at church ills.

The Jonathan Edwards Revivalist Anointing

"Give to the Lord the glory due His name; Bring an offering, and come before Him. Oh, worship the Lord in the beauty of holiness!" (1 Chronicles 16:29)

Jonathan Edwards was perhaps a likely candidate to lead a Great Awakening. He grew up in a family that was sold out to God's plans and purposes. Born in 1703 in Connecticut, his father was a pastor who raised him to emphasize the reality of awakenings.

A Yale graduate, Edwards started pastoring a Presbyterian church when he was just eighteen years old. Interestingly, the church at which he served his longest tenure fired him. But it seemed to be God's providence. Edwards was indeed born for awakening. He is perhaps best remembered for his troubling sermon, *Sinners in the Hands of an Angry God.*

"After great convictions and humbling, and agonizing with God, they had Christ discovered to them anew as an all-sufficient Savior, and in the glories of His grace, and in a far more clear manner than before; and with greater humility, self-emptiness, and brokenness of heart, and a purer, a higher joy, and greater desires after holiness of life; but with greater self-diffidence and distrust of their treacherous hearts," he wrote.

Before he passed on to glory, Edwards started serving as a pastor and missionary to Native Americans in 1751. Some of his most important writings were penned during that time. All told, he wrote seventy-three books. In 1758, he was installed as president of what is now Princeton University.

Mark Noll, an American historian specializing in the history of Christianity in the United States remarked, "Edwards' piety continued on in the revivalist tradition, his theology continued on in academic Calvinism, but there were no successors to his God-entranced world view. The disappearance of Edwards's perspective in American Christian history has been a tragedy."

Indeed, Edwards' work can be summed up in two themes: the absolute sovereignty of God and the beauty of Gods' holiness. The Jonathan Edwards revival anointing is a bold anointing that causes people to see both the ugliness of sin and the beauty of Jesus.

— *Prayer* —

Father, in the name of Jesus, would You help me balance calls for repentance for sin with calls to gaze up on Your beauty? Help me speak the truth in love. Let my words—and prayers—be seasoned with grace and mercy. Give me a bold anointing that helps people see what is at stake.

MARCH

"In revival, God is not concerned about filling empty churches, He is concerned about filling empty hearts."—Leonard Ravenhill

When the Revivalist is Ignored

"Son of man, I have made you a watchman for the house of Israel; therefore hear a word from My mouth, and give them warning from Me" (Ezekiel 3:17).

When you think of Joshua, you may think of the skilled warrior who led the Israelites into the Promised Land. But we should also remember him as a revivalist. You might say he was a pre-revivalist. Sadly, his warnings for disobedience were ignored.

Israel saw God's blessings under Joshua's leadership, but Joshua saw the potential for backsliding after his death—and he was right. Joshua 24:31 tells us, "Israel served the Lord all the days of Joshua, and all the days of the elders who outlived Joshua, who had known all the works of the Lord which He had done for Israel."

But soon thereafter, Israel started disobeying the covenant and started serving the Baals and Ashtoreths. They forsook the God of their fathers. The anger of the Lord burned against them, and their enemies swiftly conquered them. Throughout the Book of Judges, we see God raise up deliverers to save Israel only to see nation backslide again and again. Sadly, Joshua warned them ahead of time.

"Now therefore, fear the Lord, serve Him in sincerity and in truth, and put away the gods which your fathers served on the other side of the River and in Egypt. Serve the Lord! And if it seems evil to you to serve the Lord, choose for yourselves this day whom you will serve, whether the gods which your fathers served that were on the other side of the River, or the gods of the Amorites, in whose land you dwell. But as for me and my house, we will serve the Lord" (Joshua 24:14-15).

The Israelites agreed not to serve other gods. They vowed to serve the Lord, despite Joshua's warning, "If you forsake the Lord and serve foreign gods, then He will turn and do you harm and consume you, after He has done you good" (Josh. 24:20). Sadly, their children's children entered into compromise.

Revivalist, you can only give the warning. You can't make people listen.

— *Prayer* —

Father, in the name of Jesus, would You help me stay ready to release Your warnings to Your people? Would You help me model the way of faithfulness to Your Word and Your ways so people will be more likely to give heed to the words of warning You give me to speak?

Paying the Price for Revival

"For which of you, intending to build a tower, does not sit down first and count the cost, whether he has enough to finish it" (Luke 14:28).

When God called me into ministry, He spoke many things to my heart. One of the things He told me was "to count the costs and don't look back."

Some years later, the Lord asked me if I was willing to pay the price to do what He had called me to do. I answered quickly, "Yes, Lord. I am willing." After all, I had already decided to follow Him anywhere when He called me—or at least I thought I had. But He admonished, "Don't answer too quickly. Consider the costs."

With that, I went off to pray. After about a week, I returned to the Lord with a solid answer: "Yes, Lord, I am willing to pay the price." I sensed the pleasure of the Holy Spirit at my sincere answer, but I never anticipated what He would tell me next: "It will be a very dear price."

Before too long, I started paying the price—and it was a dear price indeed. Thank God that in His wisdom and mercy He shows us things to come if we simply have eyes to see and ears to hear the truth into which the Holy Spirit is trying to lead us.

Had the Holy Spirit not warned me of what was about to happen through that one line, "It will be a very dear price," I would've been devastated at what happened next. I had to leave a toxic church—and with that move I lost all my friends and ministry opportunities overnight. I was sorely persecuted on the way out the door. The cost was indeed very dear.

However, God is a rewarder of those who diligently seek Him (see Heb. 11:6). Vengeance really is His responsibility, and He really will repay evil for good (see Rom.12:19). I paid a dear price, but God repaid way more than seven times what the thief stole (see Prov. 6:31). I will always remember that lesson and it would come in handy in the context of revival. Are you willing to pay the price?

— *Prayer* —

Father, in the name of Jesus, would You help me count the cost for what I say I want? I want revival, but I may not know what it's really going to cost me to pursue Jesus until revival comes to my city. Strengthen me to count the costs—and to pay the price until I see Your revival.

MARCH 3

Armed for Revival Battles

"Stand therefore, having girded your waist with truth, having put on the breastplate of righteousness, and having shod your feet with the preparation of the gospel of peace; above all, taking the shield of faith with which you will be able to quench all the fiery darts of the wicked one" (Ephesians 6:14-16).

We need to put on—and keep on—the whole armor of God. Paul offers insight into what's available to us in Ephesians 6:12. But many have not heeded those Spirit-inspired instructions. Let's look at these verses again from the Amplified translation:

"So stand firm and hold your ground, having tightened the wide band of truth (personal integrity, moral courage) around your waist and having put on the breastplate of righteousness (an upright heart), and having strapped on your feet the gospel of peace in preparation [to face the enemy with firm-footed stability and the readiness produced by the good news]. Above all, lift up the [protective] shield of faith with which you can extinguish all the flaming arrows of the evil one."

Many in the church have taken off the belt of truth and embraced lies that it's okay to practice homosexuality or to neglect prayer or to sleep with people to whom you're not married. Many in the church have set down the Sword of the Spirit, which is the Word of God, and picked up pornography. Many others have traded church service for occultic entertainment like Harry Potter or danced to the demonic lyrics of modern music.

Many in the church have taken off the breastplate of righteousness, compromising who they are in Christ to avoid conflict in the workplace—or in the church, or even in the pulpit. Lay members laugh at dirty jokes to fit in or turn Sunday morning worship into a worldly event or preach a pretty message that never confronts sin in order to keep tithes up.

Many have traded their shoes of peace for some chic fashion designer's shoes of the season while neglecting to bring an offering to God. Oh, sure, many are still wearing helmets of salvation, but they sometimes wish they could hide that hat because they don't want to seem uncool in a contemporary society that shuns Christ. I pray God will wake us up so we can armor up and fight the good fight.

— *Prayer* —

Father, in the name of Jesus, would You remind me daily to put on the whole amor of God, for I know it doesn't do me any good in storage? Help me stay ready for battle so I can be an agent of awakening in the earth. Help me see what's at stake in my life and for those who don't know You.

Derailing the Delilah Spirit

"And it came to pass, when she pestered him daily with her words and pressed him, so that his soul was vexed to death" (Judges 16:16).

Too many in the church is playing the harlot—forsaking the Bridegroom for sin. This was a problem in ancient Israel and it's still a problem in the nations today.

Keep in mind, harlotry was ultimately Samson's downfall. The Bible says Samson went to Gaza and saw a harlot there and had sex with her (see Judges 16:1). Samson was literally sleeping with the enemy as he followed the passions of his flesh rather than the God he vowed to serve—even though he was a Nazarite called to live an uber holy life.

Later, Sampson met Delilah, with whom he fell in love—but her motives toward him were not pure. The Philistines—enemies of Israel—offered her eleven hundred pieces of silver if she could persuade him to share the source of his great strength so they could overpower him, bind him, and afflict him (see Judges 16:4-5). She asked him time and time again, and he lied to her time and time again. Samson foiled the enemy's plans until Delilah wore him down with her constant nagging.

This is a key strategy of the enemy. Daniel 7:25 reveals the enemy wearies the saints but we know that those who wait on the Lord shall not grow weary (see Is. 40:31). What's more, Galatians 6:9 admonishes us, "And let us not grow weary while doing good, for in due season we shall reap if we do not lose heart."

Samson didn't wait on the Lord. He allowed the devil's words to press him "so that his soul was vexed to death" (see Judges 16:17). That's what we do may times— we allow the enemy's persistent words to vex our hearts until we fail to fight back. We must fight for revival and awakening. We must not play the harlot, chasing after idols that appease our flesh. We must not cave in to the enemy's nefarious nagging temptations. We must not—and we shall not!

— *Prayer* —

Father, in the name of Jesus, would You help me recognize and cast down every idol I have erected in my life? I don't want to play the harlot. I don't want to be unfaithful to Your heart. Help me not to give in to the nagging temptations of the enemy that dull my soul.

MARCH 5

False Revivals Will Rise

"Beloved, do not believe every spirit, but test the spirits, whether they are of God; because many false prophets have gone out into the world" (1 John 4:1).

Intercession broke out. Travail ensued. Groanings too deep for utterance seemed to echo throughout the church—and then the spirit of the fear of the Lord fell on the entire congregation (see Is. 11:2).

Everybody froze. The intercession stopped. The travail stopped. The groanings stopped. The church was silent. The spirit of the fear of the Lord permeated the atmosphere. There was an awe among us, a reverence for God. It was a holy moment. You could hear the proverbial pin drop.

In that moment, the Holy Spirit spoke something that shook me. He told me, "False revivalists would rise up in this hour." These false revivalists don't truly have a heart for revival or awakening or transformation. Rather, they are motivated by the potential profits in the latest church trend.

Much like we saw false prophets arise amid a true prophetic reformation, and false apostles rise amid a true apostolic reformation, false revivalists are rising even as sincere believers are making an urgent appeal to heaven in desperation for a Third Great Awakening.

We've seen false revivals before, so it's not altogether surprising that false revivalists would rise in any emerging move of God. I believe the fear of the Lord is what will ultimately separate the true revivalists from the ones who are looking to the latest wind of the Spirit for an opportunity to merchandise the saints.

Unfortunately, it's time to add false revivalists to all the warnings. If you go to a meeting where something doesn't seem right, it may not be. If people try to manipulate you for money, run for the door. If ministers are pushing people down at the altar and standing on top of their "slain" bodies, from such turn away. Revivalist, discern before you get caught up in the hype.

— *Prayer* —

Father, in the name of Jesus, help me understand the reality of false revivals. It grieves my heart that some would hype up an atmosphere to build a ministry or make a name for themselves instead of building the church and promoting Your great name. Give me discernment.

Discerning Counterfeit Revivals

"Many will say to Me in that day, 'Lord, Lord, have we not prophesied in Your name, cast out demons in Your name, and done many wonders in Your name?' And then I will declare to them, 'I never knew you; depart from Me, you who practice lawlessness!'" (Matthew 7:22-23)

God is bringing a Third Great Awakening to America marked by signs, wonders, and miracles. We should expect that if the devil can't stop it—and he can't—he will try to offer a counterfeit move to fleece the sheep who are hungry for an authentic outpouring.

I am praying for a Hebrew 5:14 reality in the Body of Christ—that believers would have powers of discernment and would be trained to distinguish good from evil through practice. In these last days, we cannot take everything we see at face value. I am not suggesting suspicion. I'm advocating for righteous judgment, prophetic insight, and spiritual perception. I'm pleading with believers to study the Word of God, fellowship with the Spirit of God and pray without ceasing. Ultimately, I'm just suggesting we do what the Bible says we should do:

"Beloved, do not believe every spirit, but test the spirits to see whether they are from God, because many false prophets have gone out into the world" (1 John 4:1). You can't read a single book in the New Testament without finding a warning about deception. Jesus Himself said, "For false christs and false prophets will arise and show great signs and wonders to deceive, if possible, even the elect" (Matt. 24:24).

So how do we discern false revivals? So many critics of revival call the true false and so many undiscerning believers call the false true. False revivals lack a word of conviction or anything that resembles repentance. There is no revival without repentance. Remember, there is revival fire but there is also what the Bible calls "strange fire" (see Lev. 10:1). False revivals are marked by hype—or a counterfeit anointing.

Strong preaching that gets us up on our feet is healthy. We all need to be stirred up at times—both in our spirit and in our soul—to rise up a little higher. But hype is another story. The very definition of hype means "deception" and "publicity." Real revivals don't need advertisements or hype. The Spirit of God will do.

— Prayer —

Father, in the name of Jesus, help me discern counterfeit anointings and not fall for the hype. Help me discern the strange fire issuing from false revivalists who are in it for greedy gain and self-glory. Teach me to discern the true anointing and shun every false manifestation.

MARCH 7

Smith Wigglesworth's Word and Spirit Revival

"And there are three that bear witness on earth: the Spirit, the water, and the blood; and these three agree as one" (1 John 5:8).

We're all praying for the next great move of God. But Smith Wigglesworth, known as the Apostle of Faith, prophesied about the last great move of God in 1947. These are his words:

"During the next few decades there will be two distinct moves of the Holy Spirit across the church in Great Britain. The first move will affect every church that is open to receive it, and will be characterized by the restoration of the baptism and gifts of the Holy Spirit.

"The second move of the Holy Spirit will result in people leaving historic churches and planting new churches. In the duration of each of these moves, the people who are involved will say, 'This is a great revival.' But the Lord says, 'No, neither is this the great revival but both are steps towards it.'

"When the new church phase is on the wane, there will be evidence in the churches of something that has not been seen before: a coming together of those with an emphasis on the word and those with an emphasis on the Spirit.

"When the word and the Spirit come together, there will be the biggest move of the Holy Spirit that the nations, and indeed, the world have ever seen. It will mark the beginning of a revival that will eclipse anything that has been witnessed within these shores, even the Wesleyan and Welsh revivals of former years.

"The outpouring of God's Spirit will flow over from the United Kingdom to mainland Europe, and from there, will begin a missionary move to the ends of the earth." Amen!

— *Prayer* —

Father, in the name of Jesus, I come into agreement with Smith Wigglesworth's prophecy. I thank You for this prophetic word and I commit to warring with it. I want to see a Word and Spirit revival. Help me continue to contend with this prophetic word until we see it come to pass.

The Lou Engle Revivalist Anointing

"Truly, these times of ignorance God overlooked, but now commands all men everywhere to repent..." (Acts 17:30).

In the year 2000, Lou Engle started asking the Lord how he could be part of turning America back to God. This John the Baptist-style prophet and intercessor discerned the perils facing our nation before 9/11, before the Great Recession, before this new wave of racial tension—and before the rise of an Islamic terrorist group that is beheading Christians and threatening to "strike America at its heart."

Lou's humble question birthed TheCall, a prayer movement that has gathered hundreds of thousands of believers to stadiums in America for solemn assemblies in the spirit of Joel 2. Later, he started praying for the mantle of Frank Bartleman, an American Pentecostal writer and evangelist from the early 1900s. It seems God took him up on his petition.

As Lou tells the story, the very night he was crying out for Bartleman's mantle, his friend had a dream in which he saw a big black book with the title "Revival." In that dream, his friend opened the book to the inside cover and there was a picture of Frank Bartleman—and his face turned into Lou's face.

"From that moment on, I knew my calling was revival and I was an intercessor for revival," Lou said. "My calling is to fast and pray. I am a fire starter in prophetic intercession who calls people into fasting and prayer for breakthroughs with the end goal of seeing the spirit of revival."

Perhaps the prince of forty-day fasts, Lou is known for fasting as much as he is for prayer. Lou's ministry is marked by prophetic dreams and visions—and God uses these revelations to lead and guide him on each step of his journey.

Lou will go down in charismatic church history as a general of intercession who mobilized the church to pray; a John-the-Baptist-like prophet who called the nation to repentance; a pro-life leader who understood that the blood of abortion is on our hands; a spiritual warrior who refused to tolerate Jezebel; and, hopefully an instrument of transforming revival.

— *Prayer* —

Father, in the name of Jesus, give me an anointing like Lou Engle's that lays it all down in prayer for Your Kingdom. Give me the grace to fast. Give me prophetic dreams and visions and revelation that helps me forward Your plans in my generation for Your glory.

When Revival Hits the Children

"Have you never read, 'Out of the mouth of babes and nursing infants You have perfected praise'?"
(Matthew 21:16)

During an outpouring at Awakening House of Prayer, a little boy named Hunter came up to the altar. He wanted to be filled with the Spirit and speak in tongues. He must have come expecting because he specifically told his mother he did not want to go children's church that day. He wanted to be part of the outpouring.

The temptation for many revivalists is to send kids up to a glorified babysitter during revival meetings. But there is no junior Holy Spirit and when children are touched by the Spirit at a young age, they can become carriers of revival to their generation.

George Whitefield and Jonathan Edwards, two key figures in the First Great Awakening, seemed to understand this well. Whitefield took revival to the children's hospitals and preached to the children of the city in the parks. He wrote: "It is remarkable that many children are under convictions, and everywhere great power and apparent success attend the word preached."

In April of 1742, a minister in Edinburgh, Scotland wrote: "On June 3, Whitefield arrived for his second visit to a rapturous welcome, and the following morning, three of the little boys that were converted when I was last here, came to me and wept and begged me to pray for and with them. A minister tells me that scarce one is fallen back who was awakened, either among old or young."

Meanwhile, Edwards kept a journal that included some of his encounters with children.

"I began meeting with the children in the afternoon, though with little hopes of doing them good; but I had not spoken long on our natural state before many of them were in tears, and five or six so affected, that they could not refrain from crying aloud to God. When I began praying, their cries increased, so that my voice was soon lost. I have seen no such work among children for eighteen or nineteen years."

— *Prayer* —

Father, in the name of Jesus, help me not to ever forbid children from coming into Your presence in the throes of revival. Help me make room for the children to taste and see that You are good during the outpouring of Your Spirit. Teach me how to minister to the little ones.

Eight Ravenhill Quotes That Will Stir Your Heart

"'Is not My word like a fire?' says the Lord, 'and like a hammer that breaks the rock in pieces?'" (Jeremiah 23:29)

Leonard Ravenhill, author of *Why Revival Tarries,* had a way with words. Indeed, his words sometimes cut like a knife. I believe the Holy Spirit used his words to convict people to repent, pray and seek personal revival. Here are eight quotes that will stir your heart.

"The only reason we don't have revival is," he said, "is because we are willing to live without it!" Let us decide right now that we are not willing to live without revival!

"Revival is when God gets so sick and tired of being misrepresented that He shows Himself," he said. Let's pray that God will show up and show us who He is.

"Surely revival delays because prayer decays," he said. Lord, let our prayer never decay. Ravenhill also said, "In revival, God is not concerned about filling empty churches. He is concerned with filling empty hearts." Father, fill every empty heart with Your Spirit.

"When God-given, heaven-sent revival does come," Ravenhill said, "it will undo in weeks the damage that blasphemous Modernism has taken years to build." He also opined, "As long as we are content to live without revival, we will."

Ravenhill insisted: "At God's counter there are no sale days, for the price of revival is ever the same: travail!" Holy Spirit, lead us into travail for Your church!

"Maybe you are the key to revival in your church," he said. "Revival is the Spirit's passion within the believer to know and to obey the total will of God."

I'll leave you these Ravenhill words: "I read of the revivals of the past, great sweeping revivals where thousands of men were swept into the Kingdom of God. I read about Charles G. Finney winning his thousands and his hundreds of thousands of souls to Christ. Then I picked up a book and read the messages of Charles G. Finney and the message of Jonathan Edwards on 'Sinners in the Hands of an Angry God,' and I said, 'No wonder men trembled; no wonder they fell in the altars and cried out in repentance and sobbed their way to the throne of grace!'"

— *Prayer* —

Father, in the name of Jesus, thank You for men of God like Leonard Ravenhill who sharpen the Body of Christ. Help me to take his words to heart and shift any wrong attitudes I have toward revival. Help me to be bold for revival because the righteous are as bold as lions.

A Prodigal Awakening

"I will seek what was lost and bring back what was driven away, bind up the broken and strengthen what was sick" (Ezekiel 34:16).

It's a shocking statistic! More than eighty and up to ninety percent of children who grow up in church are leaving the church once they reach eighteen. Sadly, only forty percent return, according to Focus on the Family.

I believe, with prayer, we can overturn those statistics. Indeed, God is trying to wake up the world—and I believe He is also going to wake up a massive number of prodigals in this season. Never underestimate the power of your prayers. It got saved because of the power of a praying great grandmother and a praying grandmother.

Isaiah 55:11 (AMP) says, "So shall My word be that goes forth out of My mouth: it shall not return to Me void [without producing any effect, useless], but it shall accomplish that which I please and purpose, and it shall prosper in the thing for which I sent it."

God is in the business of saving people (see John 3:16). He sent His only begotten Son into the world to seek and save those who are lost. If we are going to see a revival among prodigals, we must pray without ceasing for it.

Pray God will break the blinders off their eyes (see 2 Cor. 3:14). Pray the prodigals will be delivered from the evil one (see Prov. 11:21). Pray that God's laws will be in their minds and on their hearts (see Heb. 8:10).

But don't stop there. Keep praying. Pray the prodigals will choose companions who are wise—not fools, nor sexually immoral, nor drunkards, nor idolaters, nor slanderers, nor swindlers (see 1 Cor. 5:11). Pray for God to remove evil, ungodly friends and influences from their lives (see Prov. 13:20).

Pray for God to send laborers in their path who will drop seeds of truth, water the Word that was sown in their hearts, and even prophesy over them with accuracy that opens their eyes to God's love for them (see Matt.9:38). Pray that God would encounter their hearts with His great love and that His kindness will lead them to repentance (see Rom. 2:4).

— Prayer —

Father, in the name of Jesus, would You give me a heart for the prodigals? So many are in the snare of the enemy. Give me compassion for the plight of the ones who have strayed from You heart. Give me a burden for Your prodigal sons and daughters and a passion to pray them back home.

The Greatest Revival in History

"The Lord is not slack concerning His promise, as some count slackness, but is longsuffering toward us, not willing that any should perish but that all should come to repentance"
(2 Peter 3:9).

"I see the greatest revival in the history of mankind coming to planet earth, maybe as never before. And I see every form of disease healed. I see whole hospitals emptied with no one there. Even the doctors are running down the streets shouting."

Those were the word of Smith Wigglesworth, the Apostle of Faith, spoken to Lester Sumrall, a 20th century Pentecostal preacher and evangelist. Sumrall recorded the encounter in his book *Pioneers of Faith*.

"He told me that there would be untold numbers of uncountable multitudes that would be saved. No man will say 'so many, so many,' because nobody will be able to count those who come to Jesus. No disease will be able to stand before God's people... 'It will be a worldwide situation, not local,' he said, 'a worldwide thrust of God's power and God's anointing upon mankind.'

"Then he opened his eyes and looked at me and said, 'I will not see it, but you shall see it. The Lord says that I must go on to my reward, but that you will see the mighty works that He will do upon the earth in the last days.'

"The idea that I would get to see this revival was almost overwhelming. And in the last decade or so, I believe we have seen this revival begin to sweep the earth. We have seen amazing moves of God in Africa.

"Recently, I was in China and met with the underground church. I was told there are at least forty-five million Full Gospel Christians in China. I discovered a depth of prayer and integrity there that I have not felt anywhere else in the world... So I believe we are seeing Wigglesworth's prophecy begin to be fulfilled. We are seeing the first stages of it."

The late Lester Sumrall said those words many years ago, but like him I still believe that revival is coming. We may think we're waiting on God. But what if He is waiting on us? Pray without ceasing.

— *Prayer* —

Father, in the name of Jesus, I agree with Smith Wigglesworth's prophecy. Remind me to wage war with this prophetic word and fight the good fight of faith for the complete fulfillment of the prophecy. Give me grace to stand and contend for this Last Days outpouring.

MARCH 13

Engaging in Warfare Repentance

"For this is what the high and majestic one says, the one who fills the eternal realm with glory, whose name is Holy: 'I dwell in high and holy places but also with the bruised and lowly in spirit, those who are humble and quick to repent. I dwell with them to revive the spirit of the humble, to revive the heart of those who are broken over their sin'" (Isaiah 57:15).

I believe every church is home to a remnant of revival-minded believers who are hungry to see God move in their generation—hungry enough to repent for sins they didn't even commit!

Your mission is to find them and gather together in repentance for your sins— and identificational repentance for the sins of the church at large. This demonstrates the spirit of the lowly and sets the stage for revival prayer God will answer.

I also call this "warfare repentance." Both individual and corporate repentance are vital for your church. Identificational repentance, or warfare repentance, is a type of prayer that identifies with and confesses the sins of one's nation, city, people group, church, or family before God, according to John Dawson, author of *Healing America's Wounds*.

I call it warfare repentance because it strips Satan's right to operate. When you can identify what gave or is giving the devil a right to hold back God's will and blessing, you can lay the axe to its root and watch God's plans flourish. You can repent for sin in the land committed even before you were born. That's what Daniel did on behalf of Israel. It takes a prophetic spirit to identify these issues.

We can make blanket repentance to the Lord, and if we lack understanding and insight this act could take us into revelation because the Lord loves a contrite heart, but ultimately we need the Holy Spirit's help to identify those things for which we need to repent that are holding back revival. This is true at a personal and corporate level.

— *Prayer* —

Father, in the name of Jesus, I repent of my sins and the sins of the church. I ask You to forgive the church for not emphasizing evangelistic outreach. Forgive us for not reaching out to the poor and the widows. Forgive us for the gossip and slander within our four walls. Forgive us and cleanse us.

What Do You Need to Lay Aside?

"Therefore since we are surrounded by so great a cloud of witnesses let us lay aside every weight and the sin which so easily ensnares us and let us run with endurance the race that is set before us" (Hebrews 12:1).

Let me paint a picture. Have you ever seen a one-hundred-meter sprint in the Olympics? It's competitive and exciting, but sometimes runners sustain injuries that should have taken them out of the race.

I've seen runners sprain ankles or tear ligaments—but they won't stop running the race. They continue on the track, hobbling along if they have to, even though the pain looks unbearable. They are determined to run their race and cross the finish line even though they are severely wounded—and even though they know they can't win the gold. It's a matter of dedication to finishing what they started.

Maybe you have been wounded on your race in life. Don't stop running. Run to Jesus. He wants to heal you everywhere it hurts. Maybe you are too wounded to run in ministry or run in a relationship in this season. But you can still run to Jesus—and you must. He is your revival.

Of course, it's much easier to run to Him when you lay aside the weights, like bitterness, resentment and unforgiveness. It's easier to run to Him when you lay aside the sins that snare your soul. That is part of continual consecration. We run to Him even when it hurts—and even when we don't feel like it.

In Romans 13:1 Paul the apostle wrote these Spirit-inspired words, "Let us lay aside the deeds of darkness and put on the armor of light." What do you need to lay aside for the sake of revival?

It's a daily choice not to allow the enemy to tempt us back into the ways of the kingdom of darkness. It's a daily choice to put on the armor of light—to lay aside the encumbrances and the childish things. It's a daily choice to seek revival.

— Prayer —

Father, in the name of Jesus, help me today to see You as You are. I repent for being too busy, too self-centered, and more concerned about what You can do for me than Who You are. Lord, if I have slipped into any of these childish ways of thinking forgive me and set me on a revival path.

The Leonard Ravenhill Revivalist Anointing

"Yes, and if I am being poured out as a drink offering on the sacrifice and service of your faith, I am glad and rejoice with you all" (Philippians 2:17).

Born in Leeds, England in 1907, Leonard Ravenhill is in many ways synonymous with revival. His famed book, *Why Revival Tarries* has marked generations of people in passionate pursuit of revival in the nations.

Ravenhill was impacted by Samuel Chadwick, one of the most influential preachers of the time. And Ravenhill was marked by an encounter with God's presence and holiness as a student at Cliff College. God used him and his fellow students to preach bold words that shook the soul of England.

Ravenhill came to America in 1950 and befriended revivalist A.W. Tozer. He spent the next forty-four years pouring out his life as a drink offering for the sake of revival. His heartfelt pleading with God to pour out His Spirit was remarkable.

In *Why Revival Tarries*, Ravenhill wrote these strong words:

"Oh that believers would become eternity-conscious! If we could live every moment of every day under the eye of God, if we did every act in the light of the judgment seat, if we sold every article in the light of the judgment seat, if we prayed every prayer in the light of the judgment seat, if we tithed all our possessions in the light of the judgment seat, if we preachers prepared every sermon with one eye on damned humanity and the other on the judgment seat—then we would have a Holy Ghost revival that would shake this earth and that, in no time at all, would liberate millions of precious souls."

Ravenhill was a no non-nonsense, non-compromising voice. Growing up in the middle of the Holiness Movement sweeping England helped shape his perspective. Tozer said of Ravenhill, "To such men as this, the church owes a debt too heavy to pay. The curious thing is that she seldom tries to pay him while he lives. Rather, the next generation builds his sepulcher and writes his biography—as if instinctively and awkwardly to discharge an obligation the previous generation to a large extent ignored."

— *Prayer* —

Father, in the name of Jesus, would You set me on fire like You did Ravenhill? Make me a person of prayer. Give me a heart for holiness. Give me a boldness to confront the lukewarm spirit that seeks to steal, kill and destroy the church. Give me an anointing like You gave Ravenhill.

Contending in the Valley of Dry Bones

"Then He said to me, 'Son of man, these bones are the whole house of Israel. They indeed say, 'Our bones are dry, our hope is lost, and we ourselves are cut off!''" (Ezekiel 37:11)

Ezekiel, a priest, prophet, and watchman who had extraordinary visions, stood in the Valley of Dry Bones.

"The hand of the Lord was upon me, and He carried me out in the Spirit of the Lord and set me down in the midst of the valley which was full of bones, and He caused me to pass among them all around. And there were very many in the open valley. And they were very dry" (Ez. 37:1-3).

Imagine this scene. The bones weren't just dry—they were "very dry." There weren't just a few bones lying around. The valley was full of bones. In this hour, too many in the church find themselves in the valley instead of on the mountaintop, persecuted by antichrist agendas and unsure how to respond—or too fearful to respond at all.

Like Ezekiel, the Lord is asking us a question, "Can these bones live?" (Ez. 37:3). Many are responding just like Ezekiel did, uncertain if it's too late for their church, their city, or their nation. They are answering, "O Lord God, You know" (Ez. 37:3). Let's listen in to what happens next:

"Again He said to me, 'Prophesy over these bones and say to them, O dry bones, hear the word of the Lord. Thus says the Lord God to these bones: I will cause breath to enter you so that you live. And I will lay sinews upon you and will grow back flesh upon you and cover you with skin and put breath in you so that you live. Then you shall know that I am the Lord" (Ez. 37:4-6).

In this hour, when so much of the church is lukewarm, dry—or even apostate— we need to rise up and prophesy God's will instead of tapping into the hopeless doom, gloom. God is in the restoration business. He is in the resurrection business. He is in the transformation business. We need to prophesy His will over our lives, churches, cities, and nations with endurance. That's what Ezekiel did:

"So I prophesied as I was commanded. And as I prophesied, there was a noise and a shaking. And the bones came together, bone to its bone. When I looked, the sinews and the flesh grew upon them, and the skin covered them. But there was no breath in them" (Ez. 37:7-8).

— *Prayer* —

Father, in the name of Jesus, would You give me a confidence to look at dry churches through the lens of Your Spirit—seeing what could be and prophesying Your will to the dry, lukewarm, and even dead things? Put Your resurrection power behind the words I say and pray for revival.

Family Revival

"Therefore a man shall leave his father and mother and be[a] joined to his wife, and they shall become one flesh" (Genesis 2:24).

God loves family. We are all part of God's family, and we all have families. Family is critical to the Kingdom of God. Remember, God put Adam and Eve in the Garden to form a family and populate the earth. Indeed, the family is the foundation upon which the rest of society is built. God wants to see strong families that pray to together and worship Him together.

But families get messy. The first family saw one brother murder another. Jesus also said in the last days we would see division, father against son and son against father, mother against daughter and daughter against mother and so on (see Luke 12:53).

The biblical family unit is increasingly under satanic attack. Divorce rates are climbing. Fatherlessness is rising. Children from fatherless homes are more likely to be poor, become involved in drug and alcohol abuse, drop out of school, and suffer from health and emotional problems.

Boys are more likely to get involved in crime and girls are more likely to get pregnant. There's an all-out attack on fathers in the media. Pornography is holding people in bondage and homosexual marriage is on the rise.

We need revival on the family mountain—in the church and in the world. We do have a promise: Malachi 4:6 says Elijah will come in the last days and "turn the hearts of the fathers to the children, and the hearts of the children to their fathers, lest I come and strike the earth with a curse."

God is calling families to rebuild the family altar and demonstrate what godly family looks like—then pray for other families who don't know Him. What is the family altar? The family altar is essentially family Bible study and worship time. A family that prays together stays together and is an effective agent of revival intercession for families that aren't surrendered to His heart.

— *Prayer* —

Father, in the name of Jesus, would You help me rebuild my family altar? Help me to stand in the gap for families that don't know You as Father. Give me the prayers to pray as I carry the burden for the salvation of families. Teach me how to release revival intercession that turns hearts.

The Illiterate Revivalist

"One thing I do know, that though I was blind, now I see" (John 9:25).

The Holy Spirit called her into ministry with Matthew 10:1—Jesus gave His disciples authority over unclean spirits, to cast them out, and to heal all kinds of sickness and all kinds of disease. The only problem is she was illiterate. When she heard Holy Spirit's instruction, she had to find someone to read her the words from the Bible.

Her name was Anna. Both her parents were dead when the Lord called her, and she goes down in revival history as one of the most authoritative messengers of awakening in the 20th century. According to German theologian Dr. Kurt Koch's writings, Anna received four songs from the Lord—Gospel messages that caused lost souls to come to Christ in Timor, Indonesia.

As Koch chronicles it, one day Anna met a blind woman. After leading her to the Lord, the Holy Spirit commanded Anna to pour water into the woman's eyes so she could be healed. The blind woman's eyesight was restored. After that, Anna asked the Lord for the power to heal the blind and went on to heal ten blind people. These miracles marked the Revival in Timor in the 1960s.

We need more Annas today. She was only twenty-five years old when the Lord called her. She couldn't read or write but she could listen and obey God, and the result was repentance, salvation, healings, and miracles. She was even bold enough to talk to pastors and government officials about their sin. In 1968, as the story goes, government officials accepted Christ after her Gospel presentation.

Yes, we need more Annas today. So why don't we see them? I believe one reason is because repentance is lacking. I believe a second reason is because we don't have the faith for it. I believe a third reason is because the church is so busy with programs that we sometimes fail to remain sensitive enough to Holy Spirit's instructions to "put your finger into his ear and pray with him" or "have him dip in the river seven times."

The good news is I believe the Annas are ready to rise. I believe the remnant is ready to receive the fullness of the Holy Spirit and accept His assignments to preach the Gospel, call people to tear down their idols, confront sin in the church, cast out demons and heal all manner of sickness and disease. I believe an end times army of prophetic messengers is being prepared even now.

— *Prayer* —

Father, in the name of Jesus, would You give me a passion for souls like You gave Anna? Would You give me the boldness Anna had to speak to people in high positions? Would You help me not to make excuses about the pain of my past and grace me to be an agent of revival in my generation?

MARCH 19

Pressing Into the Holy of Holies

"But Christ came as High Priest of the good things to come, with the greater and more perfect tabernacle not made with hands, that is, not of this creation. Not with the blood of goats and calves, but with His own blood He entered the Most Holy Place once for all, having obtained eternal redemption" (Hebrews 9:11-12).

God is inviting you to get on your face before Him and press into the Holy of Holies. We see the Holy of Holies first mentioned in Exodus 26:33: "You shall hang up the veil under the clasps, so that you may bring in the ark of the testimony within the veil; and the veil shall serve for you as a partition between the holy place and the Most Holy."

The Holy of Holies is the most holy place. In Scripture, it contained the Ark of the Covenant and only the high priest could enter once a year to atone for the sins of Israel. A veil in the temple separated man from the Holy of Holies, the epicenter of God's presence.

When Jesus died on the cross, God supernaturally tore the veil in the temple from top to bottom (see Matt. 27:50-51). This signified man was no longer separated from entering the presence of God. In fact, we can have confidence to enter the holy place through the blood of Jesus (see Heb. 10:19-20).

There's no room for the flesh in the holy of holies. It's not about enlightening your soul, either. This is the place where deep truly cries unto deep (see Ps. 42:7). This is the sacred place where your spirit communes with His Spirit at a level your mind cannot comprehend. Mere words cannot do justice to the holy of holies experience.

In the Holy of Holies, Jesus is more than a distant God you read about in the pages of your Bible. Jesus is fully alive. His glory surrounds you as He reveals His heart to you. When you enter the Holy of Holies, you move from glory to glory. You feel more than alive. You feel like you've entered another dimension—and you have. When you get there, time seems to stand still and you never want to leave.

Many Christians never enter the Holy of Holies because it costs you something. It requires you to shift your appetites, to lay aside childish things, set aside carnal desires and seek Him with your whole heart (see Jer. 29:13). But the reward is worth the price.

— *Prayer* —

Father, in the name of Jesus, would You put a desire and a determination in my heart to go deeper? I want to go deeper still. I want to dwell in the holy of holies. I want a fresh encounter with Your heart that will spur me to the greater works of prayer and the greater works in revival. I surrender to You.

The Corporate Weeping Meeting

"A time to weep, and a time to laugh; A time to mourn, and a time to dance"
(Ecclesiastes 3:4).

Nehemiah successfully rebuilt the wall around Jerusalem because the gracious hand of God was upon him. But even after the miraculous feat, sin remained in the camp. Ezra the priest came on the scene to read The Book of the Law of Moses, which brought deep conviction of sin to those who heard it. Nehemiah 8:2-3 offers:

"So Ezra the priest brought the Law before the assembly of men and women and all who could hear with understanding on the first day of the seventh month. Then he read from it in the open square that was in front of the Water Gate from morning until midday, before the men and women and those who could understand; and the ears of all the people were attentive to the Book of the Law."

Ezra was standing on a platform and all the people stood up at the reading of the Word. Ezra blessed the Lord and the people said, "Amen, Amen!" while lifting up their hands and they bowed their heads and worshipped the Lord with their faces to the ground (see Neh. 8:4-6). The Levites were on hand to help the people understand the Law. Suddenly something astounding happened: corporate weeping over sin. Verse 9 reads:

"And Nehemiah, who was the governor, Ezra the priest and scribe, and the Levites who taught the people said to all the people, 'This day is holy to the Lord your God; do not mourn nor weep.' For all the people wept, when they heard the words of the Law."

Why were they weeping? It was repentance unto national revival. *Jamieson-Fausset-Brown Bible Commentary* reads, "A deep sense of their national sins, impressively brought to their remembrance by the reading of the law and its denunciations, affected the hearts of the people with penitential sorrow. But notwithstanding the painful remembrances of their national sins which the reading of the law awakened, the people were exhorted to cherish the feelings of joy and thankfulness associated with a sacred festival."

— *Prayer* —

Father, in the name of Jesus, would You give me a deep sense of my sins so I can renounce them thoroughly? Would You show me the ripple effect sin has in my life and even on the world around me? I repent of my sins. Restore the joy of Your salvation to my heart.

John Kilpatrick's Revival Confessions

"Even them I will bring to My holy mountain, and make them joyful in My house of prayer. Their burnt offerings and their sacrifices will be accepted on My altar; For My house shall be called a house of prayer for all nations" (Isaiah 56:7).

John Kilpatrick told this story in the foreword to my book, *Revival Hubs Rising*. He tells how he went to the Brownsville church to pray. Before he locked myself in the building, he looked around to make sure the sanctuary was empty because he did not want anyone to hear him pour his heart out to God.

"My prayer started out as an apology to the Lord. I said, 'Lord, I am so blessed to be the husband of such a godly and loving wife and to be the father of two outstanding sons that have never given me a moment of trouble. I am on television worldwide, and I pastor a great congregation in a great city; but Lord, I feel so lonely…I hurt…I feel so empty. Why do I ache in my soul?'"

Immediately, he says he heard Holy Spirit say to him, "If you will return to the God of your childhood, I will touch you afresh and anew. If you will make this house a house of prayer, I will pour out my Spirit in this place in a mighty way that will astound you!"

Kilpatrick says he was literally sweating the prospect of trying to rally the troops for persistent congregational prayer; but the Lord said to him, "I will give you the plan." He did, and it was a concise plan.

"As we began to pray, it felt as though revival would break out any moment. However, as we continued to pray, and the weeks turned into months, and the months to years, it seemed that revival would never happen" he says. "We prayed two and one-half years for revival."

Then, suddenly, the God birthed the Brownsville Revival.

— *Prayer* —

Father, in the name of Jesus, would You help me to commit to prayer for revival? Would You help me not to grow weary in well praying but to stay the course? Help me to continue to expect revival to break out at any moment. Ready me for the outpouring of Your Spirit as I pray.

A Prophetic Vision of Revival Killers

"Let nothing be done through selfish ambition or conceit, but in lowliness of mind let each esteem others better than himself. Let each of you look out not only for his own interests, but also for the interests of others" (Philippians 2:3-4).

I had a prophetic vision. Two opposing teams were on a football field. I could sense in the atmosphere these were fierce rivals. These teams had moved beyond spirited competition to a spirit of violence. In fact, the violence was more pronounced than anything you've ever seen on a football field.

Personal fouls were getting a little too personal. I kept hearing referees crying aloud, "Personal foul!" and "Unsportsmanlike conduct!" All over the field, football players were throwing each other to the ground mercilessly, taunting, and trash talking.

In reality, they weren't even playing the game of football anymore. What I saw was a free-for-all on the field. People were getting seriously injured and no one cared because they felt justified in their behavior. Finally, after some time, one team punted the ball. The ball soared high and straight up into the air. God took the ball away and everyone sat down.

In this parabolic vision, this wasn't the church against the enemy. This was the church against the church. I have never seen this level of competition in the Body of Christ—so much slander, so much backbiting, so many "personal fouls," so much taunting and intimidation, so much chest pounding, and so many cheap shots. It was heartbreaking.

"Where do wars and fights come from among you? Do they not come from your desires for pleasure that war in your members? You lust and do not have. You murder and covet and cannot obtain. You fight and war. Yet you do not have because you do not ask. You ask and do not receive, because you ask amiss, that you may spend it on your pleasures" (James 4:1-3).

This is a plea for peace. Competition is the opposite of love. Strife among us confuses the world, which is looking to the church for answers. Strife pushes away new believers. Competition and unity cannot coexist, and where there's unity God commands a blessing. Competition is a revival killer we need to avoid like the plague.

— *Prayer* —

Father, in the name of Jesus, would You forgive me for competing with others for revival—or anything else? Would You forgive me for engaging in strife instead of seeking to be a peacemaker? I want to see You. I want to walk in love and unity. Help me do my part.

A Media Revival

"The lamp of the body is the eye. Therefore, when your eye is good, your whole body also is full of light. But when your eye is bad, your body also is full of darkness" (Luke 11:34).

We live in a media- and advertising-saturated society. It's difficult to drive down the street without seeing off-color messages on billboards or hearing —and much of it is laced with perversion.

But God also uses media to get His Word out. I believe if the apostle Paul were here today, he would be on social media. Look at the word media and its definition. Media is "the means of communication, as radio and television, newspapers, magazines, and the Internet, that reach or influence people widely," according to *Merriam-Webster*'s dictionary.

Media includes television, radio, video games, social media, magazines, and newspapers. Media influences people's mental health, with comparisons that lead to damaged self-esteem, body dissatisfaction, eating disorders, drug use, depression, harmful biases, violence, and other criminal behaviors. Media influences people's sexuality, leading to promiscuity, gender dysphoria, and sexual immorality.

Drug dealers are on Snapchat selling pills? Child molesters are on Facebook wooing children. Pornography is distributed through the Internet. Video games are stoking violence in youth. TV shows are sexualized. Advertisements entice us to spend money we don't have to purchase things we don't need. Media shapes our identity and renews our mind with liberal agendas and fake news.

Indeed, the world's media is corrupt. We need to prophesy in it and to it. God told me, "I will have the last say in the media." But we must war for it. We need to pray for a revival on the media mountain. I love the revival in Ephesus, in part, because of the media aspect.

"And many who had believed came confessing and telling their deeds. Also, many of those who had practiced magic brought their books together and burned them in the sight of all. And they counted up the value of them, and it totaled fifty thousand pieces of silver. So the word of the Lord grew mightily and prevailed" (Acts 19:18-20). Let's believe for this type of revival again. Do it again, Lord!

— *Prayer* —

Father, in the name of Jesus, help me to guard my eye gates and ear gates from secular media that defiles me. But help me not to turn a deaf ear to Your Spirit speaking to me about praying for revival in the media. Help me be part of the solution to a corrupt system that You want to reform.

Demonic Gatekeepers of Revival

"O full of all deceit and all fraud, you son of the devil, you enemy of all righteousness, will you not cease perverting the straight ways of the Lord? And now, indeed, the hand of the Lord is upon you, and you shall be blind, not seeing the sun for a time" (Acts 13:10-11).

Jesus pronounced woes to the religious leaders of His day because they stood against His mission on the earth. He specifically said, "Woe to you, scribes and Pharisees, hypocrites! For you shut up the kingdom of heaven against men; for you neither go in yourselves, nor do you allow those who are entering to go in" (Matt. 23:13)

The Pharisees had what today we call a religious spirit. Religion is legalistic and performance-oriented—and we see this spiritual plague in too many churches today. Religion typically makes little room for the Holy Spirit. He's an interruption to the prescheduled program. Religion often criticizes true revival.

When you move into revival you can expect resistance. You can expect manifestations of the religious spirit in your midst, perhaps criticizing the loud music or complaining about the length of the services or offended by the message to repent in their self-righteousness.

Yes, as you move into revival you can expect full-blown attacks at the hand of the religious spirit that influences people to stand against you. Remember, they are not really standing against you. They are standing against Jesus, just like they did over two thousand years ago when God walked the earth in the flesh and worked miracles in their midst.

You might not anticipate how or when—or through whom—the attack will come, but you can take authority over it in the name of Jesus. Even if the demon causes a stir before it bows, don't let the commotion distract you from the heart of God in revival.

God is there despite the resistance from religious spirits. Your job is to walk in love and authority and refuse to let the enemy's shenanigans rob from the people the move of God.

— *Prayer* —

Father, in the name of Jesus, I repent of any religiosity in my soul. Forgive me if I have ever stood in the way of revival. I break all agreement with religious spirits and ask You to give me the boldness to stand against legalism that keeps people out of Your presence.

Stirring Desperation for Revival

"Oh, do not remember former iniquities against us! Let Your tender mercies come speedily to meet us, for we have been brought very low" (Psalm 79:8).

Make no mistake. The war that was raging in the heavens has, at least in some measure, manifested in the natural realm. The only way we can turn this around is to get desperate enough in our own hearts to see the salvation of the souls the enemy has taken captive—in the world and in the church—and enter intercession from a place of victory, recognizing we are seated in heavenly places with Christ Jesus.

I hope it doesn't have to get much worse in the nations to make us desperate, but I am concerned it will. Even still, desperation alone is not enough. True desperation demands something from us. Faith without works is dead (see James 2:26).

As the Bride of Christ, we are charged with denying ourselves, picking up our cross and following Him (see Luke 9:23). We must die to ourselves daily (see 1 Cor. 15:31). We must crucify our flesh and the lusts thereof (see Gal. 5:24). We must stand for the truth even in the face of persecution. We must be so desperate that we are willing to do whatever it takes to see His revival glory.

Observing the signs of the times should help stir desperation. Famine is rising, horrific violence is running rampant in the nations. Souls are dying and going to hell every day. We need to stop arguing over who gets to lead prayer and pray without ceasing until we see breakthrough.

I pray the Lord will stir a desperation in our hearts to intercede even while no one is watching. I pray the King of glory will stir such a desperation in our hearts that we will willingly lay aside anything that gets in the way of pursuing His perfect will for our lives, our churches, and our cities.

I believe if we all just did what the Holy Spirit told us to do, we could turn our nations around. We could see a Great Awakening that ushers in salvation and reformation unto transformation in the name of Jesus.

— *Prayer* —

Father, in the name of Jesus, would You make me so desperate for revival that I will do whatever it takes to see Your Kingdom come and Your will be done on earth as it is in heaven? Would You help me die to self and live for the cause of revival and awakening that brings souls into Your family?

Jamaica's Great Revival

"And it happened that the father of Publius lay sick of a fever and dysentery. Paul went in to him and prayed, and he laid his hands on him and healed him. So when this was done, the rest of those on the island who had diseases also came and were healed" (Acts 28:8-9).

Awakening marked many nations in the 1800s. Jamaica was one of them. Facing severe spiritual decline, a remnant of Caribbean Islanders gained a glimmer of hope from the great prayer revival Jacob Lanphier initiated in New York City—and Jamaican Christians started crying out for revival. Prayer meetings started before the rising sun that would send them into the fields to work.

In the midst of this, a German Moravian missionary named Theodor Sonderman walked into his chapel in Clifton, Jamaica expecting to lead a worship service. But God instead took the occasion to answer the Jamaicans' prayer for a spiritual revival. Suddenly, waves of Holy Ghost power rushed into the St. Elizabeth Parish.

Sonderman kept a journal during those days, chronicling the revival. He writes about how some Jamaicans were weeping for joy at the outpouring while others were weeping over their sin. Still others, as in any revival, weren't sure what to think about what they were seeing. Sonderman's first instinct was to try to bring order, but as he started praying, he also became overwhelmed with emotion and decided, to "leave them to the direction of the Holy Spirit."

On September 28 a meeting started with worship and an opening prayer—but the prayer never stopped. Person after person stepped up to pray. Even children were crying out to God. The Spirit of the Lord moved in that prayer and people began to tremble under the presence of God. Some were travailing in the spirit with groans too deep to be uttered. Some were begging for mercy. The prayer meeting went on until midnight.

The revival spread through Jamaica. In Montego Bay, Bethel Town, and Mount Carey alone three thousand people turned to the Lord. When mockers came, the Jamaican Christians prayed for them until many of them bowed a knee to Jesus and accepted Him as Lord and Savior. Some mockers went deaf or mute for up to two weeks. Others would scream under the weight of their sin.

— *Prayer* —

Father, in the name of Jesus, would You help me be so sensitive to Your Spirit that I wake up when You want me to wake up, pray when You want me to pray, repent when You want me to repent, and otherwise follow Your leadership into and through revival?

Born for Revival

"Blessed are those who hunger and thirst for righteousness, for they shall be filled" (Matthew 5:6).

Bill Johnson was born for revival, but he didn't start burning and shining for Jesus until he was a full-grown man. Bill wanted to be professional baseball player.

"I would read about revivals," Bill recalls. "I would read about John G. Lake and pray for people. Nothing ever happened. I just assumed you had to have a special gift for healing and I didn't have it. I would try for a while and back off and get discouraged.

"I went to a John Wimber conference and heard him teach the same things I had been teaching for a couple of years—but they had the fruit of what they believed. I just had a theory. I realized I needed to take more risks and just not stop. It was the weirdest thing. When I came back, the miracles started."

Bill told me there was a time when his hunger for God, revival and miracles was so deep it would send him into depression. He got so discouraged at times that he became self-critical.

"I would honestly confess sins I never committed just to cover my bases in case there was a wrong thought or attitude—it just became about me," he reveals. "There's something wrong when it's all about you. It just came to this point where ... I don't want to say I made an agreement or contract with God, but it's kind of how it worked out for me. I said, 'Father, I'm in Your Word every day, every day. I don't miss a day. And You said it's like a sword. I'm inviting you to cut me deep. If I need the slap of a friend, please give me the slap of a friend.'"

In that moment, Bill stopped looking at himself and started crying out to God for fire to burn within him. He cautions believers everywhere not to let true hunger lead to an unhealthy frustration. Hunger, rather, should lead us to Jesus.

— *Prayer* —

Father, in the name of Jesus, would You give me a healthy hunger for revival that compels me to seek You first, second and always? Help me not to wallow in frustration or condemnation but to bask in Your presence so I find revival joy that I can share with the world.

Revival in the Secret Place

"Seek the Lord and His strength; Seek His face evermore!" (1 Chronicles 16:11)

It was as if I stepped into a river of Holy Ghost fire. The rain of the Spirit was falling and the wind of the Spirit was blowing. In one accord, over twenty-five thousand people worshipped Jesus with all that was in them. Some lay prostrate on the ground while others stood with hands raised and tears streaming down their faces. I thought I heard angels singing.

I was caught up in the glory when Pastors Ricardo and Patricia Rodríguez, founders of Central Mundial de Avivamiento in Bogotá, Colombia walked onto the platform. These pastors have sustained revival for thirty years. But it didn't start that way. They were once frustrated that their church had only a few members. God told Ricardo to stop worrying about numbers and start seeking His presence. Once he obeyed, that surrender revolutionized his life and his ministry.

"I started spending time with God from before the break of day until one in the afternoon," Ricardo, who was once a nominal Catholic, told me. "I would sit all day long in His presence. It was not an experience. It was a relationship with God. And I won't stop. There is not a single day when we don't seek Him."

That relationship birthed a spiritual awakening that's impacting the nations. Indeed, when I was there, the Holy Spirit told me, "Colombia is the drumbeat of Latin America."

"All this started when Ricardo sought the Lord in a passionate way in his secret place and the Lord manifested Himself," Patricia told me. "We had a one-person revival. This made us feel the same hunger, and we caught that fire. The Lord told Ricardo to bring that fire to the seventy people in our church. The presence of God came, and the musicians were not able to keep worshipping. They fell on the ground and wept. When the Holy Spirit has first place in the church, you can feel revival."

— *Prayer* —

Father, in the name of Jesus, would You help me put You first not just in word but also in deed? Help me make more room for You, to seek You with all of my heart, all of my mind, all of my soul and all of my strength. Help me to keep my eyes on You. You are my revival.

Weeping With Wilkerson

"Jesus wept" (John 11:35).

David Wilkerson preached a message many years ago that revivalists would do well to heed. In it, he addressed strange manifestations that people wrongly attribute to the Holy Ghost—and it grieved his heart.

In his sermon, Wilkerson tells a story of a woman who was confused about what was going on in her local church. She explained, "Many of our church don't know what to do. We were having wonderful services. The Spirit of the Lord was with us. But our pastor thought there was more. The church wasn't growing fast enough. And he heard of revival. He went to this revival. He came home three months ago. He got up to preach. And he started to laugh for half an hour. He couldn't control himself. He just laughed and laughed. There was no preaching. And he told us, 'This is a new move with the Holy Ghost'."

I want to stress this point: Wilkerson went on to explain that this wasn't a one-time incident at that local church. This wasn't some spontaneous outbreak of holy laughter. It went on for three solid months. There was no preaching for three months of Sundays. Only uncontrollable laughing.

Wilkerson asked a pointed question: "The Holy Ghost who wrote [the Bible], who said, 'The truth sets you free,' will He cause the minister to laugh so he cannot preach this Word?" I'm not against laughing, but three months of laughing at the neglect of equipping the saints with the Word of God?

Wilkerson called out ministries where people hiss and wiggle on the floor like snakes. He described many strange manifestations—and explained how people call it the Holy Ghost. Fighting back the tears, Wilkerson said crediting these sorts of manifestations to the Holy Ghost makes Him look like a fool. Before the end of the sermon, Wilkerson was overcome with grief and began sobbing in his hands.

Certainly, we can see strange manifestations in revival meetings, but we must be careful not to entertain demons in the name of God. Likewise, we must be careful not to criticize authentic revival manifestations of His glory because they are unfamiliar.

— *Prayer* —

Father, in the name of Jesus, would You help me not to mistake a true manifestation of Your Spirit for a false one—or a false one for a true one? I don't want to be critical, but I do want to be discerning. I want to come under the influence of Your Holy Spirit, not some other spirit.

The Tipping Point of Revival

"Then the churches throughout all Judea, Galilee, and Samaria had peace and were edified. And walking in the fear of the Lord and in the comfort of the Holy Spirit, they were multiplied"
(Acts 9:31).

There are pivotal moments in the Body of Christ and we're in one of them. A 24/7 prayer movement is crossing denominations to focus on worship and intercession, the pro-life movement is working to see laws and hearts changed, the student missions movement is going strong through organizations like YWAM, and the church is on the edge of seeing another healing movement sweep the nation.

In fact, I believe the Third Great Awakening will be greater than any individual movement we've seen—from the Voice of Healing to the Word of Faith to the Jesus Movement and so on. I believe we're going to see an outpouring more significant than all the past outpourings put together—and I believe it starts with these smaller movements until we reach a tipping point or, to put it biblically, when prayers of the saints fill the golden, heavenly bowls mentioned in Revelation 5:8, and they finally tip over.

Movements are about mobilizing people in unity around a common cause. If Christians will join—or launch—Holy Spirit-inspired movements that spur people to pray, evangelize and otherwise get engaged in our society, we can reach a tipping point in any given nation. In fact, it will be like the shot heard around the world in the Revolutionary War. Th nations need a spiritual revolution, and we're getting closer to the tipping point with every prayer we pray.

Malcolm Gladwell, author of the *Tipping Point, Blink, Outliers,* and other best-selling books that caught the nation's attention, explains it this way:

"The tipping point is a moment when an idea, trend or social behavior crosses a threshold, tips, and spreads like wildfire. Just as a single sick person can start a flu epidemic, he reasons, a small but targeted push can bring change."

You can be part of the tipping point. Join a movement. Pray without ceasing. Be part of the solution. Together, we can cooperate with the Holy Spirit to usher in the greatest movement the world has ever seen.

— *Prayer* —

Father, in the name of Jesus, You tell me in Your Word that every joint supplies. Many streams make a great river. Help me to lend my joint, my prayer, and my portion to what You are doing in my generation. I want to work with Your Spirit to see revival in my land. Let the bowls of revival prayer tip over.

MARCH 31

The Gypsy Smith Revivalist Anointing

"Behold, a great multitude which no one could number, of all nations, tribes, peoples, and tongues, standing before the throne and before the Lamb" (Revelation 7:9).

The Gypsy community has historically carried a stigma. Gypsies originated in South Asia and typically adopt an itinerant lifestyle. Gypsies are essentially nomads with a free spirit who wander from place to place. But Gypsies have frequently been marked as thieves and, because of distrust, were often enslaved, expelled, and executed in European nations.

Then along came a man they called Gypsy Smith. He was born again in 1876 and preached to more people during his ministry than anyone else at that time. Turnips were his first audience as he walked the fields alone.

Smith met and joined William Booth, the founder of the Salvation Army, in 1877. Booth sent him to minister at a church in Chatham, England, which grew from ten people to two hundred fifty people in only nine months under his leadership. From there, Smith moved on to Hull, where over one thousand people came every week came to hear him preach.

When the Salvation Army dismissed Smith for accepting a gold watch as a gift, that didn't stop him. He was invited to preach all over the United Kingdom and Europe and ran missions in South Africa. Smith also preached in America, speaking to over ten thousand people at a time. Indeed, he was known at the time as the "Greatest Evangelist in the World."

Smith was part of many revivals in his day, preaching to millions of people. But he never took the credit. He pointed people to Christ and told people revival started with them.

Smith was known to say, "Go home, lock yourself in your room, kneel down in the middle of your floor. Draw a chalk mark all around yourself and ask God to start the revival inside that chalk mark. When He has answered your prayer, the revival will be on." Amen. Are you ready? Go get your chalk!

— *Prayer* —

Father, in the name of Jesus, help me not to hold biases against people groups but to understand that You want to be bring revival—and salvation—to every tongue, tribe and nation. Help me to understand that revival starts with me and to pray with a passion for all people.

APRIL

"The chief danger of the Church today is that it is trying to get on the same side as the world, instead of turning the world upside down. Our Master expects us to accomplish results, even if they bring opposition and conflict. Anything is better than compromise, apathy, and paralysis. God give to us an intense cry for the old-time power of the Gospel and the Holy Ghost!"
—AB Simpson

APRIL 1

Catching the Next Wave of Revival

"Therefore they stayed there a long time, speaking boldly in the Lord, who was bearing witness to the word of His grace, granting signs and wonders to be done by their hands" (Acts 14:3).

Kathryn Kuhlman witnessed thousands miraculously healed by the supernatural power of the Holy Spirit. I've always admired Kathryn, with her flowing white dress, passionate presentations and, of course, flaming red hair. As I always say, we redheads have to stick together!

I believe the next generation of miracle workers is getting ready to rise up. The healing evangelists from Kathryn's day and earlier—I'm talking about Oral Roberts, Jack Coe, A.A. Allen, and William Branham—have long gone on to glory.

We've seen a few remarkable men of God, like Benny Hinn and Reinhard Bonnke, carry the miracle torch, but we've still longed for the glory days when mass miracles were a reality. The good news is I see a new wave of Christians believing for signs, wonders and miracles like the world has never seen.

I believe we're going to see a great move of God that's greater than the Voice of Healing Movement, the Jesus Movement, the charismatic movement, and the prayer movement all rolled into one. I believe a new healing movement is emerging even now.

This movement, though, won't be marked by a handful of evangelists with sparkling personalities and powerful gifts that fill stadiums and take to the airwaves. Rather, this movement will see the saints rise up and do the work of the healing evangelist with prophetic insights and pastoral care.

The next great move of God will unleash believers who have faith to lay hands on the sick and see them recover, cast out devils and even raise the dead. I believe it. I believe the day is coming soon when we'll see a revival sweep the nations marked by signs and wonders and miracles like we've never seen before. Will you believe with me?

— *Prayer* —

Father, in the name of Jesus, help me build my faith to see signs and wonders as I share the Word with people in everyday life. Give me the boldness and courage to carry revival to the marketplace, and to pray believing you will confirm Your Word with signs following.

APRIL 2

Birthing in the Prayer Closet

"But you, when you pray, go into your room, and when you have shut your door, pray to your Father who is in the secret place; and your Father who sees in secret will reward you openly" (Matthew 6:6).

God wants to break out, break in and pour out His Spirit. We often ask for an outpouring of glory, but we often need an outpouring of repentance first. I heard the Lord say this:

"If My people who are called by My name would think more about life in one thousand years than life tomorrow, they would make a greater impact in their generation. But the cares of this world, the lust of the flesh, the lust of the eyes, the pride of life and other demonic distractions have consumed many with the reality of now instead of the reality of eternity.

"Millions die and go to hell every day because My people who are called by My name are not about My business. Rights and freedoms are lost, people murdered, lives destroyed, babies aborted because My people who are called by my name are not about My business.

"I am looking for those in this hour who will look up instead of looking back; who will cry out; who will press in; who will determine in their hearts to see My Kingdom come and My will done on the earth—in your cities and families—as it is in heaven.

"I want to pour out My Spirit. I want to save souls. I want to heal sick bodies. I want to restore broken families. I am waiting on you to rise up and fight on your knees like there's no tomorrow because for many there isn't.

"Who shall I send to the closet of prayer to shape history? Who will go for Me? I will show myself strong in your life. I will take care of your needs. I will bless you and keep you. I will show you things to come if you will partner with Me in the place of prayer. I will do it, and I will be glorified."

Who will answer this call in their generation?

— *Prayer* —

Father, in the name of Jesus, would You help me to be about Your Kingdom business? Help me to do what I see you doing. Give me the grace to pray without ceasing and to birth a revival in my heart that spills over into my church, my city and my nation—and to the lost.

APRIL 3

Feeling the Pain of God's Heart

"Now as He drew near, He saw the city and wept over it..." (Luke 19:41).

As I stretched out on the carpet in the prayer room, I found myself grieving. The fear of the Lord struck my heart. I saw the persecution that is coming to America. I mourned over the blood of abortion that is on our hands. I pondered the eternal value of how I spend my time. I considered the failure of the church to be salt and light. And I felt the pain of God's heart.

I didn't sleep much that night as I pondered how so much of what I do makes no impact on anyone. The next morning, I woke up early and prayed in the spirit for over an hour trying to come to grips with the reality of where my nation is heading if we don't repent. We like to pray 2 Chronicles 7:14, but so many of us fail to live 2 Chronicles 7:14.

I watched David Wilkerson's video montage on anguish. I listened to Leonard Ravenhill's classics on revival. The Holy Spirit prayed through me with groans too deep for words (see Rom. 8:26). I considered what love really is. After all, we can pray in the tongues of men and angels, we can prophesy with the best of them, we can feed the poor, we can have mountain-moving faith, we can even die for the sake of the Gospel—but without love it's useless (see 1 Cor. 13:1-3).

Love is kind, patient, humble, selfless, not easily provoked, rejoices in the truth, believes all things, hopes all things, endures all things. Love also warns, but it does not seek to breed fear for profit's sake.

Love makes intercession. Love stands in the gap and on the wall. Love has violent faith that presses into what God is saying and doing in this hour despite what it looks like. Love hears His voice and sounds the alarm. Love carries the burden of His heart and prays until something happens. It's all about love.

— *Prayer* —

Father, in the name of Jesus, would You reduce me to love? Break my heart for what breaks Your heart. You love all people and are not willing that any should perish. You loved me enough to die on a cross for me. Help me to pick up my cross in love and follow You wherever You lead me.

Heralding the Message of Repentance

"The Lord is not slack concerning His promise, as some count slackness, but is longsuffering toward us, not willing that any should perish but that all should come to repentance"
(2 Peter 3:9).

I heard in my spirit a strong and clear word from the Lord. This encounter was at a stadium prayer event that changed my mind about the supernatural—and signs and wonders have been following me ever since.

I'll always remember it. It was January 24, 2015 at The Response prayer rally in Baton Rouge. Thousands of people were crying out to God for our nation when I heard the words below in His still small voice I so love. I waited months to release them because I wanted to gain a deeper understanding of what the Lord was saying—and I was waiting for His timing. Here is the prophecy:

"My blood is sufficient. My covenant is sure. 2 Chronicles 7:14 is truth. You need not operate in fear but embrace the power to cleanse that's inherent in repentance. I want to cleanse America. But it starts with purifying your hearts.

"The church in this hour must herald the message of repentance in the same way as preachers in the Voice of Healing movement heralded the message of healing. Then will you see the manifestation of My presence and the wells of the supernatural will be unlocked and many who are lost will be restored to My love.

"It starts with the message of repentance. This is the message that I need you to shout from the rooftops in this hour. Everything the church needs to fulfill her call in this hour flows from a contrite heart. You can sound the alarm but without repentance it will fall on deaf ears.

"Many are entering eternity every day without My Son because they have not heard this message. Some of them are sitting in the church right now. Start there with this message and it will position the church to rise up in My power for My glory."

— *Prayer* —

Father, in the name of Jesus, would You help me to herald the message of repentance with grace? Help me not to operate in a legalistic tone but to remember that it's Your kindness that leads people to repentance. Help me to be a friend to sinners just like Jesus was.

Repetitive, Passionate and Scriptural

"Having a form of godliness but denying its power. And from such people turn away!"
(2 Timothy 3:5)

When I asked the Lord how the Voice of Healing preachers heralded the message of healing, He gave me three points: repetitive, passionate and scriptural.

The Voice of Healing preachers were repetitive. You heard many of the same core messages about God's power to heal and deliver over and over again in their tent meetings. The Voice of Healing preachers were passionate.

Think of A.A. Allen jumping up and down and Jack Coe's exuberant singing. And, of course, the Voice of Healing preachers were scriptural. These preachers knew that faith comes by hearing and hearing by the Word of God (see Rom. 10:17) and they kept their messages in line with the Word of God.

We need to repent in the sense that we need to ask forgiveness of our sins and stand in the gap for our nations. Indeed, we need to see repentance in the church—widespread repentance. But it's not just changing the way we think about sin—and turning away from it—that is required in this hour. We need to change the way we think about the supernatural.

When Jesus rebuked the cities of Chorazin and Bethsaida for not repenting after they saw the mighty miracles He did (see Matt. 11:20-21), the word for "repent" in that verse is the Greek word "metanoeo." Metanoeo means "to change one's mind, i.e. to repent; to change one's mind for the better, heartily to amend with abhorrence of one's past sins."

The spirit of religion, along with a lukewarm mindset, prayerlessness, and the tradition of men, has all but stopped revival in too many churches. We need to turn away from thoughts that limit God in our lives. We need to turn away from a powerless expression of the Gospel. We need to turn back toward faith in God to heal the sick, cast out demons and, yes, even raise the dead. God is a God of miracles! Jesus walked on water.

— *Prayer* —

Father, in the name of Jesus, would You help me renew my mind to Your supernatural ways? Help me to keep trumpeting the message of revival, but not with a mere form of godliness—with Your power. Your Word says the Kingdom of God is not in talk but power. Help me speak and walk with power!

Letting Holy Spirit Take Over

"My soul thirsts for You; my flesh longs for You in a dry and thirsty land where there is no water. So I have looked for You in the sanctuary, to see Your power and Your glory"
(Psalm 63:2-3).

I've read articles and exit polls about the many reasons people leave their churches, but most of them are surface reasons. What's really going on?

Think for a moment about the many revivals throughout church history. Then think about the ministers God used to pioneer those revivals. It was God's presence and power working through those ministers that drew the people in.

Throughout history people have always craved the supernatural. I know the local church can't run in revival mode non-stop. Churches must meet both natural and spiritual needs. But a church devoid of the power of the Holy Spirit becomes dry. In these times, God's people need to encounter His presence and find refreshing.

If the presence and power of God are in manifestation and people don't like it, what of it? Do you really want people who deny God's glory in your church? Conversely, I know many spiritual people who are exiting their churches for lack of rain. They are not leaving due to offense or pride. They are not backsliding and leaving God, but they are leaving deadness and superficiality. There is a cry in the heart of many hungry believers for the waters of the Spirit and new wine.

It is amazing what leaders can build and do without God. But that doesn't mean that God's stamp of approval is on what they are building or doing. Divine power can only manifest through us when there is an end to self-sufficiency and an utter dependence on God Almighty.

I believe the local church to be the hope of the world. But God wants to move. He has a plan. He has a purpose. And if we don't line up with it, He has no choice but to move where He finds His people and His leaders hungering for His presence and power. Pray for your church—and pray for the Church—to embrace revival.

— *Prayer* —

Father, I want to be presence-hungry. Give me the gift of hunger. I want to be power-hungry, but not as the world knows it. I desire to operate in spiritual gifts, as You command in Your Word. Help me not to get in my head, but to get into Your heart and walk in presence and power.

A Vision of the War for Awakening

"Awake, awake, Deborah! Awake, awake, sing a song!" (Judges 5:12)

I saw pictures of famine, horrific violence in the Middle East and people dying from disease. Next, I looked up and saw a principality hanging over a large city from the second heaven. That principality was in the appearance of a dark cloud. From it came a voice that was commanding demons to execute a wicked agenda that included more famine, violence, immorality and the like.

Above that principality, I saw the throne of God. Jesus is seated at the right hand of the Father in heavenly places, far above all principalities, powers, might and dominion, as well as every name that is named—not only in this age but also in that which is to come (see Eph. 1:20-21).

As born-again believers, we are raised up with Christ and seated together in heavenly places in Christ Jesus (see Eph. 2:6). This is our legal position. Yet I saw clearly during this encounter that many believers are not wrestling principalities and powers, rulers of the darkness of this age and spiritual hosts of wickedness from this legal position.

Indeed, part of the church is literally wrestling against flesh and blood, which is breeding strife—even in the church. The church cannot agree on cultural or political issues, for example. We know where strife is, there is confusion and every evil work (see James 3:16).

Others in the church are engaging in spiritual immorality, as pastor after pastor falls into moral failure even while preaching against it. Part of the church is experiencing a Word famine, in large part because many are not students of the Word. Instead, many depend on man to spoon-feed them a biblical motivational message on Sunday mornings, do their praying for them and solve all their problems. Many are wrestling from a compromised position.

It's time to pray.

— *Prayer* —

Father, in the name of Jesus, make me a prayer solutionist in the war for awakening. The war is more than real, even though I don't always see it with my natural eyes. Help me to see the war in the spirit, like Elisha's servant. Help me stand and withstand for the sake of souls who don't know You.

The Dutch Sheets Revivalist Anointing

"All the ends of the world shall remember and turn to the Lord, and all the families of the nations shall worship before You. For the kingdom is the Lord's, and He rules over the nations"
(Psalm 22:27-28).

Dutch Sheets may go down in history as the man who resurrected the Appeal to Heaven Flag—America's first flag. As I wrote in my book, *The Next Great Move of God: An Appeal to Heaven for Spiritual Awakening:*

About three years before Washington rallied wearied troops at Valley Forge—a turning point in the Revolutionary War—he launched a private navy carrying a flag that symbolized the American spirit. This flag preceded both the stars and stripes Betsy Ross sewed together as the "first official United States flag" released in 1776 and the yellow-and-black "Don't Tread on Me" flag depicting a snake that also emerged in 1776 on Commodore Esek Hopkins' fleet.

In 1775, George Washington's "secret navy," as many have called it, flew a white flag with an evergreen tree in the middle and the words "An Appeal to Heaven" written across the top in bold black letters.

Just as Moses delivered the Israelites from the bondage of Pharaoh, Washington set out to deliver the patriots from the tyranny of Britain by the hand of God. Facing the reality that a battle against the mighty British army was too great for the fledgling Colonial forces, Washington would not stop petitioning Providence until he saw what he believed was God's will done in the United Colonies of North America.

In his book *Appeal to Heaven*, Dutch says, "The original American dream wasn't about wealth, but freedom—freedom to worship and freedom from tyranny. It was also about partnering with God to release the light of His word to all nations, and exporting His glorious gospel to the ends of the earth."

"We must pray intently, in agreement with the appeals of our forefathers and predecessors, in order to see a continuation of what they birthed," he wrote. "And we must actively repent of our wrongs and theirs, allowing God to reach back in time, healing our history so that blessings can flow into our present."

Are you making an appeal to heaven for your nation?

— *Prayer* —

Father, in the name of Jesus, help me pray in agreement with the appeals of men and women of God from days gone by for awakening and revival in my land. Help me to actively repent of the wrongs of past peoples and to continually seek Your heart for my revival in my nation.

Offering Identificational Repentance

"We have sinned and committed iniquity, we have done wickedly and rebelled, even by departing from Your precepts and Your judgments" (Daniel 9:5).

Have you ever heard the terminology "identificational repentance"? Intercessors that are sent to lands or people groups often enter into this type of selfless intercession. It's heavy.

John Dawson, author of *Healing America's Wounds*, coined the term the 1990s. Simply stated, identificational repentance is repentance that identifies with and confesses the sins of a nation, city, people group, church, or family before God. Until Dawson's book dusted off this ancient revelation, fewer practiced this intercessory prayer strategy.

We should always go into intercession with repentance, praise, and thanksgiving to our God. But identificational repentance is more than just asking God to cleanse you from all unrighteousness before you pray. Let's look at some definitions so we can thoroughly understand this concept.

Oxford Dictionary defines "identificational" as "relating to or involving identification." Identification is "the action or process of identifying someone or something or the fact of being identified." Repentance is "sorrow for any thing done or said; the pain or grief which a person experiences in consequence of the injury or inconvenience produced by his own conduct," according to *Noah Webster's 1828 Dictionary*.

The late C. Peter Wagner called identificational repentance the power to heal the past. We see Daniel entered into identificational repentance in Daniel 9:3: "Then I set my face toward the Lord God to make request by prayer and supplications, with fasting, sackcloth, and ashes."

Daniel goes on to pray things like "we have sinned and committed iniquity, we have done wickedly and rebelled, even by departing from Your precepts and Your judgments. Neither have we heeded Your servants the prophets, who spoke in Your name to our kings and our princes, to our fathers and all the people of the land" (Dan. 9:5-6). This touched God's heart.

Are you willing to repent on behalf of another in order to see revival?

— *Prayer* —

Father, in the name of Jesus, help me identify with the sin of peoples and nations that do not know You. Will You help me stand in the gap with a heart of repentance for a people You want to reach with the power of forgiveness?

What Will You Sacrifice for Revival?

"But as for me, when they were sick, my clothing was sackcloth; I humbled myself with fasting; and my prayer would return to my own heart" (Psalm 35:13).

While obedience is better than sacrifice, God does accept our sacrifices in prayer and fasting. James Goll offers prophetic insight into this in his excellent book *Revival Breakthrough*. He writes:

"Some people are well seasoned in this spiritual dimension of revival and prayer and fasting, spiritual warfare, and the like. While some are new to these dimensions. So let's push aside familiarity, as we look at some principles from the Word of God, from history, and from my own life so we can be equipped. If we can get hold of that revelation, then the spiritual disciplines move into a different arena where they more than only a sacrifice.

"Fasting is one of our spiritual privileges. Yes, it is a sacrifice, but it so much more than that. It is an invitation from God into a divine privilege or opportunity to partner with the Holy Spirit into His purposes in our generation. So declare a holy fast and call a sacred assembly.

"So what is fasting? 'Fasting is a deliberate act of turning away from food and or other personal appetites for spiritual purposes, especially so that we can focus our attention on God.' This is a very simple definition for this multifaceted subject. Now the nature of fasting… fasting does release power, or a display of God's blessings. Now, there is not one particular verse in the Bible that that says, 'sacrifice releases power.' You cannot find it.

"When I first started hearing that phrase years ago, I kind of scratched my head and I went like, now wait a second. There's no Bible verse that says that. And then I thought through and I searched through the Scriptures all over again and through church history and I found this principle throughout the Bible. Sacrifice does release another level of authority, another level of supernatural intervention, another level of blessing by partnering in another level with God."

Will you fast for revival?

— *Prayer* —

Father, in the name of Jesus, I am willing to fast for revival. I am willing to fast for the sake of souls that are lukewarm and even cold—and for the ones that don't yet know the King of Glory. I am willing to make a sacrifice for the cause of Christ in the earth.

The Stages of Spiritual Sleep

"Awake to righteousness, and do not sin; for some do not have the knowledge of God. I speak this to your shame" (1 Corinthians 15:34).

Did you know there are four stages of natural sleep? Each state is telling when paralleled to the spiritual realm. Indeed, there are direct correlations that will bring revelation.

During stage one, for example, your eyes are closed and there's a reduction of activity. From a spiritual sense, this activity reduction could be caused by weariness, apathy, compromise, or sin. Our eyes are closed. We don't want to see it—we may even justify it. The good news is it's easy to wake up without much difficulty during stage one. The bad news is this stage doesn't last long, so the opportunity to shake yourself loose from weariness, apathy, compromise, or sin is short.

Stage two is a light sleep. There are peaks and valleys, or positive and negative waves, as the heart rate slows and the body temperature decreases. At this point, experts say, the body prepares to enter deep sleep. Catch that! Your heart rate slows and your body temperature decreases. Can you see the spiritual parallel? In stage two, your heart is not on fire for Jesus as it once was. Your love is growing cold. You are in a dangerous place.

Stages three and four are what are called "deep sleep stages." This is when you dream; this is when you are disconnected from reality. You don't see things as they really are—or you don't see anything at all. During stage three, for example, you may sleepwalk. It looks like you're going along with the church crowd, but you are actually sound asleep—and you don't even know it.

Stage four is especially dangerous. In stage four voluntary muscles become paralyzed. You may not hear sounds in the waking world or respond to activity in the environment around you. If you are awakened, you may be disoriented. God forbid we slumber so long that we enter into stage four. And thank God that He can still wake us up no matter how deep we are sleeping.

— *Prayer* —

Father, in the name of Jesus, help me not to enter into spiritual sleep. I don't want to slumber in the spirit. I don't want my heart to grow cold. I don't want to be desensitized to Your presence. Help me stay fully awake so I can see Your glory and release Your glory for revival.

The Great Communion Revival

"Gather to me my consecrated ones who have made a covenant by sacrifice" (Psalm 50:5).

Lou Engle returned from a global communion service on Passover in Jerusalem in 2022. He had a dream he was speaking with Bill Johnson with his headphones on. I'll let him share the dream in his own words:

"With stumbling speech, I was having trouble trying to recall the Original Sacramento River dream. When I took my headphones off, suddenly my mind cleared, and I remembered and spoke out the dream with prophetic clarity. Then I exclaimed to Bill, 'It's the Great Communion Revival!' Then I began weeping in the dream.

"Pay close attention to your tears in dreams. They may be pointing you to your destiny or to what is dear to God and what should be dear to you. I'm convinced that the Lord was profoundly speaking to me,

"'Listen closely, son. Take off your headphones! I want to open your ears to listen (Isaiah 50).' I want you to be stunned with awe about what I'm going to say to you because it is so dear to me, the value of the blood of My beloved Son and it's power to heal the earth when applied in faith by my church."

With that, Lou prophesied the coming of the Great Communion Revival. He points out how eighteen years before his dream, seventy young men and women gathered in Colorado Springs to fast and pray for fifty days and nights that the U.S. Supreme Court would reverse Roe v. Wade.

"The Lord gave us a prayer that eventually spread across America and has been poured out before the court of heaven like a voice of many waters. 'Jesus, I plead your blood over my sins and the sins of my nation. God, end abortion and send revival to America.' We believe this prayer contains the key to shifting the nation into a culture of life, healing, forgiveness, and national revival."

— *Prayer* —

Father, in the name of Jesus, I plead the blood of the Lamb over the sins of my life, my city and my nation. As it is written, the blood speaks a better thing. Thank You, Jesus, for shedding Your blood at Calvary to make a way for my revival—and for revival in the nations.

APRIL 13

Becoming a Student of Revival

"Be diligent to present yourself approved to God, a worker who does not need to be ashamed, rightly dividing the word of truth" (2 Timothy 2:15).

We are called to be students of the Word. Likewise, if you want to see revival—if you want to discern between true and false revivals—and if you want to be prepared for revival when it comes, it's wise to be student of revival.

What does it mean to be a student of revival? A student of revival has a deep interest in the topic. A student of revival wants to understand the dynamics of revivals in the pages of Scripture. A student of revival seeks to gain knowledge of historical revivals throughout history.

Jesus said, "Every student of the Scriptures who becomes a disciple in the kingdom of heaven is like someone who brings out new and old treasures from the storeroom" (Matt. 13:52, CEV). Every revival has some common characteristics— old treasures. But every revival has some new wine—some new treasures to be explored.

When you are a student of revival, it demonstrates you have a passion about the subject. When you are a student of revival, you recognize revival anointings and atmospheres. When you are a student of revival, you dive deep into Scripture with a heart to see God do it again.

Students of revival long to be part of the next great move of God. Students of revival hunger and thirst after righteousness and live a lifestyle of repentance because they understand that apart from repentance, there is no revival. Students of revival are students of prayer because they know prayer ignites revival.

Students of revival are students of Jesus because Jesus is revival. George Whitfield, a powerful preacher of awakening in the 1700s, once said: "Study to know Him more and more, for the more you know, the more you will love Him." The more you love Him the more you will want others to know Him so they can love Him, too. That's part and parcel of revival.

— *Prayer* —

Father, in the name of Jesus, would You give me a hunger and thirst not just to experience revival in and of itself but also to become a student of revival? Help me build my faith for revival now by studying revivals past, both in Scripture and in modern history.

The Prophetic War for Revival

"This charge I commit to you, son Timothy, according to the prophecies previously made concerning you, that by them you may wage the good warfare" (1 Timothy 1:18).

Prophetic strategies are vital to seeing awakening manifest in this hour. Although I believe 2 Chronicles 7:14 is the foundation for transforming revival, there are specific strategies God will give to build on top of this foundation.

One of those strategies is praying out the prophecies over our cities, states, and nations. That's what I did with a group of Florida intercessors for many months. The Lord gave this prophetic strategy to a friend of mine who operates a house of prayer in Southwest Florida. She asked me to help lead the charge.

This is Scriptural. One way we fight the good fight of faith is to wield the Sword of the Spirit—and sometimes that means wielding the prophetic words of God: "This charge and admonition I commit in trust to you, Timothy, my son, in accordance with prophetic intimations which I formerly received concerning you, so that inspired and aided by them you may wage the good warfare ..." (1 Tim.1:18, AMP).

Toward the end of our first prayer call, I had a vision of an arrow being put into a quiver. The Lord told me that these prayer calls—these calls in which we pray out the many prophecies that have been declared over our state in the decades past—are an arrow in our quiver.

In other words, it's a new weapon for the season in which we find ourselves. This arrow in the quiver is a prophetic strategy that can be used to hit our prayer target. Our prayer target is revival and awakening. We still do this at my church, Awakening House of Prayer.

I believe it's a strategy that will lead to a tipping point for revivals around the world. This strategy brings victory through consistency. Decide now that you will not stop striking the ground with revival prophecies. Decide now you will strike and strike and strike and strike and strike—and keep on striking until you see God's revival manifest.

— *Prayer* —

Father, in the name of Jesus, would You help me find prophetic words over myself, my church, my city, my region and my nation? Help me to wage a good warfare with the true prophecies that were spoken out. Grace me partner with the prophetic word in prayer and intercession.

APRIL 15

The Ramabai Revivalist Anointing

"Praying always with all prayer and supplication in the Spirit, being watchful to this end with all perseverance and supplication for all the saints—and for me, that utterance may be given to me, that I may open my mouth boldly to make known the mystery of the gospel" (Ephesians 6:18).

You've probably never heard the name Pandita Ramabai, but heaven and hell certainly know her name. Ramabai was the leader of a massive revival that hit India in 1904. She wasn't born into a Christian home, rather she accepted Christ in 1883 while living in England. Ramabai later spent time in the United States before returning to her homeland to initiate social reform.

Ramabai founded the Mukti Mission, which was home to two thousand people. (The Mukti Mission is still operating today over one hundred years after her ascension to glory.) Like every revival, the Great Revival at Mukti Mission was birthed in prayer. You might say it was birthed by a praying woman. Of course, that woman was Ramabai.

"The news of the revival in Wales brought much gladness to Ramabai," Helen S. Dyer writes in *The Story of the Great Revival*. "In January 1905, she told her pupils about it, and called for volunteers to meet with her daily for special prayer for a revival in India. Seventy came forward, and from time-to-time others joined. In June five hundred and fifty were meeting twice daily in this praying band."

Ramabai took great interest in the growing the prayer movement in the earth in her day. She organized a system of what she called "prayer circles." The names of ten females were assigned to each circle and these girls and women were prayed for by name daily. Ramabai even had a magazine called *The Prayer Bell*.

Ramabai also understood the power of impartation. In her book, Dyer wrote: "News of the revival in Australia in 1903 aroused Ramabai to send thither her daughter and Miss Abrams, in order that they might catch the inspiration of the revival fire and form praying-bands for Mukti among the Australian Christians. The burden of the message, which Ramabai sent by them to, the newly revived Australian Churches was, 'Brethren, pray for us.'"

— Prayer —

Father, in the name of Jesus, would You give me an impartation of the spirit of revival? Cause my heart to break for what breaks Your heart and set me on fire for revival. Give me innovative prayer strategies that spark revival and stir souls to come to Jesus.

When Revival Falls on the Wicked

"Behold, I am the Lord, the God of all flesh. Is there anything too hard for Me?"
(Jeremiah 32:27)

One of the greatest revivals in Biblical history was in a pagan nation that set itself up as an enemy to Israel. And God used an unlikely candidate—a rebellious prophet with bias in his heart—to spark the revival.

You know the story of Jonah. God commanded him to go to Nineveh and cry out against it. Jonah needed a personal revival to obey that word, and he experienced this personal revival in the belly of the whale. The rest is revival history as laid out in Jonah 3 and demonstrates how God will hear the cries of even the most wicked nations. That should spur us to keep praying for the darkest nations in the earth. Jonah 3 reads:

"Jonah began to go into the city, going a day's journey. And he called out, 'Yet forty days, and Nineveh shall be overthrown!' And the people of Nineveh believed God. They called for a fast and put on sackcloth, from the greatest of them to the least of them.

"The word reached the king of Nineveh, and he arose from his throne, removed his robe, covered himself with sackcloth, and sat in ashes. And he issued a proclamation and published through Nineveh, 'By the decree of the king and his nobles: Let neither man nor beast, herd nor flock, taste anything. Let them not feed or drink water, but let man and beast be covered with sackcloth, and let them call out mightily to God. Let everyone turn from his evil way and from the violence that is in his hands. Who knows? God may turn and relent and turn from his fierce anger, so that we may not perish.'

"When God saw what they did, how they turned from their evil way, God relented of the disaster that he had said he would do to them, and he did not do it."

— Prayer —

Father, in the name of Jesus, would You help me remember that nothing is too hard for You? Help me not to behave like Jonah, writing off a people because of their apparent depravity. Help me pray prayers of revival and herald words of revival even for the darkest nations.

Confronting Sin in the Church

"Now all things are of God, who has reconciled us to Himself through Jesus Christ, and has given us the ministry of reconciliation, that is, that God was in Christ reconciling the world to Himself, not imputing their trespasses to them, and has committed to us the word of reconciliation" (2 Corinthians 5:18-19).

As part of revival, God begins to confront the sins in our hearts. There is no revival without conviction. But God may also call the preacher to confront sin in the church. This should not offend us. It should give us opportunity to respond to the Father's heart for us to experience total freedom.

We find a good example with Peter and Paul in Galatians 2. When Peter came back to Jerusalem from Antioch, Paul "withstood him to his face, because he was to be blamed" (Gal. 2:11). What did Peter do that deserved such a public confrontation? His actions were betraying the very Gospel he preached.

Some will argue that by calling out sin we are breeding strife and disunity, but the exact opposite is happening. When we call out the immorality in the church; when we call out the compromise with antichrist agendas in the church; when the Holy Spirit leads us to call out any type of sin in the church we aren't breeding disunity but opening the door to reunify the church with Christ's truth.

Indeed, it is those who are embracing immorality, compromise and various other sins that are causing a rift in the body of Christ. That said, we need to confront these issues with a spirit of humility—not superiority and arrogance. We need to be motivated by love when we call out sinful behaviors in hopes that we will be heard and that hearts will turn back to the unadulterated truth. Grace first. Then truth.

Love doesn't always sound like your mommy's voice tucking you into bed at night. Sometimes loves sounds like a blasting alarm that you dread hearing when you wake up in the morning. But it's for your own good. The point is this: We can't unify with churches and believers who aren't unified with Christ. Where compromise exists, there is no true unity. But our aim should always be to reconcile all things to Christ for the sake of true unity that will bring the revival we've been praying for.

— *Prayer* —

Father, in the name of Jesus, please, convict me of my sin. Convict me of unrighteousness. Convict me with Your kind voice that leads me to repentance. And help me, Lord, to be a minister of reconciliation unto revival. Help me express the goodness of God—and Your Good News.

I Pray. I Obey.

"Behold, to obey is better than sacrifice…" (1 Samuel 15:22).

David Yonggi Cho and his mother-in-law started a church in Seoul, Korea in 1958 in a venue pieced together from bits of U.S. Army tents. There were six people present at the launch. They probably didn't expect what God would do over the next years.

Yoido Full Gospel Church grew to a weekly attendance of about eight-hundred thousand people in seven Sunday services, with hundreds of licensed ministers and thousands of laypersons leading weekly small groups of ten to fifteen people.

Yonggi Cho died in 2021 at the age of eighty-six with a 24/7 prayer ministry that included hundreds of thousands of intercessors. Someone once asked David Yonggi Cho how he built such a massive ministry. His answer "I pray, I obey." That is a key to seeing revival: pray and obey.

When we pray, we petition God but we also hear from God. When we hear from God, we must obey God rapidly. Delayed obedience is disobedience. If we are a friend of revival, we will obey Jesus, who is Revival—even when it doesn't make any sense to our natural mind.

Jesus said, "If anyone loves Me, he will keep My word; and My Father will love him, and We will come to him and make Our home with him" (John 14:23). When Jesus makes His home among us—and when we steward His internal presence—it's only a matter of time before revival breaks forth in us. But it starts with being obedient to pray—and then obeying what He tells us in our conversation with Him.

A.W. Tozer, a theologian and preacher, put it this way: "Have you noticed how much praying for revival has been going on of late—and how little revival has resulted? I believe the problem is that we have been trying to substitute praying for obeying, and it simply will not work."

— *Prayer* —

Father, in the name of Jesus, would You help me to obey Your call to pray so I can obey what You say while I pray? I want to live by every Word that comes out of Your mouth. I want to pray for Your will to be done and Your Kingdom to come. Help me obey the call to pray.

Generational Revivals

"One generation shall praise Your works to another, and shall declare Your mighty acts" (Psalm 145:4).

Revivals usually only last a few years, but some have endured long enough to impact a generation. A generation is usually considered about forty years, but even a revival that endures twenty years has the potential to reach two generations.

The First Great Awakening broke the church out of established doctrinal boxes by emphasizing individual faith and salvation. New denominations were birthed out of the First Great Awakening, which lasted over twenty years. That's not quite a generation but consider that the Second Great Awakening lasted fifty years and you start to get a glimpse of generational revival.

The Second Great Awakening turned outward and focused on evangelism. Up until this time, Congregationalists and Anglicans were the largest presence in America, but the Second Great Awakening saw the rise of the Methodists and Baptists. Camp meetings with thousands—including a revival at Cane Ridge, Kentucky in 1802 that saw twenty thousand people gather—took place around the nation. This revival was transformational.

Because it lasted over a generation, the Second Great Awakening shifted America's religious landscape like nothing else up to that point. It was an evangelical movement that shunned Calvinistic tradition and emphasized that people could exercise their free will and believe in the Son of God unto salvation. The Second Great Awakening also opened the door to more women and African-Americans.

Instead of generational curses, what if we could see generational revivals? We know it's possible because God has done it before—but it's rare. Generational revival depends, at least in some measure, on generations connecting. In a generational revival, we may express a move of God in different ways but we are joined together, honoring one another, to press into the same move. We see a generational transfer of spiritual wealth, so to speak.

What if the revival that was sparked in your generation touched your children and even their children's children? Let's pray that revival becomes transforming revival!

— *Prayer* —

Father, in the name of Jesus, I see the possibility of generational revival. I believe for generational revival in my lifetime that affects my children's children. Help me to pray prayers with generational revival in mind. Grace me to share the Gospel to the generations in a way they can receive it.

Battling Antichrist Agendas

"Little children, it is the last hour; and as you have heard that the Antichrist is coming, even now many antichrists have come, by which we know that it is the last hour" (1 John 2:18).

There are two main movements in the Earth today—a Holy Spirit-inspired movement and an Antichrist movement. The Holy Spirit wants to shift us into a Third Great Awakening while antichrist spirits want to shift nations into godlessness and see Christians jailed for preaching the Gospel of salvation.

The contrast is stark—and visible. The Antichrist agenda is perverting sexuality, family, religion, education, government, and other sectors of society. We're seeing Christians jailed for standing on the Word of God, Islamic terror wreaking havoc on our soil and an onslaught of threats coming against our religious liberty.

This demonic movement has gained mass momentum in the last fifty years, but the devil always overplays his hand, and I am witnessing the church—at least a remnant within the church—waking up, praying fervently, and taking action to turn a nation back to God. Some of those actions are turning into movements, which *Merriam-Webster* defines as "a series of organized activities working toward an objective."

Antichrist is essentially anti-anointing, since the Greek word "Christos" is defined as "anointed." The antichrist spirit wants to kill the anointing on your life with an onslaught of coordinated spiritual terror attacks that wear you out. Daniel 7:25 paints a picture of the Antichrist's strategy and antichrist spirits employ the same tactics: "He shall speak words against the Most High and shall wear out the saints of the Most High and plan to change times and law."

An antichrist spirit is often behind the deception clouding the minds of those who flat out deny Christ and those who turn away from Him. Those raised in Christian homes who resist the Lord are deceived by the working of an antichrist spirit.

It may seem they followed football or girls or drugs or even a demanding career of some sort but make no mistake: an antichrist spirit worked on their emotions and reasonings to pull them away from the Father's heart. But when God pours out His Spirit on all flesh, repentance comes and the antichrist spirits must bow.

— *Prayer* —

Father, in the name of Jesus, would You teach me to discern antichrist spirits operating in the world—and in my midst—so that I don't come into any measure of agreement with these nefarious spirits? I don't want to be deceived. Help me walk in truth that keeps me free.

APRIL 21

Apostolic Women Arising

"Greet Andronicus and Junia, my countrymen and my fellow prisoners, who are of note among the apostles, who also were in Christ before me" (Romans 16:7).

Aimee Semple McPherson's Angeles Temple is still standing in Los Angeles today. I stood behind her pulpit and visited her home, which the Foursquare denomination she started preserved for historical purposes. While in Los Angeles, I felt mantles being released; mantles for healing, mantles for miracles—and mantles for apostolic women. I began to prophesy these words:

"The time is now for apostolic women to arise and indeed they are arising even now. The time is now for apostolic women to arise and take their places in their church and take their places in the marketplace and take their places in their families, in their homes.

"The time is now for apostolic women to release the revelation that I've shared with their hearts in the secret places. The time is now for apostolic women to arise and bring forth the revelation of days gone by. The time is now for apostolic women to build upon the revelation, to speak forth, to build, to build, to build and plant in the name of Jesus with the authority of the Lord Jesus Christ backing them; with all of heaven standing with them; with the ministering angels building and working alongside of them.

"The time is now for apostolic women to arise in this city and in this region and in the nation and in the nations of the world. For many years apostolic women have sat in the background waiting for permission to prophesy, waiting for permission to take their places and their God-given roles in the Body of Christ.

"And the time is now for apostolic women to come to the fore, working alongside apostolic men and prophetic believers and evangelists, pastors and teachers who have a heart to build, who have a heart to see awakening, who have a heart to see revival impact this land and who have a heart to see the glory of My Spirit go forth in the nations and cover the earth as the water covers the sea."

The time is now.

— *Prayer* —

Father, in the name of Jesus, would You help me to champion the women of revival? The religious spirit wants to tear women down. Some men shun women in church leadership. And sometimes women compete against each other. Show me how I can support the women of revival.

Revival Prayers That Never Fail

"For the word of God is living and powerful, and sharper than any two-edged sword, piercing even to the division of soul and spirit, and of joints and marrow, and is a discerner of the thoughts and intents of the heart" (Hebrews 4:12).

We can pray from our heart for revival, but we should try as much as possible to pray Biblical revival prayers. Yes, the Holy Spirit can and lead us to pray for what's on His heart, but we should seek to include Scripture-based prayers in our intercession sets.

Pray prayers of repentance: 2 Chronicles 7:14 reads, "If My people who are called by My name will humble themselves, and pray and seek My face, and turn from their wicked ways, then I will hear from heaven, and will forgive their sin and heal their land."

Pray for God's mercy on the church: Habakkuk 3:2 reads, "O Lord, I have heard Your speech and was afraid; O Lord, revive Your work in the midst of the years! In the midst of the years make it known; In wrath remember mercy." Pray that God would stir you up: 2 Timothy 1:6 reads, "Therefore I remind you to stir up the gift of God which is in you through the laying on of my hands."

Pray that God would make you hungry and thirsty: Jesus said in Matthew 6:33, "But seek first the kingdom of God and His righteousness, and all these things shall be added to you."

Pray God would revive the spirit of the lowly: Isaiah 57:15 reads, "For thus says the High and Lofty One Who inhabits eternity, whose name is Holy: 'I dwell in the high and holy place, with him who has a contrite and humble spirit, to revive the spirit of the humble, and to revive the heart of the contrite ones."

Pray Psalm 85:6-8: "Will You not revive us again, that Your people may rejoice in You? Show us Your mercy, Lord, and grant us Your salvation." Pray Psalm 80:16: "Then we will not turn back from You; Revive us, and we will call upon Your name."

— *Prayer* —

Father, in the name of Jesus, would You help me pray by the Word and by Your Spirit? Give me a revelation of the power of praying Your Word, which is sharper than any two-edged sword. Help me wield the sword of the spirit with accuracy. Let my prayers be according to Your will.

APRIL 23

Revival on the Business Mountain

"And he called his ten servants, and delivered them ten pounds, and said unto them, occupy till I come" (Luke 19:13).

In the Parable of the Minas, Jesus made it clear that He wants us to take what we have—our gifts, talents, graces, anointings, and financial blessings—and use it to increase the Kingdom.

Indeed, Luke 19:13, a man tells his servants: "Put this money to work until I come back." Other translations say, "Engage in business until I come." The idea is to take intentional action to advance the Kingdom.

We all need to be about the Father's business, and that includes influencing the business mountain. There are billions of people in the marketplace who don't know Him and without a revival they may never have another opportunity to meet Him, as most won't darken the doors of a church.

What is the business mountain? It's the marketplace as you know it, which is made up of large and small businesses alike. The business mountain incudes the economy, industries like healthcare as well as the general marketplace. Major corporations, in particular, have a major influence on society.

God wants to see revival in the business mountain because most people work there. Revival in workplaces has the potential to spread like wildfire. The problem is, we're dealing with strongholds like the spirit of Babylon. Of course, we're also dealing with the spirit of Mammon.

Babylon is a system. It's a principality over the kingdoms of this world. But we know the kingdoms of this world will become the kingdoms of our Lord and His Christ, according to Revelation 11:5. We need to contend for revival on the business mountain for the sake of multiplied millions of lost souls.

Make no mistake: There is a supernatural wealth transfer coming, and God wants us to be ready to minister to those who are part of a failing Babylonian economy. We need to be praying for strategies now to create wealth to establish His covenant in the earth (see Deut. 8:18). We need to pray for revival in the business mountain.

— *Prayer* —

Father, in the name of Jesus, most of us encounter the business mountain everyday—either at our jobs or through shopping in retail outlets, eating in restaurants and the like. Would You give me—and Your people—a heart to see revival in this sector? Give me a grace to pray for this mountain.

The Spiritual Avalanche

"But know that the Lod has set apart for Himself him who is godly; The Lord will hear when I call to Him" (Psalm 4:3).

I'll always remember when revivalist Steve Hill, a key figure in the Brownsville Revival, called to tell me about a vision he had just had a couple of days before. He described an alarming vision in which he saw "a massive, majestic mountain covered in glistening snow."

He said, "It reminded me of the Matterhorn in the Swiss Alps. Its peaks were sparkling white, and I was amazed by God's attention to detail. It was so realistic, I wanted to go skiing! But I sensed that there was more that the Holy Spirit was about to reveal." He wound up writing a book about that vision called *Spiritual Avalanche: The Threat of False Teachings that Could Destroy Millions.* The best-selling book exposes the great lies in the church today.

"Pastors and teachers worldwide have succumbed to heretical teachings including universal reconciliation, deification of man, challenging the validity of the Word of God including His judgements, and even lifting any boundaries, claiming His amazing grace is actually 'amazing freedom," Hill wrote. "You are free to live according to your own desires. Sound familiar? 'They had no king and did what was right in their own eyes' (Judges 17:6). These popular self-proclaimed ministers of the gospel are covering the "slopes" and will be held accountable for the spiritual death of millions."

In the book, Hill shares how every aspect of his vision relates to Christians today. The snow represents the false teaching that is steadily falling on the ears of many Christ followers, covering with many layers the solid foundational truth of Christ. Heresies including universalism, the deification of man, overemphasized grace, and many more that will ultimately destroy the spiritual lives of many, he said.

What happens when snow keeps falling, creating the dangerous threat of an avalanche? Those who heed the warnings are saved, but those who fail to listen are caught in a deadly trap. That was 2014. His vision is certainly coming to pass. We need revival now!

— *Prayer* —

Father, in the name of Jesus, would You give me an urgency to discern, expose and stand against the enemies of Your Gospel in the earth? Help me not to be deceived by the heretical teachings peppering the Body of Christ. Give me a hunger for Your Word. Your Word is truth.

APRIL 25

Don't Shrink Back

"If you faint in the day of adversity, your strength is small" (Proverbs 24:10).

Every region is home to principalities, powers, and various spiritual rulers that work to keep people in bondage—and actively resist revival. God places strategic voices and mantles in specific territories to establish truth, breakthrough, and blessing.

There is supernatural favor upon the voices that God sends. Of course, there is also supernatural resistance to those voices. The enemy understands that if he can silence particular voices in a territory, he can stop the work of transformation.

Apostolic and prophetic gifts expose and confront principalities and powers in a territory. Although each territory may have different spirits operating, there is a common ground in the realm of revival. Stand your ground! Keep declaring truth. Keep speaking the messages that burn in your belly.

Don't allow discouragement to stop you. Be the voice that God has called you to be. Pray for the voices of transformation in your region. Form a prayer covering that lifts them up and the work they are called to do. Together, we shall all reap the harvest.

Las Vegas has a gambling influence while San Francisco has a homosexual influence and New York has a Babylonian influence. That influence can impact the way people think. Apostolic and prophetic ministries join forces to identify these strongholds—which aren't always as blatant as the ones in our examples—and work to displace them so the King of Glory can reign.

You'll find one consistent pattern: spirits of religion and Jezebel stand hard against revival in any city where people are co-laboring with Christ to light a fire. Apostolic and prophetic gifts do not shrink back from the battle, but rally God's people against the enemy to tear down his throne and advance the Kingdom of God in a territory.

— *Prayer* —

Father, in the name of Jesus, I am grateful for the authority You have given me in the war for revival—and the war against revival. Would You help me discern the territorial demons rightly so I can war accurately in the spirit? Help me to stand strong against the enemies of revival.

APRIL 26

Handling Revival Critics

"A gentle answer turns away wrath, but a harsh word stirs up anger" (Proverbs 15:1).

I've always said some of the greatest opponents to the next great move of God will be those who participated in the last great move of God. That's because when God moves next time, it may—and probably will—look different from how God moved last time. In other words, it's not necessarily familiar.

But this statement is just as true: Some who criticize revival are those who don't know the Holy Spirit, those who attend lukewarm churches, or those who don't preach the full Gospel. We've seen cessationists insist the gifts of the Spirit are not for today, that there is no healing or miracles today. All of these personalities are prone to criticize revival.

When the Holy Spirit visited the one hundred-twenty disciples in the Upper Room and they were filled to overflowing and started speaking in new tongues, many people were amazed. But along with the supporters who praised God, the critics started swarming. Acts 2:13 tells us people criticized the move of God saying, "They are full of new wine."

It was new wine, indeed, that was poured into a new wineskin. But that new wine was the Holy Spirit. Despite their criticism, Peter did not attack back. Peter did not cut short the revival. Peter did not try to defend himself by human standards. No, Peter took the opportunity to show people what the Word of God says. It's hard to argue with the Word of God. Peter said in Acts 2:16-18:

"But this is what was spoken by the prophet Joel: 'And it shall come to pass in the last days, says God, that I will pour out of My Spirit on all flesh; Your sons and your daughters shall prophesy, your young men shall see visions, your old men shall dream dreams. And on My menservants and on My maidservants I will pour out My Spirit in those days; And they shall prophesy.'" Three thousand souls, some of them critics, got saved.

— Prayer —

Father, in the name of Jesus, would You help me accept the reality that Christians are not all on the same page? Help me not to get offended with believers who will not accept Your work of revival. Help me not to compromise my stance because of the critics and naysayers.

APRIL 27

Don't Miss His Visit

"For days will come upon you when your enemies will build an embankment around you, surround you and close you in on every side, and level you, and your children within you, to the ground; and they will not leave in you one stone upon another, because you did not know the time of your visitation" (Luke 19:43-44).

We need to live with an expectation of holy visitation. Many times we don't see God visit more because we haven't made room for Him. We haven't welcomed Him in. Or we're not expecting Him so we don't wait on Him.

Back in the day, Pentecostal Christians knew how to tarry long. They tarried, or waited, for hours and hours on end until the Holy Spirit came into the room and wrecked the place. I'm concerned many churches have lost the art of tarrying.

Jesus rebuked the Pharisees because they did not discern that the Son of God (whom they read about in Scripture) was in their midst. Instead of embracing Him, they rejected Him because He didn't come like they thought He would. How sad!

The New American Standard translation of Luke 19:44 says, "Because you did not recognize the time of your visitation." God forbid we cry out for revival and find every reason in the world to reject His presence when He comes. God forbid our love grows cold, or our lives grow too busy, or we're so much in our heads that we miss His heart.

The New International Version of Luke 19:44 says, "You didn't recognize the time of God's coming to you." *The New Living Translation* says, "You did not recognize it when God visited you." God forbid that God is pouring out His Spirit and we don't discern Emmanuel, God with us. God forbid we don't set aside the childish things to respond to His presence.

The Amplified Bible says, "You did not [come progressively to] recognize [from observation and personal experience] the time of your visitation [when God was gracious toward you and offered you salvation]."

The Pharisees should have been able to observe Jesus was who people said He was by the miracles, but they were proud and threatened by His presence. They should have been able to recognize God through personal experience, but instead their legalism caused them to reject Him. God forbid we do the same!

— *Prayer* —

Father, in the name of Jesus, I repent if I have cried out for Your presence only to miss Your visitation. Would You help me to be so sensitive to Your Spirit that I recognize You in any way You choose to grace me with Your presence? I don't want to miss a moment with You.

A Vision of Revival Hotspots

"In my Father's house are many rooms. If it were not so, would I have told you that I go to prepare a place for you?" (John 14:2, ESV)

I saw a vision of heaven's war room. Strategies and tactics for spiritual battles were outlined for the angels and the elect who would be sent into the skirmish to execute God's will on the earth.

While I could not see the Godhead in clear view, I felt the presence of Father God, Jesus, and the Holy Spirit. I saw the Father's arms at the head of the table. His fingers were crossed as He held his hands together. Sitting at the table in designated seats were angels and saints.

I could not hear every word spoken, but I discerned the intensity of this strategic meeting. The finger of God was pointing to different places on a world map. As He pointed to specific nations and cities, those areas of the map would light up with fire and glory. These are hotbeds of spiritual activity in the earth—areas where there is a battle for transforming revival that precedes what is perhaps the final harvest.

Suddenly, the Father started handing out war assignments to the angels present at the table. These were princes that would lead heavenly hosts in an epic battle. These massive warring angels were standing at attention waiting with their heads and muscular chests held high. Father was dispatching them with specific assignments on the earth. He sent one to fight death, one to fight disease and one of fight Jezebel. I did not see or hear all the assignments.

Next, I saw a weaponry chest open before my eyes. It contained many weapons, but swords sharpened for this specific battle drew my attention. I also saw oil, representing the anointing, poured out on the weapons. What did these sharpened, newly-anointed swords represent? New revelation from the Word of God that would help soldiers on earth battle enemies in the second heaven.

God wants to see revival in your city. Will you cooperate in through intercession and evangelism? Such are pillars of revival.

— *Prayer* —

Father, in the name of Jesus, I want to cooperate with Your plans and purposes for my city. I want to see revival in my church and awakening in my nation. Would You help me understand the forces at work in the spirit realm? Would You teach my hands to war and my fingers to fight?

APRIL 29

Do it Again, Lord!

"O Lord, I have heard Your speech and was afraid; O Lord, revive Your work in the midst of the years! In the midst of the years make it known; In wrath remember mercy" (Habakkuk 3:2).

You may hear revival-minded Christian crying out, "Do it again, Lord!" This is based on a Scripture. *The Message* translation of this verse really drives home the passion of the prophet's words in Habakkuk 3:2:

"God, I've heard what our ancestors say about you, and I'm stopped in my tracks, down on my knees. Do among us what you did among them. Work among us as you worked among them. And as you bring judgment, as you surely must, remember mercy."

God is the author of revival and awakening. Only He can bring it. But we must stir up a hunger and thirst for revival. Revival is sovereign. God alone decides when to pour out His Spirit, but He does so in the midst of desperation. It's not by might nor by power but by His Spirit (see Zech. 4:6).

We need to ask the Lord, like Habakkuk, to do it again! We need to ask Him to do it again, like He did at Azusa Street. We need to ask Him to do it again, like He did in the Welsch Revival. We need to ask Him to do it again, like He did in the Hebrides Revival. We need to ask Him to do it again in our generation.

We need to ask the Lord, like Habakkuk, to do it again! We need to ask Him to do it again, like He did in the Voice of Healing movement. We need to ask Him to do it again, like He did in the First Great Awakening and the Second Great Awakening. We need to ask Him to do it again, like He did in the Jesus Revolution.

We need to ask the Lord, like Habakkuk, to do it again! We need to ask Him to do it again, like He did in the Manchurian Revival. We need to ask Him to do it again and believe, at the right time that He will. Ask and keep on asking!

— *Prayer* —

Father, in the name of Jesus, I ask You to bring revivals like the ones of the days gone by—with more power, more fire, more repentance, more salvations, and more missions. You are the God of the more. You did it before and You'll do it again. Do it again, Lord!

The John Wesley Revivalist Anointing

"I rise before the dawning of the morning, and cry for help; I hope in Your word"
(Psalm 119:147).

He made the equivalent of ten circles around the earth during his ministry. That's two hundred-fifty-thousand miles. But John Wesley, leader of the Methodist Movement in the 1700s, was an efficient revivalist. Wesley read books on horseback, wrote sermons on horseback, penned letters on horseback and more. He was indeed a revivalist who redeemed the time.

"Give me one hundred men who love only God with all their heart and hate only sin with all their heart and we will shake the gates of hell and bring in the Kingdom of God in one generation," Wesley said.

Before he saddled up his horse to carry revival fire, he spent two hours every morning in his prayer closet. In fact, there's a room in his house in England that's been dubbed "The Powerhouse of Methodism" because of his long hours of intercession for souls there. Wesley once said, "Proceed with much prayer, and your way will be made plain."

Although he never intended to split from the Church of England, which was religion's governing force in England at the time, Wesley was forced out for ordaining ministers and sending them to America. "There are many doctrines of a less essential nature. In these, we may think and let think; we may agree to disagree," he said. "But, in the meantime, let us hold fast to the essentials."

Without a pulpit in which to preach, Wesley took to the great outdoors and preached to masses that couldn't fit in traditional chapels—up to tens of thousands of people. A man of one book (the Bible), his preaching style was Christ-centered and delivered in a way that the average person could understand the Gospel. For that reason, some described him as a "lunch bucket" preacher.

Wesley's preaching methods worked. He saw one hundred forty thousand people saved in his ministry. By the time Wesley went on to glory in 1791, Methodism counted seventy-nine thousand followers in England and about forty thousand in America. By 1957, that number rose to over 40 million.

— *Prayer* —

Father, in the name of Jesus, would You give me an anointing like the one that rested on Wesley? Give me the grace to redeem the time because the days are evil. Give me the ability to appeal to the masses who need to know Your Son. Help me spend extended hours in the prayer closet for souls.

MAY

"If revival is being withheld from us it is because some idol remains still enthroned; because we still insist in placing our reliance in human schemes; because we still refuse to face the unchangeable truth that It is not by might, but by My Spirit."—Jonathan Goforth

Waves of Mercy and Grace

"There is a cloud, as small as a man's hand, rising out of the sea!' So he said, 'Go up, say to Ahab, 'Prepare your chariot, and go down before the rain stops you'" (1 Kings 18:44).

Revival often comes in waves. It washes over a few praying people, then it washes over a church or community. Sometimes it even washes over a nation. Patricia King prophesied a pivotal word of revival:

"Revival is a wave of the mercy of God revealing His goodness. The wave washes over people and nations and is to result in repentance and realignment to His sovereign purposes so that He can pour out great glory. A great wave is coming soon that will hit the nations unto harvest...if you: prepare, pray watch."

King senses a fresh outpouring of the Spirit is coming that will wash over all the nations—and many will come to Christ. The Spirit of God, she says, is looking for those who will prepare their hearts before Him. He is looking for those who will serve His purposes in the foundation of this coming move. He is looking for "anchors," she says, for this wave.

"He is calling us to prepare our hearts before Him in readiness—repenting from those things that would distract us from gazing upon His goodness, mercy, and purity. The key in the preparation is to be absorbed in His goodness." This revival, she says, will not come as a result of striving but by looking at Jesus and worshipping Him. This preparation, she says, will stir expectancy within for what is coming but will also create deeper repentance from sin, compromise, and dead works.

King says many individuals, ministries, and churches will be called to fasting and prayer to birth this revival in their lives, churches, and regions. Finally, she says, we are to watch. "Look for the signs of revival with expectation. It is like looking for the rain when you see the clouds coming," she says. "Be watchful and when it comes, embrace it. Revival is often very different than what you expect it to look like."

— *Prayer* —

Father, in the name of Jesus, would You help me prepare my heart before You? Help me wait expectedly on You like the one hundred and twenty disciples waited in the Upper Room before the Day of Pentecost. Help me watch expectantly for the signs of revival rain.

Don't Quench Revival

"Do not quench the Spirit" (1 Thessalonians 5:9).

Paul issued a five-word warning to the church at Thessalonica. And we would do well to heed that five-word warning today: Don't quench the Spirit of God.

Don't quench Him. You might wonder what that really means. Well, *The New Living Translation* says, "Don't stifle the Holy Spirit." Unfortunately, some churches today only let the Holy Spirit out once a year on Pentecost Sunday. The rest of the year they keep Him in a closet like your drunk uncle at Thanksgiving.

The Berean Standard Bible says, "Do not extinguish the spirit." In other words: Don't put the fire of the Spirit. *The Amplified Bible* says, "Do not quench, subdue, or be unresponsive to the work and guidance of the Holy Spirit."

Did you catch that? Don't be unresponsive. Too many people in this hour are living life like business as usual. Revival is not business as usual. Revival is not church as usual. When God pours out His Spirit, there's nothing usual about it. It's altogether unusual and extraordinary. We must stop everything to respond to what He is doing.

The Contemporary English Version says, "Do don't turn away God's Spirit." Are you listening? Don't turn Him away. He wants to move in your church. Don't turn Him away. He wants to move on your heart. Don't turn Him away. Don't be too busy to stop and be with Him. Don't push Him off until later. Make time for Him now.

The Good News Translation says, "Do not restrain the Holy Spirit." Don't put a bridle on Him like a horse. Don't try to hold Him back or constrain Him. Let Him do what He wants to do, even if it makes you uncomfortable. Let Him move freely. *The International Standard Version* says, "Do not put out the spirit's fire." Amen!

Fire and wind come and do it again, God. Come rest on us! Ask the Holy Spirit to show you any way in which you have quenched His Spirit, and then come to Him in repentance and ask Him to revive you.

— *Prayer* —

Father, in the name of Jesus, I never want to constrain, hinder, or hold You back. I never want to stand in the way, stifle or quench Your work in my heart or in my church. Help me to come into full agreement with Your operations and the revival fire You pour out.

MAY 3

The Native American Revival

"I will cry out to God Most High, to God who performs all things for me" (Psalm 57:2).

I've been to Native American Reservations. I've seen the sorrow in the wake of suicides. I've seen the devastation of alcoholism. But I've also seen the hunger for revival in the churches. I've also seen the desperate prayers for awakening. And I am believing for a new revival among America's First Nations people—and indigenous people around the world.

In 1975, Billy Graham stood in front of a small group of Native American leaders in Albuquerque, NM and issued this proclamation:

"The Native American has been a sleeping giant. He is awakening. The original Americans could become the next evangelists who will help win America for Christ."

In 2022, Graham's grandson Will pointed back to those words as he shared with one hundred twenty-five Christian leaders representing fourteen states, two provinces and twenty-four tribes at the Native Peoples Christian Leaders Conference: "God is waking the Sleeping Giant, and I believe God will use you to bring the last great revival. This is a moment in history that can change our country forever."

It's here and it's coming. In a film called *Awakened*, directors tell the story of how native people of North America are now rising up and stepping into the spiritual destiny Billy Graham preached about. Many believe a revival among indigenous people holds the key to revival and America's future.

Richard Blackaby, son of Henry Blackaby, founder of Blackaby Ministries, offered these insights in 2019: "God often chooses to use the 'least' of the peoples, much like He used the Israelites when He delivered them out of bondage. These people are connected to indigenous peoples around the world. Should they gain a sense of divine purpose for their lives, they could travel down an established highway to carry the good news around the world."

— Prayer —

Father, in the name of Jesus, thank You for the indigenous people of my nation. I bless the indigenous people in my land, and I ask You to bless them. Father, would You pour out Your Spirit on native lands and send a revival that spreads like wildfire through the nations?

David Wilkerson's Anguish

"The wall of Jerusalem is also broken down, and its gates are burned with fire. So it was, when I heard these words, that I sat down and wept, and mourned for many days; I was fasting and praying before the God of heaven" (Nehemiah 1:3-4).

David Wilkerson agonized over the church. He once released a message, "A Call to Anguish." This anguish should mark every revivalist's heart.

"And I look at the whole religious scene today and all I see are the inventions and ministries of man and flesh. It's mostly powerless. It has no impact on the world. And I see more of the world coming into the church and impacting the church, rather than the church impacting the world. I see the music taking over the house of God.

"I see entertainment taking over the house of God. An obsession with entertainment in God's house; a hatred of correction and a hatred of reproof. Nobody wants to hear it any more.

"Whatever happened to anguish in the house of God? Whatever happened to anguish in the ministry? It's a word you don't hear in this pampered age. You don't hear it. Anguish means extreme pain and distress. The emotions so stirred that it becomes painful. Acute deeply felt inner pain because of conditions about you, in you, or around you. Deep pain. Deep sorrow. The agony of God's heart.

"We've held on to our religious rhetoric and our revival talk but we've become so passive. All true passion is born out of anguish. All true passion for Christ comes out of a baptism. of anguish. You search the Scripture and you'll find that when God determined to recover a ruined situation…

"He would share His own anguish for what God saw happening to His church and to His people. And He would find a praying man and take that man and literally baptize him in anguish. You find it in the book of Nehemiah. Jerusalem is in ruins. How is God going to deal with this? How is God going to restore the ruin?"

— Prayer —

Father, in the name of Jesus, would You share Your anguish with me? Help me see the work of the enemy in the earth the way Nehemiah saw the work of the enemy in Jerusalem—and deeply grieve over it. Give me a heart that weeps, fasts and prays for You to revival my city.

Watering the Roots of Awakening

"And the remnant who have escaped of the house of Judah shall again take root downward, and bear fruit upward" (2 Kings 19:30).

I spent a good deal of time in Wales in the very city where Evan Roberts launched the Welsh Revival. We also walked the streets of Cardiff. I was taken back by much of what I saw. Revival has more than waned in Wales, yet there is a root of awakening and God is looking for intercessors to water that root with intercession. I heard the Lord say:

"Wales, o Wales, I am calling you back to destiny. For I ordained you as a revival fire starter among the European nations. I have called you to pick up the mantle of Evan Roberts and begin to pray without ceasing again. I have called you to put aside the rebellion and the ways of the world and be an example of a burning shining lamp again, a forerunner for a new awakening in Europe.

"I will call other forerunners alongside you to pray with and for you as you take your place in the lampstand. I will give you strategies to penetrate the darkness that is invading Europe and you will be a leader among the nations even though you are among the smallest of the European nations.

"I will do all this if you will turn to Me again, if you will look to Me again, if you will cry out to Me again. I want to water the root of awakening the remains. I want to strengthen the revival history in a new generation that has long forgotten the heritage of your great land.

"Rise up and pray and watch Me move in responses to your petitions. I will deliver you and raise you up again as a voice in Europe."

This is a strong word for Wales, and I believe we can all apply this to our lives. If we turn to Him again, if we look to Him again, if we cry out to Him again, He will hear our cries and water the root of awakening.

— *Prayer* —

Father, in the name of Jesus, I cry out to You with everything in me. I cry out to You from the depths of my spirit. Lord, bring revival to Wales. Bring revival to Europe. Bring revival to my heart. Bring revival to my church, my city, and my nation. Water the roots of awakening.

Consecrated for Revival

"I beseech you therefore, brethren, by the mercies of God, that you present your bodies a living sacrifice, holy, acceptable to God, which is your reasonable service. And do not be conformed to this world, but be transformed by the renewing of your mind, that you may prove what is that good and acceptable and perfect will of God" (Romans 12:1-2).

The Great Falling Away is underway. On top of high-profile Christian leaders falling into gross sin, we're seeing notable authors, songwriters and others denying Christ as Savior. All the while, pastors continue committing suicide. We need a revival.

On my *Mornings with the Holy Spirit* prayer broadcast, I prophetically announced the season of consecration. This is part of the prophetic word:

"There is much deception rising in this hour—and even some of My elect are being deceived by doctrines of demons and spirits of suicide. And the lust of the flesh and the lust of the eyes and the pride of life is taking out some of My soldiers, whom I love.

"In this season, I'm calling you to draw yourself away, to set yourself apart. For I have set you apart for My purposes, but you must set yourself apart for My purposes in order to step into everything I've planned for you, since before the foundation of the earth.

"I'm calling you to set yourself apart. I'm calling you to consecrate yourself unto Me, now. Do not wait and do not hesitate for the enemy is raging. He is attacking left and right, back and forth, from behind and in the front. He is taking out My children, one by one by one and it grieves My heart.

"And I want to protect you. I want to hide you under the shadow of My wings. But you must fear My name. You must walk circumspectly to walk in the fullness of My protection. You must not look to escape My will, looking here, there and everywhere, for the pleasures of the world; the pleasures of the season."

"You must take your pleasure in Me. You must set yourself apart for Me because I have set you apart for Myself and together we will go into places and see things that you did not know existed."

— *Prayer* —

Father, in the name of Jesus, help me to cooperate with Your sanctifying grace by consecrating myself fully to You. Help me walk away from everything that hinders love and walk into Your loving arms. Let my consecration lead to a revival that sets people around me on fire for You.

MAY 7

Revival on the Entertainment Mountain

"For a day in Your courts is better than a thousand. I would rather be a doorkeeper in the house of my God than dwell in the tents of wickedness" (Proverbs 84:10).

Some people see entertainment as purely evil. Entertainment is not purely evil but there is evil on the entertainment mountain. Ecclesiastes 2:4 tells us, "Nothing is better for a man than that he should eat and drink, and that his soul should enjoy good in his labor. This also, I saw, was from the hand of God."

But let's face it. The world's entertainment system as we know it is largely corrupted—and it corrupts our minds when we lend our ears to it. Mental health issues in the entertainment industry are severe. Rates of suicide and suicidal thinking, depression, anxiety, and substance abuse are significantly higher among entertainment industry professionals than the general population.

At the same time, sexual harassment, sexual abuse, and sexual perversion is huge in the entertainment industry. Pedophilia is running rampant. (Just look at all the child stars who have confessed to being molested.) Racism and sexism are raging, and drug and alcohol abuse are off the charts. Think about how many stars have died of drug overdoses or suicides.

And the enemy is using the entertainment industry to introduce demonic ideologies to our children and mainstream perversion. That's because Jezebel—a spirit that propagates immorality and idolatry sits atop the entertainment mountain. Jezebel is a spirit of seduction and it's running rampant in the world and in the church. Remember, Jesus pointed out the purpose of Jezebel in Revelation 2:20: to teach and seduce.

Seduce in that verse comes from the Greek word "planao," which means "to cause to stray, to lead astray, to lead aside from the right way, to lead away from the truth, to lead into error, to deceive, to be led away into error or sin," according to *The KJV New Testament Greek Lexicon*.

The entertainment mountain needs revival. Ask God to give you a heart to pray for revival on this critical mountain.

— *Prayer* —

Father, in the name of Jesus, would You give me a heart to pray for revival on the entertainment mountain? Help me not to be a supporter of secular entertainment but an intercessor for those who create it, praying that they will see You in visions and dreams and turn from their wicked ways.

The Mike Bickle Revivalist Anointing

"And this woman was a widow of about eighty-four years, who did not depart from the temple, but served God with fastings and prayers night and day" (Luke 2:37).

Mike Bickle planned to practice medicine—but the Holy Spirit planned to use him to ignite a generation with a passion for Jesus that fuels day-and-night prayer.

"I wanted to like be J. Hudson Taylor, the missionary doctor from England who went to China in the 1800s," Bickle said. "He was my hero. I read three biographies of his life in high school. When I got accepted into medical school, a man asked me if I had asked the Lord about it. How could it not be the Lord?"

With less than one hundred of about eight thousand applicants accepted into the medical program, that was the big question. Nevertheless, Mike pressed in to pursue the Lord's will and was surprised to discover Christ the Healer had a different destiny in mind for him—a destiny that would see tens of thousands of youths impacted in his generation.

Despite Mike's choice to pursue God's call to raise up a generation of youth instead of his medical missionary dreams, he's still seen lives saved and bodies healed in the name of Jesus—the Bridegroom King—through his ministry. And he's contending in prayer to see God heal our land.

"We are in desperate need of revival and a great spiritual awakening for our nation," Mike says. "The Lord longs for His church to walk close to Him and to be vessels of His manifest power in their cities by developing strong prayer lives individually and corporately as local churches.

"In the midst of a growing crisis, I am encouraged as I see more and more people responding to the Lord in a wholehearted way. The numbers are still small, but they are increasing. I have great hope in seeing the Lord turn things around, but it will only happen as a culture of prayer is established in the church and a Third Great Awakening sweeps across America."

The Mike Bickle revival anointing is an anointing to mobilize intercessors for day and night prayer.

— Prayer —

Father, in the name of Jesus, would You give me an anointing like Mike Bickle's to rally the troops in prayer and worship, day and night and night and day? Give me the leadership gifts and talents, along with the communication skills, to cast the vision for unceasing intercession.

When Children Pave the Way to Revival

"Jesus said, 'Let the little children come to Me, and do not forbid them; for of such is the kingdom of heaven'" (Matthew 19:14).

I had a dream. I was at Awakening House of Prayer, my church in Ft. Lauderdale, and one of our worship pastors was singing "Build My Life." In the dream the congregation began to engage at a deep level. It was truly deep crying out to deep. The Holy Spirit was ministering to people individually. People were engaging with Him and He was engaging with them.

When the worship pastor looked over and saw the move of the Spirit, she began to smile widely and soon entered into an ecstatic state of joy. She started singing the chorus of the song even louder, with more passion and fervency and the service kept going higher and higher until all suddenly full-blown revival was birthed.

Indeed, we didn't plan for revival. You can't plan for revival. You can't make it happen—only God can. He visits the contrite hearts. Yes, we can fast and pray but God decides when it's prime time for a visitation.

Suddenly, in the dream, the children—from the smallest to the eldest—began to cry out together. They were praising God at the altar and dancing. Some of them were crying as the Holy Spirit touched their hearts in a unique way. When the adults saw the children in revival the whole church broke out into a revival like I've never seen before.

I have seen something similar in the past at a church in Georgia. We were in the sanctuary praising when the children's pastor texted and said revival broke out in kid's church. I was on the media team and ran over there with my camera. It was quite a hike as it was a few blocks from the main campus. I walked in to see the kids still jumping, dancing, praising, and weeping. We need to invest in worship—and we need to invest in our children.

— *Prayer* —

Father, in the name of Jesus, would You help me value worship and invest in the worship culture in my church? Help me remember that out of the mouths of babes comes praise and there is no junior Holy Spirit. Give me a burden to pray for the children of revival.

MAY 10

Reviving Contrite Hearts

"The sacrifices of God are a broken spirit, a broken and a contrite heart—these, O God, You will not despise" (Psalm 51:17).

Revival starts with contrite hearts. Contrite means feeling or showing sorrow and remorse for improper or objectionable behavior and actions. A contrite heart is different than worldly sorrow. It's an apologetic attitude, but it's not merely being sorry. It's grieving over one's sin.

David understood this when he penned the psalms. And Isaiah also understood this when he wrote the book that bears his name. God shared these words with the prophet in Isaiah 57:15:

"For thus says the High and Lofty One Who inhabits eternity, whose name is Holy: 'I dwell in the high and holy place, with him who has a contrite and humble spirit, to revive the spirit of the humble, and to revive the heart of the contrite ones.'"

Like David after Nathan confronted him in his sin with Bathsheba, Isaiah had his own moment of deep conviction with the Lord. Isaiah saw the Lord sitting on the throne, high and lifted up and the train of His robe filled the temple. He had an encounter with the holy one and his immediate response was to recognize his own sinfulness. Isaiah 6:5-7 reads:

"So I said: 'Woe is me, for I am undone! Because I am a man of unclean lips, and I dwell in the midst of a people of unclean lips; For my eyes have seen the King, the Lord of hosts.' Then one of the seraphim flew to me, having in his hand a live coal which he had taken with the tongs from the altar. And he touched my mouth with it, and said: Behold, this has touched your lips; Your iniquity is taken away, and your sin purged."

Ask the Lord to convict you of your sin. Ask the Lord to forgive you of your sin. Ask the Lord to purge you of your sin.

— Prayer —

Father, in the name of Jesus, my heart is contrite. I humble myself before Your throne and ask You to show me the depth of the sin in my heart and help me break free from it by Your blood. Wash me white as snow and help me walk circumspectly.

Receiving Revival Blueprints

"Having been built on the foundation of the apostles and prophets, Jesus Christ Himself being the chief cornerstone, in whom the whole building, being fitted together, grows into a holy temple in the Lord" (Ephesians 2:20).

God is a God of blueprints. A blueprint is a plan that provides guidance. Think of the blueprints for a house or a building. Without the blueprint—without a detailed plan or program of action—the end result may not be what was envisioned.

God gave David blueprints for the temple so Solomon could build it according to divine plans (see 1 Chron. 28:11). Much the same, God gave Moses the blueprint for the tabernacle with exacting instructions (see Ex. 25-27). And God gave Noah the blueprint for the ark that would preserve life on earth (see Gen. 6). No detail was too small in God's master blueprints.

With any revival blueprint, Jesus Christ must be the chief cornerstone (see Eph. 2:20). Everything in the revival must be aligned to Jesus, because Jesus is revival. Everything must magnify and glorify Him and make room for the Holy Spirit to move. We must follow His blueprint or we're in danger of seeing a man-made revival—or no revival at all.

Psalm 127:1 puts it this way, "Unless the Lord builds the house, they labor in vain who build it; Unless the Lord guards the city, the watchman stays awake in vain." Indeed, the Lord is not going to build a revival based on our blueprints. He is going to build it out based on His blueprints. We need to pray and ask God for His master plan.

Solomon, who took God's blueprints to complete a monumental building project that opened the door for such glory that the priest's couldn't stand to minister, understood this. He wrote, "Through wisdom a house is built, and by understanding it is established; By knowledge the rooms are filled with all precious and pleasant riches" (Prov. 24:3-4).

If we want divine revival that produces lasting fruit, we need to cry out to God not just for revival—but for a revival blueprint that helps us follow His leadership to build what He wants to build. He is the Chief Architect and wise master builder.

— *Prayer* —

Father, in the name of Jesus, would You show me Your revival blueprint?
Although there are ingredients to every revival, I know You have something
unique in mind for the revival You want to bring. Help me tap into Your thoughts
and Your ways and make room for Your revival.

A Spiritual Attack Against Revival

"O God, You are my God; Early will I seek You; My soul thirsts for You; My flesh longs for You in a dry and thirsty land where there is no water" (Psalm 63:1).

In the midst of writing a book on revival, I experienced a new kind of spiritual attack. As I put pen to paper about a Great Awakening, reformation and transformation in our nation, the enemy subtly worked to bring what I can only describe as "dryness" to my soul.

To combat this spiritual attack, I entered into worship in a deep way. I had an awareness of my need for God and set out to drink from His fountain until I no longer felt dry but could instead sense rivers of living water flowing from my spirit.

At first my mind would not become still. I was thinking about a conversation I had with David Ravenhill, the son of the famed Leonard Ravenhill. During our talk, we discussed how America is not yet desperate enough—not yet hungry enough—for a true revival unto another Great Awakening. That reality disturbed my heart, so I asked the Lord to start with me—to show me how the enemy is wreaking havoc on the souls of this generation and to put that desperation in my spirit.

Immediately, I had a vision. I saw pictures of famine, horrific violence in the Middle East and people dying from disease. Next, I looked up and saw a principality hanging over a large city from the second heaven. That principality was in the appearance of a dark cloud. From it came a voice that was commanding demons to execute a wicked agenda that included more famine, violence, immorality, and the like.

Above that principality, I saw the throne of God. Jesus is seated at the right hand of the Father in heavenly places, far above all principalities, powers, might and dominion, as well as every name that is named—not only in this age but also in that which is to come (see Eph. 1:20-21).

As born-again believers, we are raised up with Christ and seated together in heavenly places in Christ Jesus (see Eph. 2:6). If we don't pray more and more, things will get worse and worse.

— *Prayer* —

Father, in the name of Jesus, forgive me for being so concerned with me and my family that I neglected the greater call to pray for those who don't know You the way I know You—and those who don't know You at all. Would You make me a prayer solutionist?

Radical Revivalists

"Whatever you find to do with your hands, do it with all your might" (Ecclesiastes 9:10).

If we want to see revival, we're going to have to get radical about revival. We're going to have to be, as they said in the Jesus People movement, full-blown Jesus freaks.

Radical means "different from usual or traditional." That means a radical group that defies church as usual. Radical means "favoring extreme changes in existing views, habits, conditions or institutions." That means we might have to cut some programs or extend our prayer meetings. I heard the Lord say:

"Radicals are rising to steal, kill and destroy My plans and purposes in the earth—and in your life. Radical demons have wreaked havoc on churches, families, and individuals, bringing sickness, disease, poverty and mind battles that have caused many to abandon their callings and abort their purposes.

"But I am blowing a radical wind of My Spirit on the willing in this season. I am raising up radical spiritual warriors who will operate in radical obedience and press past radical enemy assignments against radical breakthrough.

"Jesus was a radical. John the Baptist was a radical. I am calling for a rise of the radicals who refuse to back down until they see My will come to pass in their hearts and see a radical outpouring of My Spirit in their communities. Rise, oh radicals, and take back what the enemy stole in this season of restoration."

Are you ready to be a radical revivalist? It all starts with radical obedience. For some of us, that means radical repentance.

Decide right now to trust God no matter what. Be willing to do anything and everything He asks without delay. Die to your own ways and your own comfort. Pray radical prayers. Worship in a radical way. Study with radical hunger. Pursue His presence with radical persistence.

— *Prayer* —

Father, in the name of Jesus, I saw yes to radical Christianity. I will pray with radical faith. I will seek revival with a radical determination. I will share Your Gospel with radical fervency. I don't want church as usual or revival as usual. I want to see a radical move of Your Spirit.

When Revival Touches Hard Hearts

"Go therefore and make disciples of all the nations, baptizing them in the name of the Father and of the Son and of the Holy Spirit, teaching them to observe all things that I have commanded you" (Matthew 28:19-20).

I heard the Lord say, "I'm working on the hardest of hearts in this hour. I'm working on the hard cases. And know this: As you preach the Word, as you pray without ceasing nothing shall be impossible. For I hold the hearts of men and women in my hands. I will encounter them with dreams, encounter them with visions, encounter them even in trances.

"I will meet them where they are. I will deal with their hurts and their wounds. So do not stop praying. Pray without ceasing, for the harvest is ripe. It's white and it's ready. So pray without ceasing, for souls are at stake and I am not willing that any should perish. Be the light."

Revival without a focus on lost souls is not the fullness of what God has in mind. God wants the church to be revived and refreshed so we can be about the Father's business. He wants us to co-labor with Jesus to turn hearts back to Him by being a witness in our city.

God wants to empower us and embolden us to share our faith even with the skeptics, knowing that we are sowing a seed that someone else will water. God will bring the increase (see 1 Cor. 3:6-9).

We need to pray not just for revival, but for a boldness to share the love of Christ in our city. We need to pray for hearts to be softened and readied to receive the Lord. Romans 10:14 asks, "How then shall they call on Him in whom they have not believed? And how shall they believe in Him of whom they have not heard? And how shall they hear without a preacher?"

You don't have to be a preacher to preach the Gospel. It requires no special oration skills to share your testimony of a life changed. It takes no other anointing than the one you already possess to pray to the Lord of the harvest and to stand in the gap for those who don't yet know Him.

— Prayer —

Father, would You give me a burning passion for the lost? Burden my heart for souls. Give me grace to be the salt and light, to burn and shine, to decree and declare, and to pray without ceasing. As You revive me, help me to be an agent to awaken others to Your love.

MAY 15

Moses the Revivalist

"Then Moses pleaded with the LORD his God, and said: 'Lord, why does Your wrath burn hot against Your people whom You have brought out of the land of Egypt with great power and with a mighty hand?'" (Exodus 32:11-14).

Moses is perhaps best known as a prophet and deliverer. But he was also a revivalist. You know the story. Egypt enslaved the Israelites and Pharoah was a cruel taskmaster, forcing them to make bricks without straw after increasing their daily quota. The Israelites started crying out to God for deliverance. God heard their cries, parted the Red Sea, and started them on a journey to the Promised Land.

But the Israelites quickly forgot the God of deliverance. When Moses was atop Mt. Sinai receiving the Ten Commandments written by the very finger of God, Aaron was down below leading a revolt against Jehovah. Aaron instructed the children of Israel to bring their gold, out of which he molded a golden calf. Then they said, "This is your god, O Israel, that brought you out of the land of Egypt!" (Ex. 32:4).

God planned to release burning hot wrath against the Israelites and consume them (see Ex. 32:7-10). Moses the revivalist immediately launched into identificational repentance. He pled in prayer with the Lord for mercy on their behalf. He called upon the covenant God made with Abraham, Isaac and Jacob— and the Lord relented (see Ex. 32:11-14).

Moses returned to the camp to find the Israelites in full-blown idolatry. He immediately destroyed the idol, ground it to power, scattered it on the water and made them drink it (see Ex. 32:30). But he didn't stop there. Moses the revivalist punished the leaders of the revolt. He called the Levites to strap on their swords and kill those who would not bow to the Lord. Three thousand men fell to the edge of the sword.

Moses again prayed, asking the Lord for His presence to remain with them. And God answered Him. Remember, revival is a turning back to God with a contrite heart in repentance. When we do, His presence is restored.

— Prayer —

Father, in the name of Jesus, would You forgive me for engaging in idolatry?
Forgive me for putting other gods before You. Forgive me for seeking other things
first instead of seeking first Your Kingdom and Your righteousness. Don't take
Your presence from me.

MAY 16

The Forerunner of Revival

"Is not My word like a fire?" says the Lord, "and like a hammer that breaks the rock in pieces?" (Jeremiah 23:29)

You've heard it said that prayer precedes revival, but have you let that sink in? Has this truth renewed your mind to the point that you will pray without ceasing for revival? Until we press into intercession for revival, we have only given a nod to this reality. Meditate on these eleven Scriptures that illustrate how prayer is the forerunner of revival.

"God heard their groaning and he remembered his covenant with Abraham, with Isaac and with Jacob, so God looked on the Israelites and was concerned about them" (Ex. 2:24-25). "Then Samuel took a suckling lamb and offered it up as a whole burnt offering to the Lord. He cried out to the Lord on Israel's behalf, and the Lord answered him" (1 Sam. 7:9). "They were helped in fighting them, and God handed the Hagrites and all their allies over to them, because they cried out to him during the battle. He answered their prayers because they trusted in Him" (1 Chron. 5:20).

"In you our fathers put their trust; they trusted and you delivered them. They cried to you and were saved; in you they trusted and were not disappointed" (Ps. 22:4). "Put on sackcloth, O priests, and mourn; wail, you who minister before the altar. Come; spend the night in sackcloth, you who minister before my God. Declare a holy fast; call a sacred assembly. Summon the elders and all who live in the land to the house of the Lord your God, and cry out to the Lord" (Joel 1:13-14).

"When the day of Pentecost came, they were all together in one place. Suddenly a sound like the blowing of a violent wind came from heaven and filled the whole house where they were sitting. They saw what seemed to be tongues of fire that separated and came to rest on each of them. All of them were filled with the Holy Spirit and began to speak in other tongues as the Spirit enabled them" (Acts 2:1-4). These are only a few of many examples. Pray on!

— Prayer —

Father, in the name of Jesus, help me catch the revelation that intercession is the forerunner of revival. Help me release Your Word in prayer like a fire that burns up enemy resistance. Help me use Your Word like a hammer that breaks the enemy's assignment into pieces.

155

MAY 17

Giving Way to Godly Sorrow

"For I do confess my guilt and iniquity; I am filled with anxiety because of my sin" (Psalm 38:18, AMP).

There's a difference between being sorry you got caught and true repentance. There's a difference between worldly sorrow and godly sorrow. In order to experience a personal revival, we need the latter. Paul the apostle explains this well, and expounds on the fruit of godly sorrow, in 2 Corinthians 7:8-11:

"For even if I made you sorry with my letter, I do not regret it; though I did regret it. For I perceive that the same epistle made you sorry, though only for a while. Now I rejoice, not that you were made sorry, but that your sorrow led to repentance. For you were made sorry in a godly manner, that you might suffer loss from us in nothing.

"For godly sorrow produces repentance leading to salvation, not to be regretted; but the sorrow of the world produces death. For observe this very thing, that you sorrowed in a godly manner: What diligence it produced in you, what clearing of yourselves, what indignation, what fear, what vehement desire, what zeal, what vindication! In all things you proved yourselves to be clear in this matter."

Charles Finney, a leader in the Second Great Awakening, put it this way, "Revival is a renewed conviction of sin and repentance, followed by an intense desire to live in obedience to God. It is giving up one's will to God in deep humility."

J.I. Packer, an English-born Canadian theologian, offered this critical insight, "Revival is the visitation of God which brings to life Christians who have been sleeping and restores a deep sense of God's near presence and holiness. Thence springs a vivid sense of sin and a profound exercise of heart in repentance, praise, and love, with an evangelistic outflow."

You might as well say it like this, "There is no revival without repentance."

— Prayer —

Father, in the name of Jesus, would You help me to enter into godly sorrow over my sin? I don't want to gloss over my sin, justify my sin or hide my sin. You see everything and I know if I confess my sin, You are faithful and just to forgive me of my sin and cleanse me of all unrighteousness.

Preaching Fire and Brimstone

"Upon the wicked He will rain coals; Fire and brimstone and a burning wind shall be the portion of their cup" (Psalm 11:6).

Many nations, including America, are seeing the judgment of God. That's a scary proposition and one that elicits a lot of emotion. Let me tell you what judgment means to me: We are reaping what we've sown.

It's been said preaching about hell is not a popular message in the 21st Century. I suppose it's never popular but that doesn't make it any less relevant in the context of revival. After all, Jesus spoke more about hell than He did about heaven.

Jonathan Edwards, an American theologian, and a key figure in America's First Great Awakening, wasn't bashful about preaching fire and brimstone messages. One of his most famed sermons is *Sinners in the Hands of an Angry God*, which defies the hyperfocus on the "God is good" messages that are so popular today. Yes, God is good. But He's also the Judge. That said, Edwards' severe sermon was steeped in the love and goodness of God despite the fear of the Lord it stirred in the hearts of those who heard it.

Edwards' sermon mentions hell an uncomfortable fifty-one times with lines such as, "There is the dreadful pit of the glowing flames of the wrath of God; there is hell's wide gaping mouth open; and you have nothing to stand upon, nor any thing to take hold of; there is nothing between you and hell but the air; it is only the power and mere pleasure of God that holds you up."

He preached, "Your wickedness makes you as it were heavy as lead, and to tend downwards with great weight and pressure towards hell; and if God should let you go, you would immediately sink and swiftly descend and plunge into the bottomless gulf, and your healthy constitution, and your own care and prudence, and best contrivance, and all your righteousness, would have no more influence to uphold you and keep you out of hell, than a spider's web would have to stop a falling rock."

It's been said that during his sermon, people cried out "What must I do to be saved?" while others grabbed the pews with all the strength they had in fear that they would descend into hell at any moment. Kindness leads people to repentance, but it seems some people only respond to fire and brimstone.

— Prayer —

Father, in the name of Jesus, would You help me know when to talk about heaven and when to talk about hell? I know Jesus was a friend to sinners. I do not want to be harsh, legalistic, and judgmental when sharing Christ. But I do not want to avoid the very real topic of hell if You lead me. Help me.

MAY 19

John Wesley's Dream of Heaven

"And he showed me a pure river of water of life, clear as crystal, proceeding from the throne of God and of the Lamb. In the middle of its street, and on either side of the river, was the tree of life, which bore twelve fruits, each tree yielding its fruit every month" (Revelation 22:1-2).

Through the ages, God has given men and women dreams of heaven and hell. John Wesley, a leader in the revival movement in the Church of England now known as Methodism, was one such man. This dream impacted his ministry in ways words cannot describe.

In the dream, Wesley died and stood at the pearly gates of heaven. He wanted to know who made it through the gates, so he had a conversation with the gate keeper that went like this:

"Are there any Presbyterians here?" "None," replied the keeper of the gate. Wesley was surprised. "Have you any Anglicans?" he asked. "No one!" was the reply "Surely, there must be many Baptists in Heaven?" "No, none," replied the keeper. Wesley grew pale. He was afraid to ask his next question: "How many Methodists are there in heaven?" "Not one," answered the keeper quickly.

Wesley's heart was filled with wonder. The angel at the gate then told Wesley there are no earthly distinctions in heaven: "All of us here in heaven are one in Christ. We are just an assembly who love the Lord."

Wesley was then taken downward to the entrance of hell. He met the keeper of the gate there. "Have you any Presbyterians here?" asked Wesley. "Oh, yes, many," answered the keeper. Wesley stood still, "Have you any Anglicans?" he asked. "Yes, yes, many," answered the keeper.

"Are there Baptists in there"? Wesley continued to ask. "Of course, many," replied the keeper. "Wesley was afraid to ask the next question. "Are there any Methodists in hell?" The keeper of the gate grinned. "Oh Yes, there are many Methodists here." Wesley could hardly speak. "Tell me, have you any there who love the Lord?" "No, no, not one, not one" he answered. "No one in hell loves the Lord."

— *Prayer* —

Father, in the name of Jesus, help me never to get bound up in denominationalism to the point that I don't love my brother who has slightly different beliefs than I do. Help me not to be so self-righteous that I condemn other religions instead of sharing Your love with them.

MAY 20

We Must Decrease for Revival to Increase

"He must increase, but I must decrease" (John 3:30).

One of the dangers of revival is the temptation to touch God's glory. Put another way, if we're not careful we can see ourselves as the center of the revival instead of making Jesus the center of revival. We can relish our names being famous instead of seeking to make Jesus' name famous.

George Whitefield, an evangelist and one of the early Methodist preachers, seemed to understand this truth. He once said, "Let the name of Whitefield perish, but Christ be glorified... Let my name die everywhere, let even my friends forget me, if by that means the cause of the blessed Jesus may be promoted."

With this heart posture, Whitefield became one of the most recognized names in revival history. By choosing to decrease so Christ could increase, He kept the focus on the Savior and Lord of revival and the results were mass awakenings.

Perhaps Whitefield took a page out of John the Baptist's revival playbook. John the Baptist saw a revival in Israel during his brief time on earth. Indeed, he was born for revival and he spent most of his life in the wilderness doing the will of the Lord. He never strived to make his name known.

Mark 1:5 tells us, "Then all the land of Judea, and those from Jerusalem, went out to him and were all baptized by him in the Jordan River, confessing their sins." But when Jesus arrived on the scene, John's movement began to wane. People started following Jesus instead. John's disciples came to him upset about it.

That's when John demonstrated the wisdom from heaven, humility, and an understanding that he was the forerunner of revival but not the author of it. The prophet said in John 3:30-31: "He must increase, but I must decrease. He who comes from above is above all; he who is of the earth is earthly and speaks of the earth. He who comes from heaven is above all."

Let's be careful not to lift up a man as the central figure of a revival, but to always give Jesus the preeminence.

— *Prayer* —

Father, in the name of Jesus, help me never to position myself—or position another human—as the author or center of the revival that You bring. Help me to continually decrease that Your love can increase in me. Help me die to any selfish ambition that would stand in the way of Your revival.

MAY 21

Dealing with the Mocking Spirit

"Others mocking said, 'They are full of new wine'" (Acts 2:13).

I'll admit it. The first time I saw people praying in tongues, it completely freaked me out. It scared me! It was 1993. I was interning at a Christian television station—though I wasn't a Christian.

Before going live on the air, the producers, cameramen, on-air talent, and others stood in a circle holding hands—and praying in tongues just as fast and hard as they could. I looked on with confusion for a few minutes; then I left and never came back. I went home and told everyone, "Those people were crazy!"

I mocked this supernatural experience. Now I pray in tongues for extended periods every day. I believe praying in tongues builds me up (see 1 Cor. 14:4, 18) as I speak directly to God (see 1 Cor. 14:2, 14). I believe praying in tongues stirs my faith (see Jude 20). I believe praying in tongues assures I'm praying God's perfect will (see Rom. 8:26-27). I believe there are many benefits to praying in tongues. That's why I do it as much as I can, and I encourage other believers to do the same. (Check out my book, *Tongues of Fire*.)

When revival fire falls, mockers rise. The disciples were mocked on the day of Pentecost in Acts 2. Some of the Greeks mocked Paul because he spoke of the resurrection of the dead (see Acts 17:32). And there are seventeen verses about Christ being mocked.

Mocking is beyond criticism. Mock means to treat with contempt or ridicule, defy, challenge, jeer, or scoff, insult, laugh at, deride, or sneer. The word mock appears in Scripture one hundred and four times. But these synonymous words like scorn and derision also appear frequently.

With all this in mind, it's no shock that speaking in tongues is going to bring modern-day mockers. We shouldn't be surprised. Jude, the man the Holy Spirit inspired to write, "Building yourselves up on your most holy faith, praying in the Holy Spirit" (Jude 20), also warned us there would be mockers in the last days (v. 16). So why do people mock revival and supernatural manifestations that come along with it? Ultimately, because they don't understand it. The unspiritual man cannot understand spiritual things. That's why we need revival to break out of the four walls of the church. We need to let the Gospel do its work.

— Prayer —

Father, in the name of Jesus, forgive me for any time in which I have mocked the move of Your Spirit—and help me to never be moved by the mockers. Give me confidence, a forehead like flint, a rod iron will, and a backbone like steal to stand for revival even in the face of mockers.

160

Derek Prince's Revival Prophecy

"And now I plead with you, lady, not as though I wrote a new commandment to you, but that which we have had from the beginning: that we love one another" (2 John 1:5).

Derek Prince is perhaps best known for spiritual warfare and deliverance. The British Bible teacher was one of the most well-known ministers of the 20th Century, touching millions of lives around the world. He wrote forty-five books translated into sixty languages.

While living in London in 1953, the Lord spoke to Him audibly. Prince told how this was the only time he had ever heard the audible voice of the Lord. God said, "There shall be a great revival in the United States and Britain." While there are many elements of revival, he broke them down into two categories in a book called *The Coming Revival: Shaping History for a New Heavenly Reality.*

Those two categories cover the positive aspects we must incorporate into our Christian experience and negative aspects we need to remove from our lives and testimony. Prince offers seven pivotal factors in his book.

First, loving others. God is love and we are supposed to love our neighbors as ourselves. In fact, Jesus said, "By this all people will know that you are My disciples: if you have love for one another" (John 13:35). Prince says loving others is the foundation of true revival.

Next is loving God. Jesus said in Luke 10:27, "You shall love the Lord your God with all your heart, with all your soul, with all your strength, and with all your mind,' and 'your neighbor as yourself." Prince said loving God is giving ourselves fully and obediently in preparation for revival.

Third is humbling ourselves. Remember, God resists the proud but gives grace to the humble (see James 4:6). That, Prince said, means surrendering pride as pride is a major obstacle to revival. Next is "Eliminating Legalism." Fifth is "Unmasking Witchcraft," which includes control and manipulation in all its forms.

The sixth principle is "Getting Desperate." That essentially means cultivating a hunger for revival. Finally, the seventh principle is "Purifying Ourselves," which indicates a total commitment to God. Who's ready?

— *Prayer* —

Father, in the name of Jesus, I say yes to revival on Your conditions. Would You help me to love others, love You, humble myself and surrender fully? Help me rid my life of legalism and control and pray desperate prayers as I seek to be a pure vessel of honor for Your use in revival.

MAY 23

Beware the Sadducee Spirit

"Jesus answered and said to them, 'You are mistaken, not knowing the Scriptures nor the power of God'" (Matthew 22:29).

For all the talk about modern-day Pharisees, there are plenty of Sadducees running around the church wreaking havoc on people who have faith to believe in the resurrection power of God at work in the lives of the saints. We get a glimpse into this mindset in Acts 23:6-9 when Paul was standing before the high priest making his defense against accusations from the Jews:

"Then Paul, knowing that one sect were Sadducees and the other Pharisees, cried out among the Sanhedrin, 'Brothers, I am a Pharisee, a son of a Pharisee. I am being judged for my hope in the resurrection of the dead.'

"When he had said this, dissension arose between the Pharisees and the Sadducees, and the assembly was divided. For the Sadducees say that there is no resurrection, nor angel, nor spirit. But the Pharisees acknowledge them all. There was a great outcry. The scribes that were from the sect of Pharisees stood up and argued, 'We find no evil in this man. But if a spirit or an angel has spoken to him, let us not fight against God.'"

That was the wisdom of God. But there is something more there. These verses expose the Sadducees. We still see them in today's churches. The Sadducees denied the resurrection of the dead, the existence of spirits, and the obligation of oral tradition. The Sadducees emphasized acceptance of the written Law alone. They were what you might call "Word without the spirit" people.

Paul said in 2 Corinthians 3:5-6, "But our sufficiency is from God, who has made us able ministers of the new covenant, not of the letter but of the Spirit. For the letter kills, but the Spirit gives life."

Modern-day Sadducees don't believe in healing. They don't believe in miracles. They don't believe in angelic encounters. The Sadducees were like those Paul described in 1 Timothy 2:5, "Having a form of godliness but denying the power thereof. From such turn away." Sadducees are revival killers.

— *Prayer* —

Father, in the name of Jesus, help me never to adopt a Sadducee mindset—and if there are seeds or leaven of the Sadducees in my soul, please deliver me from this evil. I want to embrace Your presence and power however You choose to pour it out. I stand with You.

The Charismatic Movement

"There are diversities of gifts, but the same Spirit" (1 Corinthians 12:4-11).

A forerunner to the Jesus People Movement, the Charismatic Movement saw the restoration of the gifts of the Spirit in denominations that largely rejected Pentecostalism. Baptists, Episcopals, Presbyterians, Methodists and others welcomed this renewal that officially started April 3, 1960.

A perhaps unlikely candidate, Dennis J. Bennett—an Episcopal priest—announced to his congregation he received the baptism of the Holy Spirit, complete with speaking in tongues. Soon thereafter, his church grew from five hundred to twenty-six hundred. But it wasn't just a Holy Ghost party, people were getting saved, marriages were restored, and people were growing spiritually.

The charismatic movement leans on 1 Corinthians 12:4-11: "There are diversities of gifts, but the same Spirit. There are differences of ministries, but the same Lord. And there are diversities of activities, but it is the same God who works all in all. But the manifestation of the Spirit is given to each one for the profit of all: for to one is given the word of wisdom through the Spirit, to another the word of knowledge through the same Spirit, to another faith by the same Spirit, to another gifts of healings by the same Spirit, to another the working of miracles, to another prophecy, to another discerning of spirits, to another different kinds of tongues, to another the interpretation of tongues. But one and the same Spirit works all these things, distributing to each one individually as He wills."

With that, the Charismatic Movement was underway. The national news media, including *Time* and *Newsweek* magazines, reported on the Spirit-led renewal. *Charisma* magazine, of which I am a former senior editor, was birthed in 1975 out of the Charismatic movement and still stands today. Movements like the John Wimber's Vineyard Church were also birthed during the Charismatic movement. The late Wimber offered this insight into the charismatic mindset:

"Our passion is to imitate the ministry of Jesus in the power of the Spirit. This requires we must follow Jesus out of baptismal waters, through our personal deserts, and into the harvest. We want to take the ammunition of the balanced evangelical theology with the firepower of Pentecostal practice, loading and readying the best of both worlds to hit the target of making and nurturing disciples."

— *Prayer* —

Father, in the name of Jesus, thank You for the emphasis on the gifs of the Spirit that you brought to the church during the Charismatic movement. Thank You for this renewal and reemphasis on the Holy Spirit and His power. Help me to earnestly desire after spiritual gifts.

MAY 25

When Judgment Falls

"For the time has come for judgment to begin at the house of God; and if it begins with us first, what will be the end of those who do not obey the gospel of God?" (1 Peter 4:7)

We know judgment begins in the house of God. There's no greater reminder than the story of Ananias and Sapphira, who sold their possessions and lied about keeping part of the proceeds for themselves. In Acts 5:3-6, Peter said:

"Ananias, why has Satan filled your heart to lie to the Holy Spirit and keep back part of the price of the land for yourself? While it remained, was it not your own? And after it was sold, was it not in your own control? Why have you conceived this thing in your heart? You have not lied to men but to God. Then Ananias, hearing these words, fell down and breathed his last."

I heard the Lord say, "I am beginning to judge sin in the house of God. So, repent ye therefore that times of refreshing might come upon you. Don't be caught as those who thought they were sneaking by, but be found as those who are in My heart; who are in My Word; who are walking in My spirit; walking by My precepts.

"I do not demand perfection. I understand and know that you are but flesh. I remember your frame. I know that you are but dust. But I am seeking those who will worship Me in spirit and truth. I am seeking those who will walk with Me in integrity.

"And even though you won't do it all right all the time, your heart toward obedience makes up for the times that you slip and fall. Your heart to repent makes up for the times that you slip and fall.

"For the righteous man falls seven times and he gets back up again and he runs to Me. He comes to my throne of grace boldly and he obtains mercy. He obtains grace. He obtains forgiveness. It's your heart that I'm looking at. Man looks at the outward appearance, but I am looking at the heart."

— *Prayer* —

Father, in the name of Jesus, would You help me to judge myself so I will not have to be judged? Help me to examine my heart in Your presence and show me if there is any wicked way in me. Help me not to lie to the Holy Ghost! I repent of my sins.

Revival in the Persecuted Church

"Therefore those who were scattered went everywhere preaching the word"
(Acts 8:4).

It was a Pentecost bloodbath and most Christians never heard about it. More than fifty Christians were killed on Christmas day in one of the deadliest terror attacks on Nigerians ever. Scores of gunmen rushed in to kill Christians in the midst of worship. And this is but one report.

All told, more than three hundred-sixty million Christians suffered high levels of persecution or discrimination for their faith between November 2020 and September 2021, according to Open Doors' World Watch List. One in seven Christians, worldwide, one in five in Africa, two in five in Asia and one in fifteen in Latin America, are suffering persecution as of the time of this writing.

Revival often breaks out in the midst of persecution. But we need to pray without ceasing. We need to pray for the persecuted church, and pray for revival among the persecuted church, if we want to see God's will done in the suffering. How do we pray?

Repent for apathy concerning praying for the persecuted church. Rend your heart and ask God to forgive you (see Joel 2:13). Pray God would mantle the persecuted church with His Spirit of might (see Is. 11:2). Pray intercessors would be persistent in prayer, staying alert with all perseverance for those suffering persecution.

Pray that as the persecuted church continues to open her mouth, words would be given to boldly make known the mystery of the Gospel (see Eph. 18-20; Heb. 13:3). Pray the Lord fills the persecuted church with His joy and peace in being steadfast in believing (see Rom. 15:13).

Bind every hindering and harassing spirit coming against the persecuted church. Pray demonic spirits would not succeed to disrupt the prayer movement, prophetic flow, and advancement of the church (see Acts 13:50). Pray those suffering from persecution would continue to run their race and not grow weary nor give up. Pray for revival in the persecuted church.

— *Prayer* —

Father, in the name of Jesus, I repent for not making intercession for the persecuted church. Father, You say in Your Word that You work all things together for Your good. Let the persecution lead to Your Word running swiftly in the nations and multitudes finding salvation.

King Asa's Prayer Keys to Revival

"Bow down Your ear, O Lord, hear me; For I am poor and needy" (Psalm 86:1-2).

When you read 2 Chronicles 14-20, you'll see a picture of Judah over a sixty-five-year period. Judah was in a mess. Solomon died and there was major political turmoil until Asa took the throne and started throwing down idols in the land. The result of Asa's moves: the nation saw revival. But King Asa was facing enemy invasion.

Listen in to King Asa's prayer in 2 Chronicles 14:11, "O Lord, no one but you can help the powerless against the mighty! Help us, O Lord our God, for we trust in you alone. It is in your name that we have come against this vast horde. O Lord, you are our God; do not let mere men prevail against you!"

God answered King Asa's prayer and revival was the end result. What can we learn from Asa's prayer? Humble prayer sets the stage for revival. At the point you need revival, you realize how helpless you are. Asa's prayer was rooted in humility. His heart's cry was basically, "Help!" Notice how Asa did not try to tell God how to help. He prayed in utter dependence to an omnipotent, all-wise God.

As Asa demonstrates, trusting prayer brings revival. At the point of revival, you realize God is your only hope and you have to trust Him. Asa's prayer was rooted in trusting God. Psalm 9:10 tells us, "Those who know your name trust in you, for you, O Lord, do not abandon those who search for you." Asa had confidence in God's desire to bring revival and faith that He could do it.

A motive to glorify God brings revival. Selfless prayers bring revival. It becomes about the greater good and the name of God rather than your own needs. Asa wanted to see God glorified. He prayed, "O Lord, you are our God; do not let mere men prevail against you!" It doesn't glorify God when His people are defeated. Pray like Asa.

— *Prayer* —

Father, in the name of Jesus, would You help me learn from the prayer Asa modeled in Your Word? You left it there for a record of a pattern and blueprint for revival prayers You will answer. It's not a formula, but it's the principles I want to learn. Help me put Asa's learning into practice.

A House of Revival

"For My house will be called a house of prayer for all nations" (Isaiah 56:7).

If we want to have a house of revival, we need to build a house of prayer. The phrase house of prayer first appears in Isaiah 56:7 (AMPC), where it is used twice:

"These [foreigners] I will bring to My holy mountain and give them joy in My house of prayer. Their burnt offerings and sacrifices will be accepted on My altar; for My house will be called a house of prayer for all nations."

Jesus refers to this verse when casting the money changers from the temple, as recorded in Mark 11:17: "Then He taught, saying to them, 'Is it not written, 'My house shall be called a house of prayer for all nations'? But you have made it a den of thieves'."

The heart of the house of prayer is perhaps best captured by David's heart cry in Psalm 27:4: "One thing I have desired of the Lord, that will I seek: that I may dwell in the house of the Lord all the days of my life, to behold the beauty of the Lord and to inquire in His temple."

As I write in my book, *Birthing a House of Prayer*, "The best picture of what the house of prayer aims to look like in any city can be found in the Book of Revelation, in the many descriptions of the redeemed gathered before the throne of God."

Revelation 5:8-9 reads: "The four living creatures and the twenty-four elders fell down before the Lamb, each having a harp, and golden bowls full of incense, which are the prayers of the saints. And they sang a new song, saying: 'You are worthy to take the scroll, and to open its seals; for you were slain, and have redeemed us to God by your blood out of every tribe and tongue and people and nation.'"

Are you ready to build a house of revival?

— *Prayer* —

Father, in the name of Jesus, make me a house of prayer. Change me from the inside out so that I can birth Your plans and purposes in the earth—whether that is launching a prayer ministry, a revival hub, or building out my prayer closet dedicated to intercession for revival.

MAY 29

A Personal Awakening

"He awakens Me morning by morning; He awakens My ear to listen as a disciple" (Isaiah 50:4).

Before we can see a church or a national awakening, we need a personal awakening. Maybe you are already awake, but I believe there are degrees of awakening and that we can always be more awake. Your spirit is awake but your soul is awakening to new levels.

The Bible says we move from faith to faith, strength to strength and glory to glory. Each new level of awakening is a new glory. Remember Jesus at the Mount of Transfiguration? The Bible says when they were "fully awake" they saw the glory of the Lord.

Ephesians 5:14 exhorts us "Arise, you sleeper! Rise up from the dead and the Anointed One will shine his light into you!" *The Message* puts it this way: "Wake up from your sleep, climb out of your coffins; Christ will show you the light! So watch your step. Use your head. Make the most of every chance you get. These are desperate times."

As you journey through your personal awakening, you may first awaken to repentance before you awaken to love and life. Sometimes, we don't recognize when our heart—or part of our heart—has fallen asleep.

In pursuit of a personal awakening, let's agree with the psalmists prayer in Psalm 119:130-135: "Break open your word within me until revelation-light shines out! Those with open hearts are given insight into your plans. I open my mouth and inhale the word of God because I crave the revelation of your commands.

"Turn your heart to me, Lord, and show me your grace like you do to every one of your godly lovers. Prepare before me a path filled with your promises, and don't allow even one sin to have dominion over me. Rescue me from the oppression of ungodly men so that I can keep all your precepts. Smile on me, your loving servant. Instruct me on what is right in your eyes."

Pray this prayer over and over again and watch your heart become fully awake.

— *Prayer* —

Father, in the name of Jesus, would You wake me up? Open the eyes of my heart. I want to see You as You are. You are the Great Revivalist. Revive me, awaken my heart, help me pursue You with everything in me and let my passion for Jesus be evident to a lost and dying world.

What We Can Learn from David Yonggi Cho

"Therefore I exhort first of all that supplications, prayers, intercessions, and giving of thanks be made for all men, for kings and all who are in authority, that we may lead a quiet and peaceable life in all godliness and reverence" (1 Timothy 2:1-2).

I traveled around the country for three years from 2014 through 2016 with the message of awakening and revival. We gathered in small groups of hungry people who were desperate to see change in their cities. We gathered in the mountains in cabins to preach, pray and prophesy about what God wanted to do in the nations. And we saw God do many miracles.

By 2017, though, it seemed like the season shifted. There was prosperity in the land. The economy was good. The American church was thriving and many didn't see the need for revival. A pro-Christian president entered America's White House and the fervency seemed to cool in many church circles. What many didn't understand was this: It's never time to stop pursuing revival.

I've learned plenty from the late David Yonggi Cho, a pastor in South Korea who built one of the largest prayer movements in the world with just a few faithful intercessors. He once said this:

"A new outpouring of the Holy Spirit is desperately needed. At no time in the history of the modern world has there been such an outpouring of satanic influence as there is today. The bottom of the pit of hell is belching out its filth in murder, rape, pornography, lawlessness, and violence.

"Just as the preaching of the Wesleys kept Britain from following France in revolution in the eighteenth century, so too a new outbreak of revival can bring about the social and political changes necessary to keep us from international destruction and calamity. What will bring about the revival that can lead the world away from the brink of total destruction and annihilation? The answer is a new call to prayer!"

We need a new call to prayer. Will you make the call? Will you answer?

— *Prayer* —

Father, in the name of Jesus, help me learn revival lessons—and prayer lessons—from the great men and women of God who went before me. Help me glean from their principles, victories, losses, and mistakes. Help me bang the drum for prayer that leads to revival.

MAY 31

The George Whitefield Revivalist Anointing

"Woe to you, scribes and Pharisees, hypocrites! For you are like whitewashed tombs which indeed appear beautiful outwardly, but inside are full of dead men's bones and all uncleanness" (Matthew 23:27).

George Whitefield was born in Gloucester, England in 1714 and worked his way through Oxford University. There he met John and Charles Wesley, founders of the Methodist movement, before becoming a minister and preaching in the American Colonies at their invitation.

Whitefield went up and down the east coast of what is now the United States, drawing large crowds during the First Great Awakening. But his dramatic style drew the snakes from the revival fire. Indeed, the critics came out of the woodwork. Thankfully, God gave Whitefield a forehead like flint. The persecution did not move him.

Whitefield wasn't afraid to take on the Church of England and, in doing so, stirred up the religious spirit in his day. Indeed, English, Scottish, and American clergy attacked Whitefield vigorously because he threatened the established religious system with his challenge to lukewarm Christianity.

Whitefield said things like: "You may have orthodox heads, and yet you may have the devil in your hearts." And on response to a nasty letter, Whitefield replied, "Thank you sir for your criticism. If you knew about me what I know about me, you would have written a longer letter."

Whitefield broke out of the four walls of the church and preached to average Joes in open fields with great emotion. Whitefield understood, "If you are going to walk with Jesus Christ, you are going to be opposed.... In our days, to be a true Christian is really to become a scandal."

Whitefield once opined, "It is a poor sermon that gives no offense; that neither makes the hearer displeased with himself nor with the preacher... I was honored today with having a few stones, dirt, rotten eggs, and pieces of dead cat thrown at me."

— Prayer —

Father, in the name of Jesus, would You give me a forehead like flint to stand against revival naysayers, doom and gloomers, religious establishments and other who stand in opposition to the great awakening You plan? Help me stay steady like George Whitfield despite the attacks.

JUNE

"Have you noticed how much praying for revival has been going on of late—and how little revival has resulted? I believe the problem is that we have been trying to substitute praying for obeying, and it simply will not work."—A. W. Tozer

Jehoshaphat's Revival Prayer Strategy

"Blessed are the poor in spirit, for theirs is the kingdom of heaven" (Matthew 5:3).

When King Jehoshaphat was facing enemy invasion, he prayed. He thought he was crying out to God for protection—and he was—but the ultimate result was revival. We read his prayer in 2 Chronicles 20:6-9:

"O Lord, God of our ancestors, you alone are the God who is in heaven. You are ruler of all the kingdoms of the earth. You are powerful and mighty; no one can stand against you! O our God, did you not drive out those who lived in this land when your people Israel arrived? And did you not give this land forever to the descendants of your friend Abraham?

"Your people settled here and built this Temple to honor your name. They said, 'Whenever we are faced with any calamity such as war, plague, or famine, we can come to stand in your presence before this Temple where your name is honored. We can cry out to you to save us, and you will hear us and rescue us.'"

The king's prayer continues by reminding God how He would not permit the Israelites to invade those enemy nations when they left Egypt. Jehoshaphat pleads with God to stop them and acknowledges that he cannot prevail without divine help.

What can we learn about revival from the king's prayer? Humility is always key, but in this case we see how Word-based prayer brings revival. Jehoshaphat reminded God of what He said in 2 Chronicles 7:13-14. We pray for revival by praying His Word with faith that God is not a man that He should lie (see Num. 23:19).

Our prayers for revival are based on our covenant with Him—and we need to believe our covenant-keeping God will answer. Faith is the foundation. James says a double-minded man is unstable in all his ways and should not expect to receive anything from God (see James 1:8).

— *Prayer* —

Father, in the name of Jesus, help me not to be double-minded about revival—
praying in faith one day and then getting discouraged by what I see in the church
the next day. Help me hold fast to Your Word and Your promise that the
knowledge of Your glory shall cover the earth.

0

JUNE 2

Prayer Lessons from the Original Pentecost

"When the Day of Pentecost had fully come, they were all with one accord in one place"
(Acts 2:1).

On the day of Pentecost all the believers were meeting together in one place. Suddenly, there was a sound from heaven like the roaring of a mighty windstorm, and it filled the house where they were sitting.

Then, what looked like flames or tongues of fire appeared and settled on each of them. Everyone present was filled with the Holy Spirit and began speaking in other languages, as the Holy Spirit gave them this ability.

Those are the words from Acts 2:1-4. In these four verses we find two keys to prayer that births revival: Unified prayer and desperate prayer. There were only one hundred-twenty in the Upper Room at the birth of the church. Today there over 2 billion Christians. Imagine if the church desperately prayed in unity for revival again.

John R. Mott, an American evangelist who won the Nobel Peace Prize in 1946, said: "If added power attends united prayer of two or three, what mighty triumphs there will be when hundreds of thousands of consistent members of the church are with one accord day by day making intercession for the extension of Christ's Kingdom."

Again, it's not just unified prayer for a purpose. It's a corporate desperation that births revival. Think about the scene. Jesus had just been crucified. They were essentially hiding for fear of persecution. John 20:19 says, "the doors were shut where the disciples were assembled, for fear of the Jews."

Unified prayer in desperation birthed a revival that birthed the church. It could have been different. Shortly before the Acts 2 outpouring Peter called for a new witness to the life, death, and resurrection of Christ. Two men were put forth to replace Judas: Justus and Matthias.

The disciples prayed and asked the Lord who should fill Judas' shoes. The lot fell on Matthias. It's a marvel this didn't breach the unity. Justus didn't leave the Upper Room in a huff because he wasn't promoted. He stayed in one accord with Matthias and the other apostles—and they all maintained desperation for the cause of Christ.

— *Prayer* —

Father, in the name of Jesus, would You give me a desperation for revival and help me find those of like precious faith who will stand in unity with me for Your will? Help me not to be offended with a lesser role in the great revival, but to be satisfied knowing I am serving Your purposes.

Travailing for Revival

"Before she was in labor, she gave birth; Before her pain came, she delivered a male child. Who has heard such a thing? Who has seen such things?" (Isaiah 66:8)

When we're desperate, we'll weep and travail for revival. Travailing prayer is prayer that toils. It's prayer with great physical and mental exertion. It's prayer that agonizes. It's prayer that, at times, is painful. But travailing prayer can birth revival.

Leonard Ravenhill, author of *Why Revival Tarries*, once said, "At God's counter there are no sale days, for the price of revival is ever the same: travail!"

Paul discusses the spiritual practice in Romans 8:26-29: "Likewise, the Spirit helps us in our weaknesses, for we do not know what to pray for as we ought, but the Spirit Himself intercedes for us with groanings too deep for words. He who searches the hearts knows what the mind of the Spirit is, because He intercedes for the saints according to the will of God."

These "groanings too deep for words" are one manifestation of travailing prayer. The Greek word for "groanings" in that Scripture is "stenagmos," which simply means a groaning or a sigh. *Merriam-Webster* defines "travail" as "a painful or difficult work or effort."

Samuel Chadwick was a Wesleyan Methodist Minister, a Spirit-filled preacher, author, revivalist—and a man who understood realms of prayer. He once said, "When the Church is run on the same lines as a circus, there may be crowds, but there is no Shekinah. That is why prayer is the test of faith and the secret of power. The Spirit of God travails in the prayer-life of the soul. Miracles are the direct work of His power, and without miracles the Church cannot live."

Travail must be Spirit-led, or it's just soulish or fleshly and won't accomplish the will of God. We can't manufacture revival with our emotions or even a strong will. Nevertheless, travail is a genuine form of prayer that can break through when nothing else does. Travail births but it also wars.

Cindy Jacobs, co-founder of Generals International, in her book *Possessing the Gates of the Enemy*, says, "There are times when we are called by God to pray strong prayers and help to birth the will of God into an area. Usually there is a sense of wonder after the prayer, and a sense that God has done something through it."

— Prayer —

Father, in the name of Jesus, I am willing to travail for revival's sake. Help me to pray. Pray through me. Help me yield to Your Spirit and be a midwife of revival in the earth. Escort me into travail as You will, and let miracles, signs and wonders manifest that convince the world Jesus is alive.

Hungering for the God of Revival

"Blessed are those who hunger and thirst for righteousness, for they shall be filled"
(Matthew 5:6).

It's not enough to hunger for revival. We need to huger for the God of revival. See, too many Christians seek revival for the sake of revival when we should be seeking first the Kingdom of God and His righteousness (see Matt. 6:33). When we hunger and thirst after righteousness, we will eventually see revival.

David was a man who hungered for God. In Psalm 42:2 (AMPC) he shared, "My inner self thirsts for God, for the living God. When shall I come and behold the face of God?" And in Psalm 63:1 (AMPC) he wrote: "O God, You are my God, earnestly will I seek You; my inner self thirsts for You, my flesh longs and is faint for You, in a dry and weary land where no water is."

See, it's one thing to be thirsty in the sense that your mouth is dry. It's another thing to be thirsty in the sense that your inner self is dry. We have to look at our lives and ask ourselves, "What do we crave more than God?" And then ask a follow up question, "Why do we crave this more than God?" Be honest with yourself. The answers may provide a wakeup call.

Spiritual hunger is an urgent need for what only God can provide, and it arises when we need His strength, His energy, His peace, and His presence. The good news is when we seek Him, we will find Him. In Isaiah 55:1 God promises, "Ho! Everyone who thirsts, come to the waters; and you who have no money, come, buy and eat. Yes, come, buy wine and milk without money and without price."

I heard somebody say if you aren't hungry for God, you are full of yourself. There's some truth in that. Ask God to make you hungry for Him. Decide to seek Him daily. David said, "early in the morning will I seek His face." David made that decision. You can too. And you'll be glad you did.

— *Prayer* —

Father, in the name of Jesus, take away my appetite for worldly things and exchange it for an insatiable hunger for Your Word, Your presence, Your peace—and Your revival. Help me lay aside worldly pleasures for the pleasures at Your right hand forevermore.

JUNE 5

Stop Eating at the World's Table

"Adulterers and adulteresses! Do you not know that friendship with the world is enmity with God? Whoever therefore wants to be a friend of the world makes himself an enemy of God" (James 4:4).

God wants to prepare a table before you in the presence of your enemies. But the Tempter wants to prepare a table before you and entice you to eat what the world has to offer. Indeed, there is a raging battle for your attention.

"The greatest enemy of hunger for God is not poison but apple pie. It is not the banquet of the wicked that dulls our appetite for heaven, but endless nibbling at the table of the world," said John Piper, a Baptist theologian and pastor "It is not the X-rated video, but the prime-time dribble of triviality we drink in every night."

Indeed, consider the prophets in King Ahab's reign. Four hundred and fifty prophets of Baal and four hundred prophets of Asherah ate at Jezebel's table. Keep in mind, these were false prophets. Many of the true prophets were hiding in caves eating bread and drinking water—or had fled Israel altogether under Ahab's reign.

If you have wrong appetites, you need a personal revival. Charles Finney, a leader in the Second Great Awakening, tells the story of a man who was, as he calls it, "a slave to the use of tobacco." Finally, the man was convinced it was sinful and he started waging war on his flesh. Finney relates how the nicotine addiction finally drove him to God in such agony of prayer that he got the victory and never again had desire for tobacco.

"I have heard of individuals over whom a life of sin had given to certain appetites a perfect mastery, but in time of revival they have been subdued into perfect quiescence, and these appetites have ever after been as dead as if they had no body," he said. "I suppose the fact is, that the mind may be so occupied and absorbed with greater things, as not to give a thought to the things that would revive the vicious appetite."

Are you eating at the world's table? Do you have worldly appetites? Cry out to God and ask Him to remove the desire for everything the word has to offer. Cry out for a personal revival and dine with Jesus at His bountiful table.

— *Prayer* —

Father, in the name of Jesus, forgive me for all the times I ate at the world's table. I repent for allowing worldly appetites to distract me from Your heart and my revival mission. Lord, I renounce every worldly appetite. Deliver me from evil and help me keep my eyes on You.

Too Busy for Revival?

"Now he who received seed among the thorns is he who hears the word, and the cares of this world and the deceitfulness of riches choke the word, and he becomes unfruitful" (Matthew 13:22).

Martha may miss the revival. But Mary can't miss it because she's sitting at the feet of Jesus, hanging on His every word. Consider the story of Mary and Martha in Luke 10:38-42:

"Now it happened as they went that He entered a certain village; and a certain woman named Martha welcomed Him into her house. And she had a sister called Mary, who also sat at Jesus' feet and heard His word. But Martha was distracted with much serving, and she approached Him and said, "Lord, do You not care that my sister has left me to serve alone? Therefore tell her to help me."

"And Jesus answered and said to her, 'Martha, Martha, you are worried and troubled about many things. But one thing is needed, and Mary has chosen that good part, which will not be taken away from her."

Mary was enjoying the God of revival. Martha was too busy preparing for the God of revival. Don't get me wrong, preparing for revival is important. We need to make time to prepare for revival through study, prayer, repentance, and worship. But when revival is in our midst, we must not get so busy administrating a revival that we miss the revival.

When we're too busy for revival, it means our priorities are wrong. During the First Great Awakening, Jonathan Edwards noted:

"The minds of people were wonderfully taken off from the world, it was treated amongst us as a thing of very little consequence. They seemed to follow their worldly business, more as a part of their duty, than from any disposition they had to it; the temptation now seemed to lie on that hand, to neglect worldly affairs too much, and to spend too much time in the immediate exercise of religion."

If we are too busy for revival, we need to repent. If we're too busy for Jesus, we're too busy for revival. If we're too busy for revival, we're too busy for Jesus.

— *Prayer* —

Father, in the name of Jesus, I repent for any and every time I have been too busy with the affairs of life to sit in Your sweet presence. Forgive me and help me to discern Your Spirit wooing me away. Deliver me from the bonds of busy-ness and make me spiritually fruitful.

Breaking Off a Lukewarm Spirit

"O wretched man that I am! Who will deliver me from this body of death? I thank God—through Jesus Christ our Lord!" (Romans 7:24-25)

We've all seen people in church who hunch over in their seat and scroll through social media apps during worship. Others come in and out several times during the message, distracting the hungry ones. Still others report to church out of obligation rather than passion. They are merely going through the motions.

All of the above point to an apathetic spirit. What is apathy? A lack of interest or concern. It's indifference. It's a lack of feeling or emotion. In a word, an apathetic Christian is a lukewarm Christian. A lukewarm Christian lacks conviction and serves the Lord half-heartedly.

Jesus said some startling words in Revelation 3:15-18, "I know your works, that you are neither cold nor hot. I could wish you were cold or hot. So then, because you are lukewarm, and neither cold nor hot, I will vomit you out of My mouth.

"Because you say, 'I am rich, have become wealthy, and have need of nothing'—and do not know that you are wretched, miserable, poor, blind, and naked— I counsel you to buy from Me gold refined in the fire, that you may be rich; and white garments, that you may be clothed, that the shame of your nakedness may not be revealed; and anoint your eyes with eye salve, that you may see."

Apathy toward God, His Word and His church can affect every area of your life, including your finances. Remember, the Lord rebuked the Israelites through the prophet Haggai because they lived in paneled houses while God's house lay in ruins.

Haggai 1:5-6, "Now, therefore, thus says the Lord of Hosts: Consider your ways. You have sown much, and harvested little. You eat, but you do not have enough; you drink, but you are not filled with drink; you clothe yourselves, but no one is warm; and he who earns wages earns wages to put them into a bag with holes."

When true revival comes, it will deliver us from a lukewarm spirit. The apathy will flee. But here's the key: The lukewarm are never the revival starters. Ask God to set you on fire so your testimony of Jesus can set others on fire.

— *Prayer* —

Father, in the name of Jesus, would You forgive me for any apathy, complacency or lukewarm mindsets I've adopted? Forgive me for treating church as an obligation rather than an opportunity. Set me on fire for You so I can pray in the revival fire You want to pour out.

The Nicolaus Zinzendorf Revivalist Anointing

"For whoever desires to save his life will lose it, but whoever loses his life for My sake will find it"
(Matthew 16:25).

Revivalists who walked away from wealth—or sowed their wealth into the Kingdom—are inspiring. Such is the story of Count Nicolas Zinzendorf. Zinzendorf was born into nobility. In fact, the German reformer was part of one of the most prominent noble families in his nation.

Zinzendorf started writing love letters to Jesus at the tender age of six. Unable to reach the throne room where Jesus sat, he was known to climb to the top of the castle tower and throw his prayers out the window into the courtyard. So touching was the young lad's prayer life that, as history tells it, Swedish soldiers in the Great Northern War were moved by the boy's devotion when they stormed into his bedroom.

As devoted to God as he was in his youth, Zinzendorf got a new fire during an encounter with the Holy Spirit in an art museum. He gazed upon *Ecce Homo (Behold the Man)*—an image of Jesus bound after He was scourged. In that moment, conviction overwhelmed his heart and he confessed, "I have loved Him for a long time, but I have never actually done anything for Him. From now on I will do whatever He leads me to do."

God took Zinzendorf up on his words and the young count lived up to them. In 1722, Zinzendorf offered asylum to persecuted people from Moravia and Bohemia—part of the Czech Republic today—and helped them build the village of Herrnhut on an estate property he purchased from his grandmother. Five years later, we see the Moravian Revival break out.

Zinzendorf said things like, "The world is the field and the field is the world; and henceforth that country shall be my home where I can be most used in winning souls for Christ." Zinzendorf faced much opposition and many trials in his ministry, and eventually laid down his titles and moved to America to reach the indigenous people. The count cast his crown, so to speak, at the feet of Jesus.

— Prayer —

Father, in the name of Jesus, inspire my heart to do what You lead me to do—no matter what it looks like or what it feels like. Help me lose my life in You so I can find my real life hidden in Christ. Help me focus on soul winning in the midst of the revival You bring.

JUNE 9

Prisoners of Hope

"Return to the stronghold, You prisoners of hope. Even today I declare That I will restore double to you" (Zechariah 9:12).

When things don't turn out in life as you expected—when people die though you prayed they would live, when prophecies don't come to pass as expected, or when your dreams seem dead—sometimes you lose hope. If you don't get healed from that disappointment, it dulls your spiritual hunger.

Proverbs 13:12 tells us plainly, "Hope deferred makes the heart sick…" The *Christian English Version* puts it this way, "Not getting what you want can break your heart…" And the *Good News Translation* says, "When hope is crushed, the heart is crushed."

Maybe you're disappointed because you've been praying for revival in your city for months or years and haven't seen the prayer answer. Maybe you are discouraged and ready to quit. Know this: The enemy wouldn't be trying to discourage you if your prayers weren't working.

Paul exhorted us in Galatians 6:19, "And let us not grow weary while doing good, for in due season we shall reap if we do not lose heart." That's a promise and those who put their hope in the Lord will never be put to shame (see Is. 49:23).

Yes, the voice of disappointment will speak. Yes, the voice of discouragement will shout. But don't take your hand off the revival plow. You are making progress. It may not look like it. It may not sound like it. It may not feel like it, but sooner or later those bowls are going to tip over and revival will come.

Consider Hannah. She was weeping, grieving, and going without food. That's how heartbroken she was in her barrenness. But as overwhelmed as she was, she didn't stop praying. The result: Hannah birthed Samuel and Samuel birthed a revival in Israel.

Upon learning she was pregnant, Hannah prayed, "My heart rejoices in the Lord; My horn is exalted in the Lord. I smile at my enemies, because I rejoice in Your salvation" (1 Sam. 2:1). Go ahead and smile. The answer is coming.

— *Prayer* —

Father, in the name of Jesus, forgive me for allowing the voice of disappointment to speak louder than Your voice in my life. I know when I pray anything according to Your will You hear me, and You are working behind the scenes to bring the revival we both want to see.

Avoiding Revival Snares

"The discretion of a man makes him slow to anger, and his glory is to overlook a transgression"
(Proverbs 19:11).

"People who wish to be offended will always find some occasion for taking offense," John Wesley, founder of the Methodist movement, once said. Sometimes, they have the help of spirit.

Offense can shut out—or quench—the spirit of revival in a hurry. I've witnessed believers getting offended over slight corrections, unreturned phone calls and even the way certain people say, "Holy Spirit." I've heard about believers getting offended over new relationships forming, being asked to sit out travel trips, or not being invited into a back-room meeting.

There's an actual spirit rising that's causing these unreasonable offenses. It's Satan's plot to divide believers in an hour of church history when it's absolutely critical that we unite on our common beliefs.

Offense is dangerous because "a brother offended is harder to be won than a strong city, and their contentions are like the bars of a castle" (see Prov. 18:19). But love is not touchy or easily provoked (see 1 Cor. 13:5-6).

We can't walk in revival and offense at the same time. Proverbs 19:11 tells us, "The discretion of a man defers his anger, and it is his glory to pass over a transgression" (MEV). We can't get prayer answers and walk in unforgiveness at the same time (see Mark 11:22-26; Matt. 6:9-15). We can't walk in offense and expect not to enter into resentment, unforgiveness, bitterness and hatred.

Dealing with offense in our hearts requires repentance—a change of thinking. We need to crucify our flesh, ask God for the grace of humility, stop being selfish and determine not to be offended. We need to allow the Lord to heal any past hurts, wounds, rejection, or other issues that drive us toward offense. We need to stop using the Word of God to justify our offense. We need to stop fleeing relationships and churches and repeating the same cycle. Amen?

— *Prayer* —

Father, in the name of Jesus, forgive me for taking the bait of Satan. Forgive me for allowing myself to be offended—or for being a stumbling block to others. Would You show me if there is any residue of resentment in my heart? Would You deliver me from the tendency to be offended?

A Noble Revival Financier

"The people must bring goods and livestock. They should also bring any offerings they choose to. All those gifts will be for God's temple in Jerusalem" (Ezra 1:4).

She was born in 1707 in Chartley, England into a noble family. Known as Lady Huntington, she was among England's elites but she was not consumed with privilege. Rather, she hungered after the true riches that only Christ could offer.

During the years when John and Charles Wesley were igniting an awakening in England, Lady Huntington invited the brothers to her home. They became dear friends, and she supported their efforts. But despite her alms to God, her sons died of smallpox in 1744 and her husband passed away two years later. Instead of despair, the trials sent the countess into an even deeper relationship with God.

George Whitefield, a popular preacher in the Great Awakening, became her personal chaplain. The fiery Lady Huntington eventually founded the Countess of Huntington's Connexion, a Calvinist movement within the Methodist church. Indeed, she was a financier of revival in many ways. She once said, "None know how to prize the Savior, but such as are zealous in pious works for others."

Lady Huntington eliminated many of the niceties of nobility so she would have more to sow into the Kingdom. She sold her jewelry and her luxurious residences to build chapels to serve growing churches. She founded sixty-four chapels and helped fund many others. All told, she gave more than $500,000 to the Kingdom in the years of revival. That's the equivalent of over $23 million today.

The countess also took interest in the Thirteen Colonies and issues concerning Native Americans and slaves. She raised funds for Indian missions and later in life promoted the writings and freedom of formerly enslaved Africans who knew Jesus. And she didn't want credit for any of it. In her will, she mandated that no biography be written about her until ninety years after hear death.

The countess understood Christ's words in Matthew 6:19-20, "Do not lay up for yourselves treasures on earth, where moth and rust destroy and where thieves break in and steal; But lay up for yourselves treasures in heaven, where neither moth nor rust doth corrupt, and where thieves do not break through nor steal."

— *Prayer* —

Father, in the name of Jesus, would You give me a mindset like Lady Huntington possessed? Help me not to focus on the riches of this world, but the eternal riches in heaven. Help me to sow my time, my finances, and my prayer into the cause of revival in my generation.

A Revival of Holiness

"Be holy, for I am holy" (1 Peter 1:16).

"I continue to dream and pray about a revival of holiness in our day that moves forth in mission and creates authentic community in which each person can be unleashed through the empowerment of the Spirit to fulfill God's creational intentions." Those were the words of John Wesley, founder of the Methodist Movement.

There was indeed a revival of holiness after he went on to glory. The Holiness Movement broke out as part of 19th Century Methodism and emphasized the doctrine of a second work of grace to enter sanctification for Christian perfection. The overarching concept: the Christian life should be free from sin.

Of course, we will never be fully free from sin in this lifetime, but we should nevertheless pursue holiness. Indeed, we need a new holiness revival—not exactly like the one in the 19th Century but one that spurs a passion in the hearts of believers to be holy even as God is holy (see 1 Pet. 1:16).

Sometimes, I think we lose sight of God as holy. If we're not careful, we can become too familiar with Him instead of reverencing Him. We can start walking in what some have aptly called "sloppy agape" instead of worshipping the Lord in the splendor of holiness and trembling before Him (see Ps. 96:9).

Consider the words of Isaiah 35:8, "A highway shall be there, and a road, and it shall be called the Highway of Holiness. The unclean shall not pass over it, but it shall be for others. Whoever walks the road, although a fool, shall not go astray."

God saved us and called us with a holy calling (see 2 Tim. 1:9). We are called to put on the new self, created after the likeness of God in true righteousness and holiness (see Eph. 4:24). We are called to present our bodies as living scarifies, holy and acceptable to God (see Rom. 12:1-2). Let's ask God for the grace of holiness.

— *Prayer* —

Father, in the name of Jesus, I want to be holy even as you are holy. Would You pour out the grace of holiness? Would You help me to walk worthy of my calling? Would You strengthen me in my inner man so the temptations of this world will not move me off my commitment to holiness?

JUNE 13

Watch Me Burn!

"He was the burning and shining lamp, and you were willing for a time to rejoice in his light" (John 5:35).

If you are going to be a revival carrier, you need to consistently burn and shine. John the Baptist was the forerunner of the revival Christ brought to the earth. He prepared the way of the Lord. But he didn't do it with a lukewarm spirit. No, John was on fire.

Jesus later said of him, "He was the lamp that was burning and shining, and you were willing to rejoice for a while in his light" (John 5:36). John was on fire for the plans and purposes of God in his generation and it was obvious to everyone.

"Spirit filled souls are ablaze for God. They love with a love that glows. They serve with a faith that kindles. They serve with a devotion that consumes. They hate sin with fierceness that burns," said Twentieth Century Wesleyan Methodist ministry Samuel Chadwick. "They rejoice with a joy that radiates. Love is perfected in the fire of God."

Thousands of years after John the Baptist, John Wesley, the founder of the Methodist Movement in the 1700s, started burning and shining. Someone once asked the revivalist, "What is your secret? Why do so many people come to hear you preach?" Wesley answered, "I get alone with God in prayer. He sets me on fire. The people come out to watch me burn."

Therein lies the secret to burning for God. Think about it. John the Baptist was otherworldly. He was set apart from his mother's womb. He didn't play games like other children his age. He was a Nazarite. He didn't engage in the world's entertainment system, such as chariot races or theater. He was deeply consecrated.

The Spirit will keep you burning, but so will the Word. Thomas Watson, a Seventeenth Century Puritan preacher, once said, "Leave not off reading the Bible till you find your hearts warmed. Read the word, not only as a history, but labor to be affected with it. Let it not only inform you, but inflame you. 'Is not my word like a fire? saith the Lord' (Jer. 23:29). Go not from the word till you can say as those disciples, 'Did not our hearts burn within us?'" (Luke 24:32).

— *Prayer* —

Father, in the name of Jesus, put the spirit of burning upon me. Burn away anything that hinders love; anything that doesn't look like Jesus. You created me in Your image yet I'm still being conformed into Your image. Help me live a life of bliss and glory forever and ever and ever with You.

When Evil Arises from Revival

"But he who received the seed on stony places, this is he who hears the word and immediately receives it with joy; yet he has no root in himself, but endures only for a while"
(Matthew 13:20-21).

Revival can produce evil. This was the contention of Barton Stone, widely considered to be one of the greatest preachers in the Second Great Awakening. What could he possibly mean?

"We have seen many things called revivals—great revivals. We have seen congregations greatly excited—many crying aloud for mercy, and many praising God for delivering grace. We have seen this state of things continue but a short time, and then disappear for years," he once preached.

"We have seen many of these converts soon dwindle, sicken and die, and become more hardened against the fear of God, than they were before—many of them becoming infidels, by thinking that all professors of religion are like themselves deluded by strong passion and imagination."

This can be likened to deliverance ministry. Jesus said, "When an unclean spirit goes out of a man, he goes through dry places, seeking rest, and finds none. Then he says, 'I will return to my house from which I came.' And when he comes, he finds it empty, swept, and put in order. Then he goes and takes with him seven other spirits more wicked than himself, and they enter and dwell there; and the last state of that man is worse than the first. So shall it also be with this wicked generation" (Matt. 12:43-45).

In this way, evil can rise from revival. What was lacking? Discipleship? How did the seed of the Word get choked out? Was it the cares of life? Persecution for the Word's sake? Perhaps it was all of the above.

"All must acknowledge that some good results from such revivals; but all must acknowledge that great evil also rose out of them," Stone preached. "Those, who under strong affections, believed they were born of God, and who made a public confession of faith, and fell from it, are of all people in the most pitiable situation, seldom do they ever after embrace religion. These by their example, discourage others, and fill their minds with prejudices against religion."

— Prayer —

Father, in the name of Jesus, help me not to close my eyes to the possibility of evil coming from revival. Help me stand as an intercessor not just for revival, but in the revival and even after the revival has waned so the enemy can't snatch the seeds You plant in souls.

The Francis Asbury Revivalist Anointing

"Finally, all of you be of one mind, having compassion for one another; love as brothers, be tenderhearted, be courteous" (1 Peter 3:8).

Born in 1745 in England to Methodist parents, Francis Asbury started preaching when he was eighteen years old. He traveled to America in 1771 and was the only Methodist preacher to stay there during the American Revolution.

Under his leadership, the Methodist church swelled from twelve hundred people to over two-hundred-forty-one thousand people and seven hundred ordained ministers. That's why he's known as the "Father of American Methodism." Despite having very little education himself, Asbury established Bethel Academy in Kentucky in 1790. That school became the Asbury University many know today.

A circuit riding evangelist, history suggests he preached over sixteen thousand sermons and traveled over two-hundred-fifty-thousand miles on horseback sharing the Good News. Asbury once said, "Preach as if you had seen heaven and its celestial inhabitants, and had hovered over the bottomless pit, and beheld the tortures, and heard the groans of the damned."

Asbury took what some might call a vow of poverty. He didn't own much more than he could carry on horseback. He advocated for low Methodist minister salaries. He was never paid more than eighty dollars a year. His mindset, "We live by faith in a prayer-hearing, soul-converting, soul-sanctifying, soul-restoring, soul-comforting God."

Known for his holiness, Asbury was more recognized in daily life than titans of the age like Thomas Jefferson and George Washington. And he was also known for breaking down racial and gender barriers in early America.

Asbury gave ministry opportunities to everyone, regardless of the color of their skin or social status. He empowered people to pray and preach and paved the way for Richard Allen and James Varrick to found African-American Methodist branches. The Francis Asbury revival anointing is one of holiness, piety, and unity among all.

— *Prayer* —

Father, in the name of Jesus, would You give me a revival anointing like Francis Asbury? Help me live a modest life that is focused on winning souls. Help me to be an advocate for those who face discrimination. Help me walk in holiness, piety, and unity.

Reviving Dead Churches

"Revive us again, O God! I know you will! Give us a fresh start! Then all your people will taste your joy and gladness" (Psalm 85:6).

Many people tell me they are in a church that is on life support rather than Holy Spirit support. God, they say, is not moving. The gifts of the Spirit are not manifesting. No one is getting saved, healed, delivered, or discipled.

Why don't they leave? Sometimes it's a false loyalty. Other times it's because their grandmother's name is engraved on the pews. While grandmother has graduated to glory, they are backsliding or growing lukewarm.

I always tell people to get out of what I call "dead" churches. Many people feel a responsibility to stay and pray— and end up stone cold. It's been said, "If the horse is dead, dismount."

It was John Wesley, a revival leader and founder of the Methodist movement, who once said, "Catch on fire, and people will come for miles to see you burn." If you are the only burning one in your city, you are the hope. Keep burning, keep shining until your fire wakes people up. There may be persecution, but the glory is worth it.

E. M. Bounds, who wrote many profound books on prayer, once said, "What the church needs today is not more or better machinery, not new organizations or more novel methods. She needs men whom the Holy Spirit can use—men of prayer, men mighty in prayer. The Holy Spirit does not flow through methods, but through men …. He does not anoint plans, but men—men of prayer!"

This is not about your local church but the church in nations around the world. The church universal needs an awakening. Even on-fire Holy Spirit churches can be more on fire and more Holy Spirit-filled. Let this be our prayer: Psalm 85:6, "Revive us again, O God! I know you will! Give us a fresh start! Then all your people will taste your joy and gladness."

— *Prayer* —

Father, in the name of Jesus, would You give me the courage to stop supporting half-dead works that have a form of religion but deny the Holy Spirit's power? Give me the courage to step out into a church that is contending for revival in the nations. Lead me to a church that prays without ceasing.

JUNE 17

Awakened to God's Presence

"Then Jacob awoke from his sleep and said, 'Surely the Lord is in this place, and I wasn't even aware of it!'" (Genesis 28:16)

Jacob was awakened to God's presence after he experienced a dramatic dream of angels ascending and descending on a stairway to heaven. When he woke up from his natural slumber, he was also awakened to the Spirit of God's presence. The reality is God's presence was there all along.

Indeed, God is everywhere but sometimes He manifests His presence in an undeniable way. We need to be awakened to the presence of God at another level. This is what happens in revival. In His presence, there is fullness of joy and at His right hand pleasures forevermore (see Ps. 16:11). We need His presence.

God wants us to walk in a level of awakening that makes us continually aware of His presence—not just when we are in a worship service or when we hear His voice or when we have a dramatic encounter. He wants us to be so awakened that we are sensitive to His presence even in the mundane areas of our life.

In 1 Kings 8, Solomon finished building the temple and the priests took the ark of the covenant into the holy place. Verse 10 reads, "When the priests had come out of the Holy Place, the cloud filled the Lord's house, so the priests could not stand to minister because of the cloud, for the glory of the Lord had filled the Lord's house."

When you are awakened to God's presence you will walk with a confidence that He has gone before you to make a way for you. You will have assurance that He has your back. You will know assuredly He is directing your steps into revival, favor, wisdom, and divine appointments.

— *Prayer* —

Father, in the name of Jesus, awaken me to Your presence. Give me a discerning heart to recognize Your leadership in my life. Help me, like the old Christian monk Brother Lawrence, to practice Your presence in my daily activities, and to direct my attention to You more often.

Make it Like Cane Ridge!

"Like the appearance of a rainbow in a cloud on a rainy day, so was the appearance of the brightness all around it. This was the appearance of the likeness of the glory of the Lord"
(Ezekiel 1:28).

The first time I ministered in the Cane Ridge Meeting House in Kentucky I started trembling on the inside. I had never experienced anything like it. I could hardly stand.

I visited Cane Ridge again some years later and had a different experience, though every bit as powerful. We began to pray for God to pour out His Spirit and the atmosphere was saturated with His presence. People walked in from the outside and literally fell on their faces.

Cane Ridge is a site in the Second Great Awakening. Barton Stone was the pastor and stood in the pulpit there during those days. The Cane Ridge Revival was a camp meeting, indeed the largest and most famous camp meeting of the Second Great Awakening. Historians agree nearly ten percent of Kentucky's population in 1800 visited the site.

Vanderbilt historian Paul Conkin said Cane Ridge was "arguably ... the most important religious gathering in all of American history." Just as we pray, "Do it again, Lord!" it's been said that the prayer at camp meetings in America in those days was, "Lord, make it like Cane Ridge."

So what was the fascination with Cane Ridge? Stone wrote: "The scene to me was new and passing strange. Many, very many fell down, as men slain in battle, and continued for hours together in an apparently breathless and motionless state— sometimes for a few moments reviving, and exhibiting symptoms of life by a deep groan, or piercing shriek, or by a prayer for mercy most fervently uttered. With astonishment did I hear men, women, and children declaring the wonderful works of God."

Some criticized the revival for being too emotional, but none can deny the Spirit of God was there. You can still feel the presence of God at Cane Ridge today. Lord, make it like Cane Ridge!

— *Prayer* —

Father, in the name of Jesus, make it like Cane Ridge! If You did it before, You can do it again. I know You want to bring revival, so I come into agreement with Your will for a revival that causes men to cry out for mercy and salvation. I declare Your marvelous works will manifest again.

JUNE 19

Pray to the Lord of the Harvest

"Therefore pray the Lord of the harvest to send out laborers into His harvest" (Matthew 9:38).

Revivals should and must break out of the four walls of the church. Yes, we should preach Christ and Him crucified in revival meetings, knowing there may be lost souls in the congregation seeking the Savior. But without prayer to the Lord of the harvest, those lost souls may not find their way to the building.

Yes, we should go out to the highways and byways and share the Good News of Jesus from a heart burning with revival fire. But if we don't pray to the Lord of the harvest, the revival fire in our belly may not land on their souls and convict them of sin so they can turn to Him.

In Matthew 9:36-38, we read of Christ's passion for souls: "When he saw the vast crowds of people, Jesus' heart was deeply moved with compassion, because they seemed weary and helpless, like wandering sheep without a shepherd. He turned to his disciples and said, 'The harvest is huge and ripe! But there are not enough harvesters to bring it all in. As you go, plead with the Owner of the Harvest to thrust out many more reapers to harvest his grain!'"

Again, in John 4:35-36, Jesus said, "Do you not say, 'There are still four months and then comes the harvest'? Behold, I say to you, lift up your eyes and look at the fields, for they are already white for harvest! And he who reaps receives wages, and gathers fruit for eternal life, that both he who sows and he who reaps may rejoice together."

Jesus is concerned about souls. Revival is for the church. Salvation is for the lost. As revivalists, we must not only carry the mandate to see nations awakened. We must embrace the Great Commission:

"And Jesus came and spoke to them, saying, 'All authority has been given to Me in heaven and on earth. Go therefore and make disciples of all the nations, baptizing them in the name of the Father and of the Son and of the Holy Spirit, teaching them to observe all things that I have commanded you; and lo, I am with you always, even to the end of the age'" (Matt. 28:18-20).

— *Prayer* —

Father, in the name of Jesus, would You help me remember that revival is often a forerunner to evangelism? Help me rejoice when revival comes to Your church, but help me embrace the responsibility to share the Good News that the God of revival is also the Savior of the world.

190

Entering Revival Glory

"Please, show me Your glory" (Exodus 33:18).

I will always remember the time I woke up with gold dust on my pillow. At first, I didn't know what to think! When I traveled with the message of revival, I saw the glory of God fall in our meetings so powerfully I didn't know what to do with myself.

At one event in Oklahoma, I was so overcome with the glory that I joined the worship team and started playing the bongos. People were getting healed of all manner of sickness and disease in the glory.

"The glory of God is bringing revival, and if we want more revival we must make room for the glory. This is the greatest need of the hour." So said Ruth Ward Heflin, who was considered by many to be a matriarch of modern-day Pentecostalism.

Throughout her forty years of ministry, Heflin stood in the gap as a general of prayer and intercession with a heart for Israel and to see the knowledge of the glory cover the earth as the waters cover the sea (see Hab. 2:14).

Heflin's definition of revival? "Revival is bringing an acceleration of the purposes of God in the earth," she says, "and an important part of the revival is the revealing to us of our Bridegroom."

Heflin drops some timeless nuggets in her book, *Revival Glory*. She said: "Our failure to make room for the glory in our services is the most common reason that the glory is not seen and experienced in church after church across America and around the world. I believe that most of the necessary elements are in place, but we simply don't give God a chance. We don't make room for Him to work. We don't make room for the glory."

Heflin also had some insight on what hinders revival. "What hinders us is rarely something complicated," she said. "We don't have major problems that need to be overcome, but minor adjustments that need to be made."

— *Prayer* —

Father, in the name of Jesus, would You give me a hunger to study the glory? You speak in Your Word about the knowledge of the glory of the Lord. I want to be knowledgeable about the glory of the Lord so I can discern it and respect it. Lord, pour out revival glory in my life.

JUNE 21

Spontaneous Revival

"I have declared the former things from the beginning; They went forth from My mouth, and I caused them to hear it. Suddenly I did them, and they came to pass" (Isaiah 48:3).

"Revival is spontaneous, and we must learn to be spontaneous." So said Ruth Ward Heflin, considered by many to be a matriarch of modern-day Pentecostalism. Many people do not know that Heflin was a descendent of the 18th Century revivalist Jonathan Edwards.

Revival is indeed spontaneous. Something spontaneous is not planned. You can't plan for revival. You can prepare for it through repentance, fasting and prayer, but you can't plan it. You can't manufacture it. Spontaneous revival just happens, often without warning and when we least expect it. We don't see it coming.

Spontaneous speaks of something that happens without apparent external influence, force, cause, or treatment. In other words, you aren't preaching or teaching on revival. You aren't even necessarily praying for revival the moment revival hits. It's not connected to anything you tried to do or make happen.

It's spontaneous. It's impromptu. It's unprompted and unplanned. It may even be inconvenient. It's a suddenly, sort of like the rain shower that seems to come out of nowhere. After weeks of praying in unity, "Suddenly a sound like a mighty rushing wind" and the one hundred twenty in the Upper Room were filled with the Spirit" (see Acts 2).

Expect revival. Wait with anticipation but understand you have to do your part. Like the disciples in the Upper Room, you need to pray. Like Paul and Barnabas in the prison, you need to praise. In other words, we need to create a spiritual climate over our lives that invites the Holy Spirit to work in our hearts, lives, and circumstances.

Take heart in Isaiah 48:3: "I have declared the former things from the beginning and they went forth from My mouth, and I announced them. Suddenly I did them, and they came to pass."

— *Prayer* —

Father, in the name of Jesus, help me stop trying to make revival happen and lean into the Holy Spirit, the true catalyst of revival. Help me to stay steady praying for revival day and night, day in and day out, knowing that the ignition moment of revival fire is in Your perfect timing.

A.W. Tozer Confronts Revival Prayer Errors

"[Or] you do ask [God for them] and yet fail to receive, because you ask with wrong purpose and evil, selfish motives. Your intention is [when you get what you desire] to spend it in sensual pleasures" (James 4:3, AMPC).

He was known as an evangelical mystic and goes down in Christian history as one of the most influential men of his generation. Indeed, he was often called a "twentieth century prophet"—and this was before the prophetic movement in the 1980s that restored the office of the prophet the church.

His name is A.W. Tozer and he was as much a revivalist as a mystic or a prophet.

Tozer was known to make cutting statements about many facets of church life—and the realm of revival was no exception. He said, "It is useless for large companies of believers to spend long hours begging God to send revival. Unless we intend to reform we may as well not pray. Unless praying men have the insight and faith to amend their whole way of life to conform to the New Testament pattern there can be no true revival.

"We must have a reformation within the Church. To beg for a flood of blessing to come upon a backslidden and disobedient Church is to waste time and effort. A new wave of religious interest will do no more than add numbers to churches that have no intention to own the Lordship of Jesus and come under obedience to His commandments. God is not interested in increased church attendance unless those who attend amend their ways and begin to live holy lives.

"Prayer for revival will prevail when it is accompanied by radical amendment of life; not before. All-night prayer meetings that are not preceded by practical repentance may actually be displeasing to God … We must cleanse the temple of the hucksters and the money changers and come fully under the authority of our risen Lord once more. And this applies to this writer and to this publisher as well as to everyone that names the name of Jesus. Then we can pray with confidence and expect true revival to follow."

— *Prayer* —

Father, help me to adopt a no-nonsense approach to revival. I don't want to put man's mechanisms in place and hope for fruit. I don't want to waste time begging for revival to no end. Let the reformation start with me. Reform my thoughts, my words, and my prayers so revival can come forth in my life.

How Bad to You Want Revival?

"Whom have I in heaven but You? And there is none upon earth that I desire besides You" (Psalm 73:25).

How bad do you want it? We have to be willing to take a leap of faith like the early church did. We have to be willing to pay a price to walk as they walked. We have to be willing to pray without ceasing. We have to be willing to die daily. We have to be willing to relinquish control to the Holy Spirit so He can move like He wants to move in our lives, churches, and cities.

How bad do you want it? We have to be willing to repent for the character flaws that hold us back. We have to be willing to cooperate with the grace of God to yield to His work in our souls. We have to be willing to walk in love and unity with true believers whose views on nonessentials aren't exactly the same as ours. We have to be willing to war against the spirit of compromise that is raging against the church in this age.

Despite 24/7 prayer movements that bear plenty of fruit, we don't see people waiting to stand in our shadows hoping to get healed. Despite the apostolic movement rising in this hour, we rarely see people raised from the dead. Despite large stadiums of sincere people repenting in tears before the Lord for the sins of generations, we are a far cry from the reality of the Book of Acts.

We can't do the Lord's part. We can't force miracles, signs, and wonders. But we can do our part.

We can tear down the strongholds in our own souls that are preventing us from walking in the fullness of the Spirit. We can stop tolerating worldly entertainment and fleshly lusts that tempt us to sin. We can start interceding for the fallen saints instead of playing judge. We can start living like the believers in the early church— sold out, on-fire, and ready to die for the Gospel. How bad do you want it?

— *Prayer* —

Father, in the name of Jesus, I want revival now. Help me do my part. Show me any strongholds in my soul that hold me back from Your perfect will. Convict me if I am tempted to tolerate the flesh, the world, or the devil. Help me to pray for souls instead of judging them. You are the judge.

JUNE 24

The Azusa Street Revival

"And these signs will follow those who believe: In My name they will cast out demons; they will speak with new tongues" (Mark 16:17).

A revival that changed the world and started a new Pentecostal Movement was birthed on the night of April 9, 1906 in an unassuming place with an unassuming man who goes down in revival history as one of the greatest-ever revivalists—William Seymour.

As legend tells it, Seymour and seven other men were waiting on God in a little house on Bonnie Brae Street in California. It was like a Book of Acts experience with a sudden visitation of the Holy Spirit. Except this time it wasn't the sound of a mighty rushing wind and cloven tongues of fire. It was like a lightning bolt that knocked the men off the chairs on which they sat.

"In a short time God began to manifest His power and soon the building could not contain the people. Now the meetings continue all day and into the night and the fire is kindling all over the city and surrounding towns," Seymour said.

"Proud, well-dressed preachers come in to 'investigate.' Soon their high looks are replaced with wonder, then conviction comes, and very often you will find them in a short time wallowing on the dirty floor, asking God to forgive them and make them as little children."

Speaking in tongues, miracles, worship, and physical healing marked the revival and, of course, met with criticism from secular newspapers that had no grid for such manifestations of the Holy Spirit. *The Los Angeles Times* wrote of people "breathing strange utterances and mouthing a creed which it would seem no sane mortal could understand… Devotees of the weird doctrine practice the most fanatical rites, preach the wildest theories, and work themselves into a state of mad excitement."

The Azusa Street Revival lasted only three years, but it's been said every revival since then can be traced, in some way, back to Azusa.

— *Prayer* —

Father, in the name of Jesus, would You birth a new awakening like the legendary Azusa Street revival? I want to see Your Spirit move freely, even if no one understands or accepts the new wine You are pouring out. Jesus, help Your Bride be open to the fullness of Your Spirit's move.

JUNE 25

Kneeling Revivalists

"For this reason I bow my knees to the Father of our Lord Jesus Christ, from whom the whole family in heaven and earth is named..." (Ephesians 3:14-15).

D. L. Moody and Ira Sankey, an American Gospel singer, set out toward London in 1872 to preach the good news in America and England. The result: Revival in the nations. Indeed, salvation was flowing like a river.

Prayer was key to Moody's revival success—both his prayers and the prayers of others. He one said, "Every great movement of God can be traced to a kneeling figure."

So many people responded to an altar call Moody made during one meeting that he asked everyone to sit back down while he explained the Good News a second time to make sure they understood the commitment. No one turned away. In fact, more people accepted Christ on the second call than the first.

Moody once said, "It is also hoped that those Christians whose hearts are united with us in desire for this new enduement of power, but who cannot be present, will send us a salutation and greeting by letter, that there may be a concert of prayer with them throughout the land during these days of waiting."

That hope was answered. There was an elderly woman in that British church who was too sick to attend the meetings. But one of her relatives shared the news of revival. The elderly woman opened her purse to pull out a newspaper article about Moody's ministry in the U.S. As it turns out, this ailing woman had been praying for two years that God would send Moody to her church to bring revival.

Moody gave us words to ponder: "Next to the wonder of seeing my Savior will be, I think, the wonder that I made so little use of the power of prayer." Finally, he shared the secret to his ministry success: "The men who have had power with God in prayer have always begun by confessing their sins."

— *Prayer* —

Father, in the name of Jesus, I confess my sins to You, and I know that You are faithful and just to forgive me of my sins and cleanse me from all unrighteousness. I commit to praying for revival to break out and souls to be saved so Your Kingdom can expand in my city.

A John the Baptist Revival

"Now when they heard this, they were cut to the heart, and said to Peter and the rest of the apostles, 'Men and brethren, what shall we do?'" (Acts 2:37)

When John the Baptist arrived on the scene, there had been no prophetic voice for four hundred years. After the prophet Malachi's writing, Israel entered silent years. There were no prophetic words, no dreams, no visions, no divine revelations, no visitations. Instead, we had the Pharisees and the Sadducees.

Mark 1:4-6 tells us, "John came baptizing in the wilderness and preaching a baptism of repentance for the remission of sins. Then all the land of Judea, and those from Jerusalem, went out to him and were all baptized by him in the Jordan River, confessing their sins."

Catch that. Everyone came to hear him preach. The result was a deep conviction of sin. Listen in to one of his sermons:

"Brood of vipers! Who warned you to flee from the wrath to come? Therefore bear fruits worthy of repentance, and do not begin to say to yourselves, 'We have Abraham as our father.' For I say to you that God is able to raise up children to Abraham from these stones. And even now the ax is laid to the root of the trees. Therefore every tree which does not bear good fruit is cut down and thrown into the fire."

"So the people asked him, saying, 'What shall we do then?' He answered and said to them, 'He who has two tunics, let him give to him who has none; and he who has food, let him do likewise.' Then tax collectors also came to be baptized, and said to him, 'Teacher, what shall we do?' And he said to them, 'Collect no more than what is appointed for you.' Likewise the soldiers asked him, saying, "And what shall we do?' So he said to them, 'Do not intimidate anyone or accuse falsely, and be content with your wages.'"

Notice how it wasn't just repentance of sins in this revival. There was restitution involved. There was a new way of living demanded. This is true revival.

— *Prayer* —

Father, in the name of Jesus, help me to pursue repentance that bears fruit. Help me to lay a root to every seed in my soul that births sin in my life. Help me to walk rightly, do justly and show mercy. I want to walk worthy of the sacrifice Jesus offered on the cross.

JUNE 27

Charles Spurgeon's Revival Prayer

"Likewise the Spirit also helps in our weaknesses. For we do not know what we should pray for as we ought, but the Spirit Himself makes intercession for us with groanings which cannot be uttered" (Romans 8:26).

"Brethren, if you will pray this prayer, it will be better than my preaching from it; and my only motive in preaching from it is that you may pray it. Oh, that at once, before I have uttered more than a few sentences, we might begin to pray by crying, yea, groaning, deep down in our souls, 'Wilt thou not revive us again: that thy people may rejoice in thee?'"

Those are the words of Charles Spurgeon, known as the prince of preachers in his sermon entitled "A Prayer for Revival," he writes:

"Notice the style of the praying here; it is in the form of a question, and in the shape of a plea. There are very few words, and none that can be spared. Godly men, when they prayed of old, meant it. They did not pray for form's sake, neither were they very particular about uttering goodly words and line-sounding sentences; but they came to close grips with God. They put interrogatories to him, they questioned him, they pleaded with him. They drove home the nail, and tried to clinch it.

"I see that in the very shape of the prayer, wilt thou not—wilt thou not—wilt thou not revive us again: that thy people may rejoice in thee?" Oh, that we knew how to pray! I fear that we do not. We are missing the sacred art, we are losing the heavenly mystery; we are but 'prentice hands in prayer.

"Oh, that I could but stir up my brethren and sisters to be instant in season and out of season, if there be such a thing as out of season with God in prayer! Let us get away to our closets; let us cry mightily to him; let us come to close quarters with him, and say, "Wilt thou not revive us again: that thy people may rejoice in thee?"'

— *Prayer* —

Father, in the name of Jesus, help me to be instant in season and out of season. Help me stay constant in prayer for You to rend the heavens and come down in our midst, visiting a generation with Your kindness, power, and love. Revive me, Lord, and use me as an instrument of revival.

When Revival Hits the Schoolhouse

"Behold, I send the Promise of My Father upon you; but tarry in the city of Jerusalem until you are endued with power from on high" (Luke 24:29).

The Welsh Revival had a profound impact in places far and away from Wales, including the Khasi Hills in Asam, India. In her book *The Story of the Great Revival*, Helen S. Dyer tells the story of how the Holy Spirit moved in Pandita Ramabai's Mukti Mission.

The revival broke out after years of prayer that led Ramabai to ask volunteers from her Bible School to give up their secular studies and preach the Gospel in the surrounding villages. Thirty women volunteered, meeting daily to pray for the Holy Ghost to endue them with power when revival fell.

A woman named Miss Abrams arrived and the girls were all on their knees, weeping, praying, and confessing their sins. Dyer writes:

"The next evening, while Ramabai was expounding John 8 in her usual quiet way, the Holy Spirit descended with power, and all the girls began to pray aloud so that she had to cease talking. Little children, middle-sized girls, and young women wept bitterly and confessed their sins.

"Some few saw visions and experienced the power of God and things too deep to be described. Two little girls had the spirit of prayer poured on them in such torrents that they continued to pray for hours. They were transformed with heavenly light shining on their faces.

"From that time," said Miss Abrams, "our Bible school was turned into an inquiry room. Girls, stricken down under conviction of sin while in school, or in the industrial school, or at their work, were brought to us. Lessons were suspended, and we all, teachers and students, entered the school conducted by the Holy Spirit."

Two weeks after the revival fell at the mission, Ramabai assembled revival teams and sent them out to carry revival fire to schools and missions around India. They indeed ignited revival fires everywhere they went.

— Prayer —

Father, in the name of Jesus, make me willing in the day of Your power to do the work of the evangelist and to wage war in the spirit. Raise me up as a revivalist who works tirelessly in intercession for the sake of the sleeping church and the souls of the lost.

The Prisoner of War Revival

"But I want you to know, brethren, that the things which happened to me have actually turned out for the furtherance of the gospel, so that it has become evident to the whole palace guard, and to all the rest, that my chains are in Christ; and most of the brethren in the Lord, having become confident by my chains, are much more bold to speak the word without fear" (Philippians 1:12-14).

During the Second Anglo-Boer War that spanned 1899-1902, Afrikaners were held in prisoner-of-war camps in places like Egypt, India, Sri Lanka, Bermuda, and St. Helena. As the Holy Spirit would have it, revival broke out among the prisoners in all these locations at the same time.

"Boers who went to the camps as prisoners of war unsaved returned as true born-again Christians, filled with the Holy Spirit," according to a profile by the Jericho Walls International Prayer Network. "God worked powerfully in these camps. During their time of isolation, trauma, loneliness, and horrific conditions (illness, fever, death), multitudes turned to God. Some, for the first time but others, renewed their faith. The church became the most important place in the concentration camps."

What led to these revivals? Jericho Walls points to three factors. First, the prisoners were open to the Gospel because of their desperate situation. Second, preachers came in to share the Gospel and lead people to repentance. And third, as it is with every revival, prayer was going forth.

"Pastors preached the message of repentance from sin and salvation. Often, groups of prisoners were praying for God to do something in their camp, even before there was an outpouring of the Holy Spirit," Jericho Walls reports. "In every concentration camp where revival broke out, pastors worked very hard, but without exception, they attributed the results to the extraordinary work of the Holy Spirit."

— *Prayer* —

Father, in the name of Jesus, would You remind me to pray for the darkest corners of the earth? Help me to remember that revival is not restricted by prison walls or concentration camps, but only by a lack of prayer. Remind me I can pray for prisoners even when I can't visit them.

The Barton Stone Revivalist Anointing

"Therefore whoever hears these sayings of Mine, and does them, I will liken him to a wise man who built his house on the rock: and the rain descended, the floods came, and the winds blew and beat on that house; and it did not fall, for it was founded on the rock." (Matthew 7:24-25).

Barton Stone was born in Maryland in 1772 and lived until nearly the mid-19th Century. He goes down in revival history as the pastor at Cane Ridge, a key site in the Second Great Awakening. The revival there in 1801 attracted about twenty thousand people, was multiracial and based on justification by faith.

But Stone didn't have an easy life. His father died when he was a little boy, so his mother took the family to rural Virginia when he was just seven years old. In 1790 he went to North Carolina to get a formal education at Guilford Academy. That's where he met the Lord and joined the Presbyterian church. His future indeed looked brighter than his past.

Stone started preaching in 1796, embarking on a tour in mountain states. He became the pastor of churches in Concord and Cane Ridge but soon had a falling out with his denomination. When the Second Great Awakening saw mass revival at his church in Kentucky, Stone was expelled for his beliefs in faith as the only condition for salvation.

Indeed, Stone refused to subscribe to the Presbyterian's Westminster Confession of Faith because he doubted some of those beliefs were biblically sound.

Stone once said, "I suggest we restore the church as it was in the New Testament day, rooting it firmly in the pattern set by the early disciples. With its roots there, it can sway and bend to adjust to the times, but fundamentally it would always be the same. A strong tree is still a tree whatever winds blow. And the church would still be the church despite men's opinions blowing about it."

— *Prayer* —

Father, in the name of Jesus, would You give me an anointing like Barton Stone's—an anointing that confronts error in the church and brings people to the saving knowledge of Christ? Help me to walk in such a way that I never compromise the Gospel to fit in with a denomination.

JULY

"Revival comes from heaven when heroic souls enter the conflict determined to win or die-or if need be, to win and die! The kingdom of heaven suffereth violence, and the violent take it by force'."—
Charles Finney

JULY 1

What Revival Teaches Us

"'Behold, the days are coming,'" says the Lord, 'When the plowman shall overtake the reaper, and the treader of grapes him who sows seed; The mountains shall drip with sweet wine, and all the hills shall flow with it'" (Amos 9:13).

"What is taught to us by a revival?" Charles Spurgeon, the prince of preachers, uttered these words in the 1800s in a message he preached based on Amos 9:13. His words are still as vital today as there were hundreds of years ago.

"What is taught to us by a revival? I think it is just this—that God is absolute monarch of the hearts of men. God does not say here *if men are willing;* but he gives an absolute promise of a blessing. As much as to say, *'I* have the key of men's hearts; *I* can induce the ploughman to overtake the reaper; *I* am master of the soil—however hard and rocky it may be, *I* can break it and I can make it fruitful."

"When God promises to bless his Church and to save sinners, he does not add, 'If the sinners be willing to be saved.' No, great God! Thou leadest free will in sweet captivity, and thy free grace is all triumphant.

"Man *has* a free will, and God does not violate it; but the free will is sweetly bound with fetters of the divine love till it becomes more free than it ever was before.

"The Lord, when he means to save sinners, does not stop to ask them whether they mean to be saved, but like a rushing mighty wind the divine influence sweeps away every obstacle; the unwilling heart bends before the potent gale of grace, and sinners that would not yield are made to yield by God."

The lesson: We must remember that revival begins in the church but should spill out into the streets as revived Christians catch the fire of God and lift up the name of Jesus.

— *Prayer* —

Father, in the name of Jesus, would You help me remember that good worship and preaching within the four walls of the church are not the end all of revival? Help me take the revival fire I receive from Your Spirit inside the church to the stone-cold hearts who don't know You outside the church.

Armored Up for Awakening

"Put on the whole armor of God, that you may be able to stand against the wiles of the devil"
(Ephesians 6:11).

There's a battle raging for the awakening of nations. If we are going to contend for the awakening of nations, we need to be battle-ready. This is a reminder to put on your prophetic armor. Paul offers this Spirit-inspired spiritual warfare advice in Ephesians 6:11-18:

"Put on the whole armor of God, that you may be able to stand against the wiles of the devil. For we do not wrestle against flesh and blood, but against principalities, against powers, against the rulers of the darkness of this age, against spiritual hosts of wickedness in the heavenly places. Therefore take up the whole armor of God, that you may be able to withstand in the evil day, and having done all, to stand.

"Stand therefore, having girded your waist with truth, having put on the breastplate of righteousness, and having shod your feet with the preparation of the gospel of peace; above all, taking the shield of faith with which you will be able to quench all the fiery darts of the wicked one. And take the helmet of salvation, and the sword of the Spirit, which is the word of God; praying always with all prayer and supplication in the Spirit, being watchful to this end with all perseverance and supplication for all the saints."

Paul followed his own advice. He speaks of a time when he wrestled the beast at Ephesus (see 1 Cor. 5:12). I believe that he was wrestling with a principality. Guess who won? Paul won through the power of God's might and the result was a revival in Ephesus. The fear of the Lord fell upon the city (see Acts 19).

In true revival fashion, people turned to the Lord, confessing their sins, and telling their evil deeds. Many who practiced magic brought their books together and burned them. Acts 19:20 says, "So the word of the Lord grew mightily and prevailed."

— Prayer —

Father, in the name of Jesus, help me remember there is a war for revival and to never run to the battle line without putting on the whole armor of God. Thank You, Lord, for supplying me this armor to protect me and to weaponize me to battle against the enemies of revival.

JULY 3

Retaliation for Revival

"Now when the devil had ended every temptation, he departed from Him until an opportune time" (Luke 4:13).

After the revival in Ephesus, the enemy retaliated in no small measure. Acts 19 tells the story of the aftermath of the revival, explaining there was a great commotion about the mass salvations and, in particular, the slowing sales of idols in the city.

It started with a man named Demetrius, a silversmith who made silver shrines to the goddess Diana—and earned big bucks doing it. He called the other idol makers together for a private meeting. Look what happens next in Acts 19:25-27:

"Men, you know that we have our prosperity by this trade. Moreover you see and hear that not only at Ephesus, but throughout almost all Asia, this Paul has persuaded and turned away many people, saying that they are not gods which are made with hands. So not only is this trade of ours in danger of falling into disrepute, but also the temple of the great goddess Diana may be despised and her magnificence destroyed, whom all Asia and the world worship."

There was an outcry. The men were full of wrath and began exalting Diana. Suddenly, the city was filled with confusion and the men seized Paul's travel companions and dragged them into a theater. Acts 19:32-34 tells us what happened next:

"Some therefore cried one thing and some another, for the assembly was confused, and most of them did not know why they had come together. And they drew Alexander out of the multitude, the Jews putting him forward. And Alexander motioned with his hand, and wanted to make his defense to the people. But when they found out that he was a Jew, all with one voice cried out for about two hours, 'Great is Diana of the Ephesians!' The mass confusion continued when finally the city clerk quieted the crowd."

Don't be surprised when the enemy retaliates against your revival prayers—or the revival your prayer births. Don't be paranoid. Be vigilant. That enemy of yours the devil is roaming about revival circles seeking someone to seize upon and devour (see 1 Pet. 5:8). Don't let it be you!

— *Prayer* —

Father, in the name of Jesus, I know there is staunch opposition to revival. Help me not to forget it. Help me be willing to pay the price on the battlefield and prepare me for the enemy's counterattack. Teach my hands to war and my fingers to fight and remind me I am warring from a position of victory in Christ.

JULY 4

When Revival Brings Deliverance

"Nevertheless, the Lord raised up judges who delivered them out of the hand of those who plundered them" (Judges 2:16).

Revival always brings deliverance of one type or another. For some, revival brings deliverance from a lukewarm attitude toward the faith. For others, revival brings deliverance from wrong paradigms about Jesus. For still others, revival brings deliverance from demonic oppression.

The Book of Judges chronicles the pattern of revival, oppression, and deliverance in Israel over the course of about four hundred fifty years. Over and again, the Israelites start out in prosperity. Over time, they forget the past and rebel against the Lord. Instead of serving God, they start serving idols. They engage in the worship of Baal and Ashtoreth. They violate the covenant.

God is longsuffering but eventually the stench of idolatry fills His nostrils, and He allows the Israelites to see how helpless they are without Him. Judgement comes. Israel is invaded by enemies and remains oppressed, often for decades, until the people start crying out in repentance.

Judges 10:1 seems to echo throughout the chapters, "And the children of Israel cried out to the Lord, saying, 'We have sinned against You, because we have both forsaken our God and served the Baals!'" God, being rich in mercy, responds to the Israelites. He raises up revival-minded judges that lead the nation into repentance. Then the nation finds prosperity and peace. But soon, idolatry infiltrates the land once again.

Reading the Book of Judges is sort of like watching a rerun of the same TV show over and over. The characters may be different, but the plot is the same. The cycle is clear and unfortunate, but it's no different than the cycle we see in the church today. And, if we're honest, sometimes we see this cycle play out in our own lives to one degree or another.

Revival comes when we get desperate, but the problem is we don't stay desperate. We, like the Israelites in the Book of Judges, don't understand that without God we can do nothing. We are always desperate even when we don't feel desperate. King David knew his desperation, and it drew him close to the God of revival.

— Prayer —

Father, in the name of Jesus, help me to live in a constant state of desperation to know You, to hear You and to follow You all my days. Help me never to grow lukewarm or chase after idols. You are my God and there is no other. I want to love You more.

JULY 5

The Love Song of the Welsh Revival

"Oh, sing to the Lord a new song! Sing to the Lord, all the earth" (Psalm 96:1).

Many revivals birth songs or have what some might call a theme song. The Welsh Revival in the early 1900s was no different. Welshman William Reese wrote a hymn called *Here is Love* that goes down in revival history as the love song of the Welsh Revival. It goes like this:

"Here is love, vast as the ocean, loving-kindness as the flood, when the Prince of Life, our Ransom, shed for us His precious blood. Who His love will not remember? Who can cease to sing His praise? He can never be forgotten throughout heav'n's eternal days.

"On the mount of crucifixion fountains opened deep and wide; through the floodgates of God's mercy flowed a vast and gracious tide. Grace and love, like mighty rivers, poured incessant from above, and heav'n's peace and perfect justice kissed a guilty world in love.

"In Thy truth Thou dost direct me by Thy Spirit through Thy Word; and Thy grace my need is meeting as I trust in Thee, my Lord. Of Thy fullness Thou art pouring Thy great love and pow'r on me without measure, full and boundless, drawing out my heart to Thee."

The Welsh belted out this song almost every time someone turned to the Lord. A story from the revival tells of a court case in Wales during which something extraordinary happened. Before the jury had a chance to deliberate the prisoner's case—and before the judge could convict him of his crime—he was convicted of his sin by the Holy Spirit Himself.

The prisoner started confessing his sins right there in court. The judge preached the Gospel to him, and the jury spontaneously burst forth singing *Here is Love*. There were so few crimes during the period of the Welsh Revival the police didn't make many arrests and were known to sing the love song of the Welsh revival in quartets.

— *Prayer* —

Father, in the name of Jesus, give me songs of revival and awakening. Help me sing Your praises morning, noon and night. Put a new song in my heart. Let me birth psalms, hymns and spiritual songs that exalt Your great name in the earth. I will sing of Your love forever.

When Miracles Break Out

"God also bearing witness both with signs and wonders, with various miracles, and gifts of the Holy Spirit, according to His own will?" (Hebrews 2:4)

When I traveled in revival circles, we saw miracles break out. People with cancer and HIV were healed. Hearing was restored. Blind eyes opened. Where there's revival, we should anticipate miracles. I believe were in an age of miracles.

Elijah and Elisha were the main figures in another age of miracles, with the latter performing more miracles than the former. Elijah caused the rain to cease and prayed it back in again. He raised the dead. He parted the Jordan River. Elisha worked healing miracles, restored the eyes of the blind, prophesied a birthing to a barren woman and more.

Jesus said, "And these signs will follow those who believe: In My name they will cast out demons; they will speak with new tongues; they will take up serpents; and if they drink anything deadly, it will by no means hurt them; they will lay hands on the sick, and they will recover." Jesus also told His disciples to heal the sick and raise the dead (see Matt. 10:18)

We know Paul did many unusual miracles—"even handkerchiefs or aprons were brought from his body to the sick, and the diseases left them and the evil spirits went out of them" (Acts 19:11). Peter's shadow healed people (see Acts 5:15). There were so many miracles done in the early church, all of them were not recorded in Scripture. Remember, Jesus said we would do greater works than Him (see John 14:12).

The reality is you don't have to be a Moses, an Elijah, or a Paul to work miracles. That's never been the case. In this age of miracles, all you need is faith to step out and see the wonder working power of the Lord. Are you ready to enter the age of miracles? Get equipped. Build yourself up in your most holy faith. Step out and take a risk for the sake of revival.

— *Prayer* —

Father, in the name of Jesus, I want to walk in the miraculous so that I can demonstrate that Jesus is alive. You told me signs would follow me if I believe. Lord, I believe. Help my unbelief. Help me renew my mind to the reality of miracles today so I can flow freely with Your Spirit.

JULY 7

Declaring the Coming Revival

"The heavens declare the glory of God" (Psalm 19:1).

The heavens declare the glory of God, and so should we. We need to declare revival instead of doom and gloom. We need to declare awakening instead of focusing too much on the sleeping church. We need to declare what God has said in His Word, which does not return to Him void (see Is. 55:11).

Merriam-Webster's dictionary defines "declare" as "to make known formally, officially, or explicitly." And a declaration is "the act of declaring: announcement; the first pleading in a common-law action; a statement made by a party to a legal transaction usually not under oath; something that is declared; a document containing such a declaration."

We are called to declare the works of the Lord—and revival is a work of the Lord (see Ps. 118:17). His name shall be declared throughout all the earth (see Ex. 9:16), His glory among the nations and His wonders among the people (see 1 Chron. 16:24).

I once had a dream. In the dream I was on a television show and the host was asking me about the conditions in my city. I started explaining how Jezebel, Leviathan and python spirits had a stronghold here.

Suddenly, the host looked disappointed and started shaking her head as if to tell me, "No!" When I woke up, the Holy Spirit told me to stop declaring the enemy's reign over my city and start declaring Jesus' reign. There are many principalities, but He is the Prince of Peace.

In her book *Revival Glory*, the late Ruth Ward Heflin wrote, "God has given to the Church a voice of declaration, and He is waiting for us to use it. He is quite ready to pour out His Spirit and His glory upon us in this hour, and if someone will just declare it, He will do it. This is not a declaration of your intellect; it is a declaration of heavenly intent; and when you declare something in the Spirit, God begins to put it into motion."

— *Prayer* —

Father, in the name of Jesus, I declare revival is coming. I declare revival glory will manifest in my life, my church, and my city. I declare Jesus is the Prince over my city and every demon power holding back the revival You want to bring is under His feet—and under my feet.

Hollywood's Revivalist

"Now God worked unusual miracles by the hands of Paul, so that even handkerchiefs or aprons were brought from his body to the sick, and the diseases left them and the evil spirits went out of them" (Acts 19:11-12).

Aimee Semple McPherson was marked for revival—and the enemy tried to take her out before she even got started. Today, decades after her death, the International Church of the Foursquare Gospel has over twenty-five thousand churches and three million members.

Aimee wasn't always on fire for God, though. As a teenager, she was going the way of the world. Her father invited her to attend revival meetings under Robert Semple's ministry in Ontario, Canada in 1907. There she got saved and fell in love with the revivalist. The couple was ordained and started planting churches in 1909. Tragically, the love of her life died of malaria during a mission trip to Hong Kong.

Now a single mother, Aimee married Harold McPherson in 1911 and had another child in 1913. The couple moved to Canada and launched *The Bridal Call* magazine in 1917 in the context of her evangelistic tent meetings that saw divine healings of all sorts. People who came in with crutches left them behind. Bones were healed. Eyesight was restored. Wheelchairs were abandoned.

By 1921 Aimee set her sights on something much larger. She planted a church, Angeles Temple in Los Angeles to pastor her followers. At the height of her ministry, she was preaching twenty times a week. She purchased a radio station to broadcast her messages to the masses, and her Foursquare movement gained momentum. Some may consider her Hollywood's revivalist. Movie stars of the day attender her church, and her sermons featured theatrical elements.

However, scandal marked her ministry when she disappeared in 1926, presumably drowning during a swim at Venice Beach. In truth, she was kidnapped. She was charged with falsifying police reports, manufacturing evidence and corruption of public morals, but the case was ultimately dismissed. Scandal in the form of lawsuits and divorce followed her into the '30s. No one may ever know the full truth of these matters. Aimee died of an accidental overdose of sleeping pills. But her impact is still felt today.

— *Prayer* —

Father, in the name of Jesus, would You help me to glean from the life of this great general who paved the way for so many women in my generation? Help me also to learn from her bold faith, but also to learn from her mistakes so that I don't see scandal that distracts from Jesus.

JULY 9

North Korea's Mighty Revival

"Continue earnestly in prayer, being vigilant in it with thanksgiving" (Colossians 4:2).

North Korea today is one of the most dangerous places on earth for Christians. But it wasn't always like that. God breathed on North Korea in a mighty way in 1907 in what goes down in revival history as the Pyongyang Revival. This move of God saw churches planted, revival in universities, and hundreds of thousands of converts.

Like all revivals, it was birthed in prayer. Missionaries started gathering in August 1906 for a week of prayer and Bible study. By September 1906, encouraged by news of the Khasi Hills Revival and the Welsh Revival, the missionaries made a deep commitment to prayer.

Prayer continued into 1907 and then it happened. Rev. Gil Seon-ju of the Central Presbyterian Church confessed stealing one hundred dollars, comparing it to the sin of Achan. He believed it was blocking the Lord's blessing. That launched a massive wave of repentance followed by revival. William Arthur Noble, a missionary to Korea, offers a first-hand account:

"We are having the most wonderful manifestations of the outpouring of the Holy Spirit on the native church that I have ever seen or heard, perhaps there has been no greater demonstration of Divine power since the apostles' days. At every meeting the slain of the Lord are laid out all over the church and sometimes out in the yard. Men and women are stricken down and become unconscious under the power of conviction. The whole city is mourning as the people mourn for their dead.

"Many spend whole nights in their homes agonizing in prayer, either for their own pardon or on behalf of others, who have not yet been converted. This move seems almost confined to people whom we had regarded as Christians. At the present no one thinks of leading in prayer at any meeting after the first prayer is offered. The people break out in spontaneous prayer. Hundreds of voices fill the church with a murmur that has no more discord than would the notes from so many instruments of music."

— *Prayer* —

Father, in the name of Jesus, would You send waves of repentance through Your church? Start with me. I want to see Your Spirit poured out in the darkest nations and in the darkest hearts. Show me any darkness in my heart that hinders my prayer for revival. I submit my heart to You.

Developing an Eternal Perspective

"Set your mind on things above, not on things on the earth" (Colossians 3:2).

Every revivalist needs to cultivate an eternal perspective. Our life is but a vapor (see James 4:4). This world is not our home. We are citizens of the Kingdom of heaven.

What we do in this life—our obedience to pray, share the Gospel and do the works He's called us to do—is critical to hearing Jesus say, "Well done, my good and faithful servant. Enter into the joy of the Lord" (Matt. 25:21).

How do we develop an eternal perspective?

By studying what the Word of God says about eternity, renewing our mind to eternal realities, and making adjustments in our lives in line with the truth about eternity. God is eternal. Psalm 90:2 tells us plainly, "Before the mountains were brought forth, or ever You had formed the earth and the world, even from everlasting to everlasting, You are God."

The great revivalist Leonard Ravenhill once said, "Oh that believers would become eternity-conscious!

"If we could live every moment of every day under the eye of God, if we did every act in the light of the judgment seat, if we sold every article in the light of the judgment seat, if we prayed every prayer in the light of the judgment seat, if we tithed all our possessions in the light of the judgment seat, if we preachers prepared every sermon with one eye on damned humanity and the other on the judgment seat—then we would have a Holy Ghost revival that would shake this earth and that, in no time at all, would liberate millions of precious souls."

Read those words again, and let them sink in. Time is short.

— Prayer —

Father, help me cultivate an eternal perspective. Help me not to lose sight of the big picture because of the mundanity of everyday life. Help me to set my mind on things above and not merely on the things of this earth. Help me to see myself as a citizen of heaven.

JULY 11

Preparing for Revival

"The voice of one crying in the wilderness: 'Prepare the way of the Lord; Make straight in the desert a highway for our God'" (Isaiah 40:3).

We can't plan a revival, so how do we prepare for revival? It's not about putting out more seats or learning revival songs. It's not about advertising revival meetings or making a list of guest speakers who may spark revival.

Preparation for revival begins with repentance. Martyn Lloyd-Jones, long-time minister of Westminster Chapel in London, offers some insight into preparing for revival in his book, *Revival*.

"Our essential trouble is that we are content with a very superficial and preliminary knowledge of God, His being, His cause. We spend our lives in busy activism . . . instead of realizing our own failure, (that) we are not attracting anybody to Christ and that they probably see nothing in us that makes them desire to come to Him."

Those words should strike our hearts and lead us to repentance. Once we repent and start seeking Him, we will find Him in a fresh way. We will make more room for Him. We will burn for Him.

"The inevitable and constant preliminary to revival has always been in a thirst for God, a thirst, a living thirst for a knowledge of the living God and a longing and a burning desire to see Him acting, manifesting Himself and His power, rising and scattering His enemies," Lloyd-Jones said. "The thirst for God and the longing for the exhibition of His glory are the essential preliminaries to revival."

God is always inviting us to prepare for revival. But that preparation begins not in our Sunday set list or even or sermon series. It begins in our hearts.

"God is giving us the opportunity to get ready for revival. Many people feel that they cannot give Him the time needed for revival right now. Their lives are far too complicated, and their involvements are too many," said Ruth Ward Heflin. "God is dealing with us to set our affairs in order so that we will be available for that great and glorious move of God, which is coming and, in many places, is already here."

— *Prayer* —

Father, in the name of Jesus, give me a thirst for Your Spirit and help me position myself to drink from the well of revival that never runs dry. Help me prepare my heart for revival so You can use me to help prepare others for the revival You want to birth in our midst.

214

JULY 12

Let His Kingdom Come

"Your kingdom come. Your will be done on earth as it is in heaven" (Matthew 6:10).

I have been thinking about a ninety-minute phone call I had with Myles Munroe some years ago during which he downloaded revelation about the Kingdom of God that forever changed my life. The wisdom he offered about manifestations the Kingdom of God struck me.

When I asked him, for example, what it would take to see the return of greater miracles, signs and wonders at the hands of believers, he gave me two words: Kingdom teaching.

"What we call signs and wonders and miracles are simply the evidence of the presence of another government—the kingdom. A kingdom is not a religion. It's the influence of a government over a domain or a territory. It's the impact of a king over a territory. That's why it's called a 'king-dom'—a king's domain," he told me.

"So miracles, signs and wonders are not for entertainment. Miracles are not supposed to be used as a point of attracting believers to big meetings. Miracles, signs and wonders are supposed to show that another government, another authority, another power, another kingdom is present. The more we preach the kingdom, I guarantee you the more we will see miracles taking place—I mean on a daily basis."

Any revivalist should preach the Kingdom, while in the background praying the Lord's Prayer, which reads:

"Our Father in heaven, hallowed be Your name. Your kingdom come. Your will be done on earth as it is in heaven. Give us this day our daily bread. And forgive us our debts, as we forgive our debtors. And do not lead us into temptation, but deliver us from the evil one. For Yours is the kingdom and the power and the glory forever. Amen."

When the Kingdom comes, revival, awakening, signs and wonders come with it.

— *Prayer* —

Father, in the name of Jesus, give me the boldness to preach the Kingdom like Jesus did. Help me always remember that signs and wonders are invitations to believe the good news of the Gospel. Let Your Kingdom come, let Your will be done in and through my life.

The Devil Can't Counterfeit This

"Do not be carried about with various and strange doctrines. For it is good that the heart be established by grace, not with foods which have not profited those who have been occupied with them" (Hebrews 13:9).

The devil can counterfeit all the saving operations and graces of the Spirit of God. Those are the words of Jonathan Edwards, a key figure in the First Great Awakening in America.

"The more excellent something is the more likely it will be imitated. There are many false diamonds and rubies, but who goes about making counterfeit pebbles? However, the more excellent things are the more difficult it is to imitate them in their essential character and intrinsic virtues," Edwards said. "Yet the more variable the imitations be, the more skill and subtlety will be used in making them an exact imitation. So it is with Christian virtues and graces."

In his view, the devil and men's own deceitful hearts tend to imitate things that have the highest value. He pointed specifically to counterfeited graces like love and humility. But he said some things the devil would not do even if he could.

"He would not awaken the conscience and make men aware of their miserable state caused by sin. He would not make them aware of their great need of a Savior. The devil would not confirm men in the belief that Jesus is the Son of God and the Savior of sinners or raise men's value and esteem of Him," Edwards said.

"He would not generate in men's minds an opinion of the necessity, usefulness, and truth of the Holy Scriptures or induce them to make much use of them. Nor would he show men the truth in things that concern their souls' interest. He would not undeceive them and lead them out of darkness into light. He would not give them a view of things as they really are...Therefore, we may be sure that these marks are especially adapted to distinguish between the true Spirit and the devil transformed into an angel of light."

If you want to discern a true move of God from a false one, consider the words of Edwards.

— *Prayer* —

Father, in the name of Jesus, help me keep in mind the wise words of Jonathan Edwards. The enemy is certainly counterfeiting revivals, spiritual gifts, angelic encounters, and the prophetic ministry. Help me to look for the aspects of Your Kingdom that cannot be counterfeited.

When Revival Breaks Out in the Orphanage

"Pure and undefiled religion before God and the Father is this: to visit orphans and widows in their trouble, and to keep oneself unspotted from the world" (James 1:27).

George Mueller's life work was faith and prayer—and he extended that prayer to build five orphanages that housed ten thousand Victorians. In his autobiography, he tells how revivals that broke out in the orphanages:

"Within a few days and without any special apparent cause except the very peaceful death of a Christian orphan, Caroline Bailey, more than fifty of the one hundred and forty girls in Orphan House No. 1 were under conviction of sin, and the work spread into the other departments, till about sixty were shortly exercising faith.

"In July, 1859, again, in a school of one hundred and twenty girls more than half brought under deep spiritual concern; and, after a year had passed, shewed the grace of continuance in a new life. In January and February, 1860, another mighty wave of Holy Spirit power swept over the institution. It began among little girls from six to nine years old, then extended to the older girls, and then to the boys, until, inside of ten days, above two hundred were inquiring and in many instances found immediate peace.

"The young converts at once asked to hold prayer meetings among themselves, and were permitted; and not only so, but many began to labour and pray for others, and, out of the seven hundred orphans then in charge, some two hundred and sixty were shortly regarded as either converted or in a most hopeful state."

"Again, in 1872, on the first day of the week of prayer, the Holy Spirit so moved that, without any unusual occasion for deep seriousness, hundreds were, during that season hopefully converted. Constant prayer for their souls made the orphan homes a hallowed place, and by August 1st, it was believed, after careful investigation, that seven hundred and twenty-nine might be safely counted as being disciples of Christ, the number of believing orphans being thus far in excess of any previous period."

— *Prayer* —

Father, in the name of Jesus, help me dedicate my life to faith and prayer for what is on Your heart, whether that be widows, orphans, the lost—or all of the above. Give me my prayer assignment so I can be about Your business and advance Your Kingdom in the earth.

The William Seymour Revivalist Anointing

"There is neither Jew nor Greek, there is neither slave nor free, there is neither male nor female; for you are all one in Christ Jesus" (Galatians 3:28).

Sometimes God uses the most unlikely figures to birth revival. Scripture says it this way, "But God has chosen the foolish things of the world to put to shame the wise, and God has chosen the weak things of the world to put to shame the things which are mighty" (1 Cor. 1:27).

In 1906, God used a black one-eyed holiness preacher named William Seymour to kindle the flames of revival in Los Angeles. It goes down in history as the Azusa Street Revival. Seymour was an unexpected candidate since most Bible schools were segregated in those days. He studied under Charles Parham, but because of Jim Crow laws he had to sit outside the classroom door.

The Los Angeles Times noted the cross-race revival: "Colored people and a sprinkling of whites compose the congregation, and night is made hideous in the neighborhood by the howlings of the worshippers who spend hours swaying forth and back in a nerve-racking attitude of prayer and supplication."

Parham didn't visit the revival because he was uncomfortable mixing races, but many other well-known holiness preachers of the day preached at the revival with Seymour, a man marked by humility and love. Indeed, some of Seymour's most quoted words are: "The Pentecostal power, when you sum it all up, is just more of God's love. If it does not bring more love, it is simply a counterfeit."

Frank Bartleman, an American Pentecostal writer who was there in the early days of the revival, observed "Brother Seymour generally sat behind two empty shoe boxes, one on top of the other. He usually kept his head inside the top one during the meeting, in prayer. There was no pride there.... In that old building, with its low rafters and bare floors, God took strong men and women to pieces, and put them together again, for His glory.... The religious ego preached its own funeral sermon quickly."

— Prayer —

Father, in the name of Jesus, help me walk as Seymour walked so I can see a revival like the one Seymour saw—a revival that crosses racial lines; a revival marked by love and acceptance; a revival that births Christians into holiness and humility and a love for the lost.

A Healing Revival in a Pandemic

"Then your light shall break forth like the morning, Your healing shall spring forth speedily,
And your righteousness shall go before you; The glory of the Lord shall be your rear guard"
(Isaiah 58:8).

Known as God's "Apostle to Africa," John G. Lake was a Canadian-American leader in the Pentecostal Movement. His legacy is healing power.

A businessman-turned-missionary, Lake founded the Apostolic Faith Mission of South Africa after he received the baptism of the Holy Spirit during the Azusa Street Revival in 1907. By 1910, a worldwide pandemic known as the bubonic plague killed millions of people.

The plague didn't faze Lake. He continued to minister to people in South Africa. Doctors warned him to stop, but he insisted no germ could attach itself to his body because the Spirit of God would kill it.

To prove it, Lake asked the doctor to take foam from the lungs of someone who died from the plague and put it under a microscope. The doctor saw living germs swarming. Lake then asked the doctor to put the foam on his hands. When he did, the doctor saw all the germs die instantly.

Lake told the doctor, "That is the law of the Spirit of Life in Christ Jesus… When a man's spirit and body are filled with the presence of God, it oozes out of the flesh and the pores and it kills the germs." Lake later launched "healing rooms" in Spokane, Washington. His "Divine Healing Technicians," reported over one hundred thousand healings. The Healing Rooms movement continues to this day, with thousands of healing rooms around the world.

"God was always the healer. He is the healer still, and will ever remain the Healer. Healing is for you," Lake said. "Jesus healed, 'all that came to Him.' He never turned any one away. He never said, 'It is not God's will to heal you,' or that it was better for the individual to remain sick, or that they were being perfected in character through the sickness. He healed them all. Thereby demonstrating forever God's unchangeable will concerning sickness."

— Prayer —

Father, in the name of Jesus, help me to look at the plagues the way You do. Help me to stand in the midst of pandemics with faith that You are the God of the impossible and You can get glory out of enemy attacks. Help me stand for a healing revival in the midst of pandemics.

Revival Amid Corruption

"Therefore I exhort first of all that supplications, prayers, intercessions, and giving of thanks be made for all men, for kings and all who are in authority, that we may lead a quiet and peaceable life in all godliness and reverence" (1 Timothy 2:1-2).

When I step into cities or nations, the Lord often and almost immediately speaks to my heart about what He thinks and feels. Once I traveled to my nation's capital to speak at the convocation for POTUS Shield, a council of prophets and leaders to raise up a spiritual shield in Washington, D.C.

As I sat in the cab passing by the Washington Monument, I heard the Lord say:

"Washington, oh Washington, I am doing a work in you. I am working to restore the foundations and return you to your former glory. I am rooting out corruption, and I am calling you back to the integrity that once marked you. I am calling for truth and righteousness.

"I am calling you back to your roots by rooting out that which has defiled you. I am doing this little by little, but I am doing it. I am raising up Nehemiahs who will repair the breaches and I am raising up Daniels who will interpret the signs. I am raising up those who know My heart and My will for the nation to speak into the heart of America. I am raising them up to expose, to root out, to rebuild and to restore. I am raising them up."

The corruption in my nation's government—and governments around the world—goes back decades. America is not alone in this. But I believe revival can hit presidents, parliaments, prime ministers, kings and even dictators as intercessors pray, like Daniel did, in identificational repentance.

I believe God can pour out His spirit on all flesh. I believe this because I believe in God's mercy and I believe 2 Chronicles 7:14 is true: "If my people, who are called by my name, will humble themselves and pray, and seek my face and turn from their wicked ways, then I will hear from heaven, and will forgive their sin and will heal their land."

— *Prayer* —

Father, in the name of Jesus, would You help me to obey 1 Timothy 2:1-2, even when I am in complete opposition to the ideologies and values of the people in leadership? Give me the grace to pray for their salvation and for You to pour out Your wisdom for leadership.

Breaking up the Fallow Ground

"Sow for yourselves righteousness; Reap in mercy; Break up your fallow ground, for it is time to seek the Lord till He comes and rains righteousness on you" (Hosea 10:12).

Breaking up the fallow ground is breaking up hardness in our hearts and preparing our minds to bring forth fruit unto God. Those are the sentiments of Charles Finney, the Apostle of Revival, in a sermon titled "How to Promote Revival." His wise words should spur us to plow up the hard ground of our hearts.

"The mind of man is often compared in the Bible to ground, and the Word of God to seed sown in it, and the fruit represents the actions and affections of those who receive it. To break up the fallow ground, therefore, is to bring the mind into such a state, that it is fitted to receive the Word of God," Finney wrote. "Sometimes your hearts get matted down hard and dry, and all run to waste, till there is no such thing as getting fruit from them till they are all broken up, and mellowed down, and fitted to receive the word of God."

In other words, we need revival.

"If you mean to break up the fallow ground of your hearts, you must begin by looking at your hearts—examine and note the state of your minds, and see where you are. Many never seem to think about this," Finney said. "They pay no attention to their own hearts, and never know whether they are doing well in religion or not—whether they are gaining ground or going back—whether they are fruitful, or lying waste like the fallow ground."

That, said Finney, means we have to consider our sins.

Haggai 1:7 puts it this way: "Thus says the Lord of hosts, 'Consider your ways and thoughtfully reflect on your conduct!'" Paul the apostle says, "Examine yourselves as to whether you are in the faith. Test yourselves. Do you not know yourselves, that Jesus Christ is in you?—unless indeed you are disqualified" (see 2 Cor. 13:5). And Lamentations 3:40 exhorts, "Let us examine and test our ways, and turn back to the Lord."

— *Prayer* —

Father, in the name of Jesus, would You break up the fallow ground in my heart? Help me to live a lifestyle of nearness to Your Spirit, examining myself and testing my ways. Help me to release wrong mindsets, wrong attitudes, and wrong ways and turn fully to You.

Shunning Sins of Omission

"Woe to you, scribes and Pharisees, hypocrites! For you pay tithe of mint and anise and cumin, and have neglected the weightier matters of the law: justice and mercy and faith. These you ought to have done, without leaving the others undone" (Matthew 23:23).

Maybe you've heard the prayer of repentance that cries, "Lord, forgive me of sins of omission and sins of commission." What are these sins of omission? Charles Finney, the Father of American Revivalism, has a long list to consider.

First, he mentions the sin of ingratitude. Remember the ten lepers who were cleansed and only one came back to thank the Lord? The Holy Spirit recorded this in Scripture for a reason. Second, Finney points to "want of the love of God." Third is neglect of the Bible. He offers, "Many people read over a whole chapter in such a way, that if they were put under oath when they have done, they could not tell what they have been reading." Ouch!

Fourth is unbelief. Finney asserts, "If you have not believed nor expected you should receive the blessing, which God has expressly promised, you have charged him with lying." Fifth is neglect of prayer. "Times when you omitted secret prayer, family prayer, and prayer meetings, or have prayed in such a way as more grievously to offend God, than to have neglected it altogether," Finney said.

Sixth is neglect of the means of grace. "When you have suffered trifling excuses to prevent your attending meetings," he said, "have neglected and poured contempt upon the means of salvation, merely from disrelish of spiritual duties."

Seventh is the way you have performed those duties—without faith or feeling. Eighth is the lack want of love for the souls of your fellow men. Finney asks, "How many days have there been, in which you did not make their condition the subject of a single fervent prayer, or even an ardent desire for their salvation?"

Then there's the lack of care for heathen, neglect of family duties, social duties, watching over your brethren, watch over your own life, and negligence of self-denial. Do you need to repent of sins of omission?

— *Prayer* —

Father, in the name of Jesus, I am cut to the heart over my sins of omission. There are only so many hours in the day, and yet You tell me to redeem the time. Help me find creative ways to pray more, to love more and to care for the needy more. Make a way out of what looks like no way.

Does Your Church Need Revival?

"I counsel you to buy from Me gold refined in the fire, that you may be rich; and white garments, that you may be clothed, that the shame of your nakedness may not be revealed; and anoint your eyes with eye salve, that you may see" (Revelation 3:18).

The best way to discern between a true revival and hype is looking at the marks of a genuine outpouring and its effects on the church and on the lost. Charles Finney, the Apostle of Revival, said a true revival presupposes the church is in a backslidden state.

"A revival always includes conviction of sin on the part of the church. Backslidden professors cannot wake up and begin right away in the service of God, without deep searchings of heart. The fountains of sin need to be broken up," he said. "In a true revival, Christians are always brought under such convictions; they see their sins in such a light, that often they find it impossible to maintain a hope of their acceptance with God."

But it doesn't stop there. A true revival will renew the faith of Christians and set them on fire to introduce others to Jesus. According to Finney, Christians will grieve that others do not love God and seek to persuade their neighbors to surrender to the Savior. They will burn for the salvation of souls and agonize over the lost with strong prayers and tears.

"A revival breaks the power of the world and of sin over Christians. It brings them to such vantage ground that they get a fresh impulse towards heaven. They have a new foretaste of heaven, and new desires after union to God; and the charm of the world is broken, and the power of sin overcome," Finney said.

"When the churches are thus awakened and reformed, the reformation and salvation of sinners will follow, going through the same stages of conviction, repentance, and reformation. Their hearts will be broken down and changed.

"Very often the most abandoned profligates are among the subjects. Harlots, and drunkards, and infidels, and all sorts of abandoned characters, are awakened and converted. The worst part of human society are softened and reclaimed, and made to appear as lovely specimens of the beauty of holiness."

Does your church need a revival? Do you?

— Prayer —

Father, in the name of Jesus, thank You for opening my eyes to the dynamics of true revival and our need for it. Help me keep the lost in mind when revival falls, knowing that You are reviving me not just for my sake but for the sake of sinners who need the Savior.

Assembling Revival Teams

"After these things the Lord appointed seventy others also, and sent them two by two before His face into every city and place where He Himself was about to go" (Luke 10:1).

The Welsh Revival was unique in that it birthed revival teams. As the revival spread to other churches in South Wales, Evan Roberts, leader of the revival, sent teams of young people, like Sydney Evans, Seth Joshua, Joseph Jenkins, and R.B. Jones, out to preach. The revival then took hold in North Wales. Within six months, one hundred thousand people had come to Christ in Wales.

This is biblical. Jesus sent His disciples out two by two and gave them authority. The original twelve disciples, then, became six apostolic teams that went out and preached the Gospel. That model didn't change after Jesus ascended to the right hand of the Father. Paul the apostle traveled with apostolic teams. First, it was Paul and Barnabas, then it was Paul and Silas.

Ecclesiastes 4:9-12 tells us, "Two are better than one, because they have a good reward for their labor. For if they fall, one will lift up his companion. But woe to him who is alone when he falls, for he has no one to help him up. Again, if two lie down together, they will keep warm; But how can one be warm alone? Though one may be overpowered by another, two can withstand him. And a threefold cord is not quickly broken."

Later, Paul formed larger apostolic teams. Acts 24 mentions seven people who were on his team. He traveled with Luke the physician, Zenas the lawyer, Timothy, Titus, Ubanas, Stachys, Rufus and his mother, Gaius, Erastus, Quartus and too many others to list here. Revival teams are made up strategically of role players who can accomplish the mission.

Paul understood this, and wrote, "but, speaking the truth in love, may grow up in all things into Him who is the head—Christ—from whom the whole body, joined and knit together by what every joint supplies, according to the effective working by which every part does its share, causes growth of the body for the edifying of itself in love" (Eph. 4:15-17).

— Prayer —

Father, in the name of Jesus, help me be a team player. There is no "I" in team. Help me not to be a Lone Ranger of revival, but to gather with others of like precious faith to pursue and advance revival in my city and nation. Help me to remember that teamwork makes the dream work.

When Revival Fire Falls

"I indeed baptize you with water unto repentance, but He who is coming after me is mightier than I, whose sandals I am not worthy to carry. He will baptize you with the Holy Spirit and fire" (Matthew 3:11).

Known as the "apostle of faith," Smith Wigglesworth was a pioneer of the Pentecostal Revival at the turn of the twentieth century. Born to a poor family, the British plumber gave his heart to the Lord later in life.

God more than made up for lost time, giving him a faith healing ministry that saw several people raised from the dead, along with blind eyes opened, deaf ears healed, and the paralyzed walking. Wigglesworth also had a dramatic experience with the Holy Spirit, as he recounts:

"For four days I wanted nothing but God. But after that, I felt I should leave for my home, and I went to the Episcopal vicarage to say good-bye. I said to Mrs. Boddy, the vicar's wife: 'I am going away, but I have not received the tongues yet.' She answered, 'It is not tongues you need, but the Baptism.'"

"'I have received the Baptism, Sister,'" I protested, 'but I would like to have you lay hands on me before I leave.' She laid her hands on me and then had to go out of the room. The fire fell. It was a wonderful time as I was there with God alone. He bathed me in power. I was conscious of the cleansing of the precious Blood, and I cried out: 'Clean! Clean! Clean!'

"I was filled with the joy of the consciousness of the cleansing. I was given a vision in which I saw the Lord Jesus Christ. I beheld the empty Cross, and I saw Him exalted at the right hand of God the Father. I could speak no longer in English but I began to praise Him in other tongues as the Spirit of God gave me utterance. I knew then, although I might have received anointings previously, that now, at last I had received the real baptism in the Holy Spirit as they received on the day of Pentecost."

Do you need a baptism of fire?

— *Prayer* —

Father, in the name of Jesus, baptize me in the Holy Spirit—baptize me with fire! Encounter my heart with your cleansing, purifying fire and endue me with power from on high so I can accomplish the greater works Jesus said His church would do. Fill me to overflowing.

JULY 23

Beholding the Lord of Revival

"But we all, with unveiled face, beholding as in a mirror the glory of the Lord, are being transformed into the same image from glory to glory, just as by the Spirit of the Lord" (2 Corinthians 3:18).

If we want personal revival, we need to behold the Lord of revival. Mike Bickle, director of the International House of Prayer in Kansas City, says it like this: "No one can come face-to-face with what God is like and ever be the same." That, he explains, is because His personality touches the depths of our emotions, which leads us to spiritual wholeness and maturity.

"Beholding the glory of who He is and what He has done renews our minds, strengthens us, and transforms us," Bickle says. "I believe the greatest problem in the church is that we have an entirely inadequate and distorted idea of God's heart. We can experience short-term renewal through prayer and ministry. But to achieve long-term renewal and freedom, we must change our ideas about who God is."

What does Bickle mean by this? Ask yourself these questions: In your most private thoughts, what do you believe God's personality is like? How does God feel about you when you stumble in sin and cry out to Him with a broken heart? How are you in God? How much intimacy do you really want with God? How passionate for Jesus do you want to be? How badly do you want to see personal revival that spills over into corporate revival, awakening, reformation and transformation?

"The promise of being transformed and ignited to holy passion by understanding God's glorious personality is for everyone. No matter how weak or strong we feel, regardless of our previous failures, irrespective of our natural temperaments and personalities, each one of us can be ablaze with passion for Jesus," assures Bickle.

"Passion for Jesus comes first and foremost by seeing His passion for us. Through frustration, condemnation and heartache, I came to realize what ignites a heart with passion. The same can happen for you. It can happen to anyone who wants to experience passion for Jesus."

— Prayer —

Father, in the name of Jesus, help me keep my eyes on You, the God who loves me so much He died for me. I want to burn for You and only You. I want to let my line shine for You so people can see Your goodness in me. I want to live in the beauty of holiness every day of my life.

226

JULY 24

Return to Antioch

"Come, and let us return to the Lord; For He has torn, but He will heal us; He has stricken, but He will bind us up. After two days He will revive us; On the third day He will raise us up, that we may live in His sight" (Hosea 6:1-2).

I was taking a long drive from South Florida to Orlando, praying in the Spirit, and asking the Lord to reveal some prophetic direction for 2013. I must have prayed in the Spirit for two hours before I heard these three words: "Return to Antioch." When I opened my Bible to Acts 14 later, prophetic revelation began to unfold:

After Paul and Barnabas visit to Lystra, Iconium and Antioch they returned to Antioch with clear mandate: to "strengthen the souls of the disciples, exhorting them to continue in the faith, and saying, 'We must through many tribulations enter the kingdom of God'" (Acts 14:22).

As I meditated on this verse, it became abundantly apparent how different the apostles' message was to what we hear in many local churches today. The apostles understood that we are in a spiritual war against darkness. The apostle urged and warned believers to fight the good fight of faith—not for cars and houses and bigger ministries but pure faith in Christ that refuses to compromise the gospel—and that it wouldn't be easy.

We need to "return to Antioch." We need to return to sound doctrine that strengthens the spirits and souls of the disciples, encourages them to contend for the true faith. We need to "return to Antioch" and leave behind the Hollywood Christianity. We need to "return to Antioch" and walk with Christ no matter what it costs us.

When the apostle's returned to Antioch, their message was clear. And their message rings as true in this hour as it did two thousand years ago: "We must suffer many hardships to enter the Kingdom of God." So revivalist, I implore you to return to Antioch. Strengthen the believers. Encourage them to continue in the truth faith, not the perverted "gimme-gimme" faith that is so prevalent in the Western culture. Please, return to Antioch.

— Prayer —

Father, in the name of Jesus, help me to return to the roots of Christianity. Help me to be willing to suffer hardships for the sake of advancing Your Kingdom. Help me to spit out all doctrines of demons and renew my mind to Kingdom realities. You are the God of revival.

Don't Grieve the Spirit of Revival

"And do not grieve the Holy Spirit of God, by whom you were sealed for the day of redemption" (Ephesians 4:30).

If want revival, we need to get out of the Holy Spirit's way. We need to stop grieving the Holy Spirit in our personal lives and in our churches.

Yes, the Holy Spirit can be grieved. Ephesians 4:30 tells us, "And do not grieve the Holy Spirit of God, by whom you were sealed for the day of redemption." Grieve in this verse means: to make sorrowful; to affect with sadness, cause grief, to throw into sorrow; to offend; to make one uneasy; to vex, irritate, offend, insult." God forbid.

When we sin, we grieve Him. The way we talk can grieve Him. What we watch on TV can grieve Him. Our attitude toward people can grieve Him. Our lack of passion for lost souls can grieve Him. Our thoughts can grieve Him. Our prayerless can grieve Him. Our religiosity can grieve Him. Our lack of response to His presence can grieve Him.

When we have a running dialogue with our neighbor criticizing the preacher or talking about what we're going to have for lunch during the sermon, we grieve and quench Him. When we pay more attention to Facebook than we do seeking His face, we grieve Him.

When people fall asleep in church, it grieves Him. When people leave a service during offering or prayer time because they don't want to give or pray, it grieves Him. Carnal people are like dams in the river. They are blocking the Holy Spirit's fullness by not yielding to what He is doing.

Kathryn Kuhlman once said, "If I knew that the Holy Spirit was grieved, if I knew the Holy Ghost would depart from me, I would never again walk out on this stage. I would never make a pretense of things but in that hour I would be the most ordinary person that ever lived, and nothing would happen. I could say the same words, go through the same form, do the same things, but the secret power is the Holy Ghost." Amen.

— *Prayer* —

Father, in the name of Jesus, forgive me for any and every way that I have grieved Your Spirit, vexed Your Spirit, or quenched Your Spirit. I repent for disregarding Your presence or leaving You out of my daily life. Give me an awareness of Your presence and the spirit of the fear of the Lord.

A Word to Intercessors of Awakening

"He saw that there was no man, and wondered that there was no intercessor; Therefore His own arm brought salvation for Him; And His own righteousness, it sustained Him" (Isaiah 59:16).

Intercessors are on God's heart. I was working fervently by the grace of God to press into prayer initiatives, including raising up intercessory prayer leaders when I heard the Lord say:

"When you see who I am and when you engage with Me in prayer at the level to which I am taking you, you are going to understand the work that you are doing is important to My Kingdom. So stand fast, hold fast and walk strong. For I am pouring out My grace upon you.

"I am putting my mantle of prayer on you. It is from Me. It's My mantle. It's the mantle of Christ to pray without ceasing. That is how I have equipped you. Not by your own might not or by your own power—but it's by My Spirit that you will do what I have called you to do.

"And when you begin to see the fruit of it in this next season—when you see what I am doing, when you see that I hear and answer prayer—you are going to begin to enter into the fullness of joy.

"Even your prayer times are going to change. You are going to enter into My presence a little faster in this season. You are going to enter into the peace of God a little stronger in this season.

"So look to Me and wait for Me and I will take you places in prayer that will make your jaw drop. I will take you places in prayer that will cause you to understand the authority that I have put upon you. You are not second class. You are over not under—you are over the attack. You are above and not beneath. So stand firm, stand strong and stand ready and I will make you able and nothing shall by any means harm you."

— *Prayer* —

Father, in the name of Jesus, thank You for speaking to my heart. Thank You for encouraging me to pray. Thank You for giving me instructions for how to succeed in my awakening prayer assignment. Thank You for helping me stand and withstand against the enemies of revival.

JULY 27

Would Jesus Rebuke Your Church?

"Nevertheless I have this against you..." (Revelation 2:4).

Many people quip, "If Paul the apostle were alive today, we'd be getting a letter!" Indeed, but Jesus has given us a letter—more than one. The seven letters to the seven churches in the Book of Revelation are relevant to us today. Jesus wrote these words to the church in Sardis, known as the "dead church" in Revelation 3:1-6:

"These things says He who has the seven Spirits of God and the seven stars: 'I know your works, that you have a name that you are alive, but you are dead. Be watchful, and strengthen the things which remain, that are ready to die, for I have not found your works perfect before God.

"Remember therefore how you have received and heard; hold fast and repent. Therefore if you will not watch, I will come upon you as a thief, and you will not know what hour I will come upon you."

So what would you do if Jesus rebuked you or your church? Maybe He already has. We see churches literally named Deliverance Revival Tabernacle that are more dead than the church in Sardis Jesus rebuked. But there can be no dead churches without half-dead believers sitting in the pews. I always say, "If the horse is dead, dismount. If the church is dead, get out."

Yes, any church can be revived. But if you aren't careful your love will grow cold. If you are not careful, the dead church will hinder your intimacy with the Lord by replacing prayer with programs. If you are not careful, you will start operating in religion rather than revival.

Like Leonard Ravenhill once said, "The true church live and moves and has its being in prayer." Is there a prayer meeting at your church? Do you go to it? If we don't go to the prayer meeting, we are part of the problem.

— Prayer —

Father, in the name of Jesus, thank You for correcting me when I get my focus on the wrong thing. I repent if I have clung to a dead vine instead of the Vine, Jesus. Help me to pursue intimacy instead of entertainment. Help me to pursue more prayer instead of more programs.

The Voice of Healing Movement

"Who Himself bore our sins in His own body on the tree, that we, having died to sins, might live for righteousness—by whose stripes you were healed" (Peter 2:24).

After World War II, a healing movement broke out that brought a different kind of revival to America. They called it The Voice of Healing and it ran from 1947 to 1958.

The birth of the movement is largely credited to William Branham. Branham said an angel of the Lord appeared to him and said, "I have called you to take Divine Healing to the nations… If you are sincere when you pray, and can get the people to believe you, no sickness will stand before you, not even cancer."

Oral Roberts was also a key figure in the revival, as well as A.A. Allen, Jack Coe, and a young Paul Cain. All told, over one hundred preachers were holding crusades, often under mega tents that held over twenty-thousand people. Extraordinary miracles were wrought. Cancer was cured. The lame walked. The deaf could hear.

Indeed, extraordinary may be an understatement. One of the most unusual miracles occurred in the life of a boy named Ronnie Coyne. He was only nine-years old when surgeons removed his eye after an accident. Ten months later he came to the miracle tent where Evangelist Daisy Gillock was preaching. She was the sister of Dr. T.L. Osborn. She prayed for Ronnie and he began to see through his empty eye socket.

"During my ministry, I have personally laid hands on over a million people in prayer, thousands of whom had been given up because there was no known medical cure," Oral Roberts said. "And I am convinced that no disease is hopeless—none is incurable—for God can heal all sickness. His power has no limits or barriers when we center our faith in Him."

Thousands of people got healed in the revival, and tens of thousands turned to Jesus as Savior and Lord. Missionaries were sent out. Churches were planted. And God was glorified.

— *Prayer* —

Father, in the name of Jesus, thank You for showing me what is possible not only in Bible times, but in more modern times. Would You help me renew my mind to Your will to do extraordinary miracles in my generation? Give me the courage to extend my faith and let signs and wonders follow.

JULY 29

Banks on the Revival River

"For whatever things were written before were written for our learning, that we through the patience and comfort of the Scriptures might have hope" (Romans 15:4).

When revival breaks out, there's an emphasis on repentance—but there's also an emphasis on worship, healing, signs and wonders. In that context, it can be tempting to neglect the teaching of the Word of God. But teaching offers banks on the river of revival.

Indeed, some of the excesses we've seen in revivals gone wrong were rooted in a lack of biblically sound teaching—or neglecting the Word of God in favor of the Spirit of God. We need both the Word and the Spirit to be balanced.

Paul wrote, "All Scripture is given by inspiration of God, and is profitable for doctrine, for reproof, for correction, for instruction in righteousness, that the man of God may be complete, thoroughly equipped for every good work" (2 Tim. 3:16-17). Without solid teaching, we can quickly see people—especially new coverts—become unstable.

After the outpouring of the Holy Spirit on the Day of Pentecost in Acts 2, the apostles didn't stay in the Upper Room soaking. Nor did they merely walk the streets of Jerusalem performing miracles. Indeed, they went about teaching. Peter and other apostles were put in prison, an angel opened the door and let them out and told them to go teach the people in the temple. And so they did. Acts 5:26-28 tells us the rest of the story:

"Then the captain went with the officers and brought them without violence, for they feared the people, lest they should be stoned. And when they had brought them, they set them before the council. And the high priest asked them, saying, 'Did we not strictly command you not to teach in this name? And look, you have filled Jerusalem with your doctrine, and intend to bring this Man's blood on us!'"

Yes, sometimes the Holy Spirit takes over a service. But we must be careful not to leave the teachers—and the teaching—out of revival.

— *Prayer* —

Father, in the name of Jesus, would You help me never to prioritize the Spirit of God at the expense of the Word of God. Help me to stay balanced in Word and Spirit so that the enemy cannot lead me astray. Your Spirit and Your Word bring truth that sets me free and strengthens me.

Papa Hagin's Revival Wisdom

"And whatever you do, do it heartily, as to the Lord and not to men, knowing that from the Lord you will receive the reward of the inheritance; for you serve the Lord Christ"
(Colossians 3:23-24).

Kenneth E. Hagin, father of the Word of Faith Movement, was convinced complacency—spiritual sloth and laziness—is a deadly poison that kills revival. This is his revival advice:

"There are some requirements we must fulfill to see revival explode in our generation. First, we must be spiritually hungry for more of God. Revival comes when the church is hungry to see souls won into God's Kingdom.

"It comes when both ministers and laypeople alike dare to pay the price to seek the Lord the way great men and women of God have done in times past. When God's flame of revival burns inside us, we won't be content to sit around and do nothing for the Lord.

"Secondly, before we experience a spiritual awakening, we must learn to pray persistently until victory comes. We'll have to spend time praying for the lost! We won't be concerned with praying for just our own needs to be met. Our hearts will burn with the desire to pray for others and minister to their needs.

"Thirdly, to experience revival we must be committed to what God has called us to do. We must completely sell out to God, giving Him everything we are and everything we possess. We must be committed to obey God and fulfill our part in His master plan. We should be willing to say, 'Lord, I'll obey Your call. I'll preach, witness, or help behind the scenes. I'll do whatever You want me to do.'

"Determine to be the success God intends you to be. Allow the wind of the Holy Spirit to blow through your heart and cause the desire for revival to burn brightly. Always depend on God's supernatural power and never try to bring about revival in your own strength.

"Determine to do the greater works of Jesus and not just talk about them. Revival is the cry of the hour. Don't fail to take your place. Answer your call!"

— *Prayer* —

Father, in the name of Jesus, I will answer my call to revival. Make me hungry for You so that I will turn away from childish things. I commit to praying persistently for a revival that brings lost souls out of the darkness and into the light. I am ready to execute Your master plan or my life.

The Charles Finney Revivalist Anointing

"And let us consider one another in order to stir up love and good works, not forsaking the assembling of ourselves together, as is the manner of some, but exhorting one another, and so much the more as you see the Day approaching" (Hebrews 10:24-25).

Charles Granderson Finney goes down in history as the Father of American Revivalism. Born in Connecticut in 1792, he was an attorney before he was a revivalist.

Finney's salvation experience was dramatic. At age twenty-nine he decided he needed to settle the question about his soul's salvation and make peace with God. The problem was, he was busy with work in the legal office.

Although Holy Spirit conviction was on him, he said it seemed his heart was growing harder. Finally, one evening he came to a breaking point. He started singing sacred music and began to weep.

"It seemed as if my heart was all liquid; and my feelings were in such a state that I could not hear my own voice in singing without causing my sensibility to overflow," he said. "I wondered at this, and tried to suppress my tears, but could not." Finney was gloriously saved and took over a half million souls with him to heaven through his ministry in the Second Great Awakening.

One he accepted his calling, he stopped practicing law, saying, "I have a retainer form the Lord Jesus Christ to plead His cause..." Finney is called the Father of Modern Revivalism because he wrote great volumes on revival. He wrote things like:

"When there are dissensions, and jealousies, and evil speakings among professors of religion, then there is great need of a revival. These things show that Christians have got far from God, and it is time to think earnestly of a revival."

And again, "When sinners are careless and stupid, and sinking into hell unconcerned, it is time the church should bestir themselves. It is as much the duty of the church to awake, as it is for the firemen to awake when a fire breaks out in the night in a great city."

— *Prayer* —

Father, in the name of Jesus, would You give me a revival anointing like Charles Finney? Encounter my heart with Your love and drive me to plead Christ's cause with lost men wherever I go. Help me not to get wrapped up in the ways of the church but to forward the ways of Your Kingdom.

AUGUST

"The average man is not going to be impressed by our publicity, our posters or our programs, but let there be a demonstration of the supernatural in the realm of religion, and at once man is arrested."—Duncan Campbell

The Sound of Revival

"Then Elijah said to Ahab, 'Go up, eat and drink; for there is the sound of abundance of rain'" (1 Kings 18:41).

I heard the Lord say, "There is a sound coming that has never before been heard on the earth. I am the Author of it, but I will release it through My people who are hungering and thirsting after My righteousness. I will release it through My people who are hungering and thirsting after a unity that releases a fresh anointing in the earth.

"I will release it through My people who are pressing into revival, but not just any revival—a revival that spreads like wildfire from coast to coast. It's a sound like none other you've heard. It is a sound that brings transformation. It is a sound that brings healing. It is a sound that brings miracles. Continue praying. Continue pressing. Continue contending for the release of this new sound. All those who hear it will come running."

Yes, there is a sound of revival. Consider Acts 2:1-4, "When the Day of Pentecost had fully come, they were all with one accord in one place. And suddenly there came a sound from heaven, as of a rushing mighty wind, and it filled the whole house where they were sitting. Then there appeared to them divided tongues, as of fire, and one sat upon each of them. And they were all filled with the Holy Spirit and began to speak with other tongues, as the Spirit gave them utterance."

God was the Author of this sound. It was a sound ear had not heard. The sound filled the house. It was the sound of revival coming. When people outside the upper room heard the sound, they came running.

It wasn't the sound of the people praying in tongues that caused them to come running. It was the sound like a mighty rushing wind—it was the sound of revival. It was the sound of Pentecost. It was the sound of a great awakening. Let's pray we hear that sound again soon.

— *Prayer* —

Father, in the name of Jesus, help me tune my ear to the sound of Your voice. Help me tune my ear to the wind of Your Spirit. Help me recognize any sound You release so I can respond rightly. And, Father, help me carry the sound of revival in prayer that moves Your heart.

Give Me Six More

"For where two or three are gathered together in My name, I am there in the midst of them"
(Matthew 18:20).

Evan Roberts was the principal figure in the Welsh Revival of 1904-1905. It was the largest revival in Wales in the twentieth century and sent waves of revival to other nations. W.T. Stead, author of *The Story of the Welsh Revival*, record Roberts' words:

"For a long, long time I was much troubled in my soul and my heart by thinking over the failure of Christianity. Oh! it seemed such a failure—such a failure—and I prayed and prayed, but nothing seemed to give me any relief.

"But one night, after I had been in great distress praying about this, I went to sleep, and at one o'clock in the morning suddenly I was waked up out of my sleep, and I found myself with unspeakable joy and awe in the very presence of the Almighty God.

"And for the space of four hours I was privileged to speak face to face with Him as a man speaks face to face with a friend. At five o'clock it seemed to me as if I again returned to earth."

Roberts had a vision of himself speaking to people. He was reluctant about the assignment but "the pressure became greater and greater" and he submitted to God. He gathered young people, but they initially weren't interested in what he had to say. Suddenly Holy Spirit power came down and six men responded.

"But I was not satisfied. Oh, Lord,' I said, 'give me six more—I must have six more!' And we prayed together. At last the seventh came, and then the eighth and the ninth together, and after a time the tenth, and then the eleventh, and last of all came the twelfth also. But no more. And they saw that the Lord had given me the second six, and they began to believe in the power of prayer."

That was the beginning of the revival. What's the beginning of your revival?

— *Prayer* —

Father, in the name of Jesus, help me not to be satisfied with church as usual or Christianity as usual. I want more! I want more of You so help me believe for others to stand with me in prayer for revival in church and in my city. You are the God of more than enough. I want more!

When Revival is Messy

"Where no oxen are, the trough is clean; But much increase comes by the strength of an ox" (Proverbs 14:4).

We sing songs about revival. We preach messages about revival. We pray for revival. Indeed, everybody wants revival until they see the mess it makes. Seriously, revival can be especially messy. Revival shakes things up. Revival disturbs the status quo.

When revival breaks out, certain programs may be shuttered as we make more room for the Holy Spirit. Program-oriented Christians may leave in search of a seeker-friendly church.

The numbers of people in the pews may initially decrease so that Jesus can increase. When revival comes, many people get uncomfortable as the Holy Spirit confronts their sin. Some will repent. Others will never come back. These are risks every revivalist must take.

When God pours out His Spirit, some may not like the new wine. They may prefer a form of godliness that denies the power of God (see 2 Tim. 3:5). There may be accusations of strange fire when it's truly Holy Ghost fire. There may be criticisms of unusual manifestations when there are unusual miracles (see Acts 19:11-13).

In the 1906 Azusa Street Revival in Los Angeles, people were labeled heretics for speaking in tongues. Make no mistake, the Accuser of the Brethren is attending the revival meeting.

When revival spills outside the four walls of the church, new believers will come rushing in. In the Jesus Movement in the late 1960s, many churches closed their doors to hippies who loved the Lord because of the way they looked, dressed and spoke.

Today, many new converts still dress like the world and talk like the world—and sometimes smell like the world because they are still smoking or drinking. Religious Christians will threaten to leave if the revivalist doesn't make changes.

Revival can be emotional. People may weep under the power of God. Others may manifest demons. Revival can be chaotic. Revival can be hard work. Revival can be messy. Do you still want revival?

— *Prayer* —

Father, in the name of Jesus, help me not to be shaken or stirred by the messes revival may bring. Help me to stand firm on my convictions that You are the God of revival and You can move however You want to move. Help me not to compromise the outpouring.

When Devils Manifest in Revival

"Now in the synagogue there was a man who had a spirit of an unclean demon. And he cried out with a loud voice, saying, 'Let us alone! What have we to do with You, Jesus of Nazareth? Did You come to destroy us? I know who You are—the Holy One of God!'" (Luke 4:31-34)

Jesus came to set the captives free. Indeed, Jesus cast out devils everywhere He went—and not just in the graveyards or the streets of Israel but in the synagogue. Jesus made it clear in Luke 4:18:

"The Spirit of the Lord is upon Me, Because He has anointed Me to preach the gospel to the poor; He has sent Me to heal the brokenhearted, to proclaim liberty to the captives and recovery of sight to the blind, to set at liberty those who are oppressed."

Wherever Jesus went, there was revival. That revival included repentance, healings and deliverance. He cast demons out of the boy with epilepsy. He cast demons out of the man at the Gerasenes. He cast demons out of a Greek woman's daughter. He cast seven demons out of Mary Magdalene. And He gave us authority to cast out demons.

The late Derek Prince, author of *They Shall Expel Demons*, wrote, "It is unscriptural to pray for the sick if one is not prepared also to cast out demons. Jesus did not separate one from the other." Healings are exciting. Deliverance can be chaotic.

When revival hit Samaria, demons came out in Philipp's ministry. Acts 8:5-8 reads, "Then Philip went down to the city of Samaria and preached Christ to them. And the multitudes with one accord heeded the things spoken by Philip, hearing and seeing the miracles which he did. For unclean spirits, crying with a loud voice, came out of many who were possessed; and many who were paralyzed and lame were healed. And there was great joy in that city."

Remember, deliverance is the children's bread (see Matt. 15:26). God is the God of deliverance. Perhaps part of the reason believers grow lukewarm, apathetic, and complacent in the first place was due to demonic oppression. Revival is prime time for deliverance. Expect it. Embrace it.

— *Prayer* —

Father, in the name of Jesus, I embrace the deliverance You want to bring in the midst of revival. Deliver me from evil. Deliver lukewarm believers from a spirit of complacency. Deliver the lost from the bondage of sin. Deliver Your children from demonic oppression. Bring freedom in our midst.

AUGUST 5

Revival Restitution

"Therefore bear fruits worthy of repentance" (Matthew 3:8).

Repentance leads to revival, but sometimes words are not enough. In the Welsh Revival, we saw instances of restitution. Restitution is making good on a wrong by giving something equivalent to—or more than—what was lost.

We see this biblical concept in the Old and New Testaments. Exodus 22:1 offers, "If a man steals an ox or a sheep, and slaughters it or sells it, he shall restore five oxen for an ox and four sheep for a sheep."

Verses 3-4 reads, "If the sun has risen on him, there shall be guilt for his bloodshed. He should make full restitution; if he has nothing, then he shall be sold for his theft. If the theft is certainly found alive in his hand, whether it is an ox or donkey or sheep, he shall restore double."

In the New Testament, we see a man named Zacchaeus. He was a chief tax collector. Scripture says he was rich. He wanted to see Jesus, but he was so short he couldn't see past the crowd. Zacchaeus was so hungry for personal revival he climbed up into a sycamore tree to get a better view of Jesus as He was passing by. Jesus saw the tax collector's hunger and invited Himself to Zacchaeus' house.

"Then Zacchaeus stood and said to the Lord, 'Look, Lord, I give half of my goods to the poor; and if I have taken anything from anyone by false accusation, I restore fourfold'" (Luke 19:8).

Genuine repentance should show fruits. John the Baptist said it best, "So produce fruit that is consistent with repentance [demonstrating new behavior that proves a change of heart, and a conscious decision to turn away from sin]" (Matt. 3:8, AMP). Sometimes it's too late to make restitution. But, when possible, let's allow our repentance to go beyond, "I'm sorry."

— *Prayer* —

Father, in the name of Jesus, would You help me to remember that saying "I'm sorry" is not always enough. If I have wronged anyone in any way, show me what I can do beyond mere words to make up for the harm I've caused. Help me make restitution and show the true fruit of repentance.

When Revival Hits the Pit Ponies

"Therefore, if anyone is in Christ, he is a new creation; old things have passed away; behold, all things have become new" (2 Corinthians 5:17).

When transforming revival hits a city, everything changes. An early prototype is the Welsh Revival in 1904-1905. In many ways, the whole nation was turned upside down.

Led by Evan Roberts, the Welsh Revival shut down the football teams because more people were interested in hearing the Word of the Lord than watching the football matches. The police had so much time on their hands, they formed choirs. The bars shut down and the demand for Bibles was so great it took years for printers to catch up.

When coal miners in Wales started coming to the Lord, a strange thing happened. The pit ponies stopped moving at their command. That's because unsaved miners had historically cussed at the ponies but newly-minted Christians cussed no more. The pit ponies were unresponsive to the cuss-less commands of the now gentle miners.

One historian writes, "Cursing and profanity were so diminished that... a strike was provoked in the coal mines... so many men had given up using foul language that the pit ponies dragging the coal trucks in the mine tunnels did not understand what was being said to them and stood still, confused."

In fact, the coal mines—a place Evan Roberts himself once worked—were now prayer rooms. The prayer drove revival, revival drove salvation, the salvation drove more prayer, and more prayer drove revival across Wales—and ultimately around the world.

"The vision is passing out into virtue, and men are paying their debts, and abandoning the public-house, and treating their horses well," Roberts said. "Oh, my masters! Did you say the next revival would be ethical? It is that, because it is spiritual, and you will never get an ethical revival except in this way."

If God can bring transforming revival to Wales that hits the pit ponies, He can bring transforming revival to your city that hits the abortion doctors, the prostitutes, the drug dealers and more. Let's keep contending for transforming revival.

— *Prayer* —

Father, in the name of Jesus, would You help me continue to press in for a revival that spills out of the four walls of the church and into the streets, the abortion clinics, the night clubs, the brothels, the colleges, the hospitals and beyond? Help me stand in prayer for transforming revival.

AUGUST 7

Confessing Sins of Commission

"If we say that we have no sin, we deceive ourselves, and the truth is not in us" (1 John 1:8).

Sins of omission are bad enough, but sins of commission are blatant. Charles Finney, the Father of Modern Revivalism, offered a laundry list of sins of commission—and the list is not exhaustive. Still, it's a tool that helps us examine our hearts.

First, worldly mindedness. He said, "If you have loved property, and sought after it for its own sake, or to gratify lust or ambition, or a worldly spirit, or to lay it up for your families, you have sinned, and must repent."

Next, he points to pride, then envy. Censoriousness is fifth on his list. He said, "Instances in which you have had a bitter spirit, and spoken of Christians in a manner entirely devoid of charity and love--charity, which requires you always to hope the best the case will admit, and to put the best construction upon any ambiguous conduct."

Along those lines, Finney points to slander as the sixth sin of commission. And let's not forget lying. He said, "How innumerable are the falsehoods perpetrated every day in business, and in social intercourse, by words, and looks, and actions—designed to make an impression on others contrary to the truth for selfish reasons."

Similarly, Finney cites cheating, hypocrisy and robbing God. He said, "Instances in which you have misspent your time, and squandered hours which God gave you to serve him and save souls, in vain amusements or foolish conversation, reading novels, or doing nothing…" Finney goes on to list bad temper and hindering others from being useful.

"If you find you have committed a fault against an individual, and that individual is within your reach, go and confess it immediately, and get that out of the way," Finney said. "If the individual you have injured is too far off for you to go and see him, sit down and write him a letter, and confess the injury, pay the postage, and put it into the mail immediately."

— *Prayer* —

Father, in the name of Jesus, I repent deeply for sins of commission. Sometimes it seems like a little thing in practice, but there is no small sin. Sin is sin. Help me to avoid sins of commission and give me the grace to overcome them. I want to be about Your Great Commission.

The Frank Bartleman Revivalist Anointing

"My heart is overflowing with a good theme; I recite my composition concerning the King; My tongue is the pen of a ready writer" (Psalm 45:1).

Frank Bartleman was a missionary whose tongue was the pen of a ready writer. The American Pentecostal started his writing career in 1905 and offers some of the most credible reports on record of the Azusa Street Revival. His heart was for alcoholics, wayward girls, and people who were otherwise underprivileged. He knew what they needed: revival.

"A revival almost always begins among the laity. The ecclesiastical leaders seldom welcome reformation. History repeats itself," he wrote. "The present leaders are too comfortably situated as a rule to desire innovation that might require sacrifice on their part. And God's fire only falls on sacrifice. An empty altar receives no fire!"

Bartleman started preaching in Philadelphia in 1893, over a decade before the birth of the Pentecostal Movement with William J. Seymour. He served anywhere he was needed, from the Baptist Church to the Salvation Army, to the Wesleyan Methodist church and beyond. As such, his ministry was steeped in diversity, and he walked in humility.

"God has always sought a humble people. He can use no other... There is always much need of heart preparation, in humility and separation, before God can consistently come," he said. "The depth of any revival will be determined exactly by the spirit of repentance that is obtained. In fact, this is key to every true revival born of God."

Where there is humility, there will be repentance. Where there is repentance, there will be times of refreshing in the presence of the Lord. Where there is the presence of the Lord, there will be liberty. Where there is liberty, there will be a free flow of His Spirit. Therein lies a pattern for revival. History does indeed repeat itself.

"The very truths that gave birth to the Pentecostal movement are today generally rejected as too strong," Bartleman said. Sadly, his words are true. Revival, with its messy repentance, loud deliverance and lengthy worship offends many. Nevertheless, do it again, Lord!

— *Prayer* —

Father, in the name of Jesus, thank You for raising up men like Frank Bartleman to chronicle great moves of God in church history. Help me to journal my own experiences with Your heart and what You are doing in my generation so those who read it will see faith for revival rise in their hearts.

AUGUST 9

Return to Your First Love

"Nevertheless I have this against you, that you have left your first love" (Revelation 2:4).

I got saved in a jail. I was falsely accused of a crime I did not commit and was looking at a ten-year sentence when the evangelists came through and shared testimonies of God's saving grace—and the good news of the Gospel. When I got saved, I got radically saved.

But there have been times when I've strayed from my first love. Sometimes it was the business of life. Sometimes the success of business. Sometimes trials or spiritual warfare made me dull. Thankfully, I recognized my condition through Holy Spirit conviction and returned to my first love.

Revelation 2:4-5, "Nevertheless I have this against you, that you have left your first love. Remember therefore from where you have fallen; repent and do the first works, or else I will come to you quickly and remove your lampstand from its place—unless you repent."

The great revivalist Leonard Ravenhill once quipped about how almost every Bible conference majors on today's church being like the Ephesian Church. We are told, he said in *Why Revival Tarries*, that despite our sin and carnality, we are seated with Him.

"Alas, what a lie! We are Ephesians all right; but, as the Ephesian Church in the Revelation, we have 'left our first love.' We appease sin—but do not oppose it. To such a cold, carnal, critical, care-cowed Church, this lax, loose, lustful, licentious age will never capitulate," he wrote.

"Let us stop looking for scapegoats. The fault in declining morality is not radio or television. The whole blame for the present international degeneration and corruption lies at the door of the Church!"

Remember your first love. Think about a time when you were hungry for God and the joy you had. Listen to a song that really stirred your heart in the past. Think about the day of your salvation. Gaze upon His beauty.

— *Prayer* —

Father, in the name of Jesus, if I stray from my first love please lead me to repentance with Your kindness. Help me to remember the joy of my salvation. Help me see You rightly. Help me shake off the lukewarm spirit and burn for You.

Give Me Revival or Give Me Death!

"Whoever seeks to save his life will lose it, and whoever loses his life will preserve it"
(Luke 17:33).

"Is life's span so dear and are home comforts so engrossing as to be purchased with my unfaithfulness and dry-eyed prayerlessness? At the final bar of God, shall the perishing millions accuse me of materialism coated with a few Scripture verses? "Forbid it, Almighty God! I know not what course others may take; but as for me, GIVE ME REVIVAL in my soul and in my church and in my nation—or GIVE ME DEATH!"

These are the words of the great revivalist Leonard Ravenhill. I suspect he borrowed the phrase from John Knox, a man who was willing to perish for his nation. Knox once said, "Give me Scotland or I die!" Or maybe Ravenhill was inspired by Patrick Henry, one of the Founding Fathers of the United States and the first governor of Virginia. A major figure in the American Revolution, Henry gave a stirring speech to the state legislature in 1775 in which he declared, "Give me liberty, or give me death."

Maybe still Ravenhill was moved by the words and ministry of John Hyde, a Christian missionary with the nickname "Praying John." John Hyde was an American missionary who preached in the Punjab of India. Serving the Lord in the 1800s and early 1900s, he was also known as an Apostle of Prayer. His primary focus was praying for a Jesus awakening in India.

Hyde's heart's cry was, "Give me souls, O God, or I die." What a commitment to souls and to the ministry of prayer! Indeed, "Praying John" did pass away doing the work of the ministry. His heart moved over from the left side of his chest to the right side. The doctors were baffled and told him if he didn't start resting more he would not live another six months. Yet he kept preaching.

What about you? Are you one who cries, "Give me revival, or give me death?

— *Prayer* —

Father, in the name of Jesus, give me revival or give me death! Give me such a deep passion to see souls saved, churches revived, and nations awakened that I am willing to die to worldly passions. Give me such a burden for revival that I am willing to pay the price.

AUGUST 11

The Jesus People

"For God so loved the world that He gave His only begotten Son, that whoever believes in Him should not perish but have everlasting life" (John 3:16).

Chuck Smith is widely known as the father of the Jesus People Movement. Pastor of Calvary Chapel in Costa Mesa, California in the 1960s, he was serving a small congregation when he met a hippie named Lonnie Frisbee who convinced him to open the doors of his congregation to a generation that was hungry for change. By 1971, the movement made it to the cover of *Time* magazine.

But Smith didn't birth the movement. He just gave it momentum. The Jesus People Movement was birthed during America's war in Vietnam. Posters declaring, "Make Love, Not War" were popular on college campuses. And it wasn't just the war causing despair among the youth. The near-deadly Cuba Missile Crisis, the assassination of John F. Kenney, his brother Robert, as well as Martin Luther King, Jr. rattled a generation. Race riots were common and church attendance was declining while drug use was soaring. Rebellion was in the air.

But, as with any revival, Jesus stepped into a small group of those seeking truth. A group of former hippies who called themselves Jesus Freaks sparked the Jesus People Movement in the Haight-Ashbury district of San Francisco. A Christian mission for the hippies called "The Living Room" rose up. From there, communal homes came on the scene to care for and disciple converted hippies. A then-19-year-old Frisbee traveled from San Francisco to Costa Mesa—and that's where Smith comes in.

Once Smith opened his doors to the hippies, his church rapidly grew from eighty people to over two thousand within six months—and the revival spread like wildfire. Smith and Frisbee saw two hundred salvations each week and five hundred baptisms every month for two years straight.

Moreover, hundreds were raised up and sent out to plant churches. More than two million young people came to Jesus by 1977—and the revival spread to Canada, Europe, and South America. The Jesus People Movement is a revival that touched a generation of hungry youths.

— *Prayer* —

Father, in the name of Jesus, do it again! Meet a generation of hungry young ones—those who are disillusioned by the spirit of the age and the rejection of man. Pour out Your Spirit like You did in the Jesus People Movement. Transform lives by the power of Your Spirit.

A Sneaky Enemy of Revival

"Pride goes before destruction, and a haughty spirit before a fall" (Proverbs 16:18).

Spiritual pride is a derailing force in revival. Jonathan Edwards, an American revivalist in the First Great Awakening, boldly declared that the first and worst cause of error that prevailed in his day was spiritual pride. Edwards wrote:

"The first and worst cause of errors that abound in our day and age is spiritual pride. This is the main door by which the devil comes into the hearts of those who are zealous for the advancement of Christ. It is the chief inlet of smoke from the bottomless pit to darken the mind and mislead the judgement.

"Pride is the main handle by which he has hold of Christian persons and the chief source of all the mischief that he introduces to clog and hinder a work of God. Spiritual pride is the main spring or at least the main support of all other errors. Until this disease is cured, medicines are applied in vain to heal all other diseases.

"It is by spiritual pride that the mind defends and justifies itself in other errors and defends itself against light by which it might be corrected and reclaimed. The spiritually proud man thinks he is full of light already and feels that he does not need instruction, so he is ready to ignore the offer of it.

"If spiritual pride is healed, other things are easily corrected. Our first care should be to correct the heart and pull the beam of pride out of our eye and then we shall see clearly."

When God pours out His Spirit in a single place or a single church, pride will try to find a way in to puff up preachers. But God will not share His glory with any man. Spiritual pride will quench the spirit of revival—and it creeps in subtly. Beware.

— *Prayer* —

Father, in the name of Jesus, forgive me of spiritual pride. I don't want to act like Lucifer, who thought more highly of himself than he ought. I don't want to walk into destruction. I don't want to be an agent that quenches the spirit of revival. Give me the grace of humility.

When Transforming Revival Hits

"This became known both to all Jews and Greeks dwelling in Ephesus; and fear fell on them all, and the name of the Lord Jesus was magnified" (Acts 19:17).

I had a dream one night that my city, Ft. Lauderdale, was absolutely transformed by the glory of God. We need a transforming revival—a revival that leads to genuine society transformation. The Sentinel Group, a Christian research and information agency, has documented transformation in about one thousand communities around the world.

What is a transformed community? A neighborhood, city, or nation whose values and institutions have been overrun by the grace and presence of God; a place where divine fire has not merely been summoned but has fallen; a society in which natural, evolutionary change has been disrupted by invasive, supernatural power; a culture that has been impacted comprehensively and undeniably by the Kingdom of God; and a location where kingdom values are celebrated publicly and passed on to future generations, according to The Sentinel Group. The Sentinel Group offers the following ten points along with Scriptures for your study as you build your faith for transformation in your community.

Political leaders publicly acknowledge their sin and dependence on God (see Jonah 3:6—9). New laws, curricula, and business practices are put into effect (see 2 Chron. 19:4-10). The natural environment is restored to its original life-nurturing state (see 2 Chron. 7:14). Economic conditions improve and lead to a discernible lessening of poverty (see 2 Chron. 17:3-5). There is a marked change in social entertainment and vices as Kingdom values are integrated into the rhythm of daily life (see Ezra 10:1-4).

Crime and corruption diminish throughout the community (see Isa. 60:17-18). Volunteerism increases as Christians recognize their responsibility to heal and undergird the community (see Isa. 58:10-12).

Restored hope and joy leads to a decline in divorce, bankruptcy, and suicide (see Hosea 2:15). The spiritual nature of the growing socio-political renewal becomes a hot topic in the secular media (see 2 Chron. 20:29). Overwhelmed by the goodness of God, grateful Christians take the embers of revival into surrounding communities and nations (see Acts 11:20-26).

— *Prayer* —

Father, in the name of Jesus, would You make me a catalyst for revival in my city like You did with Paul the apostle? I will not be satisfied until I see my city turned upside down for Jesus. Give me the prayer strategy and the evangelism strategy to see Your Word run swiftly through my city.

The Mariah Woodworth-Etter Revivalist Anointing

"Now it happened, when I returned to Jerusalem and was praying in the temple, that I was in a trance" (Acts 22:17).

Maria Woodworth-Etter was a Pentecostal forerunner. She saw great outpourings of God's Spirit in the Midwest before entering the West Coast to win souls for God. She bought an eight-thousand-seat tent in 1889 and packed it out with people hungry to watch God move in Oakland, Calif. God didn't disappoint. Healings, signs, wonders, miracles were commonplace in Woodworth-Etter's meetings.

Of course, miracles always draw both crowds and critics and it was no different for this female pioneer. However, she probably didn't expect attacks from fellow healing evangelist John Alexander Dowie. Dowie, himself moving in miracles, at first praised Woodworth-Etter. But later he accused her of propagating a great delusion because people were falling into trances left and right under her tent. He called it "trance evangelism."

Woodworth-Etter also drew attention from the media. *The Salem* report documents her falling into a trance on March 24, 1904, and she "had to be laid on the platform for over an hour." *The Indianapolis Star* also reported "Woodworth-Etter Goes into a Trance" in a 1904 edition. In 1913, *The Boston Globe* reported, "Took No Money for Healing; Mrs. Etter Gave God Credit for Cures." Those are just a few of the articles written about this pre-Pentecostal minister.

There are accounts of Woodworth-Etter falling into a trance at a St. Louis meeting and standing like a statue for three whole days as attendees of the World Fair looked on in amazement. It's not clear if the trance actually lasted that long, but she was known to fall into trances that left her frozen for hours at a time—and so did many others who attended her meetings.

"People fell into trances, experienced visions of heaven and hell, collapsed on the floor as if they'd been shot or had died," reports *Revival Library*. "Thousands were healed of a wide variety of sicknesses and diseases and many believers, even ministers, received mighty baptisms of the Holy Spirit."

— *Prayer* —

Father, in the name of Jesus, would You help me not to fear the persecution that comes along with an intense focus on revival and soul-winning? Help me not to quench the Spirit by resisting manifestations of His power that might bring criticism and controversy into my life.

The D. L. Moody Revivalist Anointing

"Blessed is the man who endures temptation; for when he has been approved, he will receive the crown of life which the Lord has promised to those who love Him" (James 1:12).

He was widely known as the greatest evangelist of the 19th Century—and he was a praying revivalist. Dwight Lyman Moody, better known as D.L. Moody, preached the Gospel to more than one hundred million people, founding evangelistic ministries like the Student Volunteer Movement and inspiring the late and great Billy Graham.

Moody was an agent of unity, holding "Bible Conferences" that aimed to challenge people to do the work of the evangelist. He opened his meetings to all Christians across all denominations.

Moody invited "all of God's people who are interested in the study of His Word, in the development of their own Christian lives, in a revival of the spiritual life of the Church, in the conversion of sinners, and in the evangelization of the world."

Moody was the picture of perseverance despite hardship. He was the sixth of nine children. His father tragically died in 1841. He only attained a fourth-grade education, but he had an entrepreneurial spirit. He was a pioneer in Christian publishing and his legacy still stands strong today with the Moody Bible Institute.

"I believe firmly that the moment our hearts are emptied of pride and selfishness and ambition and everything that is contrary to God's law, the Holy Spirit will fill every corner of our hearts," he said. "But if we are full of pride and conceit and ambition and the world, there is no room for the Spirit of God. We must be emptied before we can be filled."

The D.L. Moody revivalist anointing is an anointing to unify the Body of Christ in prayer for revival. He once said, "I have never known the Spirit of God to work where the Lord's people were divided."

— *Prayer* —

Father, in the name of Jesus, would You empty me of pride, selfishness, ambition and everything that doesn't look like You? Help me decrease that You might increase for the sake of revival. Fill me with Your Spirit to overflowing. Give me an anointing like You gave D.L. Moody.

The Mightiest Revival Wales Has Ever Known

"That which is born of the flesh is flesh, and that which is born of the Spirit is spirit"
(John 3:6).

Before Azusa Street in 1906, there was the Welsh Revival in 1904. It was one of the greatest revivals ever and perhaps the one with the most tragic end. Evan Roberts, a young man God used to set a nation on fire for Jesus, burned out.

As history tells it, over one hundred thousand souls in Wales came to Jesus over the course of nine months. Hundreds of thousands more would come to know the Lord over the next couple of years—and it all started in Moriah Chapel in Loughor, South Wales where Roberts gathered with a few youth and began to pray, "Bend us! Bend us!" and eventually "Bend me! Bend me!"

"It was the very next month that Roberts had his first vision. While strolling in a garden, Evan looked up to see what seemed to be an arm outstretched from the moon, reaching down into Wales," writes Roberts Liardon, author of God's Generals. "He later told a friend, 'I have wonderful news for you. I had a vision of all Wales being lifted up to heaven. We are going to see the mightiest revival that Wales has ever known—and the Holy Spirit is coming just now. We must get ready."

The pastor of his church let him start holding meetings on Oct. 31. The meetings turned into a two-week revival marked by fervent faith, strong intercession and late-night services that sometimes lasted until sunrise. Those meetings ignited a revival that spread across the world.

The Welsh Revival was marked by conversions. Drunkards were afraid to come outside—and when they did, they got saved. The fear of the Lord fell on cities across the nation. A local football team stopped playing because the Welsch preferred going to church. A local band accepted Jesus and started playing hymns. Churches were filled to the brim. And God's presence seemed to permeate the nation.

— Prayer —

Father, in the name of Jesus, would You do it again? Let a revival sweep through my city—and my nation—that brings transformation of souls, churches, businesses, and governments. Lord, do what only You can do. Ignite a passion for souls and for Your Spirit in the hearts of Your children.

Cracking Under Revival Pressure

"Come to Me, all you who labor and are heavy laden, and I will give you rest" (Matthew 11:28).

Evan Roberts ignited transforming revival in Wales and beyond. Unfortunately, he cracked under the strain of the pressure. The revival started in 1904. Within a year, he was completely burned out.

"By 1905, Roberts' mind became confused from physical and emotional exhaustion. He began hearing conflicting voices in his head and doubted his ability to distinguish the voice of the Spirit among them," Roberts Liardon writes. "He would rebuke his listeners for not being pure of heart, while he became increasingly obsessed with examining his own self for un-confessed sin. He feared most that he would be exalted instead of God and became overly critical of his audiences and church leaders."

The Welsh revival finally fizzled out in 1905 when the spirit of Jezebel allegedly operating through Jesse Penn-Lewis, a Welsh evangelical speaker and author, beguiled young Roberts. Penn-Lewis reportedly seduced and deceived the revivalist in the prime of his anointing.

Penn-Lewis, whose doctrine was largely rejected in Wales and is even now described as apostate teaching by some modern theologians, sought to ride on Roberts' coattails. She flattered him with words that aimed to ease the suffering he was experiencing from people with religious spirits in the midst of revival. But her smooth words didn't heal his soul. He suffered a nervous breakdown and went to live at this wealthy woman's home to recover.

"They built their new home around his needs, including a bedroom, prayer room and private stairway. It was there that the great revivalist was confined to bed for more than a year," says Liardon. "Evan became ever more isolated and reclusive as years passed. He refused to see friends, and eventually family. He allowed Penn-Lewis to dictate who he would see, and what he would do."

Watch out for the spirit of Jezebel. It's a revival assassin.

— *Prayer* —

Father, in the name of Jesus, would You give me a keen discernment so I can see even the most subtle operations of Jezebel spirits—and other spirits—working to infiltrate Your work of revival? Help me not to move in suspicion but in discernment that roots out demons derailing revival.

The Prayer Life of a Revivalist

"I have great sorrow and unceasing anguish in my heart" (Romans 9:2, NIV).

The prayer life of a revivalist is not the same as the prayer life of the "Everyday Joe" Christian. It's deeper. It's marked by tears of anguish for souls and cities alike. Consider the words of the late David Wilkerson, founder of Times Square Church.

"Where are the Sunday school teachers that weep over kids they know are not hearing and are going to hell? You see, a true prayer life begins at the place of anguish. You see, if you set your heart to pray, God's going to come and start sharing His heart with you. Your heart begins to cry out: 'Oh God, Your name is being blasphemed.' The Holy Spirit is being mocked. The enemy is out trying to destroy the testimony of the Lord's faithfulness and something has to be done."

"There is going to be no renewal, no revival, no awakening, until we are willing to let Him once again break us. Folks, it's getting late, and it's getting serious. Please don't tell me… don't tell me you're concerned when you're spending ours in front of the Internet or television. Come on. Lord, there are some that need to get to this alter and confess: I am not what I was, I am not where I am supposed to be. God, I don't have Your heart or Your burden. I wanted it easy. I just wanted to be happy. But Lord, true joy comes out of anguish."

"There's nothing of the flesh that will give you joy. I don't care how much money, I don't care what kind of new house, there is absolutely nothing physical that can give you joy. It's only what is accomplished by the Holy Spirit when you obey and take on His heart. Build the walls around your family. Build the walls around your own heart. It will make you strong and impregnable against the enemy. God, that's what we desire."

— *Prayer* —

Father, in the name of Jesus, would You let me feel the anguish of Your heart for the lost souls You love? Break my heart over the state of the lukewarm church, carnal Christians and compromised preachers who have forgotten their first love. Help me pray with Your anguish.

AUGUST 19

Kathryn Kuhlman's Key to Revival Power

"I affirm, by the boasting in you which I have in Christ Jesus our Lord, I die daily"
(1 Corinthians 15:31).

Kathryn Kuhlman started her ministry with Sawdust Trail revivals. In other words, her revival meetings were in temporary buildings or tents—and the floors were covered with sawdust. This humble beginning was fitting for a young girl from Concordia, Missouri. But her ministry is best remembered as one of the greatest miracle ministries of the twentieth century.

Born in 1907, Kuhlman ministered under the power of the Holy Spirit for five decades. Her father was raised Baptist. Her mother raised Methodist. She accepted Christ at a Baptist revival meeting and soon defied her parents' wishes to travel with her sister and brother-in-law leading revival meetings in 1928. Within five years, she was herself preaching. Remember, this was during the Great Depression.

"I surrendered unto Him all there was of me; everything! Then for the first time I realized what it meant to have real power," Kuhlman once said. "The greatest human attainment in all the world is for a life to be so surrendered to Him that the name of God Almighty will be glorified through that life."

In 1947, Kuhlman started focusing on her healing ministry and by 1950 her ministry grew so large she opened her own church in Pittsburgh. She held revival meetings there, in addition to traveling to larger cities like Los Angeles. At one time, she had her own weekly television show on CBS.

The long meetings and heavy travel, though, took a toll on her health. Although she was diagnosed with a heart condition, she kept preaching until she finally needed open heart surgery. She died a few days after the surgery in 1976. She was only 68.

"My purpose is to save souls, and my particular calling is to offer proof of the power of God," she said. "The only limit to the power of Almighty God lies within you and me. The Heavenly Father does not ask for golden vessels. He does not ask for silver vessels. God asks for yielded vessels."

— Prayer —

Father, in the name of Jesus, I thank You for role models like Kathryn Kuhlman
who pioneered in so many ways. Help me set myself apart to You like she did.
Help me to take risks to work miracles like she did. Help me to lay aside my own
life and find my life in You, like she did.

Your Revival Mentor

"Imitate me, just as I also imitate Christ" (1 Corinthians 11:1).

Every revivalist needs a mentor. Steve Hill—the man whose message kicked off a five-year revival known as the Pensacola Outpouring—was a mentor to me. Indeed, he taught me plenty about walking in revival—and walking with the Lord. He would call me randomly and ask, "Do you have a minute?" Of course, no matter what I was doing, my answer was, "Yes, sir."

Steve's mentor was the great British revivalist Leonard Ravenhill, author of *Why Revival Tarries*. Steve once told me a story of an encounter with Ravenhill. He shared a time when he was sitting across from Ravenhill in his office. Ravenhill called him out of his chair and asked him to "come closer."

Steve told me he walked over and stood right next to Ravenhill, but apparently it wasn't close enough. Ravenhill told him to draw closer. Steve obeyed and they were essentially face to face. Even still, Ravenhill called Steve closer. Steve brought his ear close to Ravenhill's mouth. But Ravenhill wasn't satisfied. "Closer," he whispered.

Steve's ear was so close to Ravenhill's mouth that he could feel the revivalist's breath on his ear. Finally, Ravenhill said, "Steve, the Lord has secrets ... but He doesn't shout them. You have to live close enough to God that you can hear the gentle whispers of His still, small voice." I'll never forget it.

Who's your Leonard Ravenhill? Who's your Steve Hill? In other words, who's your mentor? Who's your Elijah? There would be no Elisha without Elijah. Who's your Naomi? There would be no Ruth without Naomi. Who's your Apostle Paul? There would be no Timothy or Titus without Paul.

You can't "rent a mentor." You need a relationship. Charles Finney was a mentor to many in the realm of revival. Pray that God would bring you a Ravenhill or a Hill to teach you the secrets of revival.

— Prayer —

Father, in the name of Jesus, would You bring me a seasoned mentor who can teach me the ways of Your Spirit—and the ways of revival? Even if it's just the right books to read, I want to learn and grow. But please send someone to speak truth into my life so I can grow in the mysteries of revival.

When Prophets Lead Revival

"So the Israelites got rid of their images of Baal and Ashtoreth and worshiped only the Lord" (1 Samuel 7:4).

The Israelites felt like the Lord had abandoned them. The Ark of the Lord was not among them. But they brought it on themselves by breaking the law. Thank God for prophets of revival. In 1 Samuel, the young prophet confronts the people:

"'If you want to return to the Lord with all your hearts, get rid of your foreign gods and your images of Ashtoreth. Turn your hearts to the Lord and obey him alone; then he will rescue you from the Philistines.' So the Israelites got rid of their images of Baal and Ashtoreth and worshiped only the Lord" (1 Sam. 7:3-4).

Samuel told them to gather all of Israel so he could pray for them. The people met him there and Samuel performed a ceremony in which he drew water from a well and poured it out before the Lord. They fasted all day and confessed their sins against the Lord. The enemy saw this as a prime time to attack, and the Philistine rulers gathered their army to advance.

"The Israelites were badly frightened when they learned that the Philistines were approaching. 'Don't stop pleading with the Lord our God to save us from the Philistines!' they begged Samuel" (1 Sam. 7:7-8). Samuel sacrificed a young lamb and prayed—and the Lord answered.

"But the Lord spoke with a mighty voice of thunder from heaven that day, and the Philistines were thrown into such confusion that the Israelites defeated them. The men of Israel chased them from Mizpah to a place below Beth-car, slaughtering them all along the way" (1 Sam. 7:10-11).

That repentance had long-lasting impact. Samuel erected "the stone of help" as a memorial and the Philistines didn't invade Israel again for a long time. During Samuel's lifetime, the Lord's powerful hand was raised against the Philistines. Notice, though, how it all began with desperate repentance.

— Prayer —

Father, in the name of Jesus, would You raise up modern-day prophets and prophetic voices to prepare the way of the Lord of revival? Just as John the Baptist and Samuel paved the way for Your plans and purposes in their day, help me to be a prophetic solutionist in my day.

Common Denominators in Revival

"Call upon Me in the day of trouble; I will deliver you, and you shall glorify Me"
(Psalm 50:15).

The study of Old Testament Revivals offers insights into the conditions of the hearts of people who need revival. Most revivals, for example, came during a time of serious spiritual decline that led to despair. In 2 Chronicles 29-31, we see children sacrificed as burnt offerings to Molech before King Hezekiah's revival.

Every Old Testament revival was birthed in the heart of one person—such as Moses, Samuel, Elijah, Haggai, Josiah, and Nehemiah—before it spread like wildfire. And every single Old Testament revival relied on revisiting and proclaiming the Word of God.

Every Old Testament revival was marked by a deep conviction of sin. Kings tore their robes—and the fear of the Lord fell upon people to the point that they were eager and desperate to separate the profane from the holy in their hearts. Only the Holy Spirit can bring this level of conviction.

Every Old Testament revival was marked by a complete return to obedience and worship of Jehovah, the one true living God. In most cases, that heart turning ultimately led to the complete destruction of idols, Ashtaroth poles, Baal temples and other symbols of idolatry in the land.

Every Old Testament revival saw the return of joy and celebration of God's people. Nehemiah 8:10 is a strong example: "Go your way, eat the fat, drink the sweet, and send portions to those for whom nothing is prepared; for this day is holy to our Lord. Do not sorrow, for the joy of the Lord is your strength."

The conclusion of all this led the nation of Israel into times of peace and prosperity. It's a manifestation of the blessings of obedience listed in Deuteronomy 28. Unfortunately, the revivals didn't last. The nation backslid, grew desperate and needed revival again. Let not that be true of us.

— *Prayer* —

Father, in the name of Jesus, would You help me learn the lessons You left in the pages of Scripture through the chronicles of the Israelites' successes, failures and revivals in the Old Testament? There is such a rich history from which to glean that is relevant for today. Teach me.

The End Times Watchman's Role in Revival

"Son of man, I have made you a watchman for the house of Israel; therefore hear a word from My mouth, and give them warning from Me" (Ezekiel 3:17).

Although much of the end times watchman's role has to do with warnings of the coming judgment, the end times watchman's message is not all doom and gloom. He also has a keen interest in the prophesied end times revival.

The end times watchman calling often comes with discerning of spirits, which is the ability to distinguish between good and evil in the spirit realm. The end times watchman must watch for the King of Glory while watching for dark forces seeking to spoil God's harvest and final revival. He may also have the gifts of prophecy, mercy, and teaching, as I write in my book *The End Times Watchman*.

As the final great harvest and revival approaches, God will call more end times watchmen. The end times watchman will understand the last of the last days are growing near and feel a critical need to pray for the lost to come to the saving grace of Christ. That may manifest as warnings, but it also manifests as prayer for the evangelists to be effective in their assignments and for the word of the Lord to run swiftly through the nations (see 2 Thess. 3:1).

Jesus said, "But when He saw the multitudes, He was moved with compassion for them, because they were weary and scattered, like sheep having no shepherd. Then He said to His disciples, 'The harvest truly is plentiful, but the laborers are few. Therefore pray the Lord of the harvest to send out laborers into His harvest'" (Matthew 9:36-38).

The end times watchman assigned to evangelistic efforts understands well that the harvest is ripe and ready (see John 4:35). He understands that Jesus came to seek and save that which is lost, dying on a cross for the sin of the entire world because He's not willing that any should perish (see Luke 19:10; John 3:16-17).

— *Prayer* —

Father, in the name of Jesus, if You have called me as an end times watchman, help me step into that mantle. Even still, You have charged all believers to watch and pray. So help me watch and pray without ceasing. Help me see what You are doing and what the enemy is trying to do.

Revival is Family

"Now the multitude of those who believed were of one heart and one soul; neither did anyone say that any of the things he possessed was his own, but they had all things in common" (Acts 4:32).

You've probably seen the T-shirts that declare, "Revival is family." It's a true statement, and it's rooted in Scripture.

Richard Baxter, the most prominent English churchman of the 1600s, once said this: "You are not likely to see any general reformation, till you procure family reformation. Some little religion there may be, here and there; but while it is confined to single persons and is not promoted in families, it will not prosper, nor promise much future increase."

Family is important to God. God set the stage for the first family in the Garden of Eden. Scripture says plenty about family. We are supposed to honor our fathers and mothers so we can live long (see Ex. 20:12). We are supposed to train up our children in the way they should go (see Prov. 22:6). But revival goes beyond our blood family to our spiritual family. We are all brothers and sisters in Christ. We are all family.

Revival is family. We see it plainly in the Book of Acts: "And they continued steadfastly in the apostles' doctrine and fellowship, the breaking of bread and prayers. Now all who believed were together and had all things in common and sold their possessions and goods, and divided them among all, as anyone had need" (Acts 2:42, 44-45).

Baxter also said, "If any good be begun by the ministry in any soul, a careless, prayerless, worldly family is likely to stifle it, or very much hinder it…" Indeed, if worldly family can stifle revival, and it can, spiritual family should fuel the flames of revival.

We should, as Paul said, "Consider one another in order to stir up love and good works" (Heb. 10:24). After all, when one part of the Body suffers, we all suffer (see 1 Cor. 12:26). When one falls, we should seek to restore them in a spirit of gentleness (see Gal. 6:1). Revival is family.

— *Prayer* —

Father, in the name of Jesus, would You help me to keep in mind that revival is family? Even if my own family hasn't yet received Your Son, I have a spiritual family that is on one accord. Help me labor with my spiritual family to see a revival sweep through the families of the earth.

AUGUST 25

When Denominations Quench Revival

"For when one says, 'I am of Paul,' and another, 'I am of Apollos,' are you not carnal? Who then is Paul, and who is Apollos, but ministers through whom you believed, as the Lord gave to each one? I planted, Apollos watered, but God gave the increase" (1 Corinthians 3:4-6).

Many years ago, the Holy Spirit told me denominations were a tool the enemy uses to bring division in the church. I found out later that the very definition of denomination is "a division of part of a whole." Selah.

It's been said that Jesus didn't come to start a religion. Well, I don't believe Jesus meant for His body to be sliced and diced into 38,000 disagreeable parts, either.

Denominations can breed a measure—and sometimes a large measure—of disunity because each denomination tends to think it adheres to the truth, the whole truth and nothing but the truth, so help them God.

Many, if not most, believe other denominations are flowing in some sort of error, whether that's speaking in tongues, baptizing in the name of Jesus only rather than in the name of the Father, Son and Holy Ghost, how to receive salvation or the path to heaven, whether or not women can preach or some other doctrine. You know me. If there's major delusions going on, I call it out. But there are many issues over which it's not worth making a mountain out of a molehill.

You don't see denominations in the Book of Acts. There's no pattern for denominations in the Bible that I can find. Jesus never taught us to form sects based on the teachings of any bishop, apostle, prophet, evangelist, pastor or teacher. Rather, Jesus prayed that believers may be one, even as Father, Son and Holy Ghost are one (see John 17:10). Paul actually pled with the church at Corinth not to allow divisions (see 1 Cor. 1:10-13).

Of course, now we have denominations—some 38,000 of them. It's not likely that we will see the end to denominationalism until we see the other side of glory. But let's not be ignorant of the devil's devices. Where there is unity, God command a blessing (see Psalm 133). So that means where there's disunity, the blessing is absent. Revival is a blessing. Let's not allow denominational differences to derail it.

— Prayer —

Father, in the name of Jesus, would You help me not to get caught up in denominational differences that ultimately breed strife? Would You help me to keep an open heart over open-handed differences while standing against error and deception in the church? Bring Your Bride into unity.

Revival Demands Surrender

"Then Jesus said to His disciples, 'If anyone desires to come after Me, let him deny himself, and take up his cross, and follow Me'" (Matthew 16:24).

Martin Luther King, Jr. once said, "Every genuine expression of love grows out of a consistent and total surrender to God." Oh, how true are his words. And we could just as easily say "Every genuine expression of revival grows out of a consistent and total surrender to God."

Jesus made it clear in Matthew 16:25: "For whoever desires to save his life will lose it, but whoever loses his life for My sake will find it." Our lives are not our own. We were bought with a price. But when we forget that, we fail to surrender. When we are not living in surrender, we cannot live in revival.

Consider these questions. Be honest with yourself: Where does God's will rank in your life? Do you ask for His direction, guidance and provision or do you just wake up in the morning and start going about your business? How much do you consider God's will on a daily basis?

When everything is going well do you just chug along without considering the will of God or is He still top of mind? When someone comes to you sharing what God told them to do—and it involves you—do you just go along with it, or ask God what His will is?

If we never ask God what His will is, we are basically telling Him, "I don't need You. I can make it without You." When we live day after day without consulting God about His will and what pleases and honors Him, we are disregarding God. This is a clear violation of Proverbs 3:6, "In all your ways acknowledge Him, and He shall direct your paths."

The other side of the coin is when we know the will of God and choose not to do it. This is rebellion. There is no revival where rebellion rules. The only answer to self-will is to surrender once again. And the way to surrender anew is through repentance. Do you need to repent?

— *Prayer* —

Father, in the name of Jesus, would You help me completely and utterly surrender to Your will? Help me to yield to Your Holy Spirit's leadership. Help me to embrace the truth. Help me remember to acknowledge You and seek Your will in all things before I take a step.

AUGUST 27

Practicing the Presence of God

"O God, You are my God; Early will I seek You; My soul thirsts for You; My flesh longs for You in a dry and thirsty land where there is no water. So I have looked for You in the sanctuary, to see Your power and Your glory" (Psalm 63:1-3).

One of the greatest influences in my walk with God is a seventeenth century lay brother in a Carmelite monastery in Paris. His name was Brother Lawrence.

Brother Lawrence wrote a series of letters that was published as a book called, *The Practice of the Presence of God.* It's a must-have book for everyone who seeks a personal revival and who wants to help spread revival fire. He demystified practicing God's presence. He said things like:

"He does not ask much of us, merely a thought of Him from time to time, a little act of adoration, sometimes to ask for His grace, sometimes to offer Him your sufferings, at other times to thank Him for the graces, past and present, He has bestowed on you, in the midst of your troubles to take solace in Him as often as you can. Lift up your heart to Him during your meals and in company; the least little remembrance will always be the most pleasing to Him. One need not cry out very loudly; He is nearer to us than we think."

And again, "We should fix ourselves firmly in the presence of God by conversing all the time with Him...we should feed our soul with a lofty conception of God and from that derive great joy in being his. We should put life in our faith. We should give ourselves utterly to God in pure abandonment, in temporal and spiritual matters alike, and find contentment in the doing of His will, whether he takes us through sufferings or consolations."

And again, "I cannot imagine how religious persons can live satisfied without the practice of the presence of God. For my part I keep myself retired with Him in the depth of center of my soul as much as I can; and while I am so with Him I fear nothing; but the least turning from Him is insupportable."

What do you say? Are you ready to start practicing?

— *Prayer* —

Father, in the name of Jesus, would You help me to keep You in the center of my focus? Help me to learn the practical lessons Brother Lawrence taught through his experience in choosing to put You first in His life. Help me to practice Your presence every moment of my life.

Revival Fruit that Remains

"And when they had prayed, the place where they were assembled together was shaken; and they were all filled with the Holy Spirit, and they spoke the word of God with boldness"
(John 15:16).

We want revival that bears fruit—and fruit that remains. The first fruit of revival is repentance—a true change of heart that brings lasting results. Put another way, revival is not merely a feeling, a goosebump or deliverance. Revival turns our hearts back to God.

Revival shouldn't be a flash in the pan. It shouldn't be a temporary fix to life's challenges. Revival should bear fruit—and fruit that remains. It should compel us to share with others the fire of God that touched our hearts and changed our lives.

Jesus said, "You did not choose Me, but I chose you and appointed you that you should go and bear fruit, and that your fruit should remain, that whatever you ask the Father in My name He may give you" (John 15:16).

What is the key to bearing fruit that remains? That's found in Christ's words recorded in John 15:4-7: "Abide in Me, and I in you. As the branch cannot bear fruit of itself, unless it abides in the vine, neither can you, unless you abide in Me.

"I am the vine, you are the branches. He who abides in Me, and I in him, bears much fruit; for without Me you can do nothing. If anyone does not abide in Me, he is cast out as a branch and is withered; and they gather them and throw them into the fire, and they are burned. If you abide in Me, and My words abide in you, you will ask what you desire, and it shall be done for you."

Fruit that remains is fruit that lasts the test of time. It's fruit that's visible long after the outpouring has ceased. It's a heart that contends for the next outpouring for the sake of those who haven't tasted and seen how good the Lord is. Fruit that remains is lasting fruit. It's fruit that is ripe but doesn't rot. It's fruit that abides as we abide in Christ.

— *Prayer* —

Father, in the name of Jesus, would You give me the grace to continually abide in You so I can bear fruit that remains? I don't want to be busy with the world's work. I want to be fruitful in Kingdom work. Help me abide in You, draw from Your life source, and follow Your leadership.

AUGUST 29

A Fresh Outpouring

"Rain down, you heavens, from above, and let the skies pour down righteousness; Let the earth open, let them bring forth salvation, and let righteousness spring up together. I, the Lord, have created it" (Isaiah 45:8).

Many times, I hear people crying out for a fresh outpouring in their churches. That's a wonderful prayer, but the revivalist should seek a fresh personal infilling before they cry out for a fresh corporate outpouring.

Yes, sometimes, we need to get refilled with the Spirit. Paul suggests this in his Spirit-inspired words in Ephesians 5:18-19: "And do not be drunk with wine, in which is dissipation; but be filled with the Spirit, speaking to one another in psalms and hymns and spiritual songs, singing and making melody in your heart to the Lord."

The Holy Spirit's outpouring into hungry believers for His service wasn't restricted to the day of Pentecost. We see several infillings in the pages of Scripture. Two chapters after the Upper Room encounter, we see Peter and John releasing the power of the Holy Spirit in the name of Jesus to heal a lame man at the Gate beautiful. They were arrested and stood before the Pharisees. We read this in Acts 4:7-12:

"And when they had set them in the midst, they asked, 'By what power or by what name have you done this?' Then Peter, filled with the Holy Spirit, said to them, 'Rulers of the people and elders of Israel: If we this day are judged for a good deed done to a helpless man, by what means he has been made well, let it be known to you all, and to all the people of Israel, that by the name of Jesus Christ of Nazareth, whom you crucified, whom God raised from the dead, by Him this man stands here before you whole."

The result of this infilling was not speaking in tongues, which he already received, but a new boldness. When Peter and John were released, they returned to their own company, told them what happened, and held a prayer meeting. Guess what happened? The place they were assembled shook and they were all filled with the Holy Spirit (see Acts 4:1).

— *Prayer* —

Father, in the name of Jesus, I want to move in Your power continually. That means I need a continual flow of the rivers of living water into me so they can flow out of me wherever You send me. Would You give me boldness to press in for revival against all opposition? Fill me with Your boldness.

The Revivalist's Power Source

"But you shall receive power when the Holy Spirit has come upon you; and you shall be witnesses to Me in Jerusalem, and in all Judea and Samaria, and to the end of the earth" (Acts 1:8).

Like D.L. Moody, you may be an eloquent preacher but without Holy Ghost power you will only be so effective. You need the baptism of the Holy Spirit.

Jesus knew this, and told the disciples, "I will pray the Father, and He will give you another Helper, that He may abide with you forever—the Spirit of truth, whom the world cannot receive, because it neither sees Him nor knows Him; but you know Him, for He dwells with you and will be in you" (John 14:16-17).

Doubtless, the disciples did not fully understand what Jesus meant. After He ascended to the right hand of the Father, Jesus appeared to the disciples once again and "commanded them not to depart from Jerusalem, but to wait for the Promise of the Father, 'which,' He said, 'you have heard from Me; for John truly baptized with water, but you shall be baptized with the Holy Spirit not many days from now'" (Acts 1:4-5).

Jesus told them they would receive power when the Holy Spirit came upon them (see Acts 1:8). And Holy Spirit power is what they received. They were officially empowered as revival carriers in the Upper Room. R.A. Torrey, an early 20th Century American evangelist, pastor, educator and writer, offered these wise words about the baptism of the Holy Spirit:

"There are certainly few greater mistakes that we are making today, than that of setting men to teach Sunday school classes, and do personal work, and even to preach the Gospel, simply because they have been converted and received a certain amount of education—perhaps including a college and seminary course—but have not as yet been baptized with the Holy Spirit," he said.

"Any man who is in Christian work, who has not received the baptism with the Holy Spirit, ought to stop his work right where he is, and not go on with it until he has been 'clothed with power from on high.'"

— *Prayer* —

Father, I surrender full control of my life to You. I ask You even now to fill me to overflowing with Your Spirit, just as You have promised to do if I ask according to Your will. I ask this in the name of Jesus and believe that You are pouring out your Spirit upon me right now.

AUGUST 31

The George Mueller Revivalist Anointing

"Until now you have asked nothing in My name. Ask, and you will receive, that your joy may be full" (John 16:24).

George Mueller, a nineteenth century Christian evangelist known for building orphanages, once said: "It is not enough to begin to pray, nor to pray aright; nor is it enough to continue for a time to pray; but we must pray patiently, believing, continue in prayer until we obtain an answer."

Born in 1805, Mueller's ministry was birthed in a "Cottage Prayer Meeting" just like Paul and Barnabas' mission was birthed while believers ministered to the Lord in Acts 13. He wasn't known as a circuit rider who preached fire and brimstone or a theologian who could share the Gospel with conviction. No, Mueller was known as a man of faith and prayer.

Indeed, George Mueller's *Narrative*, which chronicles story after story of God's provision in his ministry, is credited with igniting revival fires in Ireland. A contemporary of D.L. Moody, Mueller traveled to London, Glasgow, Dublin, Liverpool and beyond following up Moody's revival work with teachings that discipled new believers.

Mueller believed he saw the answers to fifty thousand prayers in his lifetime. He once said, "I believe God has heard my prayers. He will make it manifest in His own good time that He has heard me. I have recorded my petitions that when God has answered them, His name will be glorified."

Mueller lived in a spirit of prayer and wasn't bashful about it. In fact, he confessed, "I live in the spirit of prayer. I pray as I walk about, when I lie down and when I rise up. And the answers are always coming." He said, "The joy which answers to prayer give, cannot be described; and the impetus which they afford to the spiritual life is exceedingly great."

— *Prayer* —

Father, in the name of Jesus, make me into a praying revivalist. It's not enough to seek revival, I know I need to live in a spirit of prayer. Would You give me an unction and anointing like You gave George Mueller to pray, do works of justice, and make disciples in the midst of revival?

SEPTEMBER

"There is need of a great revival of spiritual life, of truly fervent devotion to our Lord Jesus, of entire consecration to His service. It is only in a church in which this spirit of revival has at least begun, that there is any hope of radical change in the relation of the majority of our Christian people to mission work."—Andrew Murray

SEPTEMBER 1

When Complacency is Like a Cancer

"For the turning away of the simple will slay them, and the complacency of fools will destroy them" (Proverbs 1:32).

"Complacency is the deadly enemy of spiritual progress. The contented soul is the stagnant soul. When speaking of earthly goods Paul could say, 'I have learned to be content,' but when referring to his spiritual life he testified, 'I press on toward the mark.' So stir up the gift of God that is in thee." Those are the words of A.W. Tozer, a preacher and magazine editor from the mid-1900s.

What is complacency? Self-satisfaction—and it's a deception. We can never satisfy ourselves. Only God can satisfy us. There's a hole in our hearts and only He can fill it. Complacency is like the snake in the garden—the deception is subtle. So how do you discern it?

We are complacent when we have every excuse in the world why we don't have time to get in the Word of God—and when we spend more time on our outward appearance than our inner appearance. Peter said, "Don't be concerned about the outward beauty of fancy hairstyles, expensive jewelry, or beautiful clothes. You should clothe yourselves instead with the beauty that comes from within, the unfading beauty of a gentle and quiet spirit, which is so precious to God" (1 Pet. 3:3-4).

We are complacent when we plow through our days without praying and acknowledging God; when we skip church to sleep in because we were out late the night before; when we are content to sit in a dead church where the Holy Spirit is shut up in a closet; when we're no longer sensitive to the Spirit of God, the voice of God, or the conviction of God; and when we get offended with preaching that challenges us out to get of our comfort zone.

Jesus was talking to complacent Christians in Revelation 3:15-16 when He said, "I know your works, that you are neither cold nor hot. I could wish you were cold or hot. So then, because you are lukewarm, and neither cold nor hot, I will vomit you out of My mouth."

Are you complacent?

— *Prayer* —

Father, in the name of Jesus, forgive me for any and every way that I have waxed complacent. I don't want to be lukewarm or cold. I don't want to be apathetic and unconcerned. I want to be like Jesus when He walked the earth—He was always about Your business, and He was fervent in prayer.

268

The Black Woman Who Breathed Revival

"A woman who fears the Lord, she shall be praised" (Proverbs 31:30).

There's a lot of talk about William Seymour, the central figure of the Azusa Street Revival, and there should be. But have you heard of Elder Lucy? Her name was Lucy Turner Smith and she was the founder and pastor of All Nations Pentecostal Church in Chicago—a church that is still standing today.

Elder Lucy was the first black woman to pastor a megachurch in Chicago. She was not loud or flashy when she preached. She walked in a peace, though, that attracted the Holy Spirit—and thousands of hungry people—into her meetings.

As history tells it, Elder Lucy witnessed about two hundred thousand miracles in her ministry. Indeed, she decorated the walls of her church with crutches and wheelchairs that once belonged to the sick. It was a sight to see!

Elder Lucy started her ministry with a one-room prayer meeting in her home with only two people. She wasn't concerned with the numbers because she had a revelation of Matthew 18:20, "For where two or three are gathered together in my name, there am I in the midst of them."

Her one-room prayer meeting didn't stay small for long, though. Within three years she moved into a larger space. In 1926, at the ten-year mark of her ministry, she built a $65,000 facility—that's $1 million in today's terms. Attendance hit about five thousand by the 1930s. Keep in mind this was in the middle of the Great Depression.

The three-hundred-pound faith healer was a woman of firsts. She was the first to broadcast a radio program from a black church in 1933—and people sent in letters testifying to the healing power of God touching them from a distance. When she went on to glory in 1952, over sixty thousand people came to her memorial service.

— *Prayer* —

Father, in the name of Jesus, people like Elder Lucy inspire me. Help me not to allow economic conditions or societal demands sway me from Your high calling on my life. Help me to stay steady in what You've called me to do against all odds for Your glory. Give me determination like Elder Lucy.

SEPTEMBER 3

Calling a Collective Fast

"So the people of Nineveh believed God, proclaimed a fast, and put on sackcloth, from the greatest to the least of them" (Jonah 3:5).

Sometimes, fasting alone is not enough. In the same way that one can put a thousand to flight and two can put ten thousand to flight, there are dynamics of the collective fast that gets God's attention.

Indeed, collective fasting—along with united prayer, the Holy Spirit's supernatural gifts, and public praise and worship—become weapons to gain victories that are both powerful and dramatic, according to the late Derek Prince. Esther called a corporate fast during a life-and-death situation. You know the story:

Esther's uncle Mordecai learned that wicked Haman was plotting to wipe out the Jewish race, of which she was a part. He wanted her to approach the king and plead for her people. At first, she was fearfully reluctant, but Mordecai warned her that if she didn't speak up she would not escape Haman's plot.

"Then Esther told them to reply to Mordecai: 'Go, gather all the Jews who are present in Shushan, and fast for me; neither eat nor drink for three days, night or day. My maids and I will fast likewise. And so I will go to the king, which is against the law; and if I perish, I perish!'" (Esther 4:15-16). Long story short. Haman was exposed and the Jews were saved in response to the collective fast and prayer.

Ezra the priest also called a collective fast for protection. Ezra 8:21-23 reads: "Then I proclaimed a fast there at the river of Ahava, that we might humble ourselves before our God, to seek from Him the right way for us and our little ones and all our possessions.

"For I was ashamed to request of the king an escort of soldiers and horsemen to help us against the enemy on the road, because we had spoken to the king, saying, 'The hand of our God is upon all those for good who seek Him, but His power and His wrath are against all those who forsake Him.' So we fasted and entreated our God for this, and He answered our prayer." And God answered.

— *Prayer* —

Father, in the name of Jesus, would You give me a deeper revelation of the power of a collective fast to break chains, disrupt the enemy's plans, rescue souls and even birth revival? Help me find those with whom You would lead me to fast with for the revival You want to bring.

When Revival Births a Church

"Confess your trespasses to one another, and pray for one another, that you may be healed"
(James 5:16).

It was 1908 and revival was in the air. Azusa Street and the Welsh Revival were the headline-making outpourings but there were revival sparks the world over. Manchuria, which was controlled by imperial Japan at the time, was one of them.

God used Jonathan Goforth, a missionary to China, to birth the Manchurian Revival in prayer. Reading about the fire in the Welsh Revival inspired him. He was also an eyewitness to the Pyongyang Revival in 1907. In his hunger to see souls saved and the nation awakened, he pressed into intercession for God to move in China the way He did in Wales and Korea. Basically, his cry was, "Do it again, Lord!"

After much resistance, Goforth broke through in prayer. The result was a deep conviction among the Chinese. A single message under the anointing of the Spirit led an elder to confess he kept some of the church money for himself during the Boxer Rebellion. That led to godly sorrow in the congregation of nearly one thousand people that lasted four days. One by one, church elders and deacons confessed their sins publicly.

The unknown author of *Days of Grace in Manchuria*, wrote, "The point of Mr. Goforth's message on which the emphasis rested was this 'It is not by might, nor by power, but by My Spirit, saith the Lord.'

"This doctrine, presented in many aspects, reiterated and amply illustrated, certainly formed the distinguishing theme of Mr. Goforth's ministry in Manchuria. The holiness of God, the exceeding sinfulness and destructive nature of sin, the absolute helplessness of man without God's Holy Spirit, the possibility, of keeping back the Holy Spirit from working His miraculous work in and through us—these were the preacher's principal subjects."

Keep in mind Goforth did not call for a public confession of sins. It was the Holy Spirit who led people to confess idolatry, theft, murder, adultery, gambling, opium smoking, disobedience to parents, hatred, quarreling, lying, cheating, fraud, division, resistance to the Spirit, and indifference to the salvation of souls. But it wasn't just revival for revival's sake. The revival birthed the Manchurian Chinese Church.

— *Prayer* —

Father, in the name of Jesus, I see Your pattern to birth churches through revival. Help me understand that when revival comes—when the Great Awakening floods the earth—we will need more churches than we have. Help me to be a champion for unity in the church and abolish competition.

SEPTEMBER 5

When the Enemies of Revival Repent

"For a great and effective door has opened to me, and there are many adversaries"
(1 Corinthians 16:9).

Jonathan Goforth, the missionary to China who birthed the Manchurian Revival in prayer, experienced great grief before his ministry spurred a great outpouring. Five of his eleven children died in sickness.

Goforth himself suffered a sword attack during the Boxer Rebellion just a few years earlier. But at least he survived. Many of the thirty-two thousand Chinese who participated in the prayer movement lost their lives. So did one hundred eighty-eight foreign missionaries and their children.

Understanding the severity of the assignment through personal experience, Hudson Taylor, the great missionary to China, commissioned Goforth with these words:

"We understand North Honan is to be your field; we, as a mission, have tried for ten years to enter that province from the south, and have only just succeeded. It is one of the most anti-foreign provinces in China . . . Brother, if you would enter that province, you must go forward on your knees."

And so he did. Goforth was a man who met with and overcame opposition to revival. When he faced trouble with the hosts of his meetings in Mukden, he prayed and asked God, "What is the use of coming here? These people are not seeking after Thee. They have no desire for blessing. What can I do?"

Goforth tells how the Lord responded to him, "Is it yours or Mine? Can I not do a sovereign work?" In that moment, Jeremiah 33:3 was impressed on his heart: "Call to Me, and I will answer you, and show you great and mighty things, which you do not know."

Goforth persevered and eventually those who opposed him started supporting him. It was the manifestation of Proverbs 16:7, "When a person's ways are pleasing to the Lord, He causes even his enemies to make peace with him."

— Prayer —

Father, in the name of Jesus, would You give me an apostolic grit like Jonathan Goforth so I can take a stand against the opposition to the revival You want to bring into my territory? I want see souls saved, churches revived and nations awakened. Use me.

SEPTEMBER 6

A Plea for the Spirit of Prayer

"So he went up and looked, and said, 'There is nothing.' And seven times, he said, 'Go again'"
(1 Kings 18:43).

With every revival finding its genesis in prayer, we can safely conclude one reason we don't see more revival is because we don't see enough prayer. We need the spirit of prayer.

The Holy Spirit is the spirit of prayer. Charles Finney, a preacher and intercessor, understood this all too well. He once wrote, "If people know not the spirit of prayer, they are very apt to be unbelieving in regard to the results of prayer. They do not see what takes place, or do not see the connection, or do not see the evidence. They are not expecting spiritual blessings."

The spirit of prayer is an anointing that helps us pray effectively and without ceasing. We may start out in the flesh but when we repent of our sins and lift up the name of Jesus, we attract the Holy Helper into our intercession. He begins to work with us to release perfect petitions. Indeed, we must press into a deeper revelation of our need for the spirit of prayer so we won't release vain repetitions.

In the book *Days of Grace in Manchuria*, an unknown author who chronicled the Manchurian Revival, wrote these poignant words of confirmation:

"The spirit of prayer has been wonderfully manifest. Sometimes half a dozen would start at once, and on one occasion the entire congregation of seven or eight hundred people were all praying together. But there was not the slightest feeling of discord. One felt they were all of one heart and one mind. The spirit of giving offerings has been wonderful. Men have promised land and houses, as well as money, to the Lord's cause. I don't know how many offered to give part of their time to voluntary service for the Master."

The Holy Spirit made it clear that we need His help to make intercession. We would do well, as we set out praying, to let one of our first prayers be, "Lord, let Your spirit of prayer descend upon me."

— *Prayer* —

Father, in the name of Jesus, give me a spirit of prayer. Indeed, let the spirit of prayer rest upon me so I can pray effective, fervent prayers for revival according to Your will. Let the spirit of prayer fall upon me so I can pray without ceasing for revival when my natural strength fails me.

273

SEPTEMBER 7

Don't Run Out of Oil

"There is desirable treasure, and oil in the dwelling of the wise..." (Proverbs 21:20).

In prolonged revivals, revivalists need to be careful not to run out of oil. We have to keep our lamps burning so others can see the path to revival. If we run out of oil—if we don't press into a fresh anointing day by day—we won't have anything to pour out to hungry souls. Even worse, we will eventually burn out.

Jesus was clear on the need to keep oil in our lamps. Consider the Parable of the Wise and Foolish Virgins. We could, for sake of our discussion, call it the Parable of the Wise and Foolish Revivalists. Matthew 25:1-13 warns us:

"Then the kingdom of heaven shall be likened to ten virgins who took their lamps and went out to meet the bridegroom. Now five of them were wise, and five *were* foolish. Those who were foolish took their lamps and took no oil with them, but the wise took oil in their vessels with their lamps. But while the bridegroom was delayed, they all slumbered and slept.

"And at midnight a cry was heard: 'Behold, the bridegroom is coming; go out to meet him!' Then all those virgins arose and trimmed their lamps. And the foolish said to the wise, 'Give us some of your oil, for our lamps are going out.' But the wise answered, saying, 'No, lest there should not be enough for us and you; but go rather to those who sell, and buy for yourselves.' And while they went to buy, the bridegroom came, and those who were ready went in with him to the wedding; and the door was shut.

"Afterward the other virgins came also, saying, 'Lord, Lord, open to us!' But he answered and said, 'Assuredly, I say to you, I do not know you.'"

Do you need some fresh oil? Don't waste another minute. Start cultivating the oil of intimacy now. Invest your time with Him. Sow to the Spirit. It's worth spending the time now to see a continual flow of oil later.

— Prayer —

Father, in the name of Jesus, would You release fresh oil on my life? I need the oil of Your anointing to continue in the work of revival. There is so much at stake. Apart from You I can do nothing, but with You I can do all things. Anoint me to do the impossible for the sake of souls.

SEPTEMBER 8

Cultivating the Oil of Intimacy

"For your love is better than wine" (Song 1:2).

One symbol of the Holy Spirit in Scripture is oil. The oil is symbolic of the Holy Spirit touching our minds and hearts as we spend time with Him.

Mike Bickle taught me this oil touches our hearts in at least four ways: It tenderizes our heart, making us able to feel more of God's desire for us. It makes us hungrier for Him as we encounter His perfect love for us. It opens our understanding and gives us revelation of His magnificent beauty. And it imparts zeal to live holy and righteous, which helps us overcome besetting sins.

We must not pursue revival at the expense of pursuing His heart. God is always our first priority. Everything else flows out of our relationship with Him. Now is the time to cultivate the oil of intimacy in your life—to invest in a deeper relationship with the Holy Spirit—so we can stay steady in revival.

Just as Moses used oil to anoint the priests and consecrate them for service, we need to set ourselves apart to receive His anointing so we can faithfully execute His call on our lives.

So how do you cultivate that intimacy with God? In a word, spend time fellowshipping with His Spirit and in His word. You might say we buy the oil with our time. Understand how beautiful He is, how much He loves you, and your utter dependence on Him.

Reading the Song of Solomon reveals the love God has for us in a beautiful allegory. In our pursuit of the oil of intimacy, we need to gain a revelation of Jesus as not only King and Judge, but also Bridegroom.

Song of Songs 4:9-10 reads, "You have ravished my heart, my sister, my bride; you have ravished my heart with one glance of your eyes, with one jewel of your necklace. How fair is your love, my sister, my bride! How much better than wine is your love, and the fragrance of your oils than any spice!"

— Prayer —

Father, in the name of Jesus, give me a hunger and thirst for You. I want to go deeper into Your heart. I want to know You more. Help me press past the distractions of the world and the works of the flesh and enter into the joy of my Lord. Help me cultivate the oil of intimacy.

SEPTEMBER 9

A Prayer Orchestra

"So when they heard that, they raised their voice to God with one accord and said: 'Lord, You are God, who made heaven and earth and the sea, and all that is in them'" (Acts 4:24).

Willis C. Hoover, an American Methodist, may have seemed an unlikely candidate to birth a revival in Chile, but he answered the call as a missionary and was faithful to the assignment. In 1889, Hoover launched his ministry there teaching English in a city named Iquique. In 1902, he took the pastorate of a church in Valparaiso. In 1909 a unique revival broke out.

How did it happen? With a new church building half-way constructed, he called for an all-night prayer meeting on New Year's Eve 1908. What happened next surprised him—but it didn't surprise the Spirit of God.

"We observed, as we had ever done, the evangelical week of prayer. On the first prayer night a strange thing happened. After the usual preliminary exercises the usual call to prayer was given; but instead of the usual successive response of prayer by one and then another and another, the whole congregation, numbering above a hundred persons, broke forth simultaneously in audible prayer," wrote Hoover.

"It was an astonishing thing, but there was given the comforting assurance that God was pleased with us; for we were seeking a revival and the baptism with the Holy Spirit; and here God was meeting us in the very beginning. This prayer lasted ten or fifteen minutes and the 'sound as of many waters' subsided. This experience was repeated now and again."

Two weeks later, a man in Hoover's church had a vision of Jesus with a message to Hoover: "Go to your pastor and tell him to call some of the more spiritual brothers and tell them to pray every day, because I am going to baptize them with tongues of fire."

Five people met to pray the next day and committed to meeting every day at 5 p.m. to pray until the prophecy was fulfilled, sort of like the believers in the Upper Room before the day of Pentecost. That evolved into Saturday night prayer meetings that went on until dawn. By mid-April, revival broke out marked by weeping and laughter and groaning in the spirit. And the revival fires spread throughout Chile.

— Prayer —

Father, in the name of Jesus, would You help me step out in faith to follow You down the path to revival, even if I don't see the whole blueprint? Help me walk by faith into revival one step at a time, one day at a time. Fill me to overflowing with Your Spirit so my dedicated life influences others.

Revival Manifestations Revealed

"For these are not drunk, as you suppose, since it is only the third hour of the day" (Acts 2:15).

While some manifestations in revival can be pure emotion, there are authentic manifestations of the Spirit in revivals that are worth noting.

For example, in the 1909 Chile Revival, manifestations included a powerful conviction of sin—which is part and parcel with most revivals. Other manifestations included laughter, weeping, shouts, singing, speaking in tongues, visions, trances, visits to heaven, speaking with Jesus or angels, joy, praise, prayer, love, and the fruit of the Spirit multiplied in the lives of believers present.

David Brainerd, an American missionary to Native Americans, once wrote this in his journal regarding revival manifestations: "And as there has been no room for any plausible objection against this work, in regard of the means; so neither in regard of the manner in which it has been carried on.

"It is true, persons concern for their souls has been exceeding great, the convictions of their sin and misery have risen to a high degree, and produced many tears, cries, and groans: but then they have not been attended with those disorders, either bodily or mental, that have sometimes prevailed among persons under religious impressions.

"There has here been no appearance of those convulsions, bodily agonies, frightful screaming, swooning, and the like, that have been so much complained of in some places; although there have been some who, with the jailer, have been made to tremble under a sense of their sin and misery—numbers who have been made to cry out from a distressing view of their perishing state—and some that have been, for a time, in a great measure, deprived of their bodily strength, yet without any such convulsive appearances."

Yes, there can be fanaticism, emotionalism, and even demonic manifestations in the midst of revival. There's nothing wrong with excitement. In fact, when the Holy Spirit shows up you can expect excitement. People make shake or tremble, appear drunk in the spirit, fall under the power of the Spirit, enter travail and more. Let's be careful not to label true fire as strange fire.

— *Prayer* —

Father, in the name of Jesus, help me never to criticize a manifestation of Your Spirit moving upon someone because I don't understand it—or because it seems contrary to my experience. In fact, help me Lord to be more concerned with what You are doing and what You want to do.

SEPTEMBER 11

Revival Prostrations

"Oh come, let us worship and bow down; Let us kneel before the Lord our Maker"
(Psalm 95:6).

Doubtless, you've seen people laying prostrate on the ground during worship or prayer. This is biblical—and can be a manifestation of revival.

Moses was known to fall on his face (see Num. 20:6). The angels in heaven lay prostrate (see Rev. 7:11). Abram fell on his face before God (see Gen. 7:13). The Israelites fell on their faces (see Lev. 9:24). Even Jesus lay prostrate in the Garden of Gethsemane (see Luke 5:12).

Speaking of the Lewis Revival—a revival in the Island of Lewis in 1949-1952, evangelist Duncan Campbell wrote these words:

"I have seen this happen over and over again during the recent movement in the Western Isles. Suddenly an awareness of God would take hold of a community, and, under the pressure of this divine presence, men and women would fall prostrate on the ground, while their cry of distress was made the means in God's hand, to awaken the indifferent who had set unmoved for years under the preaching of the Gospel.

"I have known men out in the fields, others at their weaving looms, so overcome by this sense of God that they were found prostrate on the ground. Physical manifestations and prostrations have been a further feature. I find it somewhat difficult to explain this aspect, indeed I cannot; but this I will say, that the person who would associate this with satanic influence is coming perilously near committing the unpardonable sin.

"Lady Huntingdon on one occasion wrote to George Whitefield respecting cases of crying out and falling down in meetings, and advised him not to remove them from the meetings, as had been done. When this was done it seemed to bring a dampener on the meeting. She said, 'You are making a great mistake. Don't be wiser than God. Let them cry out; it will do a great deal more good than your preaching.'"

— Prayer —

Father, in the name of Jesus, teach me how to focus on You to the point that I will lay on my face in Your presence and get caught up in Your Spirit. Help me not to pay attention to what others around me may be doing, but to focus solely on Your face and Your voice and get lost in holy moments.

278

Is This Holding Back Revival?

"Let all bitterness, wrath, anger, clamor, and evil speaking be put away from you, with all malice" (Ephesians 4:31).

If you are reading these words, I know you are believing God for a mighty revival. I know you are praying for a Great Awakening. But let me ask you a sobering question: Are you harboring unforgiveness in your heart?

In 2016, The Holy Spirit showed one of the reasons why we haven't seen the next great move of God is because of all the resentment, bitterness and unforgiveness in the church. So many members of the Body are holding grudges against other members of the Body.

While we don't need the entire Body of Christ on fire to see a Third Great Awakening—every great revival always started with two or three people—some who are laboring in prayer for transforming revival aren't heard in heaven because of the hardness of their heart.

Indeed, when you don't forgive, it affects your prayer life—God won't hear your prayers when you walk in unforgiveness. In Mark 11:25, Jesus tells us, "And whenever you stand praying, if you find that you carry something in your heart against another person, release him and forgive him so that your Father in heaven will also release you and forgive you of your faults."

When you don't forgive, your spirit is dull. In other words, you are not fully awake spiritually. It's time for us to search our hearts to see if there is any unforgiveness, bitterness or even the slightest residue of resentment in our hearts toward anyone—or anything. It's time to forgive.

In Matthew 6:14-15, Jesus said, "For if you forgive men when they sin against you, your heavenly Father will also forgive you. But if you do not forgive men their trespasses, neither will your Father forgive your trespasses."

Ask yourself this question: What if the Lord forgave you in the same proportion that you forgive the people who hurt you? What if someone died and went to hell because you didn't share the love of God in your bitterness. Selah.

— *Prayer* —

Father, in the name of Jesus, I choose to forgive all who abused me, accused me, or harmed me in any way. My relationship with You is the most important thing in my life and I don't want to grieve Your heart. I want You to hear and answer my revival prayers. Give me the grace to forgive.

SEPTEMBER 13

When the Holy Spirit Rocked Mockers

"Oh, the joys of those who do not follow the advice of the wicked, or stand around with sinners, or join in with mockers" (Psalm 1:1).

With Catholic strongholds in Latin America, it seems the Holy Spirit was intent on giving Jesus the preeminence there. In 1925 Venezuela, a great revival swept South America during the fifth anniversary of G. F. Bender's church in Barquisimento. That revival saw Catholics turn away from Mary to the true Savior. Barquisimento writes:

"The revival did not break out with the Baptism in the Holy Ghost and speaking in other tongues; it started with such deep conviction for sin that the people all thought they were lost. For almost a month they wept and cried to God, paid their debts, and got all grudges out of the way. I said: 'Oh, Lord, this looks like the real thing.'

"In a Tuesday afternoon prayer meeting there fell on the audience such conviction, such weeping and moaning and crying out for sin, and we just let them cry on. Two of them wept their way through to God that afternoon, and when they came through they had the whole neighborhood together. The people came running to see what was happening in the Protestant church. They call us 'devils,' and they wanted to see what had happened among 'the devils.'

"About that time, these two women that had broken through, turned on the crowd and exalted Jesus Christ and His Blood, and told them that the virgin Mary could not save them. How those two women preached that afternoon! We could not close the meeting so we let it go on, and we went about our work. And that kept up until two days before our fifth anniversary. Wrongs were righted, they sought their enemies and humbled themselves before then."

We need to see a revival that will bring Catholics, Buddhists, Muslims, Hindus, Mormons, Freemasons, Christian Scientists, Scientologists, Humanists, Atheists and Satanists firmly into the Kingdom of God.

— *Prayer* —

Father, in the name of Jesus, would You give me a heart for religious people groups the enemy has deceived? Many people follow a path that leads to destruction while feeling secure in their religiosity. Give me a heart to pray for revival among those following the wrong path.

United for Revival

"Behold, how good and how pleasant it is for brethren to dwell together in unity!"
(Psalm 133:1)

There's so much strife and division in the Body of Christ. We see denominational strife, prophetic strife, theological strife and more. Paul was clear in his admonition:

"Now I plead with you, brethren, by the name of our Lord Jesus Christ, that you all speak the same thing, and that there be no divisions among you, but that you be perfectly joined together in the same mind and in the same judgment" (1 Cor. 1:10)

Read that again. Paul was pleading with the church at Corinth. There was no such pleading with people in the Upper Room. The disciples instead pled in unison for the promise of the Father—the Holy Spirit. When the disciples were waiting on the promise of the Holy Spirit, there was no strife. There was unity, then there was revival. Let Acts 2:1-4 serve as a reminder.

"On the day Pentecost was being fulfilled, all the disciples were gathered in one place. Suddenly they heard the sound of a violent blast of wind rushing into the house from out of the heavenly realm. The roar of the wind was so overpowering it was all anyone could bear!

"Then all at once a pillar of fire appeared before their eyes. It separated into tongues of fire that engulfed each one of them. They were all filled and equipped with the Holy Spirit and were inspired to speak in tongues—empowered by the Spirit to speak in languages they had never learned!"

When we unify under the banner of Jesus, it attracts the Holy Spirit. The reality is, we probably all have some points of doctrine that are incorrect. Unless it's serious error and heresy, we can set aside those points and pray together. When we stop the name calling and call out to Father in the name above all names—the name of Jesus—then we'll see the outpouring of the Holy Spirit and revival in our churches.

— *Prayer* —

Father, in the name of Jesus, help me lay aside my personal biases and preferences and adopt Your bias for souls and Your preference for a church on fire. Forgive me if I have operated in strife and give me the grace of humility to prefer others in honor. Make me an agent of unity.

SEPTEMBER 15

The William Booth Revivalist Anointing

"Then He will answer them, saying, 'Assuredly, I say to you, inasmuch as you did not do it to one of the least of these, you did not do it to Me'" (Matthew 25:45).

He and his family were key players in 19th Century revivals. And his name still marks humanitarian missions today. General William Booth, a Methodist minister, founded The Salvation Army in 1865 with a mission to bring salvation to the poor, destitute and hungry by meeting their physical and spiritual needs.

"While women weep, as they do now, I'll fight. While little children go hungry, as they do now, I'll fight," Booth said. "While men go to prison, in and out, in and out, as they do now, I'll fight. While there is a drunkard left, while there is a poor lost girl upon the streets, while there remains one dark soul without the light of God, I'll fight. I'll fight to the very end!"

Booth and his wife Catherine became traveling revivalists. In *The Life of William Booth*, Harold Begbie writes, "His popularity was embarrassing, his success as a revivalist amazing and all the accounts of that time show him as a fiery preacher, not only able to crowd and pack large buildings with a breathless audience; not only able to sway the emotions of enormous congregations but able to permanently change the lives of sinful men.

"In the middle of his successes, where he was compared with John Wesley, William would drop into despair again and again. Part of this was his indigestion, but more probably because he was harassed, criticized and opposed by the Church. Some did not like the emotionalism, some thought he was too young and some were jealous. As a passionate revivalist the rigors of so much preaching would have worn out a very healthy man, let alone a man like William."

Today, the organization has a membership of over 1.7 million. One of Booth's famous quotes, "You cannot warm the hearts of people with God's love if they have an empty stomach and cold feet." Amen!

— *Prayer* —

Father, in the name of Jesus, would You help me advocate for a people group that You have assigned me to? I want to do works of justice that pave the way for people to see Jesus through me. Would You give me an anointing like the anointing that rested on General William Booth?

May College Awakenings Arise

"Rejoice, O young man, in your youth, and let your heart cheer you in the days of your youth"
(Ecclesiastes 11:9).

The Collegiate Day of Prayer, a united, multi-generational day of prayer for revival and awakening on college campuses in America, is over two hundred years old. I firmly believe campus awakenings were birthed through these organized prayer meetings.

"Throughout American history our colleges have been repeatedly blessed and transformed by intense seasons of spiritual awakening. The early records of many of our best universities read like a virtual history of spiritual revival. In fact, no other nation has ever enjoyed as many student awakenings for as many consecutive years as the United States of America," according to The Collegiate Day of Prayer.

In the United States alone, we've seen numerous college revivals. Revival historian Edwin Orr recorded many such revival during 1949 and 1950. In fact, he cites over a dozen college campus revivals in the U.S. in during that period.

Perhaps the best remembered is the Wheaton College revival that lasted nearly a week. A deep recognition of God's holiness led to deep conviction of sin. *Time* magazine reported on one meeting that lasted forty-two hours.

"Singly and in little groups, sweatered and blue-jeaned undergraduates streamed onto the stage, filling up the choir chairs to await their turn. Hour after hour they kept coming," *Time* reported. "All night long, all the next day, all through the following night, and half the following day, students poured out confessions of past sins and rededicated themselves to God."

In that same year, Lee College in Cleveland, Tenn. saw an outpouring with conviction and confession as well as the gifts of the Holy Spirit manifesting through teachers and students alike. While this was occurring, we saw Wilmore, Kentucky's Asbury College break out in revival. It started as a holy hush followed by the power of the Spirit of God blowing through the place. We've seen more revivals in the sixties, seventies, and even in the 2020s. Do it again, Lord!

— *Prayer* —

Father, in the name of Jesus, do it again on college campuses! Pour out Your Spirit and heal a generation of hurting youth, fill a generation of youth who are curious about the supernatural. Lord, awaken their hearts and save their souls and let revival fire spread swiftly on school grounds worldwide.

SEPTEMBER 17

The One-Eyed Revivalist of Wales

"Therefore most gladly I will rather boast in my infirmities, that the power of Christ may rest upon me" (2 Corinthians 12:9).

Many remember William Seymour, a black one-eyed preacher who led the Azusa Street Revival. But there was another one-eyed preacher who fewer know about. His name was Christmas Evans.

Born in 1776, Evans' father died when he was a young boy. His family was so poor his mother sent him to live with her brother to work on his farm. Unfortunately, his uncle was a mean drunk. At the age of 17, Evans still couldn't read.

Evans almost died several times. He was stabbed once and almost drowned on another occasion. He fell from a tree with a knife in his hand and later fell victim to a runaway horse that nearly took his life. Despite the enemy's efforts to snuff him out, though, God had a plan for Evans. Repeatedly, his life was spared.

Evans got saved at a revival but was soon beaten with sticks by his unbelieving friends. That attack caused him to lose sight in one eye. That didn't stop him from learning to read and certainly didn't stop him from praying. He was known to wrestle in prayer with God for an outpouring of the Holy Spirit and his persistence led to revival.

Evans had an obvious infirmity. His past was abusive. The spiritual warfare was real. And, with one eye, he had natural limitations. But we all have limitations—whether we can see them or not. Evans' story should encourage us all that we can see revival despite an abusive past, despite spiritual warfare, and despite physical limitations.

Like Evans—and Paul the apostle—we all have a thorn in our side. God is saying the same thing to you that He said to Paul, "My grace is sufficient for you, for My strength is made perfect in weakness" (2 Cor. 12:4).

So go ahead, gladly boast in your infirmities that the power of Christ may rest upon you. Take pleasure in infirmities, in reproaches, in needs, in persecutions, in distresses, for Christ's sake. For when you are weak, then you are strong.

— *Prayer* —

Father, in the name of Jesus, help me to stop looking at what I don't have and what I think I need—and what obstacles are against me—and start looking at You. When I am weak, You are strong in me. Help me remember that You are the strength of my life.

The Lifestyle of a Revivalist

"And do not present your members as instruments of unrighteousness to sin, but present yourselves to God as being alive from the dead, and your members as instruments of righteousness to God"
(Romans 6:13).

Revivalists live a little differently than typical Christians. You might say they have a different lifestyle. So, what is the lifestyle of a revivalist?

First, let's look more closely at what a revivalist is. Every Christian can experience revival, but not every Christian is a revivalist. A revivalist is one who preaches, prays and prophesies revival. A revivalist is one who carries revival fire to lukewarm believers. A revivalist is one who calls people out of complacency and sin and into repentance and revival.

A lifestyle is a particular way of living, according *to Merriam-Webster*'s dictionary. A lifestyle is the typical way of life of an individual. Your lifestyle includes attitudes, behaviors, moral standards and habits. The lifestyle of revivalist is a set apart life.

The lifestyle of a revivalist is a lifestyle of holiness. Jonathan Edwards, a key figure in the First Great Awakening said, "Holiness appeared to me to be of a sweet, pleasant, charming, serene, calm nature; which brought an inexpressible purity, brightness, peacefulness and ravishment to the soul."

The lifestyle of a revivalist is a lifestyle of intercession. Revivalist Leonard Ravenhill put it this way: "Prayerlessness is disobedience, for God's command is that men ought always to pray and not faint. To be prayerless is to fail God, for He says, 'Ask of me'."

The lifestyle of a revivalist is a lifestyle of passion for souls. The late Canadian pastor Oswald J. Smith once said, "Oh, to realize that souls, precious, never dying souls, are perishing all around us, going out into the blackness of darkness and despair, eternally lost, and yet to feel no anguish, shed no tears, know no travail! How little we know of the compassion of Jesus!"

The lifestyle of a revivalist is a lifestyle of hard work, dedication, determination, and commitment to the cause of Christ. The lifestyle of a revivalist is a lifestyle of preparation, stewardship and Kingdom exploits. The lifestyle of a revivalist is intense, but if you are called to it there is grace for it.

— *Prayer* —

Father, help me embrace the lifestyle of a revivalist. I am all in for revival. Show me anything in me that resists the lifestyle of a revivalist. Help me lay aside the weights and sin that so easily beset me. Let Your revival fire consume anything that hinders holiness in my life.

The Key to Staying on Fire

"Therefore I remind you to stir up the gift of God which is in you through the laying on of my hands" (2 Timothy 1:6).

When revival fire falls, it makes an undeniable impact on the souls that have cried out to God for the outpouring. Suddenly, even backsliders become fervent. But we must maintain that fervency—that fire—in between outpourings.

Paul said in Romans 12:11 we should be fervent in spirit, serving the Lord. The Amplified version says to be aglow. The International Standard Version says to "be on fire with the Spirit."

Merriam-Webster defines the word "fervent" as very hot or glowing. When something is fervent, it is "exhibiting or marked by a great intensity or feeling." Let's drill down a little deeper to the roots of the word. The English word "fervency" comes from the Greek word "zeo." It literally means "to boil."

A fervent spirit is on fire for God. A fervent spirit is a passionate spirit. A fervent spirit is a zealous spirit. God likes fervency. Again, He expects us to be fervent in spirit. The Bible has plenty to say about fervency. The Holy Spirit started to use the word "fervency" in the Book of Acts.

We can't be as fervent as we need to be without the Holy Ghost. That's why the Apostle Paul admonishes us to "be not drunk with wine, wherein is excess; but be filled with the Spirit" (see Eph. 5:18). In the Greek, the phrase "be filled" literally means to "be being filled" with the Spirit, signaling the need to be continually filled with the Holy Ghost.

So how do stay fervent? Paul gives Timothy some direct advice: "Therefore I remind you to stir up the gift of God which is in you through the laying on of my hands" (see 2 Tim. 1:6). Other translations say, "fan into flame the gift of God" or "kindle afresh" or "keep ablaze." And how do you do that? A lifestyle of repentance, a lifestyle of prayer, and a lifestyle of seeking the Lord. If you do those three things, you'll keep burning and shining in any season.

— *Prayer* —

Father, in the name of Jesus, I want to burn for You and for the revival You want to bring in my generation. Light a fire under me and help me fan the flame with prayer, worship and meditation on Your Word. Help me to stay fervent in spirit as I serve You while I wait on revival.

The Dynamic Duo of Revival

"And being let go, they went to their own companions and reported all that the chief priests and elders had said to them" (Acts 4:23).

When you think of revival, you probably think of William Seymour, Jonathan Edwards or Evan Roberts. You've probably never heard the names Peggy and Christine Smith. But you should know them—and know how instrumental they were to revival. Every revival needs such a dynamic duo.

The Smith sisters were key figures in the Hebrides Revival of 1949-1952, led by Duncan Campbell. Peggy and Christine were in their eighties at the time. Peggy was blind. Christine had such severe arthritis that she was nearly bent over double, like the woman Jesus loosed in Luke 13:12.

Although the Smith sisters couldn't attend the revival meetings, they played a critical role in the outpouring on Lewis Island. God gave them a promise: "I will pour water upon him that is thirsty and floods upon the dry ground" (see Is. 44:3). Peggy and Christine pled with God several nights a week from 10 p.m. to 3 a.m. to bring that promise to pass.

Then, one day, Peggy got a revelation that the church would be filled with young people. She sensed God was getting ready to bring revival. With that, she made a bold request to the reverend: Call the elders and deacons together to wait upon the Lord. People were desperate for revival and answered the call. Prayer increased.

One night, a young deacon read from Psalm 24:3-5, "Who may ascend into the hill of the Lord? Or who may stand in His holy place? He who has clean hands and a pure heart, who has not lifted up his soul to an idol, nor sworn deceitfully."

When he finished reading the passage, he closed his Bible and said, "It seems to me to be so much humbug to be praying as we are praying, to be waiting as we are waiting, if we ourselves are not rightly related to God." Then he prayed, "God, are my hands clean? Is my heart pure?"

Suddenly there came an overwhelming awareness of God. The presence of God permeated not only the room but the island. The Smith sisters saw the promise come to pass. And a history-making revival broke out.

— *Prayer* —

Father, in the name of Jesus, help me find the right prayer partners to engage with for the sake of revival. Help me find a family of serious-minded intercessors who will sacrifice in prayer for a city, state, and a nation. Lead me and guide me to my revival prayer tribe.

Supernatural Revival Signs

"You are the God who does wonders; You have declared Your strength among the peoples" (Psalm 77:14).

In response to desperate prayer, revival hit the Scottish island of Lewis in the village of Barvas in what goes down in history as the Hebrides Revival in 1949-1952.

Legalism marked the churches on the island in those days. People went through the motions of religious form, but the power of the Holy Spirit was nowhere to be found. There was no hunger. But two elderly women had a word from the Lord and sparked a revival that saw young people set on fire.

The sisters, Peggy and Christine Smith, called Duncan Campbell after the revival started. Strangely, nothing happened during his first meeting there, despite a hungry audience of three hundred. But one young man went into prayer and at 11 p.m. they called Campbell back in to witness hundreds of people spontaneously entering the church, drawn by God himself.

"The Hebrides Revival in many ways was a young people's phenomenon. Many teenagers and those under the age of forty were converted, relates R.T. Kendall, a writer, speaker and pastor. Kendall recounts the story of a mother with her twenty-one-year-old son, William, who were walking down a country road. Suddenly William was overcome with emotion and began to cry. His mother said to him, "Oh Willie, at last you have come home."

The Hebrides Revival was marked by supernatural phenomenon. Kendall says, "Many people walked several miles to reach the church, some twelve miles each way, and never got blisters on their feet or felt tired." Beyond this, he said, lights appeared to show people the way home in the dark.

Another time, a home was shaken as if from an earthquake while people were praying, just like the place where the disciples was shaken when they prayed! People were functioning on little to no sleep. The crowds did not want to leave. In fact, it was typical for people to get home from revival meetings at 5 am and go to work at 7 am.

— *Prayer* —

Father, in the name of Jesus, would You help me believe You for an unusual revival that leaves its mark on the youth? Just as Paul performed unusual and extraordinary miracles, help me contend for an extraordinary revival that satisfies the curiosity of young people to meet the Holy Spirit.

What it Means to Carry Revival

"If the household is worthy, let your peace come upon it. But if it is not worthy, let your peace return to you" (Matthew 10:13).

Some people are igniters of revival. Other people are carriers of it. What does that mean? It's one thing to pray until revival comes. It's another thing to carry the spirit of revival—to carry revival fire—beyond the four walls of the local church.

Carry means transport, but it also means to communicate. Carry means to influence by emotional appeal but it also means to wear something. Carry means to bear like a mark or attribute, but it also means to sustain the weight or burden of a thing. Carry means to gain a victory for someone, but it also means to reach or penetrate at a distance.

Being a carrier of revival, then, means to talk about revival, influence others to pursue revival, bear the scars of the war for revival, possess a prayer burden for revival, see the victory in lukewarm churches through revival, and to transport revival far and wide. A carrier of revival is consumed with the message of revival. Are you a carrier of revival?

Men like Charles Finney were carriers of revival—and so was Jonathan Goforth. Goforth was a missionary to China under Hudson Taylor's ministry. Once he read Finney's writings, which carried the message of revival, and was so convicted to pursue revival that he said, "If Finney is right, I'm going to prove it."

Leonard Ravenhill carried revival in a different way. He published resources for the masses like *Why Revival Tarries*, *Revival God's Way* and *Revival Praying*. He used his writing skills to pen convicting messages on the need for revival and how to pursue it God's way that are still stirring God's people decades after he went on to glory.

Decide in your heart to be a carrier of revival, not just a pursuer of it. Choose to carry revival outside the four walls of your church into your family, into your workplace, and into the retail stores in your city. Revival is critical. Carry it well.

— *Prayer* —

Father, in the name of Jesus, make me a carrier of revival. Help me use my God-given gifts and talents to talk about revival, influence others to pursue revival, bear the scars of the war for revival, possess a prayer burden for revival, and steward revival. Let me be consumed with the message of revival.

Overcoming Mind Battles

"Casting down imaginations, and every high thing that exalteth itself against the knowledge of God, and bringing into captivity every thought to the obedience of Christ" (2 Corinthians 10:5, KJV).

Every great revivalist comes under enemy fire. The devil hates revival because he wants to keep souls—even Christian souls—out of the abundant life Jesus died to give them (see John 10:10). Revivalists carry the fire that burns away indifference to the Gospel, so if the enemy can put out your fire, he can keep that fire from spreading.

Evan Roberts, leader of the Welsh Revival in 1904-1905, faced his fair share of spiritual warfare. Specifically, the enemy launched imaginations against his mind. He wrote a letter to Florrie Evans, a young woman on his team of traveling revivalists, that exposed how the enemy was meddling in his mind:

"Oh! I am quite happy this week and throughout the last. But, nevertheless, it has been a grand fight with the tempter. But, thanks be to God, I am now a conqueror. He tried to destroy my faith—and by saying—What did I want at Loughor while there are so many ministers to be had? Why did I waste my time? And then he said that God's Spirit was not with me, and that these grand effects were only the results of my relating the signs and visions I had seen."

What amazing insight into the battle revivalists face! The Holy Spirit told me many years ago, "The battle is in the mind, but the war is for your heart." The enemy attacks our minds relentlessly hoping to change what we believe in our hearts about ourselves, others, and God. He knows if a lie gets in our heart, we'll speak it out of our mouths and it will be our reality.

Here's some strategic advice from a revivalist called Paul the apostle: "For the weapons of our warfare are not carnal but mighty in God for pulling down strongholds, casting down arguments and every high thing that exalts itself against the knowledge of God, bringing every thought into captivity to the obedience of Christ, and being ready to punish all disobedience when your obedience is fulfilled" (2 Corinthians 10:4-6).

— Prayer —

Father, in the name of Jesus, would You help me gird up the loins of my mind and guard my heart with all diligence? Help me to pay attention to the thoughts rolling around in my mind, and to cast down the thoughts the enemy is trying to plant in my soul, and to speak Your truth out of my mouth.

Understanding the Ulster Revival

"Then those who gladly received his word were baptized; and that day about three thousand souls were added to them" (Acts 2:41).

William Harding chronicled the Ulster Revival—an awakening in 1859 Ireland. As he describes it, the Ulster Revival was a transforming revival that kindled apostolic zeal without any "famous" revivalists to fan the flames.

To appreciate this revival, you need to understand the corruption in Ireland during those days. Churches were dead, cold, prayerless and worldly. One minister reported people were hostile toward prayer meetings and salvation was rare. But things started changing in 1856 when a Baptist missionary from England named Mrs. Colville helped influence a young man named James McQuilkin to surrender to Christ.

McQuilkin held prayer meetings with three young Irishmen every Friday night starting in September 1857. By the end of the year, the prayer group grew to fifty. By 1859 the prayer meetings drew crowds so large the balconies in the Presbyterian church where they met started bending under the weight of the people. Mass conviction of sin resulted. All told, there were over one hundred different prayer meetings each week in barns, schools, workplaces, and homes.

Harding wrote, "Although the churches and other meeting-places were crowded, the revival was marked by such heart-stirrings that even large buildings were not able to contain the multitudes that assembled. Hence, meetings were held on the highways, in the fields, or at any popular rallying point. A Belfast visitor, invited to speak at the village of Broughshane, found his congregation to consist of about five thousand people, the meeting-place being a quarry."

The Ulster Revival saw one hundred thousand people turn to Christ—that was a whopping ten percent of Ireland's population at the time. A true societal transformation, crime rates decreased fifty percent in a matter of months. Bars shut down because no one wanted to drink. Even Catholics turned to Christ by the time the revival ended in 1874. Do it again, Lord!

— *Prayer* —

Father, in the name of Jesus, help me believe for revival in the most antagonistic cities in the world. Help me to pray without ceasing for cities and nations that are hostile to the good news of the Gospel. Teach me to persevere until Your Spirit comes from heaven to invade earth.

Why Revival Ends

"And the fire on the altar shall be kept burning on it; it shall not be put out. And the priest shall burn wood on it every morning, and lay the burnt offering in order on it; and he shall burn on it the fat of the peace offerings" (Leviticus 6:12).

If you notice, there is no perpetual revival. Revivals have a start date and an end date. You might say the revival fire burns out. But why does it? And should it? If we look at revival like an event, it's hard to sustain forever. But if we look at revival like a lifestyle, it's a different thrust.

In his book, *Open Heavens*, Bill Johnson, senior leader of Bethel church, says each story in Scripture and in Church history provokes him to a pursuit of all that God has made available in his lifetime. But the problem he has with most studies on revival is that conclusions are made based on the history of revival, and not on the nature or promises of God.

"That means that when a revival ended due to greed, competition, self-promotion or the like, it is assumed that it was God's will for it to end. And while it is God who can bring an end to such an outpouring of the Holy Spirit, it was not because God no longer wanted a revival. It was because He refused to align His outpouring with the soulish attempts of His people to control and direct Him," Johnson wrote.

"Perhaps the best illustration for this is the biblical responsibility of priests of the Old Testament, with the fire on the altar. It was God who lit the fire on the altar, but it was the priests who kept it burning. It is the same today. God initiates the mighty outpouring of His Spirit (fire), and we sustain or correctly steward the outpouring for His glory and the transformation of cities and nations, which is still in His heart."

A revival event may end. An outpouring may end. But the revival fire that fell should set you on fire to the point that you sustain the fire you caught. A visitation may end. A time of awakening may end. But when you let revival fire do its work in you, you can walk in personal revival and become an agent to spark the next corporate revival.

— *Prayer* —

Father, in the name of Jesus, I know "revival mode" in a church doesn't last forever but let me live in revival mode. Help me sustain the fire that You pour out, then spread it person to person. Help me never to grow lukewarm but to cultivate a red-hot fiery walk with Your Spirit.

There's Revival in the Fire

"For our God is a consuming fire" (Hebrews 12:29).

Many people tend to shy away from the refiner's fire. The revivalist, by contrast, welcomes it. That's because the revivalist understands the necessity of the fire.

Our faith is tested by fire (see 1 Pet. 1:7). Fire is symbol of the Holy Spirit (see Acts 2). Fire represents the presence of God (see Ex. 3:2). When we're on fire, people will come to not only watch us burn but to catch the fire that awakens, cleanses, purifies, and empowers.

In the prayer room at Awakening House of Prayer in South Florida, I heard the Lord say, "There's freedom in the fire. Don't be afraid of the fire for I am the all-consuming fire. Don't be afraid of Me but yield to Me. I won't take anything you need, but I'll take the things that hold you back. I'll burn up the things that get in the way of your first love. Do not be afraid. Don't run away. Let me have My way.

"My way is better. You'll like it if you just yield—if you just let Me do My work in you. You'll like yourself more because you're going to look more like My Son. So don't resist My fire. Let me do the work in you.

"I will have My way. You already said yes so don't turn back now. Keep looking up. Keep looking at My face. I will comfort you even in the fire. You will feel My presence even in the fire. You will know My voice in the fire. You will encounter My heart in the fire.

"You're going to learn to love the fire because it's cleansing. it's purifying, it's making a way for more intimacy with My heart. I will not burn away anything that you need. I'll just burn up the things that get in the way, so yield. Yield to my fire. I won't burn you. I'll make you better. I'll heal you by fire. It's healing. It's cleansing. It's freedom. There's freedom in the fire."

— Prayer —

Father, in the name of Jesus, I submit to Your all-consuming fire. I submit to the furnace of affliction. I submit to the coals of burning fire to cleanse my mouth. Help me yield to Your fire when it falls and not run away from the spirit of burning. Remind me of the purpose of the fire so I can embrace it.

SEPTEMBER 27

Nine Conditions of Revival

"But first and most importantly seek (aim at, strive after) His kingdom and His righteousness [His way of doing and being right—the attitude and character of God], and all these things will be given to you also" (Matthew 6:33, AMP).

Although you can't predict revival like you can predict the weather, there are conditions that are common to almost every revival. We see these conditions— conditions both before and after revival—throughout the pages of Scripture.

In essence, revival is made possible by encountering God, according to Bill Johnson, senior leader of Bethel Church in Redding, Calif. That encounter, he says, regardless of how extreme or how subtle, carries with it the seed of revival, which is the seed of reformation—that which could change a nation if stewarded well.

"Look at it this way: There's an oak tree in an acorn if the acorn is taken care of properly. But there is also a forest of oak trees available through the seeds of the one oak tree," he writes in his book, *Open Heavens: Position Yourself to Encounter the God of Revival.*

"The outcome is written into the nature of the seed, but it requires proper stewardship by the caregivers, in this case, those affected by the revival. So it is with one touch from God. It carries the seed of transformation, not only for our lives, but is enough for a nation. This is the responsibility that comes with encountering God."

Johnson points to nine ingredients of revival: (1) they occurred in times of moral darkness and national depression; (2) each began in the heart of a consecrated servant of God who became the energizing power behind it; (3) each revival rested on the Word of God, and most were the result of proclaiming God's Word with power.

He continues, (4) all resulted in a return to the worship of God; (5) each witnessed the destruction of idols where they existed; (6) in each revival, there was a recorded separation from sin; (7) in every revival the people returned to obeying God's laws; (8) there was a restoration of great joy and gladness; and (9) each revival was followed by a period of national prosperity.

— Prayer —

Father, in the name of Jesus, help me understand the conditions of revival so that I can do my part, under Your leadership, to set the stage for a visitation of Your Spirit. Let me be part of a revival that sees souls saved, believers revived, bodies healed and the miserable delivered.

Activating Angels of Awakening

"Bless the Lord, you His angels, who excel in strength, who do His word, heeding the voice of His word" (Psalm 103:20).

Angels are on assignment—and we need to activate them. I wrote about this in my book, *Angels on Assignment Again*. Tim Sheets has a grand revelation of this reality in his book, *Activating Angel Armies*. He writes:

"We need angels for the convergence of the ages. We need them to assist this awesome move of God. We need angels to help us overcome hell's strongholds, tear down demonic thrones in regions, and help with the harvest. Jesus said angels assist His Kingdom as harvesters and reapers. You can see that in Matthew 13:39. Angels do all of this and they do so much more. the Holy Spirit knows this and He has begun to supervise the release of millions and millions of angels upon this planet.

"I was at the lake praying and I could take you to the exact spot when Holy Spirit captured my attention as He said, 'I will now lead another campaign similar to Acts 2 in your times.'

"But then He said, 'This time I am going to be bringing far more of the angel armies.' I remember when it happened, I didn't know what to do or what to say. I sat there for probably an hour saying nothing. I was almost afraid to move because I knew something so big and significant was about to take place.

"This was a 'wind word' that the Holy Spirit was blowing through the church and is now speaking to the remnant. 'This time I am bringing far more of the angel armies.' From that point until today angel activity began to be revealed to me and dramatically so on certain occasions.

"I saw how the Holy Spirit was using angels locally, regionally, and around the world. Angel activity increased in unexpected and yet very clear ways to me. I began to see their work and their ministry everywhere, even in everyday life. I knew the Holy Spirit was giving me another key to this end-time surge."

— *Prayer* —

Father, in the name of Jesus, help me believe that angels really are on assignment, working behind the scenes to help execute Your will in the earth. Help me not to neglect the ministry of angels or stand in the way of their assignment with faithless words. Help me to make decrees that release angels of awakening.

When Opposition Hits Hard

"Lord, how they have increased who trouble me! Many are they who rise up against me" (Psalm 3:1).

Retaliation is one thing, flat out opposition to what God wants to do or is doing is another. And it's usually not the secular world that opposes revival. Rather, it's the lukewarm church that refuses to let Jesus in when He knocks on the door.

No, it's not usually the world. It's the hard-hearted believers that resist the Holy Spirit's conviction. It's the program-oriented church that won't make room for the Holy Spirit. It's the religious church that calls a move of God "strange fire." It's a denominational church that is jealous because revival started somewhere else.

Many revivals saw opposition but the Hebrides Revival in 1949-1952 documents intense hostility. Duncan Campbell faced contention on many levels. Pastors of other churches in the region told their congregants not to attend his meetings because they didn't believe the revival was God-breathed. Other pastors stood against Campbell's teaching on the baptism of the Holy Spirit.

But it wasn't just the move of God or the teaching they resisted. The persecuted Campbell with petty comments. One example: they despised his brown shoes. Most ministers in that day wore black shoes. The sentiment was, "Could God really use a preacher wearing brown shoes?"

Beyond the move itself and God's messenger, many opposed the manifestations of revival. People testified to hearing angels singing. Others fell into trances. Still others testified to seeing demons flying out of the church buildings. At certain times groups of people appeared frozen like statues or had shaking fits.

Those who opposed the revival missed out. Author and pastor R.T. Kendall said, "The town of Stornoway—the capital of the Isle of Lewis—was completely bypassed. The revival came only to small towns or villages in the Hebrides. The reason for this was thought to be that the ministers in Stornoway opposed the revival."

Don't let the opposition to the move of God—or the personal persecution you face when you step out as a revivalist—stop you. Pray for the opposers lest they miss the day of their visitation. God wants to touch them, too.

— *Prayer* —

Father, in the name of Jesus, would You help me not to get angry, resentful, frustrated, or bitter over the opponents and persecutors of the revival You are bringing? Help me, rather, to pity them and pray for them to have an encounter with the God of revival.

The Charles Spurgeon Revivalist Anointing

"Therefore I say to you, whatever things you ask when you pray, believe that you receive them, and you will have them" (Mark 11:24).

"Revival begins by Christians getting right first and then spills over into the world." These are the poignant words of Charles Spurgeon, a 19th Century Englishman known as the prince of preachers.

The British Baptist got saved at age fifteen and started preaching a year later. Above all, he was a preacher of the cross who focused much of his preaching on the new birth. And he continually called the church to revival—true revival. He wrote:

"The word 'revival' is as familiar in our mouths as a household word. We are constantly speaking about and praying for a 'revival;' would it not be as well to know what we mean by it? Of the Samaritans our Lord said, 'Ye worship ye know not what,' let him not have to say to us, 'Ye know not what ye ask.' The word 'revive' wears its meaning upon its forehead; it is from the Latin, and may be interpreted thus—to live again, to receive again a life which has almost expired; to rekindle into a flame the vital spark which was nearly extinguished."

Despite his legacy for preaching, Spurgeon viewed the prayer meeting as the most important gathering of the week. He once said:

"The power of prayer can never be overrated. They who cannot serve God by preaching, need not regret it if they can be mighty in prayer. The true strength of the church lies there. This is the sinew which moves the arm of omnipotence. If a man can but pray, he can do anything. He that knows how to overcome the Lord in prayer, has heaven and earth at his disposal. There is nothing, man, which thou canst not accomplish if thou canst but prevail with God in prayer."

Spurgeon didn't see revivals at his church, but eternity may show that his prayer meetings birthed many revivals in his era. The Spurgeon revival anointing is an anointing to pray for revival.

— *Prayer* —

Father, in the name of Jesus, so many strive to be great preachers but help me seek first to be a great intercessor. Give me a revelation that prayer is the principal thing, and that my words to men will be more powerful if they are preceded by prayers to You. Give me an anointing like Spurgeon's!

OCTOBER

"A revival does two things. First, it returns the Church from her backsliding and second, it causes the conversion of men and women; and it always includes the conviction of sin on the part of the Church. What a spell the devil seems to cast over the Church today!"—Billy Sunday

OCTOBER 1

Combatting a Revival of the Devil's Witchcraft

"For rebellion is as the sin of witchcraft, and stubbornness is as iniquity and idolatry" (1 Samuel 15:23).

Just as angels are painted with a humanistic brush in pop culture, demons are often glorified in mass media. Wikipedia actually publishes an A-to-Z list of fictional demons—and there are nearly 600 of them. I imagine the list is not exhaustive.

Watching old videos of healing evangelists like Kathryn Kuhlman, A.A. Allen, Jack Coe, and Oral Roberts is one of my favorite things to do. I've consumed hundreds of hours of videos showing the miracle-working power of God and bold revival preaching that makes no apologies for the Rock of Offense.

While watching an A.A. Allen miracle reel on YouTube, my ears perked up when I heard him declare a revival of the devil's witchcraft. Of course, this was back in the 1950s. What was a revival of witchcraft then has turned into a full-blown movement today.

"An awful lot of people are sick, diseased and afflicted under a curse, under a spell because of the present revival of witchcraft around the world," Allen declared. "There has never been a time in history when there has been such a devil's revival of witchcraft."

Think about it for a minute. In Allen's day, there was no such thing as Harry Potter. Allen made this declaration before popular TV shows like *Bewitched, Charmed* and *The Witches of East End*—and before films like *Rosemary's Baby, The Blair Witch Project,* and *Season of the Witch.* Indeed, it was before children's media like *Meg and Mog, The Witch Family* and *Witches in Stitches* hit the mainstream.

A generation of youth has been exposed to witchcraft games, television shows, movies and more. The enemy is seducing people who are looking for the supernatural into a counterfeit movement that could have dangerous eternal consequences. In the Book of Revelation, God has made clear the fate of those who practice such things: sorcerers will have their portion in the lake that burns with fire and brimstone (see Rev. 21:8). Let's keep pushing back this darkness.

— *Prayer* —

Father, in the name of Jesus, show me if I have any agreement with witchcraft so I can repent and renounce it. Help me to discern even the most subtle forms of witchcraft so I can stand against it. Give me prayer strategies to combat the revival of the devil's witchcraft.

A Holy Expectation

"Confess your trespasses to one another, and pray for one another, that you may be healed. The effective, fervent prayer of a righteous man avails much" (James 5:16).

Every Easter Sunday, New Zealanders gathered at Ngaruawahia—and it was no different in 1936 except that year believers were expecting revival. As providence would have it, revival historian J. Edwin Orr was queued up to speak. Intercessors were pressing into revival prayer and faith was high.

Before Easter Sunday, students at the local Bible Training Institute fell under the power of conviction after Orr made a call for prayer. Students entered deep repentance. This was the ignition point of the revival, which was then fueled at a tent meeting when a man stood up to ask for prayer, confessing that he was dead inside. That confession sparked weeping, praying and singing.

At that point, revival was in the birth canal, but had not fully come forth. During Orr's meetings, a group of spiritually hungry young men asked to meet with him privately. Orr shared with them hindrances of revival and asked them, "Do you really believe that God is going to give us revival?" The young men agreed and set out to pray again for revival. But sin was laying heavy on one man's heart.

"I want to confess openly that I have been criticizing you behind your back. Will you forgive me? I think I ought to get right with you first," he said to a friend. His friend, in turn, confessed he had committed the same sin. Conviction swept through the tent, and they all confessed their sins to each other. Orr left but the prayer didn't end. The prayer meeting went viral and a dozen prayer new meetings launched.

Revival was now underway—and critics immediately rose up. "We have come to Ngaruawahia for revival," Orr said. "Revival has begun. Take heed that you do not hinder the work of the Spirit. Mark my words, you may see revival sweep the camp tonight." Orr's prophetic wisdom helped stoke the fire on the altar. That same night, a holy hush manifested in his meeting and more sin confessions came forth.

Orr's words proved prophetic. He stepped up to the pulpit Saturday evening and preached for an hour. A holy hush of conviction came over the crowd. When an invitation was given, twenty young people responded to confess their sins. Many in tears knelt at the front. They expected revival, and revival they got. Are you expecting revival?

— *Prayer* —

Father, in the name of Jesus, help me to anticipate revival, to expect revival, to confess revival, to pray for revival, to stand for revival and to make room for the power of conviction to move in my heart. Help me to walk in transparency with my brothers and sisters so no sin in the camp can hold back Your revival.

OCTOBER 3

Joel's Prophecy to the Lukewarm Church

"Now, therefore," says the Lord, 'Turn to Me with all your heart, with fasting, with weeping, and with mourning'" (Joel 2:12).

Joel prophesied a message to Israel concerning the Day of the Lord. And his prophecy should ring in our ears today as a call to prepare for Christ's Second Coming. Indeed, the Book of Joel is almost like an abbreviated Book of Revelation with many parallels, including the locust plague, God's judgment on the nations, and God's blessings on His people.

Joel 2 is a prophecy for the ages. The prophet begins by sounding the alarm about the coming Day of the Lord, filled with darkness and gloominess. He speaks of earthquakes and trembling heavens, the sun and the moon growing dark and the brightness of the stars diminishing. Joel wonders who can endure it, then prophesies these words in Joel 2:12-17:

"'Now, therefore,' says the Lord, 'Turn to Me with all your heart, with fasting, with weeping, and with mourning.' So rend your heart, and not your garments; Return to the Lord your God, for He is gracious and merciful, slow to anger, and of great kindness; And He relents from doing harm. Who knows if He will turn and relent, and leave a blessing behind Him—a grain offering and a drink offering for the Lord your God?

"Blow the trumpet in Zion, consecrate a fast, call a sacred assembly; Gather the people, sanctify the congregation, assemble the elders, gather the children and nursing babes; Let the bridegroom go out from his chamber, and the bride from her dressing room.

"Let the priests, who minister to the Lord, weep between the porch and the altar; Let them say, 'Spare Your people, O Lord, and do not give Your heritage to reproach, that the nations should rule over them. Why should they say among the peoples, 'Where is their God?'"

It's time to weep over our condition—and the conditions of our churches, cities, and nations. It's time to stand in the gap and make intercession for God's people—and the lost. It's time to travail in agony before it's too late.

— *Prayer* —

Father, in the name of Jesus, it doesn't take a prophet to see the days are growing darker. Would You help me to redeem the time because the days are evil? Would You inspire me to deeper realms of intercession for the church and the lost so that we can hasten Your return?

302

Keys to Stewarding Revival

"We must keep our eyes on Jesus, who leads us and makes our faith complete"
(Hebrews 12:1, CEV).

Just as every revivalist has strengths, we also have weaknesses. All revivals end at some point, but we don't want to see revival end before God has fulfilled His purpose in the outpouring. So, then, how do we steward revival? There is a natural side and a spiritual side this equation.

"Our stewardship of natural things prepares us for the stewardship of the spiritual," Bill Johnson, senior leader of Bethel Church, wrote in his book *Open Heavens*. "The apostle Paul coined this phrase in his instruction to the church at Corinth. He was teaching them about the mystery and necessity of the resurrection."

Johnson points to 1 Corinthian 15:46, "However, the spiritual is not first, but the natural; then the spiritual." There are natural aspects to stewarding revival, such as taking care not to wear out the staff, the financial cost of revival and, unfortunately, in some cases security concerns.

From a spiritual perspective, we steward revival by keeping our eyes on Jesus, who is Revival. Hebrews 12:1 (CEV) tells us, "We must keep our eyes on Jesus, who leads us and makes our faith complete." It's easy to put our eyes on fiery preachers or a worship team as the sustainer of revival. We need fiery preachers and worship teams, but without Jesus it's all pointless. Jesus must remain the center of it all.

People have many thoughts on stewarding revival, but beyond a Christ-centered mandate the key to true sustainability is the same key that births revival: prayer. When revival hit Herrnhut under Count Nikolaus Von Zinzendorf's leadership in Germany, he understood this principle.

With God's wisdom, Zinzendorf built a twenty-four-hour prayer watch to stoke the flames of revival. Historian A. J. Lewis writes, "For over a hundred years the members of the Moravian Church all shared in the 'hourly intercession.' At home and abroad, on land and sea, this prayer watch ascended unceasingly to the Lord."

— *Prayer* —

Father, I focus so much on praying in the revival that I may be unprepared to rightly steward the revival You bring, first in my heart, then in my church, and then through my city. In the name of Jesus, would You teach me the principles of stewarding revival in my life so I can help steward it at greater scales?

OCTOBER 5

Revival Prayers God Answers

"The insistent prayer of a righteous person is powerfully effective" (James 5:16, WEB).

James, the apostle of practical faith, made it clear: the effective fervent prayer of a righteous man avails much (see James 5:16). If there are effective prayers, there must be ineffective prayers. If we want revival, we need to pray effective prayers. Let's look at James 5:16-18 in the Amplified translation:

"The heartfelt and persistent prayer of a righteous man (believer) can accomplish much [when put into action and made effective by God—it is dynamic and can have tremendous power]. Elijah was a man with a nature like ours [with the same physical, mental, and spiritual limitations and shortcomings], and he prayed intensely for it not to rain, and it did not rain on the earth for three years and six months. Then he prayed again, and the sky gave rain and the land produced its crops [as usual]."

But effective prayer must be fervent prayer. It's not rote prayer. It's not a standard list prayed through out of religious obligation. It's fiery prayer that refuses to doubt the God of revival hears and will respond at the right time. It's boiling hot prayers of passion that petition heaven for a visitation.

An effective prayer is the right kind of prayer for the specific situation. In the context of revival, effective prayers start with repentance. In the context of revival, effective prayer cries out for an outpouring and an infilling. In the context of revival, effective prayer is prayer without ceasing for God to revive us and our churches.

Charles H. Spurgeon wrote this: "Oh! men and brethren, what would this heart feel if I could but believe that there were some among you who would go home and pray for a revival—men whose faith is large enough, and their love fiery enough to lead them from this moment to exercise unceasing intercessions that God would appear among us and do wondrous things here as in the times of former generations."

— *Prayer* —

Father, in the name of Jesus, would You help me pray effective fervent prayers? I want to tap into dynamic power that shifts atmospheres, convicts hearts, and moves Your Spirit to release a great outpouring in the earth. Set me on fire as I pray Your will.

OCTOBER 6

No-Compromise Revivalists

"Even so then, at this present time there is a remnant according to the election of grace"
(Romans 11:5).

There is a remnant—and the remnant is rallying in prayer for revival. We don't need the whole Body of Christ in agreement. We just need the remnant.

I heard the Lord say: "I have preserved a people in this generation to speak forth My Word without compromise. Their voices will continue to rise in boldness for the cause of righteousness but few will listen. Just like the days of old, my prophetic voices are crying out to a nation with deaf ears who continue serving idols instead of the life giver.

"Yet the remnant is rising and their voices are growing louder. And there will come an hour when the circumstances of the day will demand that a wicked generation take notice of the righteous remnant and turn their hearts back toward Me. Some will continue to mock My Son, but many will break free of the deception that besets the land. So continue to cry out and continue to call out in My name because I hear you and I am answering you for My Son's sake. I will not turn my back on those who fear me. I will not."

The remnant is rising and refuses to bow down to the principalities and powers that have targeted churches, cities, and nations for destruction. The remnant is humbling itself on behalf of nations whose pride is pushing it toward a fall. The remnant is praying fervently for God's Kingdom to come and His will to be done in our land, just as it is in heaven. The remnant is seeking His face. The remnant is repenting on behalf of a nation that has slipped from its former glory.

And God hears from heaven. And God will forgive our sins. And God will heal our lands. Until then, walk by faith and not by sight. Don't stop praying even if evil appears to be overcoming good. If the remnant stops praying, who will declare God's will for our nations?

— *Prayer* —

Father, in the name of Jesus, I count myself as part of the remnant. Help me to stay consecrated to You. Help me not to grow weary in praying for a lukewarm church that doesn't see the need for revival. Help me to pray for my nation as if my life depended on it.

Raising Up Revival Chroniclers

"Write the things which you have seen, and the things which are, and the things which will take place after this" (Revelation 1:19).

Old Testament prophets recorded Biblical events—the good, the bad and the ugly. Samuel chronicled the ministry of Saul and David. And the Books of First and Second Chronicles were thought to have been written by Ezra. As far as New Testament chroniclers, we think of Luke, who documented Jesus' life and ministry and, later, the Acts of the Apostles.

Really, much of the Bible is a chronicle inspired by the Holy Spirit. What would we do without the Word of God? How could we learn the character and will of God without the historical accounts of how He responded to people? How would we know the pattern for the apostolic church without the Book of Acts? How would we know that Jesus talked to His apostles about the Kingdom of God for forty days after His ascension? Chronicling is so important that God chose to manifest Himself and to communicate to all mankind His character, His will, and His way through chronicles.

Consider Gordon Lindsay, who published over two hundred fifty volumes of historical and doctrinal books on the Voice of Healing Movement. Many of those texts preserved the revelations we stand on today. We don't have to redig those wells. Think about Frank Bartleman, an American Pentecostal writer, evangelist, and missionary who penned columns for Christian periodicals and documented the events that led up to the Azusa Street Revival.

What is the ministry of a chronicler of revival? It's one who records what God is doing. We need to chronicle prophetic words, significant events and spiritual battles. Luke chronicled the changing of the guard from the old to the new covenant. While Old Testament prophets chronicled natural wars, New Testament chroniclers should be documenting significant spiritual wars.

Revival chroniclers are curious and must be savvy about the move of the Spirit. They must have integrity, perseverance, and commitment to the cause. They need to be dependable, have initiative and write with pinpoint accuracy. They must be involved, but objective, disciplined and bold to write contrary to man's carnal opinions. They must have eyes to see and ears to hear what says the Spirit of God.

— *Prayer* —

Father, in the name of Jesus, would You remind me to chronicle what I see the Holy Spirit doing in my life, my church—and my generation? Help me make record of what You are doing and saying to me and the church so that people who come after me might see Your faithfulness.

When Witches Repent

"I tell you, no; but unless you repent [change your old way of thinking, turn from your sinful ways and live changed lives], you will all likewise perish" (Luke 13:3, AMP).

We know the story of Simon the Sorcerer who got saved in Acts 8. But a few chapters later we see full-blown revival in a city marked by witchcraft.

Paul the apostle was doing what Paul the apostle did: preaching the Gospel, getting people filled with the Holy Spirit, working miracles and casting out devils. Look at this scene from Paul's ministry and let this fill your heart with hope for a revival among those who practice witchcraft. Acts 19:11-20 reads:

"Now God worked unusual miracles by the hands of Paul, so that even handkerchiefs or aprons were brought from his body to the sick, and the diseases left them and the evil spirits went out of them. Then some of the itinerant Jewish exorcists took it upon themselves to call the name of the Lord Jesus over those who had evil spirits, saying, 'We exorcise you by the Jesus whom Paul preaches.' Also there were seven sons of Sceva, a Jewish chief priest, who did so.

"And the evil spirit answered and said, 'Jesus I know, and Paul I know; but who are you?'

"Then the man in whom the evil spirit was leaped on them, overpowered them, and prevailed against them, so that they fled out of that house naked and wounded. This became known both to all Jews and Greeks dwelling in Ephesus; and fear fell on them all, and the name of the Lord Jesus was magnified.

"And many who had believed came confessing and telling their deeds. Also, many of those who had practiced magic brought their books together and burned them in the sight of all. And they counted up the value of them, and it totaled fifty thousand pieces of silver. So the word of the Lord grew mightily and prevailed."

Do it again, Lord!

— Prayer —

Father, in the name of Jesus, help me walk in the spirit of the fear of the Lord so that I can release the spirit of the fear of the Lord in cities where I preach, pray and prophesy. Help me believe for mass salvation of the darkest people groups in the earth. Nothing is impossible with You.

OCTOBER 9

The Auntie Cooke Revivalist Anointing

"Yet you do not have because you do not ask" (James 4:2).

They called her Auntie Cooke, though her given name was Sarah. She may have been one of the most fervent revival intercessors that has ever walked the earth, but few know her name. Like many great intercessors in history, she worked behind the scenes for the glory of God.

Auntie Cooke beat the drum on the power of prayer, writing: "I was in a meeting in Illinois where more than twenty preachers were present, every day a prayer meeting was held at six o'clock. Three mornings the hour came, but not one of the twenty preachers were there. My soul was stirred within me. If alive to God, would they not have been there to take hold of the blessing of God for the people who would gather there through the day? Awake beloved preacher of the Gospel! You have not, because you ask not."

You may have heard the story of how two intercessors approached D.L. Moody after his message and told him, "You need power." Auntie Cooke was one of those intercessors.

Imagine the boldness to go up to a megachurch pastor and make such a statement! But thanks to Auntie Cooke's obedience, Moody was endued with power. Beyond Moody, Auntie Cooke had influence on many revivalists in her day, including the likes of Samuel Bringle, a Commissioner in the Salvation Army, S.B. Shaw, and B.T. Roberts.

Auntie Cooke walked in holy boldness. Bringle once said, "She let no opportunity pass by to speak to saint or sinner of Christ's great salvation. Dr. Campbell Morgan tells how he stepped onto a streetcar one day and saw a man sitting alone in one of the seats. He felt an impulse to speak to him about his soul, but hesitated to gather his courage. When he turned to take the seat he found it occupied by a little woman, who was now earnestly speaking to the man."

— *Prayer* —

Father, in the name of Jesus, would You give me an anointing like You gave Auntie Cooke? Give me a holy boldness to do what You tell me to do no matter the personal cost. Give me a holy fire to speak Your words to whomever You send me despite any consequences.

A Cross-Denomination Revival

"For you are still carnal. For where there are envy, strife, and divisions among you, are you not carnal and behaving like mere men?" (1 Corinthians 3:3)

John Hus founded the Moravian Church in 1457. Hundreds of years later, Count Nicolaus Zinzendorf, a leader in the Moravian church, birthed a cross-denomination revival that has marked prayer movements in every generation since.

In 1772, Zinzendorf made way for refugees from Roman Catholic persecution to find freedom in Germany in a village on his property known as Herrnhut, which means "the Lord's watchful care" or "the Lord's protection." Over the course of five years, Herrnhut was home to two-hundred twenty believers of varying denominational backgrounds.

There were Baptists, Lutherans, Moravians, Presbyterians and Schwenkfelders living together—but not in unity. Indeed, there was no lack of strife, judgmentalism and even bitterness between the brothers and sisters in Christ. This grieved Zinzendorf's heart, and he started making personal visits to pray with the families and study what the Bible says about unity.

Those visits led to the Brotherly Agreement, which resulted in a measure of unity but stopped short of true brotherly love. Having done all he could, he took it to the Lord in prayer. The only answer was revival. On August 5, 1727, he gathered with a dozen others for an all-night prayer meeting. They were seeking the Lord for an outpouring of His Spirit when, at midnight, the Holy Ghost touched their hearts. The next day, revival began to spread among the children at Herrnhut.

By August 13, the community was primed for full-blown revival. Zinzendorf preached about the cross and the Holy Spirit came rushing in. Zinzendorf said, "A sense of the nearness of Christ bestowed, in a single moment, upon all the members present; and it was so unanimous that two members at work twenty miles away, unaware that the meeting was being held, became at the same time deeply conscious of the same blessing."

The outpouring spurred more prayer and worship. Indeed, a twenty-four-hour prayer ministry was launched—a prayer meeting that lasted for one hundred years. From that prayer movement, a missionary movement was birthed that brought salvation to the nations.

— *Prayer* —

Father, in the name of Jesus, would You give me a revelation of how critical unity is to the cause of revival? How can we pray in revival when we are biting and devouring each other? I repent of any discord I have caused. Convict Your church of the unity needed to see You move in our midst.

OCTOBER 11

Telling it Like it Is

"You will say, 'How I hated discipline! If only I had not ignored all the warnings!'" (Proverbs 5:12).

Mentored by Leonard Ravenhill, Steve Hill had a reputation for telling it like it is. Before he passed away, he asked me to write an article with him. The article is called, *Warning: Sugar-Coated Ear Candy Gospel is Weakening the Saints.* Let this excerpt stir you up.

"We've all heard the adage that a spoonful of sugar helps the medicine go down. That may be true. But today, in the spiritual sense, there is no medicine coming behind the ear candy. The doctors of the Word, the clergy, are afraid to prescribe the medicine that was made available from heaven's pharmacy two thousand years ago. They see the disease but are afraid to properly treat it for fear of offending. They have become tolerant.

"From God's perspective, the diagnosis and treatment have always been clear: Sin is the disease. The blood of Christ is the cure. Repentance is God's method for putting the two together.

"If we want to be relevant, if we want to be effective, we must preach the cross, the blood, repentance and sacrifice. We must preach Jesus Christ and Him crucified. Today's junk-filled jargon, all in the name of Jesus, reminds us of the trouble in Isaiah's day when the people said, 'Do not prophesy to us right things; speak to us smooth things, prophesy deceits. Get out of the way, turn aside from the path, cause the Holy One of Israel to cease from before us'" (Is. 30:10-11).

"John Wesley, George Whitefield and Charles Finney never preached soupy, self-centered, society-pleasing sermons. Their words challenged people to live a life of no compromise that included acknowledging and repenting of sin and receiving God's forgiveness. We need to get back to offering this type of fare. There are hungry souls both inside and outside the church who need a fresh, cutting word from the heart of God. Let's stop giving them a soft, sweet substitute. No more sugar. It's time to start a detox program!"

— *Prayer* —

Father, in the name of Jesus, help me find the balance between grace and truth. I know grace must come before truth—but truth must come. Help me never to share a Gospel that doesn't come with sacrifice. Help me to challenge people's minds about their eternity and show them Jesus.

Revival Praying

"And I have also heard the groaning of the children of Israel whom the Egyptians keep in bondage, and I have remembered My covenant" (Exodus 6:5).

Not all prayer is the same. There's everyday prayer for the needs of life—"Give us this day our daily bread." There's prayer for protection—"Lead us not into temptation but deliver us for evil." There's prayer for healing, prayer for deliverance—but there is revival praying. If we want to see revival, we need revival praying.

See, revival praying is desperate prayer but it's more than desperation. Revival praying is repentance prayer, but it's more than godly sorrow. In his book, *Revival Praying*, Leonard Ravenhill helps clarify the distinction so we can get the answers to our revival prayers. He writes:

"Prayer is, I think, the language of heaven. A sage of old spake of prayer as thinking God's thoughts after Him. But in the spirit-born prayer, I believe we pray Gods burden into and through our hearts. With God we share in prayer. Prayer is no magic transformation of words into heavenly language just because we close our eyes. Words are not prayer because we utter them on our knees, nor because we say them in the pulpit, nor yet because they are breathed within the confines of the church.

"Concerning our praying today, a phrase from Shakespeare often comes into my mind: 'What do you read, my Lord?' Polonius asked Hamlet. To this the melancholy man replied. 'Words! Words! Words!' Likewise in prayer what do we often say? Words! Words! Words! We can use words without praying, and we can pray without using words. We can also pray when words are used.

"But there is a language of the spirit beyond words groanings that cannot be articulated, that defy language, that are above language, that are beyond language, that are the yearnings of the heart of God committed to those who seek to know His will and to care for a lost world and feeble church."

— Prayer —

Father, in the name of Jesus, would You help me master the realm of revival prayer? Put the words in my mouth that You want me to pray. Help me pray in with understanding prompted by Your Spirit and to pray in my heavenly language. Help me to release Your perfect will through my prayers.

When Revivalists Need to Repent

"When I kept silent, my bones grew old Through my groaning all the day long. For day and night Your hand was heavy upon me; My vitality was turned into the drought of summer" (Psalm 32:3-4).

Revivalists seem expert in calling people to repentance—and we should be. But sometimes the revivalist also needs to repent. Don't get mad at me and skip to the next page. You may think, "I've repented enough." But repentance is not a once and for all issue. Repentance is a lifestyle.

We can't fight the good fight of faith when we're walking in sin—and whatever is not of faith is sin (see Rom. 14:23). Words of revival prayer mixed with words of contention, competition and criticism don't reach God's ears. Repentance is a key to seeing accurately so we can pray accurately.

God told Isaiah, "What good is fasting when you keep on fighting and quarreling? This kind of fasting will never get you anywhere with me" (Is. 58:4). And again, Gold told the prophet, "When you spread out your hands, I will hide My eyes from you; Even though you make many prayers, I will not hear. Your hands are full of blood" (Is. 1:15). And Solomon wrote, "He who covers his sins will not prosper, but whoever confesses and forsakes them will have mercy" (Prov. 28:13).

Repentance seems to offend some believers, but it should not offend revivalists. The gift of repentance empowers revivalists for victory in the war against the enemies of revival. 1 John 1:18 says, "If we say that we have no sin, we deceive ourselves, and the truth is not in us."

The truth is, we have all fallen short of the glory of God (see Rom. 3:23). In fact, we all fall short of the glory of God every day. That's why we need a Savior and that's why we are charged with working out our own salvation with fear and trembling (see Phil 2:12). Let's lay aside the sin that besets us (see Heb. 12:1). Let's run to Him instead of away from Him when we sin. Our sin could block someone else's revival by diminishing our effectiveness.

— *Prayer* —

Father, in the name of Jesus, help me not to point a finger at others—calling others to repentance—until I have first pointed a finger at myself. Help me walk in a lifestyle of repentance that attracts Your Spirit into every aspect of my life. Help me to run to You instead of away from You when I sin.

Avoiding Carnal Revival-Killers

"As charcoal is to burning coals, and wood to fire, so is a contentious man to kindle strife"
(Proverbs 26:21).

Strife will kill the spirit of revival just about as fast as anything. When you yield to strife—a work of the flesh—you open the door to the demonic. Strife spreads like wildfire. So, what does strife look like and what causes it?

Where you see power struggles and exertion of superiority, you can't automatically blame Jezebel, witchcraft or religious spirits. Strife is very often the motivator. When you see arguing or contending over anything, it's not always rebellion. Strife is typically lurking. When you see double standards, strife could be at the root.

"Now the works of the flesh are manifest, which are these; Adultery, fornication, uncleanness, lasciviousness, idolatry, witchcraft, hatred, variance, emulations, wrath, strife, seditions, heresies, envyings, murders, drunkenness, revellings, and such like: of the which I tell you before, as I have also told you in time past, that they which do such things shall not inherit the kingdom of God" (Gal. 5:19-21, KJV).

Strife is an abomination to God (see Prov. 6:16-19). How can we wield His mighty weapons when we're engaged in an abomination? Strife affects the anointing and the flow of the Holy Ghost (see Ps. 133:1-3).

Strife grieves the Holy Spirit (Eph. 4:30). How can we gain victory in battle without the His Spirit? Strife is rooted in anger (see Prov. 29:22), hatred (see Prov. 10:12), pride (see Prov. 13:10) and a quarrelsome, self-seeking spirit (see Gal. 5:14-18; Luke 22:24-27). Strife plays in the field of flesh with all manner of sin.

It was James who also said this: "But if ye have bitter envying and strife in your hearts, glory not, and lie not against the truth. This wisdom descendeth not from above, but is earthly, sensual, devilish. For where envying and strife is, there is confusion and every evil work" (James 3:14-16, KJV).

— *Prayer* —

Father, in the name of Jesus, would You forgive me for any and every way that I have engaged in strife—breeding strife or sowing seeds of discord? I repent and renounce strife in all its manifestations. Help me not to walk in the works of the flesh but in the fruit of the Spirit.

The Jeremiah Lanphier Revivalist Anointing

"Continue earnestly in prayer, being vigilant in it with thanksgiving" (Colossians 4:2).

"It was exactly 12 noon on September 23, 1857—a little more than one hundred years ago. A tall, middle-aged former businessman climbed creaking stairs to the third story of an old church building in the heart of lower New York City.

"He entered an empty room, pulled out his pocket watch and sat down to wait. The placard outside read: 'Prayer Meeting from 12 to 1 o'clock—Stop 5, 10, or 20 minutes, or the whole hour, as your time admits.' It looked like no one had the time. As the minutes ticked by, the solitary waiter wondered if it were all a mistake."

That's how the story of Jeremiah Lanphier's Layman's Revival is laid out in *America's Great Revivals*, a compilation of revival history in the U.S. from 1734-2000. Lanphier was himself a Christian businessman, and part of the Presbyterian church. His first foray into ministry was evangelism—visiting local businesses and passing out tracts. But that wasn't bearing fruit, so he shifted his strategy.

Lanphier's journal tells more of the story. "One day as I was walking along the streets," Lanphier wrote, "the idea was suggested to my mind that an hour of prayer, from twelve to one o'clock, would be beneficial to businessmen."

Lanphier's initial prayer meeting at first looked like a dud. It was 12:30 before anyone joined him. Then another joined, and another. All told, they were six men praying. The following week the meeting swelled to twenty, then forty the week after that.

By October, Lanphier was hosting daily prayer meetings and by 1828 there were twenty such prayer rooms in New York. He even rented Burton's Theatre, with a three-thousand-seat capacity, to hold the crowd. Ultimately, ten thousand men gathered daily for prayer.

The result was the Layman's Revival, a revival birthed in prayer and led by laymen. The revival hit two years before the Civil War and spread all over America and inspired revivals in foreign lands.

— *Prayer* —

Father, in the name of Jesus, help me take a cue from Lanphier's strategy: prayer precedes revival. Help me be willing to shift my strategy if what I am doing is not bearing fruit. Help me to hear Your voice leading me to preach and pray in a way that sets the stage for revival.

Beware False Repentance

"For godly sorrow produces repentance leading to salvation, not to be regretted; but the sorrow of the world produces death" (2 Corinthians 7:10).

During revival, some people may come to the altar with tears streaming down their faces. But just because the tears are flowing doesn't mean the repentance is genuine.

False humility is one thing. False repentance is another. When the Lord sent Elijah with a word of condemnation to Ahab, he appeared to repent but it wasn't sincere. Elijah prophetically spoke these words:

"Behold, I will bring calamity on you. I will take away your posterity, and will cut off from Ahab every male in Israel, both bond and free. I will make your house like the house of Jeroboam the son of Nebat, and like the house of Baasha the son of Ahijah, because of the provocation with which you have provoked Me to anger, and made Israel sin.'

"And concerning Jezebel the Lord also spoke, saying, 'The dogs shall eat Jezebel by the wall of Jezreel.' The dogs shall eat whoever belongs to Ahab and dies in the city, and the birds of the air shall eat whoever dies in the field" (1 Kings 21:21-24).

How did Ahab respond? "He humbled tore his clothes and put sackcloth on his bod, and fasted and lay in sackcloth, and went about mourning" (2 Kings 21:27).

Although the repentance put off God's judgment, Ahab's heart really didn't change. Therefore, it was false repentance. It's like the kid who says he's sorry because he got caught but goes right back out and does the very same thing again.

Ahab tore his garments but not his heart. We know this because Ahab did not forsake his idols, he did not return Naboth's vineyard, and he did not bring Jezebel in order. In fact, he went on in the next chapter to put Micaiah in prison because he wouldn't prophesy a lie. Ultimately, actions speak louder than words. Ahab remained Jezebel's puppet until the day he died.

Look for the fruit of repentance in yourself and in others.

— Prayer —

Father, in the name of Jesus, would You help me get past surface level repentance and pursue a true change of heart by Your Spirit. And, Lord, help me recognize false repentance. Help me discern those who are not sincerely sorrowful over what they have done so I can walk carefully.

Discerning True Repentance

"Therefore bear fruits worthy of repentance" (Matthew 3:8).

We can say "Lord, forgive me" all day without entering into true repentance. There's true repentance and there's false repentance. There's no power in false repentance. There's shallow repentance and there's deep repentance. There's only a little power in shallow repentance.

As revivalists we need to walk in power, so we need to walk in repentance. I am not talking about walking around with a sin consciousness. I am talking about walking around with a righteousness consciousness. I am talking about cultivating a sensitivity to the Holy Spirit's conviction so we can repent quickly and shut the enemy out.

Repentance is merely coming into agreement with God's heart for us, which is holiness, and breaking agreement with darkness in our hearts. The enemy targets revivalists with temptation because if he can dilute our power and dilute our prayers, he can hold back God's will through us.

There are many benefits to repentance. Besides refreshing, there's proximity to God. Psalm 34:18 tells us, "The Lord is near to those who have a broken heart, and saves such as have a contrite spirit." And Psalm 51:17 reads, "The sacrifices of God are a broken spirit, a broken and a contrite heart—these, O God, You will not despise."

Sin compromises your legal position. Legally you are seated in heavenly places with Christ, but you can't sin in His seat. When your living condition doesn't match your legal position, your authority is diminished. Sin opens the door to the devil. You can't take authority over the devil when you are acting like the devil. The wages of sin is death. Rebellion is as the sin of witchcraft (see 1 Sam. 15:23).

Repentance brings us back into close proximity to God so we are under the canopy of His protection. Ecclesiastes 8:5 tells us: "He who keeps his command will experience nothing harmful; and a wise man's heart discerns both time and judgment." Repentance paves the way to more revival prayer answers. 1 John 3:22 assures, "And whatever we ask we receive from Him, because we keep His commandments and do those things that are pleasing in His sight."

— *Prayer* —

Father, in the name of Jesus, would You show me explicitly how the enemy is leveraging unconfessed or repetitive sin in my life to hold me back from Your high calling? May my heart break over my own sin. May I observe the ripple effect of sin's consequences in my life and deeply repent.

Reaching Revival Critics

"Who are you to judge another's servant? To his own master he stands or falls. Indeed, he will be made to stand, for God is able to make him stand" (Romans 14:4).

God has a way of reaching the hardest hearts. And John Wesley, founder of the Methodist movement, knew this all too well. He tells the story of a man he called J.H. who was standing against revival. Listen in and let this encourage you in the face of your critics.

"Being informed that people fell into strange fits at the societies, he came to see and judge for himself. But he was less satisfied than before; inasmuch, that he went about to see his acquaintances one after another till one o'clock in the morning, and labored above measure to convince them it was a delusion of the devil.

"We were going home when one met us in the street, and informed us that J. H. was fallen raving mad. It seems he sat down to dinner but had in mind first to end the sermon he had borrowed on Salvation by Faith. In reading the last page, he changed color, fell off his chair and began screaming terribly, and beating himself against the ground.

"He immediately fixed his eyes upon me, and stretching out his hand cried, 'Aye, this is he who I said was a deceiver of the people. But God has overtaken me. I said it was all a delusion. But this is no delusion.'

"He then roared out, 'O, thou devil! thou cursed devil! yea, thou legion of devils! thou canst not stay. Christ will cast thee out! I know His work is begun. Tear me to pieces if thou wilt, but thou canst not hurt me!' He then beat himself against the ground again, his breast heaving at the same time, as in the pangs of death, and great drops of sweat trickling down his face.

"We all betook ourselves to prayer; his pangs ceased and both his body and soul were set at liberty."

God has a way of reaching the hardest hearts. Don't let the critics stop you.

— *Prayer* —

Father, in the name of Jesus, give me a forehead like flint so that I can stand confidently against all opposition to the revival You are bringing. Help me not to get caught up in who is saying what about the move of God and focus my attention on stewarding what You have poured out.

The Billion Soul Harvest

"The harvest truly is great, but the laborers are few; therefore pray the Lord of the harvest to send out laborers into His harvest" (Luke 10:2).

Bob Jones, a seer prophet, went home to be with the Lord in 2014. But it wasn't the first time he experienced heaven. He tells a story of how he died and went to heaven in 1975. He would have stayed, he said, but the Lord sent him back with what we now call the billion-soul harvest prophecy.

"[God] put his arm out in front of me and said, 'No. I want you to go back. The enemy killed you before your time. I want you to go back', and I told him, 'I don't want to go back, I wasn't doing any good in the first place.' He said, 'You're a liar, because you quoted my Word and My Word always does good.'

"I said, 'it's painful back there, I've suffered persecution and it was terrible.' And He said, 'Well you're sort of cowardly too, but you have a love for souls and that's why I moved on you the way I did. I want you to go back and if you don't want to, I want you to look at this line right over here and if you can look at them and still want to come home, I'll take you home.'

"I looked at that line and that old Baptist in me sort of rose up and said, 'I'll go back for one soul Lord'. He said, 'I don't want you going back for one soul, I want you going back for one billion youth.' And I wish I could go back to touch the leaders because I am going to honor myself in one of the greatest awakenings of all time. It will be over six billion people on the earth at the time I'm speaking it. Which is now.

"And I'm going to bring youth in from every place of that number. And they're going to need leaders to bring them in.' And I said, 'I'll go back for that', I mean look at that line was one of the most horrible things I've ever seen. So all of a sudden, I was back and I leaped out of my body, and that towel was still around my face. And I looked and there was two huge angels." Let it be so, Lord!

— *Prayer* —

Father, in the name of Jesus, I am believing for the billion-soul harvest Bob Jones prophesied. Help me stand strong and firm in prayer for the laborers to go out into the ripe harvest fields and share the Good News with those who don't yet know Your gracious heart.

Circuit Rider Revivalists

"But you shall receive power when the Holy Spirit has come upon you; and you shall be witnesses to Me in Jerusalem, and in all Judea and Samaria, and to the end of the earth" (Acts 1:8).

Circuit riders were at the forefront of early Methodism. These preachers like John Wesley, Peter Cartwright, and Francis Asbury traveled from place to place on horseback preaching to the masses. In fact, the First Discipline of the Methodist church said, "Be merciful to your Beast. Not only ride moderately, but see with your own eyes that your horse is rubbed and fed."

Circuit riders were sort of like itinerant evangelists today, but without cars or airplanes. Because of geographic limitations to traveling on horseback, circuit riders were assigned territories. This was the first manifestation of a "preaching circuit." Some circuit riders traveled hundreds of thousands of miles on horseback during their ministry.

Circuit riders left families who never knew if or when they would return home due to the dangers of the assignment. They were selfless and sold out to the cause of Christ. Instead of church meetings, they held camp meetings that lasted up to a week or more.

"A Methodist preacher, when he felt that God had called him to preach, instead of hunting up a college or biblical institute, hunted up a hardy pony, and some traveling apparatus, and with his library always at hand, namely, a Bible, Hymn book, and Discipline, he started, and with a text that never wore out nor grew stale, he cried, 'Behold, the Lamb of God, that taketh away the sin of the world,'" Cartwright wrote in his autobiography.

"In this way he went through storms of wind, hail, snow, and rain; climbed hills and mountains, traversed valleys, plunged through swamps, swollen streams, lay out all night, wet, weary, and hungry, held his horse by the bridle all night, or tied him to a limb, slept with his saddle blanket for a bed, his saddle-bags for a pillow. Often he slept in dirty cabins, ate roasting ears for bread, drank butter-milk for coffee; took deer or bear meat, or wild turkey, for breakfast, dinner, and supper. This was old-fashioned Methodist preacher fare and fortune."

— *Prayer* —

Father, in the name of Jesus, let the modern-day circuit riders arise! Let bold men and women with a call to travel up and down the highways and byways of cities and nations go forth in the power of the Holy Spirit with the Word of God in their mouth to stir revival and awakening.

OCTOBER 21

The Revivalist's Cry

"But when He saw the multitudes, He was moved with compassion for them, because they were weary and scattered, like sheep having no shepherd" (Matthew 9:36).

You may be familiar with the beautiful hymn called *Spirit of the Living God, Fall Afresh on Me*. Inspired by a sermon on the Holy Spirit during an evangelical crusade in 1926, Daniel Iverson wrote the words that are essentially a cry for personal revival.

The hymn's lyrics are inspired by Acts 11:15, "And as I began to speak, the Holy Spirit fell upon them, as upon us at the beginning." The Holy Spirit was poured out on the Day of Pentecost, but there was a fresh outpouring that resembled the first encounter. The hymn's lyrics read: "Spirit of the Living God, fall fresh on me, Spirit of the Living God, fall fresh on me. Melt me, mold me, fill me, use me. Spirit of the Living God, fall fresh on me."

Long before Iverson penned this classic hymn, revivalist Evan Roberts prayed a similar prayer in Wales. Roberts first heard his contemporary, Seth Joshua, cry out "Lord, bend us." When young Roberts heard that prayer, it gripped his heart.

"I felt a living power pervading my bosom. It took my breath away and my legs trembled exceedingly. This living power became stronger and stronger as each one prayed, until I felt it would tear me apart. My whole bosom was a turmoil and if I had not prayed it would have burst ...

"I fell on my knees with my arms over the seat in front of me. My face was bathed in perspiration, and the tears flowed in streams. I cried out, 'Bend me, bend me!!' It was God's commending love which bent me ... what a wave of peace flooded my bosom ...

"I was filled with compassion for those who must bend at the judgement, and I wept. Following that, the salvation of the human soul was solemnly impressed on me. I felt ablaze with the desire to go through the length and breadth of Wales to tell of the savior."

— *Prayer* —

Spirit of the Living God, fall fresh on me. Melt me, mold me, fill me, use me. Spirit of the Living God, fall fresh on me. Bend me. Father, in the name of Jesus, this is my prayer. This is my desire. This is my pursuit. Help me position myself to receive everything You want to pour out.

The Bold-as-a Lion Revivalist

"The wicked flee when no one pursues, but the righteous are bold as a lion" (Proverbs 28:1.)

Revival demands bold preachers, not ear ticklers. I will go so far as to say perhaps we wouldn't need revival if we didn't have so many ear ticklers.

Paul told his spiritual son Timothy, "Preach the word! Be ready in season and out of season. Convince, rebuke, exhort, with all longsuffering and teaching. For the time will come when they will not endure sound doctrine, but according to their own desires, because they have itching ears, they will heap up for themselves teachers; and they will turn their ears away from the truth, and be turned aside to fables. But you be watchful in all things, endure afflictions, do the work of an evangelist, fulfill your ministry" (2 Tim. 4:2-5).

The time Paul spoke of has manifested in our midst.

Robert Barr, who started preaching at seventeen years old in South Africa in the 1940s, put it this way: "This is what our age needs, not an easy-moving message, the sort of thing that makes the hearer feel all nice inside, but a message profoundly disturbing. We have been far too afraid of disturbing people, but the Holy Spirit will have nothing to do with a message or with a minister who is afraid of disturbing.

"You might as well expect a surgeon to give place to a quack who claims to be able to do the job with some sweet tasting drug, as expect the Holy Spirit to agree that the tragic plight of human souls today can be met by soft and easy words.

"Calvary was anything but nice to look at, blood-soaked beams of wood, a bruised and bleeding body, not nice to look upon. But then Jesus was not dealing with a nice thing; He was dealing with the sin of the world, and that is what we are called upon to deal with today. Soft and easy words, soft-pedaling will never meet the need."

— *Prayer* —

Father, in the name of Jesus, help me be willing to receive words that bring conviction and correction to my soul. I don't want to stray from Your heart. And raise up a generation of preachers who are not afraid of the persecution that comes with bold Gospel preaching.

OCTOBER 23

Revival Midwives

"Therefore God dealt well with the midwives, and the people multiplied and grew very mighty" (Exodus 1:20).

Every revival needs a midwife—or two or three or more—to birth the move of God. Just as a midwife labors to help a woman birth a child, a revival midwife labors in the spirit through prayer until revival comes forth. Also called birthing intercessors, a midwife intercessor assigned to revival will tarry long in the prayer closet even unto travail until the rain of revival floods in.

Elijah served as a midwife, as well as a prophet, in Israel. There was a long famine in the land—and there was no revival. Elijah told Ahab to bring his false prophets to Mt. Carmel for a contest.

Elijah's challenge: Each would build an altar and the god who answered by fire would prove to be the real god. You know the story. The Baal prophets labored long and saw no results after many hours of crying out and even cutting themselves. Elijah simply called on God and fire fell and consumed the sacrifice immediately.

The purpose of the showdown with the false prophets was to bring the Israelites to repentance, which was the first step to revival. After the Israelites turned back to God, Elijah announced an end to the drought and transitioned from warrior mode to midwife mode.

1 Kings 20:42 tells us, "Elijah went up to the top of Carmel; then he bowed down on the ground, and put his face between his knees." Let the reader understand: This was the position of a woman giving birth in those days.

Elijah essentially entered into travail for rain. He was a midwife working on God's behalf to help birth His purposes in the earth. We don't know how long it took to birth the revival—we don't know how many hours he prayed—but we do know he sent his servant six times to look for signs of rain before he finally saw a rain cloud on the seventh trip.

Revival midwives need a word of the Lord and a persevering spirit to press through the opposition and bring revival from the womb of God through the birth canal and into the earth. Are you a revival midwife?

— *Prayer* —

Father, in the name of Jesus, I am willing to be used as a revival midwife. I don't want or need the credit. I just want Your will to be done—Your revival to come—to earth. I want to see the drought end and the rain of revival fall down upon a dry and thirsty land. Help me persevere through the dry seasons for revival's sake.

OCTOBER 24

Burning With a Burden

"For I could wish that I myself were accursed from Christ for my brethren, my countrymen according to the flesh, who are Israelites, to whom belongs the adoption as sons and daughters, the glory, the covenants, the giving of the Law, the temple service, and the promises" (Rom. 9:3-4).

You may be burning for revival, but are you burdened for revival? You can be both burning and burdened, but one without the other won't birth revival.

When we're burning, we're on fire. We have an intensity to pursue revival. It's an urgency in a desperate heart. A burden is a spiritual load. It's feeling the Holy Spirit's concern. We can burn all day, but without the burden we might not pray.

See, some people conference hop for the thrill of a prophecy or to witness signs and wonders. They are burning for the experience of revival but they are not necessarily burdened to the degree that they fall to their knees and cry out the God of revival through intercession.

Are you burdened for revival? Does your heart hunger for awakening in your nation? Dave Butts, president of Harvest Prayer Ministries, offers some insight:

"Revival comes to those who are desperate for it. Many today are talking about spiritual awakening and even beginning to pray about it. But have we allowed God to place within us the burden necessary to pray desperately for God to show up in our midst?

"Are we willing to 'pray the price' to see God move in a powerful way in the Church today? As I continue to learn how to move my prayers into alignment with God's will, praying Scripture has become increasingly important. As I pray God's Word, I find myself praying in ways I would never have found myself praying before. So it is as we begin to place ourselves before the Lord in asking for a burden for revival."

Many are willing to carry revival fire. Fewer are willing to carry the revival prayer burden, compelled by a compassion for the lost and an unselfish concern for others. Paul had this kind of burden for the churches he stewarded, praying for the Galatians, "My little children, for whom I labor in birth again until Christ is formed in you..." (Gal. 4:19).

— *Prayer* —

Father, in the name of Jesus, I want to burn and shine—but I also accept the burden. I am not just in it for the outpouring of Your Spirit. I want to carry Your heart for the lukewarm church—and for those who don't yet know Your Son. Give me a burden for revival that compels me to pray and share Your Gospel.

From Revival to Reformation

"Then Samuel spoke to all the house of Israel, saying, 'If you return to the Lord with all your hearts, then put away the foreign gods and the Ashtoreths from among you, and prepare your hearts for the Lord, and serve Him only; and He will deliver you from the hand of the Philistines" (1 Samuel 7:3).

Most revivals only last a few years. Even the Welsh Revival in 1904-1906 that saw sweeping reforms eventually waned—and so did the reforms. In my visit to Wales in 2018, you couldn't tell there had ever been a revival there. So what do we do?

Cindy Jacobs, co-founder of Generals International, proposes a massive paradigm shift back to a biblical worldview on every level. To reform means "to amend what is corrupt; to return things to their God-ordained order and organization."

As she sees it, many today are talking about the transformation of their nations, but transforming a nation is only "changing the outward form or appearance." Without a reformation, she says, we will never see lasting transformation.

"How we see truth depends on our starting point. The war for our minds and the way we think has largely been won by the way we have all been taught to see the world. This is why I want to bring up the subject of worldview. Most of us, even strong believers, see the world through a lens polluted by humanistic thinking, and on a deeper level than we could ever imagine," she writes in her book *Reformers Arise*.

"Even those of us who truly believe God's Word is the final authority have had our margins moved outside of scriptural bounds by the society in which we were educated. This education has not only been in the classroom but through media and supposedly neutral programs termed as 'scientific.' The more I've delved into the subject of the biblical discipleship of nations, the more I've realized that my own worldview has been affected by secularistic thinking."

Cindy's counsel? Engage both your heart and mind to become willing to make a radical shift in your thinking. To do that, ask the Holy Spirit to expose to you any way that you have been affected by secularism or any other "ism" that is ungodly.

— *Prayer* —

Father, in the name of Jesus, I want to see reformation in my city and nation, but I know reformation begins with me. Help me to make radical shifts in my thinking where I am out of line with Your Word. Expose and deliver me from any "isms" that pervert Your truth.

The Secret to Revival

"Then He spoke a parable to them, that men always ought to pray and not lose heart"
(Luke 18:1).

Horatius Bonar knew the secret to revival—and he shared it. Bonar, a Scottish churchman and poet in the 19th Century, offers this lasting insight: Revival men were men of prayer.

"It is true that they labored much, visited much, studied much, but they also prayed much. In this they abounded. They were much alone with God, replenishing their own souls from the living fountain that out of them might flow to their people rivers of living water.

"In our day there is doubtless among many a grievous mistake upon this point. Some who are really seeking to feed the flock, and to save souls, are led to exhaust their energies upon external duties and labors, overlooking the absolute necessity of enriching, ripening, filling, elevating their own souls by prayer and fasting.

"On this account there is much time wasted and labor thrown away. A single word, coming fresh from lips that have been kindled into heavenly warmth, by near fellowship with God, will avail more than a thousand others. If Christ's faithful ministers would act more on this principle, they would soon learn what an increased fruitfulness and power are thereby imparted to all their labors.

"Were more of each returning Saturday spent in fellowship with God, in solemn intercession for the people, in humiliation for sin, and supplication for the outpouring of the Spirit, our Sabbaths would be far more blessed, our sermons would be far more blessed, our sermons would be far more successful, our faces would shine as did the face of Moses, a more solemn awe and reverence would be over all our assemblies, and there would be fewer complaints of laboring in vain, or spending strength for naught.

"What might be lost in elaborate composition, or critical exactness of style or argument, would be far more than compensated for by the 'double portion of the Spirit' we might then expect to receive."

— *Prayer* —

Father, in the name of Jesus, give me a double portion of Your Spirit so I can pray twice as long, praise twice as long, worship twice as long, evangelize twice as long, and labor for Your Kingdom twice as long. Help me to keep first things first and continually sow to the Spirit.

OCTOBER 27

All We Need Is Love

"Let all that you do be done with love" (1 Corinthians 16:14).

While Jonathan Edwards is famous for his sermon *Sinners in the Hand of an Angry God*, David Brainerd took the exact opposite approach in his ministry to the Native Americans in 1745. He turned their hearts to Christ with love.

"In the morning I discoursed to the Indians at the house where I lodged: many of them were then much affected, and appeared surprisingly tender, so that a few words about their souls' concerns would cause the tears to flow freely, and produce many sobs and groans.

"In the afternoon, they being returned to the place where I had usually preached amongst them, I again discoursed to them there. There were about fifty-five persons in all, about forty that were capable of attending divine service with understanding. I insisted upon 1 John 4:10, "Herein is love." They seemed eager of hearing; but there appeared nothing very remarkable, except their attention, till near the close of my discourse; and then divine truths were attended with a surprising influence, and produced a great concern among them.

"There was scarce three in forty that could refrain from tears and bitter cries. They all, as one, seemed in an agony of soul to obtain an interest in Christ; and the more I discoursed of the love and compassion of God in sending his Son to suffer for the sins of men, and the more I invited them to come and partake of his love, the more their distress was aggravated, because they felt themselves unable to come. It was surprising to see how their hearts seemed to be pierced with the tender and melting invitations of the gospel, when there was not a word of terror spoken to them."

In revival, we must pray about what message will reach the listeners and turn hearts toward Christ. Edwards emphasized the reality of hell and the spirit of the fear of the Lord fell. Brainerd emphasized the reality of a loving Savior and it melted the hearts of the indigenous people.

— *Prayer* —

Father, in the name of Jesus, would You inspire my heart to share Your unconditional love with people who have only known love with strings attached? Would You help me witness Your unfailing love to people who have wrong perceptions of Your heart?

Releasing Revival

"Let us hear the conclusion of the whole matter: Fear God and keep His commandments, for this is man's all" (Ecclesiastes 12:13).

Charles Finney walked in such revival power that, at one point in his ministry, revival broke out when he showed up, without speaking a word. In his autobiography, he writes:

"The next morning, I went into the factory, to look through it. I observed there was a good deal of agitation among those who were busy at their looms, and their mules, and other implements. On passing through one of the apartments, where a great number of young women were attending to weaving, I observed a couple of them eyeing me, and speaking very earnestly; and I could see that they were a good deal agitated, although they laughed.

"I went slowly towards them. They saw me coming, and were evidently much excited. One of them was trying to mend a broken thread, and her hands trembled so that she could not mend it. I approached slowly, looking at the machinery, as I passed; but this girl grew more and more agitated, and could not proceed with her work.

"When I came within eight or ten feet of her, I looked solemnly at her. She was quite overcome, sunk down, and burst into tears. The impression caught almost like powder, and in a few moments nearly all in the room were in tears. This feeling spread through the factory Mr. W——, the owner was present, and seeing the state of things, he said to the superintendent, "Stop the mill, and let the people attend to religion; for it is more important that our souls should be saved than that this factory run."

"The gate was shut down, and the factory stopped; but where should we assemble? The superintendent suggested that the mule room was large; and, the mules being run up, we could assemble there. We did so, and a more powerful meeting I scarcely ever attended. It went on with great power. The revival went through the mill with astonishing power, and in the course of a few days nearly all in the mill were hopefully converted."

— Prayer —

Father, in the name of Jesus, I marvel at the power and presence Charles Finney walked in. It reminds me of how Peter's shadow healed people. Help me steward my spiritual life to the point that I look like Jesus. Let rivers of living water that convict hearts of the reality of Christ flow through me.

OCTOBER 29

The Lost Souls of Revival

"For the time will come when they will not endure sound doctrine, but according to their own desires, because they have itching ears, they will heap up for themselves teachers" (2 Timothy 4:3).

We read over and over again about conversions in revival. Any true revival leads to the salvation of many, and that means unbelievers—the curious and even critical seekers—need to hear the Gospel. Charles Finney, the father of Modern Revivalism, had some thoughts on how to be a soul-winner. He's one to listen to—he won over half a million souls to Christ in his ministry.

Finney pounds the drum called conviction of sins. We must not present a seeker-friendly Gospel that makes promises without repentance. He writes, "It is absurd to suppose that a careless, unconvicted sinner can intelligently and thankfully accept the Gospel offer of pardon, until he accepts the righteousness of God in his condemnation."

Once and only once that conviction comes, can the rescue come. Finney stresses the need for a Savior and how Christ paid the price for sin. He writes: "The truth should be preached to the persons present, and so personally applied as to compel everyone to feel that you mean him or her."

Souls need instruction in accordance with the measure of their intelligence, Finney writes, and a few simple truths, when wisely applied and illuminated by the Holy Ghost, will convert children to Christ: "I say wisely applied, for they too are sinners, and need the application of the law, as a schoolmaster, to bring them to Christ, that they may be justified by faith."

Finney offers these strong words: "Instead of attempting to please our people in their sins, we should continually endeavor to hunt and persuade them out of their sins. Brethren, let us do it, as we would not have our skirts defiled with their blood. If we pursue this course, and constantly preach with unction and power, and abide in the fullness of the doctrine of Christ, we may joyfully expect to save ourselves and them that hear us."

— Prayer —

Father, in the name of Jesus, would You help me be so convinced that what Your Word says is true that I will boldly proclaim it? Help me to never water down the truth to win people to Christ. Put Your very words in my mouth as I share the compassion of Christ with the lost.

The Character of the Revivalist

"He who walks with integrity walks securely, but he who perverts his ways will become known"
(Proverbs 10:9).

We've seen revivals where the revivalist lived one life in public and an altogether different life in private. Character matters—and Finney knew this. Charles Finney, the father of Modern Revivalism, offers some tips for developing the character of an effective revivalist.

"Constantly maintain a close walk with God. Make the Bible your book of books. Study it much, upon your knees, waiting for divine light. Keep yourself pure—in will, in thought, in feeling, in word and action. Be diligent and laborious, 'in season and out of season.'

"See that your own habits are in all respects correct; that you are temperate in all things free from the stain or smell of tobacco, alcohol, drugs, or anything of which you have reason to be ashamed and which may stumble others. Bridle your tongue, and be not given to idle and unprofitable conversation.

"Be sure to teach them as well by example as by precept. Practice yourself what you preach. Guard your weak points. If naturally tending to gayety and trifling, watch against occasions of failure in this direction. If naturally somber and unsocial, guard against moroseness and unsociability. Avoid all affectation and sham in all things. Be what you profess to be, and you will have no temptation to 'make believe.'

"Let simplicity, sincerity, and Christian propriety stamp your whole life. Never let the question of your popularity with your people influence your preaching. Be sure to 'commend yourself to every man's conscience in the sight of God.' Be 'not a lover of filthy lucre.' Avoid every appearance of vanity. Maintain your pastoral integrity and independence, lest you sear your conscience, quench the Holy Spirit, forfeit the confidence of your people, and lose the favor of God.

"Repel every attempt to close your mouth against whatever is extravagant, wrong, or injurious amongst your people. Be an example to the flock, and let your life illustrate your teaching. Remember that your actions and spirit will teach even more impressively than your sermons. See that you personally know and daily live upon Christ."

— *Prayer* —

Father, in the name of Jesus, character trumps gifts so help me refine my character. I know I cannot change myself, but You can change me. You can conform me into the image of Christ, who is revival. You can move me from glory to glory. Make me an example to the flock.

OCTOBER 31

The A.B. Simpson Revivalist Anointing

"This is the word of the Lord to Zerubbabel: 'Not by might nor by power, but by My Spirit,' says the Lord of hosts" (Zechariah 4:6).

With a deacon dad, A.B. Simpson's family pressured him to go into the ministry. But the young Canadian was conflicted.

A fourteen-year-old Simpson went to Toronto's Knox College to train to become a Presbyterian minister but had an emotional and physical breakdown in the process. He convinced himself he could die at any moment and was afraid he might die without knowing God. He surrendered fully to Christ in 1858.

By 1865, Simpson graduated and started pastoring at Knox Church in Hamilton, Ontario. With twelve hundred members, it was the second-largest church in Canada. He added seven hundred fifty members during his tenure there before moving to Louisville, KY in 1874 to pastor a church during the American Civil War. Still struggling with his health, his father was concerned he was killing himself.

Five years later, Simpson moved to New York City to pastor the Thirteenth Street Presbyterian Church. That's where he caught a revelation of God's healing power and started teaching on divine healing. God healed his heart in 1881 and he launched into ministering to Manhattan's immigrants. He also published missionary journals and magazines and set out into multicultural missions. He wrote:

"The chief danger of the Church today is that it is trying to get on the same side as the world, instead of turning the world upside down. Our Master expects us to accomplish results, even if they bring opposition and conflict. Anything is better than compromise, apathy, and paralysis. God give to us an intense cry for the old-time power of the Gospel and the Holy Ghost!"

Simpson founded The Christian and Ministry Alliance, a society devoted to experiencing the "deeper life" in Christ and completing the Great Commission and coined the doctrine of The Fourfold Gospel of Christ—our Savior, Sanctifier, Healer and Coming King.

Speaking from personal experience, Simpson said: "God is not looking for extraordinary characters as His instruments, but He is looking for humble instruments through whom He can be honored throughout the ages."

— *Prayer* —

Father, in the name of Jesus, would You help me catch a revelation in my generation that helps birth an awakening among those who don't know You? I want to turn the world upside down for Jesus. Would You give me an anointing like A.B. Simpson?

NOVEMBER

"The depth of our repentance will determine the depth of our revival."—Frank Bartleman

Determined To See Revival

"Do you not know that those who run in a race all run, but one receives the prize? Run in such a way that you may obtain it" (1 Corinthians 9:24).

Many years ago, the Holy Spirit told me, "Put your determination where your desire is." Ultimately, that's what we do whether we know it or not. If we are determined to see a new movie, we will go see it. If we are determined to eat a hamburger after church, we will go eat it. If we are determined to see revival, we will press into it.

Here's the point: When you want something bad enough, you'll make sacrifices to get it. You will do whatever it takes for however long it takes. And you will see revival—but not without a fight. Remember, the Kingdom of God suffers violence, but the violent take it by force (see Matt. 11:12).

First of all, the enemy is going to fight your personal revival because he knows once you get on fire, you'll set others on fire. The enemy knows once you are on fire, you'll burn him. He knows once you are on fire, others will want what you carry.

Your flesh is going to fight your personal revival because your flesh is hostile toward God. Your flesh wants what it wants when it wants it. Your flesh wants to sit in front of the TV with some popcorn and ice cream. The determining factor in personal revival is your will.

God wants to revive you. God wants you to walk in His peace, joy, love and security. It goes back to a simple question: How bad do you want it? How determined are you to get it?

Leonard Ravenhill "I know not what course others may take; but as for me, GIVE ME REVIVAL in my soul and in my church and in my nation—or GIVE ME DEATH!"

Paul said, "I die daily." It's a daily decision to walk in revival. It's a daily decision to crucify the flesh and pursue God and His will. Surrender demands determination.

— *Prayer* —

Father, in the name of Jesus, I surrender to Your will. I want what You want more than anything. Change the desires of my heart if they don't line up with what You want for me. I know we both want revival, so give me a determination to see revival in my generation.

No More Hasty Repentance

"Do you see a man hasty in his words? There is more hope for a fool than for him"
(Proverbs 29:20).

A.W. Tozer, an American pastor, author and magazine editor, once said these cutting words: "Do not hurry to get it over with. Hasty repentance means shallow spiritual experience and lack of certainty in the whole life. Let godly sorrow do her healing work. Until we allow the consciousness of sin to wound us we will never develop a fear of evil. It is our wretched habit of tolerating sin that keeps us in our half-dead condition."

"Hasty repentance means shallow spiritual experience…" These are strong words, indeed. But can we take them to heart? Sometimes, we're not fully aware of our sin and its impact. David sinned with Bathsheba, had Uriah the Hittite murdered, and went on with business as usual in the Kingdom of Israel for months before God sent a prophet to confront him and bring him to repentance.

When David's eyes were fully opened to the sin, he didn't gloss over it. He told Nathan, "I have sinned against the Lord." David started crying out for mercy. He fasted and laid all night on the ground pleading with God. This was not hasty repentance, but a deep sorrow.

Too many Christians seem to thing saying, "Sorry God" and moving on is sufficient. It's not sufficient. You say sorry when you bump into someone. Sorry isn't enough when we sin. We need to repent. We don't have to beat ourselves up, but we should not treat our sin lightly.

I was in a meeting in the Midwest where revival was birthed before my eyes. Many twenty-somethings were sitting at the altar when a word of knowledge came forth about sexual sin. It got very quiet for some time. To say that the atmosphere was tense is an understatement.

The Holy Spirit brought such a deep conviction of sin that these young people began crying out loud, "God, forgive me of pornography." "God forgive me for jealousy." "God forgive me of my pride." This went on for about twenty minutes. There were tears everywhere as these young people publicly cried out, confessing their sins. And revival went on for months after that ignition.

— *Prayer* —

Father, in the name of Jesus, I renounce all hasty repentance. No longer will I treat my sin lightly. Forgive me for being oblivious to how sin affects my relationship with You and others. Forgive me for merely being sorry but not changing my mind—for not truly repenting.

NOVEMBER 3

Snakes in the Revival Fire

"Behold, I give you the authority to trample on serpents and scorpions, and over all the power of the enemy, and nothing shall by any means hurt you" (Luke 10:19).

Make no mistake there are snakes in the revival fire. When the fire gets hot, the heat will drive out the snakes. If you don't expect the snakes, you might get bit! You might be caught off guard—even blindsided by the snake bites.

What are the snakes? The snakes are those who oppose revival. The snakes are those who don't believe in manifestations of the Holy Spirit, such as travail or trembling under the power of God. There are snakes are the critics who come out of the fire to quench the Spirit rather than embracing what God is doing. There's a snake that questions if the move is real or if people are just overly emotional.

Paul the apostle knew about snakes in the fire. Consider what happened when he landed in the Isle of Malta, shipwrecked. Let's look at Acts 28:1-6:

"But when Paul had gathered a bundle of sticks and laid them on the fire, a viper came out because of the heat, and fastened on his hand. So when the natives saw the creature hanging from his hand, they said to one another, 'No doubt this man is a murderer, whom, though he has escaped the sea, yet justice does not allow to live.'

"But he shook off the creature into the fire and suffered no harm. However, they were expecting that he would swell up or suddenly fall down dead. But after they had looked for a long time and saw no harm come to him, they changed their minds and said that he was a god."

Notice how this wasn't a garden snake. It was a poisonous snake. When revival fire starts burning, the deadly snakes come out with an assignment to kill the move of God. But revival fire will also cause the poison from past snake bites to manifest in people who needed deliverance. If there's poison in us from past hurts and wounds, the heat of the Holy Spirit will drive it to the surface for freedom's sake.

— Prayer —

Father, in the name of Jesus, get the poison out of me. I don't want to oppose the revival You are bringing. Help me to be wise as a serpent, knowing that the snakes will slither out of the revival fire to put a damper on Your will. Help me, like Paul, to shake off the snakes.

NOVEMBER 4
Mountain-Shaking Revival Prayer
"Oh, that You would rend the heavens! That You would come down! That the mountains might shake at Your presence" (Isaiah 64:1).

How bad do you want revival? How bad you want to see His presence permeate your heart, your city, and your nation? Do you want it bad enough to cry out day and night and night and day, week by week, month by month and year by year? Isaiah cried, "Oh, that You would rend the heavens"

Many grow weary in well doing and give up right before the bowls tip over and His Spirit is poured out. We need to persevere in prayer until we see the promise of revival. We need to release petitions that touch God's heart, like Isaiah did. We need to stand and withstand in the evil day until awakening comes. We need to stand like Isaiah. Isaiah 64 is titled, "A Prayer for Help" in my Bible.

In Isaiah 64:1-5, Isaiah cries out, "Oh, that You would rend the heavens! That You would come down! That the mountains might shake at Your presence—as fire burns brushwood, as fire causes water to boil—to make Your name known to Your adversaries, that the nations may tremble at Your presence!

"When You did awesome things for which we did not look, You came down, the mountains shook at Your presence. For since the beginning of the world men have not heard nor perceived by the ear, nor has the eye seen any God besides You, who acts for the one who waits for Him. You meet him who rejoices and does righteousness, Who remembers You in Your ways. You are indeed angry, for we have sinned—in these ways we continue; And we need to be saved."

The New Living Translation of Isaiah 64:1 puts it this way, "Oh, that you would burst from the heavens and come down." *The New American Standard Bible* cries, "Oh, that You would tear open the heavens and come down." *The Contemporary English Version* reads, "Rip the heavens apart! Come down, Lord." These are violent connotations prayed in the context of violent repentance and violent intercession. Pray Isaiah 64 repeatedly.

— *Prayer* —
Oh, that You would rend the heavens God and come down. Oh, that You would burst forth and come and visit Your people today, right here and right now. That is my heart's cry. That is what I want more than anything. There's nothing I desire more than Your presence.

When Holy Spirit Refreshing Comes

"Repent therefore and be converted, that your sins may be blotted out, so that times of refreshing may come from the presence of the Lord" (Acts 3:19).

Scripture speaks loud and clear about how to step into times of refreshing. It's not the way of the world. It's not a vacation or a nice dinner and movie on the weekend. It's a spiritual refreshing—a deeper refreshing only the Holy Spirit can bring. That spiritual refreshing can ripple through every part of our life—and it starts with repentance.

"So repent [change your inner self—your old way of thinking, regret past sins] and return [to God—seek His purpose for your life], so that your sins may be wiped away [blotted out, completely erased], so that times of refreshing may come from the presence of the Lord [restoring you like a cool wind on a hot day]" (Acts 3:19, AMP).

Refresh means to restore strength and animation. But refresh also means to revive. So when we talk about times of refreshing, we're talking about times of revival. We're talking about times where God breaks in and washes over you with His love, peace, and joy.

Indeed, many revivalists release fire but they need to enter a different type of revival in their own life. They don't need a goosebump. They need a refreshing. A refreshing restores strength to the weary—to those who have emptied themselves of themselves by pouring out their lives as a drink offering for those who need salvation. The refreshing restores virtue in us.

Refresh also means to "freshen up." Think of women who go to the restroom to freshen up their makeup. But this is a spiritual refreshing. Maybe your relationship with the Holy Spirit has become too routine, almost stale. God wants to bring a refreshing. Perhaps you are not receiving revelation like you once did. God wants to freshen up your revelation and freshen up your anointing as the wind of the Spirit blows over you.

Refresh also means to restore or maintain by renewing a supply. Times of refreshing, then, are times of restoration. What part of your life needs restoration? Is it your family? A friendship? Your finances? God wants to restore what the enemy stole—with interest—during times of refreshing.

— *Prayer* —

Father, in the name of Jesus, I repent of my sins that hold back the fullness of Your presence in my life. Forgive me, Lord, and let Your winds of refreshing blow in my life even now. Blow away all the weariness and worry and blow over me with peace and joy in Your presence.

A Militant Revival

"For I also am a man under authority, having soldiers under me. And I say to this one, 'Go,' and he goes; and to another, 'Come,' and he comes; and to my servant, 'Do this,' and he does it.' When Jesus heard it, He marveled, and said to those who followed, 'Assuredly, I say to you, I have not found such great faith, not even in Israel!" (Matthew 8:9-10)

You've probably seen the viral video of U.S. Marines singing *Days of Elijah* in unison. It's touching, but it's only the first fruits of what we long to see in the military. We want to see full-blown revival hit militaries around the world. Anything is possible with God (see Matt. 19:26). Of course, we won't see it if we don't pray for it.

So how do we pray for revival among soldiers, sailors, airmen and other members of militaries in the nations of the earth?

Pray for the word of the Lord to run swiftly throughout militaries (see 2 Thess. 3:1). Pray for revival to come to barracks around the world. Pray the kindness of God would lead soldiers to repentance. Pray for those in battle to call upon the name of the Lord so they will be saved (see Rom. 10:13).

Pray soldiers would know God intimately like never before and hear His battle strategies. Pray military personnel would trust in the Lord with all their hearts and lean not on their own understanding as they seek to protect and defend (see Prov. 3:5). Pray that military personnel will not be deceived by the enemy.

Pray for military warriors who have a heart like David's for our God and who believe in Him at all costs (see Acts 13:22, Psalm 18:2, Heb. 10:5). Pray for the military warriors to become sold out Jehovah worshippers like David, who never lost a battle.

Pray for the Lord to be their Rock, who trains their hands for war and fingers for battle (see Ps. 144:1). Pray that the testing of their faith will produce perseverance. Pray that righteous militaries will be mature and complete, not lacking anything. Pray that they would walk in His wisdom (see James 1:2-5).

— *Prayer* —

Father, in the name of Jesus, I thank You for righteous militaries that uphold Your will and protect people in times of war. Father, bring salvation to soldiers in every nation—to them and their families. Help them get on Your side like Joshua did, no matter what nation they serve.

NOVEMBER 7

The Mother of the Holiness Movement

"Village life ceased, it ceased in Israel, until I, Deborah, arose, arose a mother in Israel" (Judges 4:7).

While Charles Finney goes down in history as the Father of Modern Revivalism, Phoebe Palmer takes her place in the chronicles of revival as the Mother of the Holiness Movement. Palmer was born in 1807 and turned to Christ during the Methodist revival in the 1830s. She sold out completely and started leading others to the presence and power of God through salvation in Christ.

Historian Fred Day offers these words about Mother Palmer: "There's a great story related to her travels as an evangelistic speaker where she is riding a steamer. And the boiler catches fire. And the ship is on fire and there is great panic. And she calmed the crowd by leading a hymn sing. and the story goes that when the ship docked in New York one of the passengers was heard to say, 'Thank God for the Methodists.'"

Palmer was a preacher before women were supposed to be preachers. She led Bible studies. She published her writings in books. And she preached at more than three hundred camp meetings during the revival. But her influence in Christianity didn't come without personal trials. She lost her husband and three of her six children in an oil lamp fire in their home.

God used her despite the tragedy. According to Christian History Institute (CHI), Palmer was the most influential woman in the largest, fastest-growing religious group in the mid-19th Century—Methodism. CHI Offers:

"By her initiative, missions were begun, camp-meetings instituted, and many thousands attested to the transforming power of divine grace. She mothered a nationwide movement that birthed such denominations as the Church of the Nazarene and the Salvation Army, bridged 18th-century Methodist revivalism to 20th-century Pentecostalism, and pioneered in social reform and female ministry."

While some today still don't believe God can use women to do anything more than cook, clean, pray and tend to children, Palmer proved that, like Deborah and Anna the prophetess before her, women are part and parcel of God's plans for revival.

— Prayer —

Father, in the name of Jesus, would You help me to stop looking at what I don't have and submitting to the limitations of the world and the church that doesn't understand my calling? Help me to defy the odds and complete the work You sent me to do despite the naysayers.

The Martin Lloyd-Jones Revivalist Anointing

"But God forbid that I should boast except in the cross of our Lord Jesus Christ, by whom the world has been crucified to me, and I to the world" (Galatians 6:14).

On his tombstone are words from 1 Corinthians 2:2, "For I determined not to know anything among you, save Jesus Christ, and him crucified." He was a Welshman's Welshman known for his fiery preaching and logic.

Although he never led a revival, Martin Lloyd-Jones understood revival like few others in his generation. He was a true student of revival. He passed away in 1981 after serving as the minister of Westminster Chapel in London for nearly thirty years.

"Revival, above everything else, is a glorification of the Lord Jesus Christ, the Son of God. It is the restoration of Him to the center of the life of the Church. You find this warm devotion, personal devotion, to Him," he said.

"The essence of a revival is that the Holy Spirit comes down upon a number of people together, upon a whole church, upon a number of churches, districts, or perhaps a whole country. That is what is meant by revival. It is, if you like, a visitation of the Holy Spirit, or another term that has often been used is this--an outpouring of the Holy Spirit.

"What the people are conscious of is that it is as if something has suddenly come down upon them ... What are these things of which they become so aware? First and foremost, the glory and the holiness of God. Have you ever noticed, as you read your Bibles, the effect on these people as they suddenly realized the presence of God?

"Like Job, they put their hands on their mouths or like Isaiah they say, 'Woe is unto me! For I am undone; because I am a man of unclean lips.' They have just had a realization of the holiness and of the majesty and the glory of God. That always happens in a revival."

Martin Lloyd-Jones' revival sermons are still inspiring audiences in the 21st Century. When you read them, I pray you will catch his heart for revival.

— Prayer —

Father, in the name of Jesus, would You give me the perseverance and the hunger to study the dynamics of revival so I can articulate what true revival is—and what it's not? Give me a spirit of wisdom, revelation and understanding about revival like you gave Martin Lloyd-Jones.

NOVEMBER 9

Revival in the Education Mountain

"Train up a child in the way he should go, and when he is old he will not depart from it" (Proverbs 22:6).

Parents around the world are voicing concerns about what their children are being taught—or not being taught—in classrooms. Add to that vaccine mandates, school shootings and perverse indoctrination and you've got a recipe for revolt.

See, the late Nelson Mandela got it right when he said, "Education is the most powerful weapon which you can use to change the world." The problem is education can also be used to warp the minds of God-loving children, or pull them into antichrist ideologies before they even have the opportunity to meet their Lord and Savior Jesus Christ.

If we want to take nations back for Christ, we need to actively pray for the educational system, which has tremendous opportunity to sway young minds toward good or evil.

Decree the children are the Lord's and are off limits to perverse teachings and unhealthy ideologies (see Jer. 1:5; Luke 18:16). Declare each child is a gift from God and has the right to know his or her Maker, to be taught God's Word, and truthful representations of history (see James 1:17; Ps. 127:3).

Pray parents take to heart God's directive to teach and train up a child in the way they should go—a way of righteousness and serving the Lord as King (see Prov. 22:6; Eph. 6:4). Forbid school board associations, district and school leadership, and curriculum developers from teaching evil doctrines of demons to children in our educational system (see 3 John 1:4; Prov. 16:12).

Pray God will raise up and send godly people to the educational mountains who will not compromise the Word of God (see Ex. 18:21; Matt. 20:26). Pray God will pour out His Spirit on the schools and let His manifest presence rest upon students will lead to a revival that sweeps through campus (see Acts 2:17; 2 Cor. 3:17).

— *Prayer* —

Father, in the name of Jesus, would You forgive me for not keeping the children and the education system in prayer? Help me to stand for Your will for the next generation. Help me to pray without ceasing for the education mountain, least children be led astray.

When God Says 'Aloha'

"The blind see and the lame walk; the lepers are cleansed and the deaf hear; the dead are raised up and the poor have the gospel preached to them" (Matthew 11:5).

Titus Coan saw revivals under Charles Finney's ministry. The American missionary wanted to see God do it again in his mission field: Hawaii. Coan landed in the islands in 1834, started learning the language and launched a college to train the locals.

Coan also traveled to preach the Gospel up to five times a day in different locations across the Hawaiian Islands. The message of the Good News was so irresistible the people did not want to go home. In what reads like a scene out of Jesus's earthly ministry, Coan once said:

"When I supposed they would return to their homes and give me rest, they remained and crowded around me so earnestly that I had no time to eat, and in places where I spent my nights they filled the house to its entire capacity, leaving scores outside that could not enter."

In Puna, miracles started breaking out. The lame and maimed were healed. The blind regained their sight. The power of God was so strong that the high priest of the volcano in Puna surrendered his life to Christ. Once known for murder and adultery, he was set on fire for the Jesus.

During his sermon, *Repentance Toward God and Faith in the Lord Jesus*, one man in the large crowd cried out for mercy. Coan tells the rest of the story: "His weeping was so loud, and his trembling so great, that the whole congregation was moved as by a common sympathy. Many wept aloud, and many commenced praying together. The scene was such as I had never before witnessed.

"I stood dumb in the midst of this weeping, wailing, praying multitude, not being able to make myself heard for about twenty minutes. When the noise was hushed, I continued my address with words of caution, lest they should feel that this kind of demonstration atoned for their sins, and rendered them acceptable before God. I assured them that all the Lord required was godly sorrow for the past, present faith in Christ, and henceforth faithful, filial, and cheerful obedience."

Do it again, Lord!

— *Prayer* —

Father, in the name of Jesus, I long to see Your supernatural power manifest again. Would You give me the grace of surrender to do Your will, to go where others don't want to go and to step out in faith to work miracles? I know You are the same yesterday, today and forever.

Billy Graham's Revival Exhortation

"Let your light so shine before men, that they may see your good works and glorify your Father in heaven" (Matthew 5:15-17).

Billy Graham was one of the greatest evangelists of the 20th Century—indeed, perhaps one of the most influential of all time. He was a praying man—and a man who prayed for revival. Here is his exhortation to believers everywhere who want to see revival:

"Begin to live the Christian life, not passively nor indifferently but wholeheartedly for Christ. Let your light shine. Let people see that you have a faith that works, a Christ who gives you victory. And earnestly pray for a spiritual awakening. Pray for revival in your church, your community, your city and your country, all the while asking God to use you and lead you in winning others. A worldwide spiritual revival is our only hope if we are to survive as a human race.

"God is the author of revival. We Christians can prepare the atmosphere through our earnest prayer, exemplary living and being contrite and humble. But only God can revive the spirit and revive the heart of a person.

"Many are asking these days, 'What will revival do for the world?' 'What would a worldwide revival do in practical terms?' A spiritual awakening will create moral stamina and consciousness, bring back the sanctity of the home, make marriage an institution instead of an experiment, strengthen the bulwarks of freedom and bring integrity back to people.

"I pray that men and women from shore to shore at this desperate and crucial hour in history will lift their hearts to God in repentance from sin and faith in Christ, and that they will begin living the Christian life."

— *Prayer* —

Father, in the name of Jesus, help me actively live the Christian life with passionate pursuit of Your presence and Your will. Give me the fortitude to add works to my faith that people can see I am serious about Your Kingdom. Use me to win souls.
Help me see what revival will do for the world and be inspired to go all in.

The Rise of Revival Teachers

"Be diligent to present yourself approved to God, a worker who does not need to be ashamed, rightly dividing the word of truth" (2 Timothy 2:15).

Teachers are a critical gift before, during and after revival. The five-fold teacher establishes accurate belief systems and strong biblical foundations, renews the corporate mindset and steers the body away from deception.

While we want revival fire and wind, we must recognize and embrace the need for the teacher's grace in revival. Teachers have massive responsibilities in the Kingdom of God. The words teachers speak under the anointing directly impact the minds of believers. Bible-based teaching is absolutely key for birthing and sustaining true revival, as I wrote in my book, *Revival Hubs Rising*.

Of course, the Bible also speaks of false teachers whose instruction is not sound and tickles ears of those who don't love the truth (see 2 Tim. 4:3-4). Peter also warns about false teachers who bring in destructive heresies, even denying the Master who brought them (see 2 Peter 2:1). False teachers will arise in revival, and we need to hold fast to the truth.

Like true teachers, false teachers affect the belief systems of those who listen—and this poor influence can spread far and wide. Social media is full of "Christian" teachers whose doctrine does not line up with the Word of God.

In the midst of revival, believers must come into their full identity with no hindrances. They must know, understand, and activate the power of God in their lives so that they can be a Kingdom connection, releasing God's power to others. False teaching and wrong believing will block the flow.

In a healthy revival, teachers will lock arms with the rest of the five-fold to advance truth that leads to transformation, first of minds, then of bodies of believers, then of cities and regions.

— *Prayer* —

Father, in the name of Jesus, would You help me to appreciate the gift and grace on the life of a teacher who can prepare us for revival, warn us of revival errors, and put banks on the river of revival fire? Help me avoid false teachers in the midst of revival and to rightly divide the word of truth.

Divine Revival Connections

"And it shall come to pass in the last days, says God, that I will pour out of My Spirit on all flesh; Your sons and your daughters shall prophesy, your young men shall see visions, your old men shall dream dreams" (Acts 2:17).

In those early days of the Lord's move in China, Watchman Nee fasted and prayed every Saturday for the entire day, according to Witness Lee, one of his disciples, in *The History of the Church and the Local Churches*. Nee was a Chinese church leader in the 20th Century. Here's the account:

"For about a year, he fasted and prayed on Saturday and preached on the Lord's Day. During that time nearly all his classmates were saved. The entire atmosphere of his school changed. Everywhere at the school, students could be seen reading the Bible, praying together, or fellowshipping together.

"During this time of revival, Brother Nee and some other young brothers with him heard that in Nanking, far away from their hometown, a young Christian had been raised up by the Lord named Ruth Lee," Lee wrote. "She agreed to come and would make the trip by boat."

Nee had an Acts 2-type dream that night. The dream featured Sister Lee. When he woke up the next day, he set out to meet the woman, still not completely sure if his dream was divine. He had never seen her before, but sure enough, when she stepped off the boat, she was the woman he saw in the dream.

"He did not relate his dream to Miss Lee until about four years later in 1927. The Lord arranged an environment in which she was forced to give up her work in Nanking. Then she came to Shanghai, and from that time she worked with Brother Nee," Lee wrote.

"The meetings which Brother Nee held in Foochow when Miss Lee came brought in a big revival. Because the saints there did not have a big hall, they eventually met in an open field. Everyone in the congregation brought a chair with him. If someone did not bring a chair, he had to stand. Many were saved during this time, and that was the first revival among us. The news of this revival spread to many places, and many were helped to become clear about the assurance of salvation."

— Prayer —

Father, in the name of Jesus, would You give me dreams of the revival that You want to bring in my life, in my church, and in my city, nation and generation? Give me divine connections for the sake of revival. Bring me divine appointments with people of like precious faith.

From Revival to Resurrection Power

"The Spirit of Him who raised Jesus from the dead dwells in you..." (Romans 8:11).

Paul said, "I want to know Christ and experience the mighty power that raised him from the dead. I want to suffer with him, sharing in his death, so that one way or another I will experience the resurrection from the dead!" (Phil. 3:10-11)

Do you remember when you experienced the power of His resurrection? The same power that raised Christ from the dead raised you from spiritual death. But getting saved is just the beginning. Jesus said signs and wonders would follow those who believe.

So, yes, we want to walk in revival. But we want to move from revival to resurrection power. The Spirit that raised Christ from the dead dwells in us (see Rom. 8:11). Put another way, resurrection power lives in us. That resurrection power is what makes us more than conquerors in Christ Jesus (see Rom. 8:37). That resurrection power is what sets the stage for us to walk in the supernatural.

We need to understand the power of His resurrection. When you understand the power of His resurrection, you will walk in divine health and emotional wholeness; you will release signs, wonders and miracles; you will be free from every tie that binds; you will find safety in the midst of the storm. When you understand the power of His resurrection, it will change your whole life and position you as a change agent in the earth.

The power of His resurrection is the Holy Spirit. Jesus operated in resurrection power and plainly said, "I am the resurrection and the life." He was filled with the Holy Spirit without measure. This was key to His ministry.

So, yes, revival is a goal. But walking in resurrection power is the higher calling. Resurrection power brings salvation. Resurrection power brings healing from all manner of sickness and disease. Resurrection power brings deliverance from demon oppression. Resurrection power brings rescue from natural and spiritual danger. Cry out for resurrection power!

— *Prayer* —

Father, in the name of Jesus, would You give me a revelation that there's more than revival? Help me to press past revival and awakening to resurrection power that flows from my belly like rivers of living water. Help me to extend my faith to pray for miracles so people can see Jesus is alive.

The Andrew Murray Revivalist Anointing

"But you, when you pray, go into your room, and when you have shut your door, pray to your Father who is in the secret place; and your Father who sees in secret will reward you openly" (Matthew 6:6).

"A true revival means nothing less than a revolution, casting out the spirit of worldliness and selfishness, and making God and His love triumph in the heart and life." So said Andrew Murray.

Murray was a South African writer, teacher and pastor whose ministry spanned the 19th and 20th centuries. He wrote over two hundred books and tracts over sixty years of ministry. His materials still help Christians everywhere mature in Christ.

But more than anything, Murray was a man of deep prayer. Murray learned this from his father. Every night for thirty-six years, his father prayed for revival. When his parents sent him to live with his uncle in Scotland to be educated, he was exposed to powerful Reformed preachers, such as Dr. Chalmers and William Burns, who helped shape his theology.

"The coming revival must begin with a great revival of prayer," Murray once said. "It is in the closet, with the door shut, that the sound of abundance of rain will first be heard. An increase of secret prayer with ministers will be the sure harbinger of blessing."

Murray's prayer eventually birthed a revival. While he was ministering at Worcester on Pentecost Sunday on The Ministration of the Spirit, revival fire fell. As a result, prayer meetings increased. People were convicted of their sin. And people fell on their faces crying out for mercy.

"There is need of a great revival of spiritual life, of truly fervent devotion to our Lord Jesus, of entire consecration to His service," Murray once said. "It is only in a church in which this spirit of revival has at least begun, that there is any hope of radical change in the relation of the majority of our Christian people to mission work."

— *Prayer* —

Father, in the name of Jesus, would You give me a spirit of prayer like You gave Andrew Murray? Give me a deep revelation of how critical prayer is not just to revival—but to every aspect of our lives. Lord, teach me to pray for revival without ceasing until I see it and seize it.

Deliverance Ministry 101

"But Jesus rebuked him, saying, 'Be quiet, and come out of him!'" (Mark 1:25).

Every revivalist needs to embrace deliverance ministry because demonized people will show up—and even the staunchest Christians in your church could manifest. If you don't know how to cast out devils—and your authority to do so in Jesus' name—you may find yourself like the Sons of Sceva. Acts 19:13-16:

"Then some of the itinerant Jewish exorcists undertook to invoke the name of the Lord Jesus over those who had evil spirits, saying, 'I adjure you by the Jesus whom Paul proclaims.' Seven sons of a Jewish high priest named Sceva were doing this. But the evil spirit answered them, 'Jesus I know, and Paul I recognize, but who are you?' And the man in whom was the evil spirit leaped on them, mastered all of them and overpowered them, so that they fled out of that house naked and wounded."

My Book *Deliverance Protocols & Ethics* is an important read for revivalists. Let me give you the basics of deliverance ministry. It's more than saying, "Come out!"

As mentioned, you need to know your authority in Christ. Jesus said, "Look, I give you authority to trample on serpents and scorpions, and over all the power of the enemy. And nothing shall by any means hurt you. Nevertheless do not rejoice that the spirits are subject to you, but rather rejoice that your names are written in heaven" (Luke 10:19-20).

Make sure your own heart is clean before you go into a deliverance session. Repent of any unconfessed sin. Discern the demonic stronghold by the Holy Spirit. Some demons insist on being called out by name before they will come out in the name of Jesus.

Pray against retaliation. Satan will be angry that you've evicted demons from their hosts. After the person you are ministering to exits the scene, the team should stay behind and pray for one another. Plead the blood of Jesus over yourselves. Break and bind all retaliatory attacks. Get deliverance training at www.schoolofthespirit.tv.

— *Prayer* —

Father, in the name of Jesus, would You help me embrace the ministry of deliverance in the church? You are the Deliverer and it is by Your power that demons are cast out and captives are set free. Teach me to cooperate with Your grace to bring liberty to those in spiritual bondage.

NOVEMBER 17

Evan Roberts' Blueprint for Revival

"And I will give you the keys of the kingdom of heaven, and whatever you bind on earth will be bound in heaven, and whatever you loose on earth will be loosed in heaven" (Matthew 16:19).

There's no lack of articles in Christian magazines offering "keys to revival." Many of them hold truths, but many offer opinions with no basis of experience in revival. Evan Roberts, the key figure in the Welsh Revival, had both experiential truth and opinions that hold true today.

Roberts wrote a letter to his friend Sydney in 1904. In it, he shares about his meetings with a youth group in the church he attended in Loughor.

"Dear Syd," he writes, "I have been to Loughor .... I have been a blessing and have been blessed since then...I felt a wave of love for my fellow-men flowing into my soul... Praise God. I passed the football field, and I said, "Oh! that God would thunder over their heads."

"A glorious week, the Spirit working with power. This is the plan ... We begin by asking someone to read, another to give out a hymn, and another to pray. Then I say a few words. This is what is said every night:

"1. We must confess before God every sin in our past life that has not been confessed. 2. We must remove anything that is doubtful in our lives. 3. Total Surrender. We must say and do all that the Spirit tells us. 4. Make a public confession of Christ.

"That is the plan that the Spirit revealed to me. Sixty-five have stood up to confess Christ, and the effect in their lives is some strange joy within them, their lives are purer, and a desire to say more of Jesus, and do more for him. This is the song of the girls now—religion. That is the question, 'How do you feel?' Religion from morn till night. Many of the differences that people had between themselves have been removed. I wish I could write more."

In summary, Roberts' blueprint for revival is confession of sins, removing doubt, surrendering wholeheartedly to God and publicly confessing Christ. That formula led to one hundred thousand conversions in Wales.

— Prayer —

Father, in the name of Jesus, would You help me learn this blueprint and learn it well? This is a pattern for revival. Help me to continually confess my sins, battle against all doubt that rises up in my mind, surrender to You completely and confess You power continually.

When Revival Goes Viral

"Finally, brethren, pray for us, that the word of the Lord may run swiftly and be glorified, just as it is with you, and that we may be delivered from unreasonable and wicked men; for not all have faith" (2 Thessalonians 3:1).

Content creators today have a goal: to go viral. When something goes viral, it becomes popular and spreads rapidly across the Internet. The Asbury Revival in 2023 is a modern-day example of a revival that went viral. But it was not the first.

Long before television or the Internet, the Welsh Revival went viral under Evan Roberts' leadership. This is Scriptural. Paul told Timothy, "Finally, dear brothers and sisters, we ask you to pray for us. Pray that the Lord's message will spread rapidly and be honored wherever it goes, just as when it came to you" (2 Thess. 3:1, NLT).

The Welsh Revival saw one hundred thousand converts to Christ in just nine months. This was reminiscent of the Book of Acts: "Then the word of God spread, and the number of the disciples multiplied greatly in Jerusalem, and a great many of the priests were obedient to the faith" (Acts 6:7).

The Welsh Revival spread like wildfire through Wales and other continents. Thousands of revivals were ignited because of the Welsh Revival. Sam Storms, past-president of the Evangelical Theological Society, wrote:

"If it be asked why the fire of God fell on Wales, the answer is simple: Fire falls where it is likely to catch and spread. As one has said, 'Wales provided the necessary tinder.' Here were thousands of believers unknown to each other, in small towns and villages and great cities, crying to God day after day for the fire of God to fall.

"This was not merely a 'little talk with Jesus,' but daily, agonizing intercession.... One thing is clear: the revival was not the product of someone's personality or of another person's preaching or of anyone's planning, but of God's gracious response to the prayers of his people!"

What makes revival go viral? Ultimately, only the Holy Spirit can make revival go viral. But He responds to the hungry.

— *Prayer* —

Father, in the name of Jesus, I want to see a revival go viral—not for the sake of notoriety but for the sake of the lukewarm church and the stone-cold souls who are dying and going to hell. Help me to pray prayers that are viral and let Your Word run swiftly through the nations.

A Concert of Prayer

"And they were helped against them, and the Hagrites were delivered into their hand, and all who were with them, for they cried out to God in the battle. He heeded their prayer, because they put their trust in Him" (1 Chronicles 5:20).

Not many people realize that in the wake of the American Revolution there was a moral slump. Drunkenness became an epidemic. Out of a population of five million, three-hundred thousand were confirmed drunkards.

In fact, fifteen thousand drunks were buried each year. Profanity was of the most shocking kind. For the first time in the history of the American settlement, women were afraid to go out at night for fear of assault. Bank robberies were a daily occurrence.

This is the report of revival historian Edwin Orr in his book, *The Role of Prayer in Spiritual Awakening:*

"What about the churches? The Methodists were losing more members than they were gaining. The Baptists said that they had their most wintry season. The Presbyterians in general assembly deplored the nation's ungodliness. In a typical Congregational church, the Rev. Samuel Shepherd of Lennox, Massachusetts in sixteen years had not taken one young person into fellowship.

"The Lutherans were so languishing that they discussed uniting with Episcopalians who were even worse off. The Protestant Episcopal Bishop of New York, Bishop Samuel Provoost, quit functioning: he had confirmed no one for so long that he decided he was out of work, so he took up other employment. The Chief Justice of the United States, John Marshall, wrote to the Bishop of Virginia, James Madison, that the Church 'was too far gone ever to be redeemed.' Voltaire averred, and Tom Paine echoed, 'Christianity will be forgotten in thirty years.'"

"Take the liberal arts colleges at that time. A poll taken at Harvard had discovered not one believer in the whole of the student body. They took a poll at Princeton, a much more evangelical place: they discovered only two believers in the student body, and only five that did not belong to the filthy speech movement of that day ... How did the situation change? It came through a concert of prayer."

— *Prayer* —

Father, in the name of Jesus, would You help me not to focus so much on the problems in society that I lose sight of Your power to transform situations through prayer? Help me find others of like precious faith with whom I can gather in a concert of prayer.

When Darkness Pervades a Nation

"For behold, the darkness shall cover the earth, and deep darkness the people; But the Lord will arise over you, and His glory will be seen upon you. The Gentiles shall come to your light, and kings to the brightness of your rising"
(Isaiah 60:2-3).

Revivals often come with controversy and the Timor Revival in Indonesia was no exception. To understand the Timor Revival, we need to look at the history of Christianity in Indonesia.

The Dutch colonized the nation in the 1600s, but the people did not completely forsake the occult practices that were normative in the land. There was a mixture within Christianity that left people partially deceived.

In 1964, Indonesian people started having visions. One man had a vision of God's judgment while another woman had a vision of Jesus talking to the woman at the well. The visions spurred people to pray for revival in the land.

God answered that prayer, in part, through the ministry of Johannes A. Ratuwala, an Indonesian healing evangelist who operated in the miracle realm. Indeed, people were healed of all manner of sickness and disease during his visit.

But that was just the beginning. Other ministries, like Pastor Binjamin Manuain and German lecturer Detmar Scheunemann started holding evangelistic campaigns in the Asian nation. Holy Spirit conviction rained down and Christians began burning their amulets and charms, just like at Ephesus. Conversions started rising rapidly in Timor, especially among the youth.

As God poured out His Spirit, more young people were having visions. Prophecy was prevalent, as were miracles, healings, and even dead raisings. There were even reports of water turning into wine for the sake of having communion services and clothes were supernaturally washed. People walked on water. There were miraculous manifestations of food and light shining in the dark to lead people home at night.

— *Prayer* —

Father, in the name of Jesus, would You help me to continually remember that darkness cannot overcome the light of Christ? Give me a steadfast spirit as I stand for revival in dark nations. Help me release light through prayer into dark societies.

Revival That Wrecks Racism

"All Scripture is given by inspiration of God, and is profitable for doctrine, for reproof, for correction, for instruction in righteousness, that the man of God may be complete, thoroughly equipped for every good work" (2 Timothy 3:16-17).

Racism is nothing new in South Africa, and it was running rampant in the 1800s. But there was a remnant in the nation that was pressing in for revival—and revival they saw.

Dutch Reformed Church pastors called for prayer in 1859. In fact, they used the secular media to help spread their mandate. The South African Evangelical Alliance published a call to prayer in the newspaper, stating:

"That a revival in our faith is necessary and earnestly desired is a fact that no one who is at all knowledgeable about the conditions of the churches in this Colony can deny. That such an awakening can occur through the abundant outpouring of the Holy Spirit, and that the gift of the Holy Spirit is promised in answer to prayer are truths that are clearly taught in Scripture."

The efforts toward revival didn't stop there. Pastors were "called upon to preach a series of sermons on consecutive Sundays on the character of God, the role of the Holy Spirit, and the need for both corporate and private prayer for the outpouring of the Spirit on the souls of Christians."

Leaders looked to the Layman's Revival for inspiration and printed an eighty-five-page book about Jeremiah Lanphier's work in America that birthed revivals across the nation. Even with all this, the prayer meetings were at first poorly attended.

Leaders were so intent on revival that they held a conference about the prayerlessness. But it didn't move the needle much. Still, persevering prayer ultimately won out and the wildfire of revival hit cities all over South Africa starting in 1860 under the leadership of Andrew Murray. Christians across the nation shook off prayerlessness. Person-to-person evangelism saw salvations daily and church growth swelled.

Missionaries were raised up and sent out. Bible Schools were birthed. Giving increased. Families were reconciled. Unity manifested. Prisons sat empty. Businesses instituted stronger ethics. The ripple effect of the 1860 revival lasted over fifty years.

— *Prayer* —

Father, in the name of Jesus, help me see racism for the wicked work that it is—
and to pray against it while praying for the church to break free from old
paradigms. You are coming back for every tongue, tribe, and nation. Let revival
eradicate racism in our churches.

Driving Out Witch Doctors

"Praying always with all prayer and supplication in the Spirit, being watchful to this end with all perseverance and supplication for all the saints" (Ephesians 6:18).

Witch doctors, occult worship and other abominations marked Argentina in 1949. It was what many might call an evangelist's graveyard because the missions work there was so fruitless. A Catholic stronghold and the hostility toward protestants made matters worse. But nothing is too hard for God!

The spiritual climate in Argentina started changing after God sent American missionary Dr. R. Edward Miller to pastor a church in Mendoza—but not without a fight. Miller's first few weeks there proved more than challenging.

No one was coming to his tent meetings. He almost gave up, but God whispered a verse from Zachariah, "Not by might nor by power but by my Spirit." Miller sensed God calling him to pray eight hours a day for revival. Miller responded to the call, after months of intense prayer, God answered.

By 1984, it seemed Miller's momentum was lost. The nation had the lowest percentile of Protestants in Latin America, and the ground was once again hard. In essence, the nation backslid into the occult. A military dictatorship led to the Dirty War and, at the same time, the nation was at war with the United Kingdom over the Falkland Islands.

Because prayers never die, I believe those prayers bled over into the 1954 and 1984 Argentine revivals. And God raised up a new Miller. His name was Pastor Alberto Scataglini. He led a group of six hungry young people to pray for months on end, which eventually resulted in conviction of their own sin. That six-person prayer meeting grew to two hundred, and they started going out to preach the Gospel. The church ballooned to five hundred, then to twenty thousand in one year.

Revival broke out through the ministry of a then-unknown evangelist named Carlos Annacondia, who worked with Scataglini. During an eight-month campaign in La Plata, fifty thousand people came to Christ. People were healed and delivered. Miracles broke out. Christian radio and TV programs were birthed. The revival lasted twenty years.

— *Prayer* —

Father, in the name of Jesus, would You help me not to be discouraged by the size of the task but to be encouraged by the size of Your heart? You are an all-powerful God and nothing is too hard for You. No matter the strongman against revival in my city, You are the stronger man.

NOVEMBER 23

A Hunger Revival

"For He satisfies the longing soul, and fills the hungry soul with goodness" (Psalm 107:9).

In some ways, we're seeing a Word famine in the church. Studies show many Christians don't read the Bible regularly—much less study it. That leaves the mind unrenewed and a door open for enemy deception. We need a hunger revival.

Jesus said those who hunger and thirst after righteousness shall be filled (see Matt. 5:6). Is it any surprise that many believers feel empty, only darken the door of the church on average once a month, and neglect to give into Kingdom works? We need a hunger revival.

British evangelist and healer Smith Wigglesworth once said, "There are four principles we need to maintain: First, read the Word of God. Second, consume the Word of God until it consumes you. Third believe the Word of God. Fourth, act on the Word of God."

King David was a hungry man. He wrote these words in Psalm 63:1, "O God, You are my God; Early will I seek You; My soul thirsts for You; My flesh longs for You in a dry and thirsty land where there is no water." We see the results of this hunger and thirst in Psalm 107:9, "For He satisfies the longing soul, and fills the hungry soul with goodness."

If we are not in the Word, we risk not following the Spirit accurately. There are many spirits talking. We want to listen to the Spirit of Holy. Wigglesworth put it this way: "Some people read their Bibles in Hebrew, some in Greek; I like to read mine in the Holy Ghost. You must everyday make higher ground. You must deny yourself to make progress with God."

Indeed, Wigglesworth said it best: "God was and is looking for hungry, thirsty people."

Thankfully, no matter how far we've strayed from His heart because of busy schedules, trials of life or plain apathy, He has an open-door invitation. Isaiah 55:1 tells us, "Ho! Everyone who thirsts, come to the waters; And you who have no money, yes, come, buy wine and milk without money and without price."

— *Prayer* —

Father, in the name of Jesus, I hunger for You. Make me hungrier still. Give me the gift of hunger that I would hunger for You so deeply that nothing of this world will satisfy the craving in my heart for more of You. Father, give those around me the same gift of hunger so we can seek Your face together.

When Revival is Mercy

"Mercy triumphs over judgment" (James 2:13).

The cry for revival is, in some ways, a cry for mercy. When the Israelites sinned their way into bondage, they essentially cried out for mercy. Revival is God showing mercy on a people who have strayed away from His heart. Mercy sent Jesus to die on a cross for our sins.

Indeed, God is rich in mercy (see Eph. 2:4). The Lord is good to all, and His tender mercies are over all His works (see Ps. 145:9). All the paths of the Lord are mercy and truth, to such as keep His covenant and His testimonies (see Ps. 25:10). Mercy triumphs over judgment (see James 1:13).

David understood the mercy of God. Remember when David called for a census? He wanted to know the state of his military, which equaled strength. Satan tempted him to go against God's Word. The census demonstrated a lack of trust in the Lord as protector—the Lord who had historically protected him and given him victory over all his enemies. After he commanded Joab to count the soldiers, David's heart condemned him and he asked for forgiveness.

But his sin was not without consequence. The prophet Gad prophesied three options as punishment: seven years of famine, three months of fleeing before his enemies while they pursued him or three days of plague. David's response: "I am in great distress. Please let us fall into the hand of the Lord, for His mercies are great; but do not let me fall into the hand of man" (2 Sam. 24:14).

Yes, some may use God's grace and mercy as a license to sin. But I believe more people need a revelation of His mercy so they will run back to Him when they do sin. Too many are afraid of God because they don't understand His lovingkindness. Remember, it's the kindness of God that leads people to repentance (see Rom. 2:4). Revivalist, be sure to emphasize the mercy of God and His great love for His people.

— *Prayer* —

Father, in the name of Jesus, send a mercy revival. So many people have a wrong paradigm of You. They see You as a mean old man in the sky with a mallet of condemnation to punish them in their sin. Pour out Your mercy on a generation and demonstrate Your kindness that leads us to repentance.

Warring Women of Revival

"Now Zion's women are left to gather the spoils" (Psalm 68:12).

I was meditating on the Word in the presence of the Lord one morning when a passage leaped off the page. Psalm 68:11-12 became a rhema word. It says, "God Almighty declares the word of the gospel with power, and the warring women of Zion deliver its message: 'The conquering legions have themselves been conquered. Look at them flee!' Now Zion's women are left to gather the spoils.'"

The Holy Spirit began to speak to me about a revival among the warring women. See, many times it's more than a pretty prayer that brings revival. Sweat and tears are part and parcel of revival prayer in hard territories. God is calling forth women who will lay aside a few hours a week to war for the revival He wants to bring in the darkest parts of the earth.

Think of Book of Judges chapters four and five. Israel was harshly oppressed by the Canaanite King Jabin. When the children of Israel cried out to the Lord, he raised up Deborah as a deliverer. Deborah was judging Israel at that time and received a warfare strategy directly from heaven. Judges 4:6-9:

"Then she sent and called for Barak the son of Abinoam from Kedesh in Naphtali, and said to him, 'Has not the Lord God of Israel commanded, 'Go and deploy troops at Mount Tabor; take with you ten thousand men of the sons of Naphtali and of the sons of Zebulun; and against you I will deploy Sisera, the commander of Jabin's army, with his chariots and his multitude at the River Kishon; and I will deliver him into your hand'?'"

Barak wouldn't go to war without her. You know the end of the story. Israel defeated Jabin and revival broke out in the land. Deborah led the nation in praising Jehovah and the land had rest for forty years. God is calling forth the warring women of revival. Do you know one?

— *Prayer* —

Father, in the name of Jesus, I call forth the warring women of revival from the north, the south, the east and the west. I call women in both free nations and oppressed nations to pray in the revival that You want to bring. Lord, raise up Deborahs in this hour who will lead the charge for revival.

NOVEMBER 26

Beware Revival Burnout

"But those who wait on the Lord shall renew their strength; They shall mount up with wings like eagles, they shall run and not be weary, they shall walk and not faint" (Isaiah 40:38).

When revival hits, there is great excitement but there's also the potential for great burnout. When revival burnout comes, excitement turns into physical, mental, emotional, and spiritual exhaustion.

Burnout leaves you feeling like you've got nothing left to give because you don't. Burnout destroys your motivation, overwhelms your sensibilities, and drives you into hopelessness. You may develop anxiety, get sick more often, find it hard to pray or read the Word or otherwise feel detached from the revival. This is a very real danger and strategic enemy of revival.

Charles Finney, the Father of Modern Revivalism, had a colleague named Edward Norris Kirk (1802-1874). Kirk was a Christian missionary, pastor, teacher, evangelist, and writer. He was also a revivalist who founded the Fourth Presbyterian Church in Albany, New York. Educated at Princeton Theological Seminary, Kirk adopted Finney's revivalism preaching style, known to evoke stroke emotion in the audience. His preaching led to D.L. Moody's conversion.

Kirk also used outlines like Finney. He used the outlines as a skeleton to put his thoughts on paper but when he got into the pulpit, he threw himself on God. Kirk found this especially helpful when he was suffering from revival burnout. He was so busy he had no time to read or prepare his messages. He once said, "I have pulled on the old chord until I am expecting every day to hear it snap... Send me some skeletons."

So how do you avoid revival burnout? Balance. Listen to your body. Rest when you need to rest and learn to rest in the Lord. If you don't stay filled up, you can't overflow. You can't pour from a dry well. Redig the wells of revival in your life through prayer, fellowship with the Holy Spirit, and reading the Word. Get into God's soothing rhythms of grace.

— Prayer —

Father, in the name of Jesus, I want to burn for You—but I don't want to burn out. Help me to walk in Your soothing rhythms of grace. Help me to do what I need to do in the natural to take care of my body, which is a temple of the Holy Spirit. And help me stay close to You day by day.

NOVEMBER 27

The Womb of Revival

"He saw that there was no man, and wondered that there was no intercessor; Therefore His own arm brought salvation for Him; And His own righteousness, it sustained Him" (Isaiah 59:16).

Prayer and intercession are the baseline—the foundation—of every revival. The very first outpouring of the Holy Ghost happened in an upper room where united believers were in constant prayer (see Acts 2:1-4)—and every other outpouring since has been preceded by strong intercession. A revival that is not built on the bedrock of intercession is no revival at all.

What is intercession? Simply stated, it is standing in prayer for another person, place, region, family or ministry. Intercession is the activity of prayer in which you give yourself over to spiritual warfare on behalf of another. Intercession is forming an aggressive wall of prayer to push back the evil strategies of hell and unlock the glorious exploits of heaven. It is in intercession that revivalists do battle for the assigned territory and people.

Samuel Chadwick, a 19th Century Wesleyan Methodist minister, said, "The one concern of the devil is to keep Christians from praying. He fears nothing from prayerless studies, prayerless work, and prayerless religion. He laughs at our toil, mocks at our wisdom, but trembles when we pray." And Matthew Henry, a 17th century minister and author, once said: "When God intends great mercy for His people, the first thing He does is to set them a-praying."

Charles Haddon Spurgeon, a 19th Century British Particular Baptist preacher, once preached these words: "Oh, men and brethren, what would this heart feel if I could but believe that there were some among you who would go home and pray for a revival of religion—men whose faith is large enough, and their love fiery enough to lead them from this moment to exercise unceasing intercessions that God would appear among us and do wondrous things here, as in the times of former generations." Amen!

These quotes probably make your spirit leap because you bear witness to the truth contained in such profound words. Put a high value on prayer because it not only unlocks revival, but it also unlocks revival strategies for the region.

— *Prayer* —

Father, in the name of Jesus, would You help me stay steady in my intercession for revival in my region even when I am not seeing any results? Help me hold down the fort, stand in the gap, make up the hedge, climb in my watchtower and watch and pray for the revival You are sending.

Tears of Revival

"Hear my prayer, O Lord, and give ear to my cry; Do not be silent at my tears; For I am a stranger with You, a sojourner, as all my fathers were" (Psalm 39:12).

In *Revival God's Way*, Leonard Ravenhill's words have moved countless revivalists to tears. They certainly move me to tears. He wrote:

"Many of us have no heart-sickness for the former glory of the Church because we have never known what true revival is. We stagnate in the status quo and sleep easy at night while our generation moves swiftly to the eternal night of hell. Shame, shame on us! Jesus whipped some money changers out of the temple; but before He whipped them, He wept over them.

"Notice that he does not say they are enemies of Christ; they are, rather, the enemies of the cross of Christ. They deny or diminish the redemptive values of the cross. There are many like this today.

"The church of Rome does not stand as an enemy of Christ; it traces heavily on His holy name. Yet it denies the cross by saying that the Blessed Virgin is co-redemptive. If this is so, why was she not also crucified?

"The Mormons use the name of Christ, yet they are astray on the atonement. Have we tears for them? Shall we face them without a blush when they accuse us of inertia at the Judgment Seat saying that they were our neighbors and an offense to us, but not a burden because they were lost?

"The Salvationists can scarcely read their flaming evangelical history without tears. Has the glory of the evangelical revival under Wesley ever gripped the hearts of the Methodists of today?

"Have they read of the fire-baptized men in Wesley's team? Men like John Nelson, Thomas Walsh, and a host of others whose names are written in the Book of Life; men persecuted and kicked in the streets when they held street meetings? Yet as their blood flowed from their wounds, their tears flowed from their eyes."

Revivalist, do these words move you to tears? If not, read them again and ask the Holy Spirit to touch your heart.

— *Prayer* —

Father, in the name of Jesus, break my heart for what breaks Yours. Help me remember that the cause of revival is not just to awaken churches but to awaken lost souls to the reality of the saving work of Christ's cross. Help me pray for people in the enemy's snare who call on another God.

NOVEMBER 29

A Supernatural Revival

"Having a form of godliness but denying its power. And from such people turn away!"
(2 Timothy 3:5).

Duncan Campbell, a Scottish evangelist known for revival, grieved over the state of the church in his day—and it's even worse today. He wrote:

"Yet, how is it that while we make such great claims for the power of the gospel, we see so little of the supernatural in operation? Is there any reason why the Church today cannot everywhere equal the Church at Pentecost?

"I feel this is a question we ought to face with an open mind and an honest heart. What did the early Church have that we do not possess today? Nothing but the Holy Spirit, nothing but the power of God. Here I would suggest that one of the main secrets of success in the early church lay in the fact that the early believers believed in unction from on high and not entertainment from men.

"Pentecost was its own publicity. I love that passage in Acts that tells us that 'when this was noised abroad, the multitude came together.' What was noised abroad? That men and women were coming under deep conviction. That was God's method of publicity, and until the Church of Jesus Christ rediscovers this and acts upon it, we shall at our best appear to a mad world as a crowd of common people in a common market babbling about common wares. The early Church cried for unction and not for entertainment. Unction is the dire and desperate need of the ministry today.

"In many quarters there is today a growing conviction that unless God moves, unless there is a demonstration of the supernatural in the midst of men, unless we are moved up into the realm of the Divine, we shall soon find ourselves caught up in a counterfeit movement, but a movement that goes under the name of evangelism.

"There are ominous sighs today that the devil is out to sidetrack us in the sphere of evangelism, and we are going to become satisfied with something less than Heaven wills to give us. Nothing but a Holy Spirit revival will meet the desperate need of the hour."

— *Prayer* —

Father, in the name of Jesus, would You spur me to pursue You, the God of the supernatural, in my prayer life? You tell me in Your Word that signs and wonders will follow those who believe. I believe, Lord. Help my unbelief. I don't want to be counted among the religious who deny Your power.

The Billy Sunday Revivalist Anointing

"O foolish Galatians! Who has bewitched you that you should not obey the truth, before whose eyes Jesus Christ was clearly portrayed among you as crucified?" (Galatians 3:1)

Born in 1863 in a log cabin in Iowa just before his father died in America's Civil War, Billy Sunday's mother gave him up for adoption because she was too poor to provide for her three sons. Billy ran away at age fifteen and took on a job as a stable boy. He eventually became a professional baseball player for the then-Chicago White Stockings.

But Sunday is best known for leading revivals. His preaching style was far different from others in his day. He was animated, jumping and running on stage at times as he preached his heart out. He converted about three-hundred-thousand people during his fifty-year ministry. He was a true revivalist.

"When is a revival needed? When carelessness and unconcern keep the people asleep," Sunday said. "When may a revival be expected? When the wickedness of the wicked grieves and distresses the Christian."

Sunday reached the pinnacle of his ministry in 1916 Boston. There he built a brick-and-steel tabernacle that seated eighteen thousand with a fifteen-foot-high platform. He invested in massive choirs and instruments and attacked sin headlong.

"A revival does two things," Sunday said. "First, it returns the Church from her backsliding and second, it causes the conversion of men and women; and it always includes the conviction of sin on the part of the Church. What a spell the devil seems to cast over the Church today!"

Sunday was criticized for his blunt messaging and his flamboyance on stage, but no one can argue with his results. His bold preaching helped usher in prohibition in in 1919. The criticism continued, but it did not stop Sunday.

"Trying to run a church without revivals can be done when you can run a gasoline engine on buttermilk," he said. "They tell me a revival is only temporary; so is a bath, but it does you good."

— *Prayer* —

Father, in the name of Jesus, would You give me a boldness like You gave Billy Sunday? I don't want to be offensive, but I do not want to be seeker-friendly either. Help me to share Your heart for revival with a sober mind and a soft heart toward the people You love.

DECEMBER

"History is silent about revivals that did not begin with prayer."—Edwin Orr

When Children Lead the Prayer Meeting

"Like arrows in the hand of a warrior, so are the children of one's youth" (Psalm 127:4).

When revival hit Herrnhut, the children played a key role in the awakening. Children were alongside adults, prostrate on the ground, praying, weeping and singing. One eyewitness said: "The spirit of prayer and supplication at that time poured out upon the children so powerful and efficacious that it is impossible to give an adequate description of it in words."

Can you imagine? The Moravian Revival birthed a twenty-four-hour prayer meeting that lasted one hundred years. Children were part and parcel of the intercession for souls, taking a slot in the rotation for God's glory.

"All the children, were seized with an extraordinary impulse of the Spirit, and spent the whole night in prayer. From this time, a constant work of God was going on in the minds of the children, in both places. No words can express the powerful operation of the Holy Spirit upon these children, whose lives were so transformed," said William E. Allen in his book, *The History of Revivals of Religion*.

The Moravian prayer meeting stood on Leviticus 6:13, "Fire shall be kept burning continually on the altar; it is not to go out." With children crying out to God alongside adults, doubtless even those who were once riddled with doubt or unbelief were moved to join in by faith.

"The children, also touched powerfully by God, began a similar plan among themselves. Those who heard their infant supplications were deeply moved," said John Greenfield in his book, *Power on High*. "The children's prayers and supplications had a powerful effect on the whole community."

The Moravians started their twenty-four-hour prayer watch with just twenty-four men and twenty-four women. Each person committed to praying one hour a day. Pete Greig, author of *Awakening Cry*, wrote, "The number of intercessors actually increased as the years rolled on, especially amongst the children, generating a power center that radiated to the ends of the earth for more than a century."

— Prayer —

Father, in the name of Jesus, would You remind me to invest in the next generation of intercessors and revivalists? I know there is no Junior Holy Spirit. The same Holy Spirit is in all Your children—young and old. Help me find ways to include the children in revival prayer.

Wisdom for Would-Be Revivalists

"But the wisdom that is from above is first pure, then peaceable, gentle, willing to yield, full of mercy and good fruits, without partiality and without hypocrisy" (James 3:17).

Do you want God to use you in revival? What kind of person does God use for revival? I once read an article by R.A. Torrey, an American evangelist who lived from 1856 to 1928, about the characteristics of a person God will use to birth and spread revival. Torrey uses D.L. Moody, American urban ministry pioneer, as an example of such a person.

First, Moody was a surrendered man. Torrey said: "Every ounce of that two-hundred-and-eighty-pound body of his belonged to God; everything he was and everything he had, belonged wholly to God."

Second, Moody was a man of prayer. "Yes, D. L. Moody was a man who believed in the God who answers prayer, and not only believed in Him in a theoretical way but believed in Him in a practical way," Torrey said. "He was a man who met every difficulty that stood in his way—by prayer. Everything he undertook was backed up by prayer, and in everything, his ultimate dependence was upon God."

Third was being a "deep and practical student of the Bible." Fourth was humility: "The entire shore of the history of Christian workers is strewn with the wrecks of gallant vessels that were full of promise a few years ago, but these men became puffed up and were driven on the rocks by the wild winds of their own raging self-esteem."

Fifth, Moody was entirely free from the love of money. Sixth, he had a consuming passion for the salvation of the lost. Torrey said: "Oh, young men and women and all Christian workers, if you and I were on fire for souls like that, how long would it be before we had a revival? Suppose that tonight the fire of God falls and fills our hearts, a burning fire that will send us out all over the country, and across the water to China, Japan, India, and Africa, to tell lost souls the way of salvation!"

And, finally, he was endued with power from on high. May God fill us all with the same Holy Ghost and fire.

— *Prayer* —

Father, in the name of Jesus, refine my character. Conform me into the image of Christ. Change me from glory to glory. Give me the grace and wisdom to adopt actions that become habits that transform my thinking and living. Make me a revivalist with the character of the Savior.

Not Your Grandfather's Revival

"These who have turned the world upside down have come here too" (Acts 17:6).

"How is the church to be lifted up to the abundant life in Christ, which will fit her for the work that God is putting before Her? Nothing will help but a revival, nothing less than a tremendous spiritual revival. Great tides of spiritual energy must be put into motion if this work is to be accomplished.

"Now there may be great differences in what we understand by revival. Many will think of the work of evangelists like Moody and Torrey. We need a different and mightier revival than those were in them the chief object was the conversion of sinners, and incidentally, the quickening of believers."

These are the words of the late Andrew Murray, a South African, writer, teacher, and pastor. Murray says the revival we need calls for a deeper and more entire upheaval of the church. The great defect of the revivals of Moody and Torrey, he insisted, was that the converts were received into a church that was not living at a high level of consecration and holiness, and speedily sank down to the average standard of ordinary religious life.

"Even the believers who had been roused by it, also gradually returned to their former life of clouded fellowship and lack of power to testify for Christ. The revival we need is a revival of holiness, in which the consecration of the whole being is to the service of Christ, and that for the whole life shall be counted possible," he said.

"And for this there will be needed a new style of preaching in which the promises of God to dwell in His people, and to sanctify them for Himself, will take a place which they do not now have. When our Lord Jesus gave the promise of the Holy Spirit, He spoke of the New Covenant blessing that would be experienced—God dwelling in His people. 'If a man love Me, he will keep my words; and My Father will love him.'"

— *Prayer* —

Father, in the name of Jesus, it's clear we need a spiritual revival—a great awakening that will quicken believers and prick the hearts of lost souls who are searching for answers in life. Lord, raise up a new style of preachers that call us back to Your heart and Your Word.

Our Only Hope

"Now may the God of hope fill you with all joy and peace in believing, that you may abound in hope by the power of the Holy Spirit" (Romans 15:13).

Revival was and is and always will be the only hope of a church that looks too much like the world. Jesus Christ, who is Revival, is our living hope (see 1 Peter 1:3). Duncan Campbell, a 20th Century Scottish evangelist, understood this.

Campbell points to Isaiah 64:1-2, "Oh, that You would rend the heavens! That You would come down! That the mountains might shake at Your presence—As fire burns brushwood, as fire causes water to boil—to make Your name known to Your adversaries, that the nations may tremble at Your presence!"

"You will observe that in that prayer of the prophet two fundamental things are suggested. That unless God comes down, mountains will not flow and sinners will not tremble," Campbell wrote.

"But if God comes down, if God manifests His power, if God shows His hand, if God takes the field, mountains will flow...mountains of indifference, mountains of materialism, mountains of humanism, will flow before His presence, and nations, not just individuals, but nations, shall be made to tremble."

Campbell went on to say—and I agree—that we haven't seen nations trembling. We have seen some churches tremble and even some communities tremble. But we haven't seen nations tremble.

"We have seen crowded churches. We have seen many professions. We have seen hundreds, yes, and thousands responding to what you speak of here as the altar call," he continued. "But I want to say this, dear people, and I say it without fear of contradiction, that you can have all that without God! Now, that may startle you, but I say again, you can have all that on mere human levels!

"Howard Spring was right when he wrote, 'The Kingdom of God is not going to advance by our churches becoming filled with men, but my men in our churches becoming filled with God.' And there's a difference! Oh, no! Crowded churches, deep interest in church activity is possible on mere human levels leaving the community untouched!"

— *Prayer* —

Father, in the name of Jesus, help me not mistake a crowded church for a community-minded church. Help me not mistake numbers for power. Better is a remnant of sold-out revivalists than tens of thousands of lukewarm believers who don't let faith show through their works.

DECEMBER 5

Holy Spirit Encounters

"And when they had prayed, the place where they were assembled together was shaken; and they were all filled with the Holy Spirit, and they spoke the word of God with boldness" (Acts 4:31).

D.L. Moody was a great revivalist in the 1800s. He was known as an urban ministry pioneer. He started the Moody Bible Institute, which still blesses the Body of Christ with resources today.

Before God used Him in revival, Moody needed a power encounter. Indeed, God called him and anointed him. He was accomplishing great things for the Lord in Chicago. But there still was something missing.

As history tells it, some elderly ladies came to his meetings to watch and pray. They came up to him after every meeting and said, "We're praying for you." He said, "Why don't you pray for the people." They said, "You need power."

That would have insulted many preachers today. And, keep in mind, Moody had the largest church in Chicago at the time. But these women insisted he needed to be anointed for special service.

"I asked them to come and talk with me, and we got down on our knees. They poured out their hearts that I might receive the anointing from the Holy Spirit, and there came a great hunger into my soul. I did not know what it was. I began to pray as I never did before. I really felt that I did not want to live if I could not have this power for service. The hunger increased. I was praying all the time that God would fill me with His Holy Spirit," Moody said.

"I went to preaching again. The sermons were not different; I did not present any new truths; and yet hundreds were converted. If we are filled with the Spirit and full of power, one day's work is better than a year's without."

Every revivalist needs the baptism of the Holy Spirit. Every revivalist needs to be endued with power from on high. Every revivalist needs Pentecost fire burning within them. That's because the forces of hell don't fight fair. When you are filled with the Spirit, rivers of living water drown out the enemies of revival.

— *Prayer* —

Father, in the name of Jesus, would You baptize me in the Holy Spirit—baptize me with fire. Give me a fresh infilling of the Holy Ghost. Endue me with power from on high. Help me to continually seek a refill of Your power in my life so I can be effective in revival exploits.

Making an Appeal to Heaven

"Consider and hear me, O Lord my God; Enlighten my eyes, Lest I sleep the sleep of death"
(Psalm 13:3).

In the seventeenth century, Bible commentator Matthew Henry wrote, "When God intends great mercy for His people, He first sets them praying." God is a God of mercy, but we need to cry out for that mercy. I believe when we do, God hears us—and answers us.

It's time to make an appeal to heaven. Ezra 9:5-8 is a powerful model prayer you can adapt for your state or nation. You can pray this out loud in your prayer closet or have one person read it aloud in a corporate prayer meeting as intercessors agree in their hearts:

"At the evening sacrifice I arose from my fasting; and having torn my garment and my robe, I fell on my knees and spread out my hands to the Lord my God.

"O my God, I am ashamed and embarrassed to lift up my face to You, my God, because our iniquities have expanded over our heads and our wrongdoing has grown up to the heavens. Since the days of our fathers until this day, we have been in a great guilt. It is because of our iniquities that we, our kings, and our priests have been delivered—by the sword, by captivity, by spoil, and by being shamed—into the hand of the kings of the lands. This day is like that, too.

"Yet now for a little while, there has been a favorable response from the Lord our God—leaving us a remnant to escape, giving us a tent peg from His holy place, having our eyes enlightened by our God, and giving us a little reviving in our bondage."

Notice how the petition started with Ezra leading the Israelites into corporate repentance. He took the pain of God's heart upon himself, acknowledging the guilt as his own even though he had held up a standard of righteousness. Also notice how he acknowledges God's kindness and mercy. An appeal to heaven should include all these elements: repentance, and faith in a God who loves us enough to revive us.

— *Prayer* —

Father, in the name of Jesus, help me craft an appeal to heaven that touches Your heart. Help me learn from Daniel and Ezra how to pray in line with Your will for repentance that opens the door for You to restore and revive. Teach me how to make an appeal to heaven that moves Your hand.

DECEMBER 7

The Stuttering Revivalist

"But Moses argued with the Lord, saying, 'I can't do it! I'm such a clumsy speaker! Why should Pharaoh listen to me?' Then the Lord said to Moses, 'Pay close attention to this. I will make you seem like God to Pharaoh, and your brother, Aaron, will be your prophet'" (Exodus 6:30-7:1).

Reuben "Uncle Bud" Robinson was born in a simple log cabin in the Tennessee mountains. His father passed away when he was just sixteen years old, which radically change his life. But God soon revealed Himself as Bud's Heavenly Father.

Uncle Bud came to know the Lord in 1880 during a camp meeting, and sensed a call to preach. The challenge: he had no education and stuttered badly. In fact, he could hardly speak his name rightly because of the stutter. But that didn't stop him from peaching fire. This was Uncle Bud's prayer:

"O Lord, give me a backbone as big as a saw log, and ribs like sleepers under the church floor. Put iron shoes on me and galvanized breeches, and hang a wagonload of determination in the gable end of my soul. And help me to sign the contract to fight the devil as long as I have vision, and bite him as long as I have a tooth, and then gum him till I die! Amen!"

During the first year of his ministry, Uncle Bud saw three hundred people saved. Robinson traveled about two million miles during his ministry, preached over thirty-three thousand sermons, ultimately saw over one hundred thousand conversions. Like King David, Uncle Bud gave from his personal wealth to build the Kingdom. All told, he sowed more than $85,000 to help young people with Christian education. That would total over $2 million in today's monetary value.

Known for his wit and heart to preach the Gospel to the everyday Joes, Uncle Bud also wrote fourteen books that sold more than half a million copies. Uncle Bud's revival story is a testament that prayer works. Prayer works! We can pray this same prayer over our lives and believe for the results Robinson saw. Imagine the fruit we'd bear for the Kingdom!

— *Prayer* —

Father, in the name of Jesus, help me not to look at what I don't have or what I can't do and keep my eyes on the One who can do and will do great exploits through me—Jesus Christ. Teach me never to make excuses for not following Your Spirit into the adventures You have ordained for me.

Martyrs of Revival

"I saw the woman, drunk with the blood of the saints and with the blood of the martyrs of Jesus"
(Revelation 17:6).

We don't hear much about martyrs in our day, though Open Doors records over five thousand Christians every year are killed for their faith. Martyrdom is not a new phenomenon. Stephen, a deacon in the early church, was murdered for his faith. He goes down in history as the first Christian martyr. Sadly, he was not the last.

Foxe's Book of Martyrs is a classic that makes the hairs on your neck stand up. The martyrs have a voice in Revelation 6:9-10:

"When he opened the fifth seal, I saw under the altar the souls of those who had been slain for the word of God and for the witness they had borne. They cried out with a loud voice, 'O Sovereign Lord, holy and true, how long before you will judge and avenge our blood on those who dwell on the earth?'"

Robert Jermain Thomas was the first protestant martyr in Korea. He literally laid down his life for the sake of revival. Forty years before the famed Pyongyang Revival in Korea, Thomas was on the ground.

As legend tells it, Robert was on a ship to Korea to distribute Bibles. When the ship came to shore in Pyongyang, he jumped off board and started handing out Bibles to a hostile crowd while shouting "Jesus, Jesus." He gave out his last Bible to the man who killed him. Many Christians who experienced revival decades later can point back to that day Thomas handed them a Bible.

These are his words: "I trust to give myself more completely than ever to the noble work on which I have just entered, but at present I feel weighed down by deep grief. I am sure I have your sympathy and prayers that no trial however grievous should separate me from this glorious cause, but rather thank God for her peaceful, painless end, and say, 'The Lord gave, the Lord hath taken away, blessed be the name of the Lord.'"

— *Prayer* —

Father, in the name of Jesus, I want to live for You. But if necessary, I will die for You. Help me be willing to live for Christ and to die for the sake of the Gospel. You tell me in Your Word that those who seek to save their life will lose it, but those who lose their life in Christ will find it. I am all in.

DECEMBER 9

A Psalmist's Cries for Revival

"In my distress I called upon the Lord, and cried out to my God; He heard my voice from His temple, and my cry came before Him, even to His ears" (Psalm 18:6).

Throughout the pages of the Psalms, we see a heart's cry for revival. The word "revival" is not always used but the intention is clear. When we pray the Word, we'll see results because God's Word never fails. It doesn't return to Him void.

We don't know how many times David released these petitions but thank God the Holy Spirit inspired these revival prayers that God will answer. Let's look at a few of them. Pray them aloud as you read them.

"Restore us again, O Lord God of Hosts; cause Your face to shine, and we shall be delivered" (see Ps. 80:19). "Restore us, O God; Cause Your face to shine, and we shall be saved!" (see Ps. 80:3) "O God, You have cast us off; You have broken us down; You have been displeased; Oh, restore us again!" (see Ps. 60:1)

"Restore us, O God of our salvation, and put away Your indignation toward us. Will You be angry with us forever? Will You draw out Your anger to all generations? Will You not revive us again, that Your people may rejoice in You? Show us Your mercy, O Lord, and grant us Your deliverance" (see Ps. 85:4-7).

"Remember this, that the enemy has scorned, O Lord, and that the foolish people have blasphemed Your name. Do not give the life of Your turtledove to a wild animal; do not forget the life of Your poor forever. Have regard for the covenant; for the dark places of the earth are full of the habitations of violence. May the oppressed not return ashamed; may the poor and needy praise Your name. Arise, O God, plead Your own cause; remember how the fool insults You daily. Do not forget the voice of Your enemies, the tumult of those who rise up against You continually (Ps. 74:18-23).

David didn't see revival in his day, per se. He was a man of war, but he lived in revival. He walked in personal revival in tough times, after times of sin and in times of battle. David's prayers are model prayers for revival.

— *Prayer* —

Father, in the name of Jesus, remind me to release fervent prayers for revival like David did. Help me keep You at the center of my focus and make You my one thing, like David did. Help me war for revival like David warred for the peace of Jerusalem. I want to be found faithful.

Revival Hits Intercession-Soaked Regions

"God of the Angel Armies, who is like you, powerful and faithful from every angle?"
(Psalm 89:8, *The Message*)

"Great revival fire will now begin to burn through intercession-soaked regions as My awakening begins to roll. The regions will now become activated by My glory. My shaking has come. I am shaking earth. I am shaking heaven. Walls, strongholds, obstacles, and hell's defenses are being shaken down, and My remnant is being shaken free. My shaking will open ancient wells of revival. The revival in the womb of My intercessors will now be birthed."

Tim Sheets, author of *Angel Armies*, prophesied those words. He went on to prophesy: "The revivalist mantle is descending upon My righteous evangelists. The fire shut up in their bones will now become words of fiery passion. With My gospel, I will shake open the capped wells of evangelism. I will shake open the ancient healing wells. Miracles will multiply. My angels are pumping those wells and they are opening new wells, new roads, new inroads, new mantles, new vision, new harvest. Behold I will do a new thing, and you will see it. Now it will spring forth."

"Because your cries have come before Me, because you have pursued My Presence, because your worship has become sweet savor—the Lord of Angel Armies decrees over His remnant people, you shall now begin reality church—no more acting, no more actors, no more pretending. Real church, real disciples, real Christianity, real worship, real power, real glory, real miracles, real healings. It is ordained reality church."

"I am now coming to My remnant. And I am now coming as Lord Sabaoth-Lord of Angel Armies. Because of alignment with My purpose, I will now align My hosts to assist aggressively. There is now a convergence of the angel armies and the church's prayer army into a divine coalition; the coalition of My willing; those who run to battle, not from it."

This is a word to war with! Use it as a sword for awakening!

— *Prayer* —

Father, in the name of Jesus, help me cooperate with heaven's angel armies for the sake of revival. Help me continually declare Your Word, knowing that angels hearken to the voice of Your Word, according to Psalm 103. Help me use Your Word like a sword against revival enemies.

Former Slave Sets Captives Free

"We are hard-pressed on every side, yet not crushed; we are perplexed, but not in despair; persecuted, but not forsaken; struck down, but not destroyed" (2 Corinthians 4:9).

She was once a back slave. But God used her as an evangelist to the nations. Born in 1837 in Maryland, Amanda Smith was one member of a family of slaves—but she was also a member of a family of prayer warriors.

Despite her limited education and the tragic death of her husband in America's Civil War, she persevered in the will of God through poverty. When sickness attacked her body, God healed her. When her second husband abandoned her with a child, she was once poverty-stricken for a second time. When her next three children died in infancy, she did not give up. When her second husband passed away, she did not turn away from the Lord.

In fact, she turned fully to the Lord in her sorrow and answered the call to be a full-time missionary who lived by faith. She started preaching at camp meetings with a message of holiness and salvation. By 1878, invitations from overseas came flooding in. She spoke at the Keswick Convention in England and was a favorite at revival meetings in Britain.

From there, she went to India where she saw revival break out in her meetings for eighteen months. She then traveled to Africa and spent eight years preaching the Gospel in Liberia and Sierra Leone. Finally, she returned to the United States in 1892, wrote about her travels, and started tackling issues of racism and sexism. She also started an orphanage before passing on to glory at age seventy-eight.

Reverend Canon J. John offers three insights into her life. "First, she depended upon God. Amanda was a poor woman with limited education working against widespread racial prejudice. Yet those very limitations forced her to rely on God and on His strength. The life of Amanda Smith is a reminder that God does most through those who count themselves least.

"Second, she had a desire for God. The nineteenth-century emphasis and enthusiasm for 'holiness teaching' is unfashionable today. Amanda made it her priority to seek God and to reflect that knowledge and experience of him in her life. It's a good priority to make our own. Third, she demonstrated the grace of God."

— *Prayer* —

Father, in the name of Jesus, would You help me learn a lesson from Amanda
Smith, who persevered despite all odds to make an eternal impact for Your
Kingdom? Teach me to look at my challenges and obstacles through Your eyes so
I can see the way through.

End Times Revivalists

"Now as He sat on the Mount of Olives, the disciples came to Him privately, saying, 'Tell us, when will these things be? And what will be the sign of Your coming, and of the end of the age?'"
(Matthew 24:3)

What comes to mind when I say the words "end times revival." The phrase carries all sorts of connotations, but we must first understand there's a difference between the last days and the end times. Technically, we've been in the last days since Jesus ascended to the right hand of the Father. The end times is altogether different. The end times is the end of the end.

The end times begins with the events Jesus lists in Olivet Discourse in Matthew 24. Jesus discusses the signs of the times, including wars and rumors of wars, famines, pestilences, and the like. The Book of Revelation speaks of the four horsemen of the apocalypse that represent the four types of judgment God will release at the beginning of the Tribulation.

As I write this devotional, the signs of the times are all around us. But the tribulation is not yet here. We'll see, as Isaiah prophesied, "darkness shall cover the earth, and deep darkness the people; But the Lord will arise over you, and His glory will be seen upon you. The Gentiles shall come to your light, and kings to the brightness of your rising" (Is. 60:1-2).

Before the end, we will see a great harvest. Jesus said in Matthew 24:14, "And this gospel of the kingdom will be preached in all the world as a witness to all the nations, and then the end will come." I believe before we see the final harvest, we'll see a great revival.

In his book, *The End-Time Shaking and Revival*, Guillermo Maldonado writes: "As we respond to the shaking with repentance and wholehearted devotion to God, we will be prepared to take an active role in the coming last-days revival in which God's sovereign glory will be revealed There will be an all-inclusive supernatural movement characterized by miracles, healings, salvations, financial provision, prophetic visions, renewed holiness, powerful worship, strong discipleship, and profound love."

— *Prayer* —

Father, in the name of Jesus, would You help me discern the signs of the times?
Help me watch and pray, knowing that as darkness encroaches Your light will
shine brighter. Help me to shine my light through prayer and sharing the Good
News of Jesus. Light up the path to the end times revival.

DECEMBER 13

If My People...

"If My people who are called by My name will humble themselves, and pray and seek My face, and turn from their wicked ways, then I will hear from heaven, and will forgive their sin and heal their land" (2 Chronicles 7:14)

Although 2 Chronicles 7:14 relates to Israel, I believe it holds the key not only to revival, but an awakening and transformational move of God that heals the land. Notice how it starts with "My people who are called by my name..."

Revival always starts with God's people praying and seeking the Lord with hungry hearts. It's easy to go through the motions to walk out 2 Chronicles 7:14, however it's not the volume of words but the depth of godly sorrow in our hearts that moves God to heal the land.

Christians in Cali, Colombia took this verse to heart and saw revival results. For decades, the city of Cali carried a notorious reputation as the cocaine capital of the world. No institution escaped the ruling cartel's ruthless and corrupting hand. In the mid-1990s, however, the drug lords' icy grip was finally broken when desperate believers surged into local soccer stadiums to hold all-night prayer vigils.

Likewise, Almolonga, Guatemala's "Big Carrots" community was made famous by The Sentinel Group's widely distributed *Transformations* video. Formerly a town of idolatrous and drunken brawlers, Almolonga is now a bustling, Christ-centered farming center. With eighty-five percent of its nineteen thousand inhabitants claiming a born-again experience, the secular media has dubbed it the "Ciudad de Dios," which means the City of God.

Shillong, India, is the capital of Meghalaya, one of only three Christian-majority states in India. In 1905-1906, the area experienced revival, but the fire eventually died out. A century later, local believers prayed fervently for three years that God would come again—and He did! An outpouring in 2006-2007 saw thousands converted, healed, and delivered. Distilleries closed, and children spoke forth the Word of God.

You can't argue with these results. Let's walk out 2 Chronicles 7:14, but not just with an abundance of words. Let's walk it out with a desperate heart to see God heal the land.

— *Prayer* —

Father, in the name of Jesus, teach me out to walk out 2 Chronicles 7:14.
Encourage me to adopt this assignment to see the land healed through
transforming revival. Help me to walk in humility knowing that I am helpless as a
revival agent without Your leadership.

Tozer's Revival Challenge

"Speaking the truth in love, may grow up in all things into Him who is the head—Christ—from whom the whole body, joined and knit together by what every joint supplies, according to the effective working by which every part does its share, causes growth of the body for the edifying of itself in love (2 Chronicles 7:14).

A contemporary and friend of the hard-hitting revivalist Leonard Ravenhill, A.W. Tozer was a man cut from a similar cloth. He was bold in his writings about revival. Consider these quips from the man of God who challenged us to press past self and into revival God's way.

"Have you noticed how much praying for revival has been going on of late—and how little revival has resulted?" he asked. "I believe the problem is that we have been trying to substitute praying for obeying, and it simply will not work." Indeed, does God even hear our prayers for revival when we are not obeying His commands unto revival? Selah.

"Our mistake is that we want God to send revival on our terms. We want to get the power of God into our hands, to call it to us that it may work for us in promoting and furthering our kind of Christianity," Tozer said.

"We want still to be in charge, guiding the chariot through the religious sky in the direction we want it to go, shouting 'glory to God,' but modestly accepting a share of the glory for ourselves in a nice inoffensive sort of way. We are calling on God to send fire on our altars, completely ignoring the fact that they are our altars and not God's."

Tozer once said, "I believe that the imperative need of the day is not simply revival, but a radical reformation that will go to the root of our moral and spiritual maladies and deal with causes rather than with consequences, with the disease rather than with symptoms."

Finally, Tozer opined, "Our error today is that we do not expect a converted man to be a transformed man, and as a result of this error our churches are full of substandard Christians. A revival is among other things a return to the belief that real faith invariably produces holiness of heart and righteousness of life."

Let these words convict and challenge you to rise higher!

— *Prayer* —

Father, in the name of Jesus, would You give me a bulldog tenacity to stand for the truth in a lukewarm, compromised, secular age? Help me never to compromise Your conditions for revival but to trumpet them with a bold compassion that hopes to see the saved revived and the lost saved.

DECEMBER 15

The E.M. Bounds Revivalist Anointing

"But when they did not find them, they dragged Jason and some brethren to the rulers of the city, crying out, 'These who have turned the world upside down have come here too'" (Acts 17:6).

Born in 1835, E.M. Bounds was an American author, attorney, and Methodist clergy member best known for his volumes on prayer. But much of his prayer centered on revival.

In fact, after the brush arbor revival meeting in 1857, Bounds shut down his law office and moved to Missouri to attend a seminar. Two years later he started pastoring a Methodist church at the age of 24.

Marked by awakening, he continued in prayer and led a spiritual revival in the Franklin Methodist Episcopal Church during the Civil War, where he served as a chaplain with the Confederacy. He spent a year and a half in prison after Union Troops arrested him.

As I wrote in my book, *The Intercessor's Devotional*, Bounds started writing what are now classic books on prayer at the age of 58. He also engaged deeply in intercessory prayer. Inspired by John Wesley, he prayed from 4 a.m. until 7 a.m. every day before he set out to write his books.

Bounds wrote words like these: "A revival of real praying would produce a spiritual revolution." He also said, "Every mighty move of the Spirit of God has had its source in the prayer chamber."

Bounds opined, "To look back upon the progress of the divine kingdom upon earth is to review revival periods which have come like refreshing showers upon dry and thirsty ground, making the desert to blossom as the rose, and bringing new eras of spiritual life and activity just when the Church had fallen under the influence of the apathy of the times."

Bounds understood the role of the Holy Spirit in revival, saying, "What the Church needs to-day is not more machinery or better, not new organizations or more and novel methods, but men whom the Holy Ghost can use—men of prayer, men mighty in prayer. The Holy Ghost does not flow through methods, but through men. He does not come on machinery, but on men. He does not anoint plans, but men—men of prayer."

— *Prayer* —

Father, in the name of Jesus, would You give me a revelation on the power of prayer like You gave E.M. Bounds? Moreover, give me an anointing to pray for revival and to articulate how to pray for revival like You gave Your servant Pastor Bounds. I want to pray effectively.

Rend Your Hearts, Not Your Garments

"So rend your heart, and not your garments; Return to the Lord your God, For He is gracious and merciful, Slow to anger, and of great kindness; And He relents from doing harm"
(Joel 2:13).

Throughout the pages of the Bible, we see kings, prophets and priests tear their clothes. Some even wore sackcloth and ashes as an outward demonstration of repentance and debasement. It symbolized brokenness. However, not everyone who tore their garments was truly brokenhearted.

That's why the Lord prophesied these words through Joel: "So rend your heart, and not your garments; Return to the Lord your God, for He is gracious and merciful, slow to anger, and of great kindness; And He relents from doing harm" (Joel 2:13).

The New Living Translation puts it this way, "Don't tear your clothing in your grief, but tear your hearts instead." *The Contemporary English Version* offers, "Don't rip your clothes to show your sorrow. Instead, turn back to me with broken hearts. I am merciful, kind, and caring. I don't easily lose my temper, and I don't like to punish." *The Good News Translation* puts it this way, "Let your broken heart show your sorrow; tearing your clothes is not enough."

And the *Amplified Bible* expounds on the theme: "Rip your heart to pieces [in sorrow and contrition] and not your garments. Now return [in repentance] to the Lord your God, For He is gracious and compassionate, Slow to anger, abounding in lovingkindness [faithful to His covenant with His people]; And He relents [His sentence of] evil [when His people genuinely repent]."

God is offering the same invitation to people around the world right now who compromised the revival fire in their hearts for the fleeting pleasures the world has to offer. *Matthew Henry's Commentary* puts it this way:

"There must be outward expressions of sorrow and shame, fasting, weeping, and mourning; tears for trouble must be turned into tears for the sin that caused it. But rending the garments would be vain, except their hearts were rent by abasement and self-abhorrence; by sorrow for their sins, and separation from them."

— *Prayer* —

Father, in the name of Jesus, I never want to show an outward expression of repentance without a deep sorrow in my heart for my sin and the sin in my city. Help me go deeper than outward expressions of discontent and feel the pain of Your heart so deeply that I serve as a change agent.

DECEMBER 17

Wanted: Modern-Day Hezekiahs

"In the first year of his reign, in the first month, he opened the doors of the house of the Lord and repaired them. Then he brought in the priests and the Levites, and gathered them in the East Square" (2 Chronicles 29:3-4).

Though a flawed man who saw the discipline of God later in life, King Hezekiah was behind one of the greatest revivals in Israel's history. Hezekiah was twenty-five years old when he ascended to the throne and Scripture says he did what was right in God's sight.

We read about Hezekiah's revival in 2 Chronicles. The young king moved quickly to make changes in Judah. Hezekiah's first act as king was to cleanse the temple. His second act was to make a covenant with the Lord. His third act was to restore temple worship. He reinstated the Passover celebration and made other religious reforms. Essentially, he set the nation back to Kingdom order. Hezekiah called the nation to repentance in 2 Chron. 30:6-8:

"Children of Israel, return to the Lord God of Abraham, Isaac, and Israel; then He will return to the remnant of you who have escaped from the hand of the kings of Assyria. And do not be like your fathers and your brethren, who trespassed against the Lord God of their fathers, so that He gave them up to desolation, as you see.

"Now do not be stiff-necked, as your fathers were, but yield yourselves to the Lord; and enter His sanctuary, which He has sanctified forever, and serve the Lord your God, that the fierceness of His wrath may turn away from you."

The result: People broke the sacred pillars in pieces, cut down the wooden images, and threw down the high places and the altars—from all Judah, Benjamin, Ephraim, and Manasseh—until they had utterly destroyed them all (see 2 Chron. 31:1).

Hezekiah's revival doesn't look like Pentecost. It looked like repentance and reformation—and this is important to understand because much of what is called revival today is just good worship and celebration. Hezekiah's revival led to God's favor on the nation, victory over their enemies, and the restoration of land. Revival is not always flashy. Just as often it's about our heart posture.

— Prayer —

Father, in the name of Jesus, would You give me a determination like young Hezekiah to do my part in bringing Your Kingdom to earth as it is in heaven? Teach me to war in the spirit for reformation in the natural. Empower me to roll up my sleeves and do the work of a revivalist.

Revival Hubs Rising

"And when he had found him, he brought him to Antioch. So it was that for a whole year they assembled with the church and taught a great many people. And the disciples were first called Christians in Antioch" (Acts 11:26).

Revival hubs are rising. What is a revival hub? That's a question many are asking in this hour as God breathes on this ministry model. Revival hubs are emerging and evolving and take on different flavors—and not everyone uses the term revival hub. Some call them apostolic centers, houses of prayer, missions bases, Kingdom centers, glory hubs and so on.

Although you don't see the term revival hub in the Bible, it's a new wineskin—or perhaps better called a resurrection of the original model of church—that is clearly presented in the Book of Acts. Here is the definition of a revival hub from a book I co-authored, *Revival Hubs Rising*: a center that is focused on digging and maintaining a rich well of revival and Spirit-led ministry unto equipping, awakening and societal transformation. A revival hub is a base of tactical operation, organization, and deployment.

Father is placing people in small towns and big cities to dig deep wells of revival and refreshing. He is establishing ministries that will, when they mature, serve as a hub of awakening in their region.

Radical revivalists whose heart cry is to see a Third Great Awakening will steward divine outpourings in revival hubs. The vision is not merely to build a ministry that blesses people but to release the spiritual destiny of a city or region, host the presence of God, and facilitate a radical transformation in hearts and minds that ultimately changes the spiritual climate.

What would it look like if a group of people gathered in unity and holiness to cry out to the Lord? What would it look like if people in your region began to share the Gospel with signs and wonders following? What would it look like if the church in your region was alive and fully awake to the spirit realm? What would it look like if God was encountering people in your region and drawing them to salvation? I submit to you, it would look much different than it does now.

— *Prayer* —

Father, in the name of Jesus, help me find a revival hub of people who will gather in unity and holiness to cry out to the Lord of revival. Give me a boldness to walk with a company of people who are on fire, releasing signs and wonders that prove Jesus is alive. Equip me so I can equip others.

DECEMBER 19

A New Wineskin

"Nor do they put new wine into old wineskins, or else the wineskins break, the wine is spilled, and the wineskins are ruined. But they put new wine into new wineskins, and both are preserved" (Matthew 9:17).

When revival comes, God pours new wine into new wineskins. Some churches will reject the new wine God pours out. They don't have the wineskin to receive it. We need to begin crying out now for God to help us become that new wineskin so we can receive the new wine in our churches.

Sometimes, that means we need to retool our lives or ministries. It surely means more prayer meetings and fewer board meetings. It may mean more worship and fewer workshops. It may mean more teaching on holiness rather than seeker-friendly messages. I heard the Lord say:

"I am raising up a new model, which is not a new model at all. I am causing revival-minded believers to return to the Book of Acts and giving them revelation on the original model of My Church.

"This model is a new wineskin in which I will pour out My Spirit. This model will sustain My glory because it will steward My presence. This model will focus on equipping and sending rather than gathering and grooming. This model will establish leaders, mature intercessors, and make an impact on the cities and regions in which they are established. This model will manifest both the apostolic and the prophetic and rely on five-fold gifts working in unison to advance the Kingdom.

"This model will be rejected and despised by the religious leaders of the day but make no mistake: I am working in this model. I am restoring the church to its original model. I am coming back for a church without spot or wrinkle and that means cleaning up the structure and truly preparing the Bride for Christ's return.

"Those who truly embrace this model will feel the wind of My Spirit blowing over them, My favor resting upon them, My grace empowering them, and My anointing to set the captives free and bring lost souls into the Kingdom with them. It's all in the Book of Acts, a book which has no end because you are living in it. Seek My model."

— *Prayer* —

Father, in the name of Jesus, help me to seek Your model instead of man's model for church—and for revival. Give me a hunger to live a Book of Acts lifestyle that glorifies Jesus through demonstrations of His love and power. Make me a new wineskin and ready me for the new wine.

Agonizing Conviction

"And when He has come, He will convict the world of sin, and of righteousness, and of judgment"
(John 16:8).

When conviction falls, it sometimes falls hard. But the fruit of such deep conviction is revival. Listen in to some of the stories from the greats of revival:

"In the midst of my discourse I saw a powerful looking man fall from his seat. As he sunk he groaned and then cried or shrieked out, that he was sinking to hell. He repeated that several times," writes Charles Finney, a leader in the Second Great Awakening.

"Of course this created a great excitement. It broke up my preaching; and so great was his anguish that we spent the rest of our time in praying for him. The next morning I inquired for him; and found that he had spent a sleepless night in great anguish of mind."

William Carvosso, a Wesleyan leader in the 18th and 19th century, wrote: "I had not spoken many words to her before she burst into tears and loud cries. She continued to groan under the weight of her guilty load. The cries and wailings of her broken heart were deeply affecting."

In the memoir of William Bramwell, an English Methodist itinerant preacher in the 18th and 19th century, we read:.

"The Spirit of the Lord was poured out abundantly and many cried aloud for mercy. Near the close he was like a flame of fire; the people burst into tears on every side, and could say, 'Lo, God is here, of a truth! 'Many cried, yea groaned, aloud for mercy, and God delivered them.

"Many were deeply convicted and cried out for mercy; an old woman about seventy years of age, was struck in a moment. She fell to the ground, making a frightful noise, and continued speechless and in an agony for above an hour. When she came to herself she jumped off the chair on which she had been placed, clapped her hands, and praised the Lord."

— *Prayer* —

Father, in the name of Jesus, let my heart agonize over what agonizes Your heart. Help me never to be desensitized to the sinful world around me and the reality that millions of people are on a highway to hell. Teach me to pray with Your heart for the revival You want to bring.

DECEMBER 21

The Man with Calloused Knees

"For this reason I bow my knees to the Father of our Lord Jesus Christ, from whom the whole family in heaven and earth is named, that He would grant you, according to the riches of His glory, to be strengthened with might through His Spirit in the inner man" (Ephesians 3:14-21).

They called him the man with calloused knees—and would that every revivalist was called such. His name was John Smith, a common name for an uncommon revivalist. He lived from 1794 to 1831, born to a fervent preacher of the Gospel. Although he only lived thirty-one years, he made a mark on revival history through his intercession.

"Constant communion with God was at the foundation of Mr. Smith's great usefulness. In this he was surpassed by none of any age," wrote David Smithers in *Old Paths* magazine. "Whole nights were often given up to prayer. He arose at four o'clock in the morning, and throwing himself before the mercy-seat, for three hours wrestled with God in mighty prayer…"

There's something about praying on your knees. It's a powerful exercise that demonstrates humility. Scripture says every knee will bow to Jesus one day. Praying on your knees is bowing our hearts to Him, acknowledging our helplessness and our heart to obey His commands.

Praying this way, especially for long periods, is uncomfortable at best. But John Wesley wore grooves in the wood at his prayer altar—and we know the fruit of his prayer life. He, too, had calloused knees.

"Immediately after breakfast and family worship he would again retire with his Bible into his study, and spend until near noon in the same hallowed employment," Smithers writes. "Here unquestionably was the great secret of his power in public prayer and in preaching. The Lord who sees in secret, rewarded him openly. Every sermon was sanctified by prayer."

Jesus, at times, prayed on His knees. Peter knelt down to pray and saw a miracle. Solomon knelt down to pray after the temple was completed. All prayer is powerful. But there is something about consistently praying on your knees. It's as if our hearts are bowing before Him in worship as our mouths utter our petitions.

— *Prayer* —

Father, in the name of Jesus, would You give me a deeper revelation of the power of praying on my knees? Remind me to bow a knee to You in prayer. Teach me the power of praying with a bended knee and a bended heart. I want to unlock the secret of praying on my knees for revival.

The Southern Revivalist

"Adulterers and adulteresses! Do you not know that friendship with the world is enmity with God? Whoever therefore wants to be a friend of the world makes himself an enemy of God"
(James 4:4).

You might say there would be no Billy Graham without Mordecai Ham (1877-1961). Ham was one of the best-known preachers in American's south during his days, and three-hundred thousand people were converted in his crusade meetings.

The Kentucky-born Ham said things like, "There are a lot of Christians who are halfway fellows. They stand in the door, holding on to the Church with one hand while they play with the toys of the world with the other. They are in the doorway, and we can't bring sinners in."

As history tells it, Ham was grieved about the "den of inquiry," a house across the street from a local high school where sexual immorality among young people was raging. Ham was preaching against it and Billy Graham was nominated to go check out his meetings. Despite the hard-hitting messages on sin, Graham went back night after night. A. young Billy Graham accepted Jesus in Ham's meeting in North Carolina in 1934.

The man whose preaching spanned six decades said things like, "Now they always accuse me of carrying around a sledge hammer with which to pound the church members. Yes sir, I do pound them, every time I come down, I knock one of the halfway fellows out of the doorway, and every time I knock one out I get a sinner in."

Ham boldly confronted spiritual deadness in churches. With such bold words, it's no surprise this Southern revivalist had bitter enemies. One such enemy attacked him on the way out of his hotel room. He was struck on the back of his head from behind. But that didn't stop him.

"We want a revival to come just in our way," Ham said. "You never saw two revivals come just alike. We must let them come in God's way. People are ashamed to admit they need a revival."

— *Prayer* —

Father, in the name of Jesus, I am not ashamed to admit I need revival. Help me not to stand by idly while believers backslide, and sinners fall by the wayside. Give me a bold-as-a-lion anointing that loves the sinner but hates the sin—and confronts with truth and grace everything that hinders revival.

DECEMBER 23

The Saint Patrick Revivalist Anointing

"Behold, I send you out as sheep in the midst of wolves. Therefore be wise as serpents and harmless as doves" (Matthew 10:15-16).

St. Patrick's legacy has been smeared by a holiday that gets you pinched if you don't wear green on March 17. Many don't know him as a revivalist and a reformer. Born in Fifth Century Britain, Patrick was considered the apostle of Ireland and brought Christianity to the nation.

Born into a Christian family, Patrick landed in Ireland after Irish raiders kidnapped him and carried him into slavery. For six years, he served as a herdsman. But the captivity only fueled his faith in God. Patrick escaped for a short time but was captured a second time before his ultimate release.

"Daily I expect to be murdered or betrayed or reduced to slavery if the occasion arises," Patrick said. "But I fear nothing, because of the promises of heaven."

In a vision, God called Patrick to return to Ireland for the work of the ministry. One might understand why he would be reluctant to do obey that command. He wrote, "And there I saw in the night the vision of a man...coming as it were from Ireland, with countless letters. And he gave me one of them, and I read the opening words of the letter, which were, the voice of the Irish...and thus did they cry out as with one mouth: We ask thee, boy, come and walk among us once more."

Patrick set out for Ireland with little confidence in himself but much confidence in the Lord. Like the apostle Paul, he lived in constant danger of martyrdom. Nevertheless, he persevered. He planted a church in 432 A.D. on the site of the present-day St. Patrick's Memorial Church in Saul. It was the first-ever Christian church in the nation.

Patrick's ministry spanned twenty-nine years. He ultimately planted over three hundred churches and baptized over one hundred twenty Irishmen. Rev. Sean Brady told CBN News, "He was a man who came to face and help his former enemies who had enslaved him. He came back to help them and to do them a great favor— the greatest favor he possibly could."

— *Prayer* —

Father, in the name of Jesus, help me rethink how I see St. Patrick. Teach me how to be self-less as a bondservant to Christ. Give me the courage to face enemies of the cross with a love. Put in me a determined spirit to see Your will done in my city and nation.

The Shantung Revival

"Moreover Josiah put away those who consulted mediums and spiritists, the household gods and idols, all the abominations that were seen in the land of Judah and in Jerusalem..."
(2 Kings 23:23).

It goes down in church history as a revival that touched every province in China. Given the vastness of the Asian nation, it's a remarkable move of the Holy Spirit—and it was Southern Baptists who stewarded the Pentecost-like revival.

Indeed, although many Baptists today reject the baptism of the Holy Spirit, Baptist missionaries to Shantung believed fully in the infilling of the Holy Ghost. It's hard to deny something you experience for yourself.

"In the revival here at Huangxian last spring, the Bible school came in for a great blessing. Every one of the faculty got a distinct blessing, and nearly every one of them was filled with the Holy Spirit. It has become a new school," writes C. L. Culpepper in *The Shantung Revival.*

One must understand the conditions of China in those days. The nation was facing tumultuous times. The churches were indifferent, complacent, cold, and many were empty. A great number of missionaries walked away because the territory was so hard. The missionaries who stayed saw a deep spiritual need for a true encounter with Christ.

"The Holy Spirit fell in great power upon the Southern Baptist missionaries and Chinese believers at Huangxian, and they cried out in prayer for four days and four nights. Everyone present came under conviction and confessed their sins. Toward the end of the meeting, the Chinese Christians told the missionaries, 'We thought you considered yourselves above us. Now we are all one,'" Eloise Glass Cauthen wrote in *Higher Ground.*

Like all revivals, the Shantung revival was birthed in prayer. The cry was, "Lord, revive Thy Church, beginning with me." The revival broke out in 1927 in Chefoo during meetings held by Norwegian Lutheran missionary Marie Monsen. Monsen had seen healings in her ministry and it was no different in Shantung. God showed up. The revival at Shantung saw people saved, healed and delivered. Churches grew and so did Bible College enrollments. The Chinese destroyed their family idols.

— *Prayer* —

Father, in the name of Jesus, do it again in China! Give me a heart for the church of China, where so many believers are hidden underground for fear of persecution. Give me a prayer burden for the church in Asia, knowing that nothing is too hard for You. You want to bring revival.

Jesus is Revival

"And the Word became flesh and dwelt among us, and we beheld His glory, the glory as of the only begotten of the Father, full of grace and truth" (John 1:14).

"God is one pent-up revival," Leonard Ravenhill.

People define revival in so many ways—and many of them are right and good. But if you had to boil it down to the foundation, Jesus is revival. If the revival is not Christ-centered, it's not a revival at all. Consider the words of the apostle Paul in this light from Colossians 1:15-20:

"He is the image of the invisible God, the firstborn over all creation. For by Him all things were created that are in heaven and that are on earth, visible and invisible, whether thrones or dominions or principalities or powers. All things were created through Him and for Him.

"And He is before all things, and in Him all things consist. And He is the head of the body, the church, who is the beginning, the firstborn from the dead, that in all things He may have the preeminence. For it pleased the Father that in Him all the fullness should dwell, and by Him to reconcile all things to Himself, by Him, whether things on earth or things in heaven, having made peace through the blood of His cross."

Jesus is revival and Jesus should have the preeminence in every revival. Remember, one of the Holy Spirit's roles is to exalt Jesus. When someone is exalted, they have preeminence. Preeminence means to be first, hold first place, have paramount rank, dignity or importance. It means to be supreme.

Bill Johnson, senior leader of Bethel, put it this way, "Jesus is revival personified… Revival is rediscovering the beauty and wonder of Jesus. He, through the working of the Holy Spirit, comes to the forefront of our thinking once again in every great move of God. For me it is His power, His love, His wisdom, and His purity. Those four things express to me who Jesus is. And they express the nature of revival."

— *Prayer* —

Father, in the name of Jesus, help me see You as the all in all. Help me to see You as the revival that I need—that my church, my city, my nation, and the world needs. Grace me to press into a Christ-centered revival where the Holy Spirit moves freely, saves souls, heals bodies and works miracles.

Staying on Fire for God

"For our God is a consuming fire" (Hebrews 12:29).

Once revival fire hits your soul, the enemy will surely come to put out your fire. He'll use circumstances, vain imaginations, raging emotions, sickness—and people—to quench that fire. Here's three words of advice: Don't let him. Determine now that you will stay on fire for God come hell or high water.

But how do you do that? How do you stay on fire for God after the wave of revival passes? Stay as desperate now as you were before the revival fire was poured out. The hunger that fueled your personal or corporate revival will fuel a fire on the altar that never goes out. We need to live in a state of desperation—total dependence on Him.

When we're desperate, our prayer life will swell. We won't stand for prayerlessness but will stand and pray without ceasing. We'll pray in the spirit and with our understanding. We'll pray day and night. We'll pray with holy hands lifted up. We'll pray everywhere and at all times. Prayer will be like breathing and the breath of the Holy Spirit will stoke the flames of the fire within us. Our first instinct when something goes wrong will be prayer.

When we're desperate we'll keep ourselves stirred up in the Holy Spirit whether we feel like it or not. We'll walk by faith, not by our fickle emotions that are up one day and down the next. We'll lean on Him and not our own understanding and acknowledge Him in all our ways.

When we're desperate we'll avoid the Martha mindset that stays too busy to be fruitful. We'll adopt the Mary mindset that sits at the feet of Jesus and hangs on His every word. When we're desperate, we'll stay in the Word and let it correct us, renew our minds, edify us, comfort us, challenge us, lead us and guide us.

The desperate soul has one desire: to dwell in His presence and inquire in His temple. With that mindset, you can't lose your revival fire. It will only burn brighter and attract others to Jesus with His eyes like flaming fire.

— *Prayer* —

Father, in the name of Jesus, help me steward this revival fire. Help me not compromise the fire that You have ignited within me. Help me fan the flames. Help me stay desperate. Help me stay focused on You. You are my one thing. Remind me to gaze into Your fiery eyes of love.

DECEMBER 27
Revival Glory in the Harbor

"For the earth will be filled with the knowledge of the glory of the Lord, as the waters cover the sea" (Habakkuk 2:14).

During Jeremiah Lanphier's Layman's Revival of 1857, the fire spread to other continents—but not before touching the ports of New York City.

Revival historian J. Edwin Orr chronicled how the Spirit of God moved upon the face of the waters, and a multitude of seamen saw a great light. It was as if a vast cloud of blessing hovered over the land and sea. And ships, as they drew near the American ports, came within the zone of heavenly influence. Orr writes:

"The North Carolina—a battleship of the United States Navy—lay in the harbor of New York. Her complement was about a thousand men. Amongst these were four Christians who discovered their spiritual kinship and agreed to meet for prayer. They were permitted to use a very retired part of the ship, on a deck far below the water line. Here, then, they gathered one evening. They were only four men, but they were a united band. They represented three denominations, one being an Episcopalian, another a Presbyterian, while two were Baptists."

As Orr tells it, these four men were so touched by the Holy Spirit they burst out in song. The sound rose to the decks above and what happened next was revival. Their unsaved shipmates came running down to mock the demonstration of God's power, but the Holy Spirit gripped them and they entered into repentance.

"Great fellows, giants in stature, and many of them giants in sin, were literally smitten down, and knelt humbly beside the four, like little children. A most gracious work straightway began in the depths of the great ship," Orr wrote. "Night after night the prayer meeting was held, and conversions took place daily. Soon they had to send ashore for help, and ministers joyfully came out to assist. A large number were added to the various churches, and the battleship became a veritable House of God!"

— Prayer —

Father, in the name of Jesus, help me believe not just for revival in the land, but revival in the sea—and revival in the air. You are an omnipresent God. You can encounter hearts with Your revival fire anywhere. Help me pray audacious prayers for Your Spirit to move upon all creation.

The Fruit of Revival

"You did not choose Me, but I chose you and appointed you that you should go and bear fruit, and that your fruit should remain, that whatever you ask the Father in My name He may give you" (John 15:16).

Just like repentance, revival should bear fruit. What is the fruit of revival? Charles Spurgeon, the prince of preachers, offered this wisdom on the fruit of revival in the lives of people:

"It simply brings them to the condition in which they ought always to have been; it quickens them, gives them new life, stirs the coals of the expiring fire, and puts heavenly breath into the languid lungs. The sickly soul which before was insensible, weak, and sorrowful, grows earnest, vigorous, and happy in the Lord. This is the immediate fruit of revival, and it becomes all of us who are believers to seek this blessing for backsliders, and for ourselves if we are declining in grace."

Holiness is a fruit of true revival, for who can receive a touch from the spirit of Holy and not be made more holy? In revival, pursue holiness without which no one can see the Lord (see Heb. 12:14).

Passion for Jesus is a fruit of revival, for who can encounter the Christ, experience His passionate love for them and not be moved with passion for Christ? In His passion, He died for us so we could live with passion for Him. Compassion is a fruit of revival, for who can have a passion for Christ without also carrying a compassion for the lost?

Obedience is a fruit of revival, for who can but obey the One who loves them and the One whom they love with all of their heart, mind, soul and strength? Forgiveness is a fruit of revival, for who can hold a grudge against man when God has forgiven him of so much.

The fruit of the Spirit is the fruit of revival in a believer who has encountered the Holy One: "But the fruit of the Spirit is love, joy, peace, longsuffering, kindness, goodness, faithfulness, gentleness, self-control" (Gal. 5:22-23).

— Prayer —

Father, in the name of Jesus, would help me bear the fruit of revival in my heart? Help me manifest the fruit of the Spirit and put it on display for the souls who don't yet know You. Ignite in me a burning passion for Your heart and for the concerns of Your heart. I choose to follow You.

DECEMBER 29

The Power of Testimony

"And they overcame him by the blood of the Lamb and by the word of their testimony, and they did not love their lives to the death" (Revelation 12:11).

Revival history tells of outpourings that, while birthed in prayer, were often ignited by testimonies. Consider the Welsh Revival. Florrie Evans testified to a group of teenagers and young adults: "What does the Lord Jesus Christ mean to you?" Her heartfelt answer set heart ablaze: 'If no one else will, then I must say that I love the Lord Jesus Christ with all my heart.'"

David testified to the goodness of God over and over and over. Psalm 27:25 tells us, "I have been young, and now am old; Yet I have not seen the righteous forsaken, nor his descendants begging bread. He is ever merciful, and lends; and his descendants are blessed."

What's your testimony of Jesus? What has He done for you that no one else could? What's your story of His love? The world is waiting to hear it.

God's Word encourages us to share our testimonies. Peter put it this way: "But honor the Messiah as Lord in your hearts. Always be ready to give a defense to anyone who asks you for a reason for the hope that is in you" (1 Pet. 3:15). Our testimonies inspire hope in the hearts of those who are going through hard times—and even those who don't know the Lord. David said, "I will tell of your name to my brothers; in the midst of the congregation I will praise you" (Ps. 22:22, ESV).

Someone needs to hear your testimony. I got saved listening to someone's testimony about how they overcame a heroin addiction. I love stories. It's scientifically proven that we learn and retain information through stories. Stories intrigue us. That's why we like to go to movies and read books or watch TV.

Your testimony is your story—and it's a compelling story even if it doesn't seem so to you. Your story will touch and move people's heart to believe in God and His Word unto salvation. Ultimately, your testimony gives glory to God and builds faith in God to bring revival.

— *Prayer* —

Father, in the name of Jesus, would You help me to share my story of Your saving grace, keeping power, and healing work in my life? Teach me how to articulate my story in a way that pierces hearts and demonstrates Your kindness and love so they, too, will want to know You like I do.

If We Do Not Wake Up

"They profess to know God, but in works they deny Him, being abominable, disobedient, and disqualified for every good work" (Titus 1:16).

There are dire consequences for falling asleep at the wheel, and I fear too many believers—even some leaders in the church—have dozed off on the highway of life while breaking the speed limit. If backslidden Christians don't wake up to their spiritual condition, a crash is inevitable. That crash is called The Great Falling Away.

Paul prophesied a great apostasy and that prophesy cannot be prayed away. Just as masses will turn to Jesus before His Second Coming in a final harvest, masses will become offended and turn away from Him. Working for the Lord is not the same as working with the Lord. Now that you have fresh fire, it's time for you to help others. Jesus offered these words in Revelation 3:1-3 (AMP):

"These are the words of Him who has the seven Spirits of God and the seven stars: 'I know your deeds; you have a name (reputation) that you are alive, but [in reality] you are dead. Wake up, and strengthen and reaffirm what remains [of your faithful commitment to Me], which is about to die; for I have not found [any of] your deeds completed in the sight of My God or meeting His requirements.

"So remember and take to heart the lessons you have received and heard. Keep and obey them, and repent [change your sinful way of thinking, and demonstrate your repentance with new behavior that proves a conscious decision to turn away from sin]. So then, if you do not wake up, I will come like a thief, and you will not know at what hour I will come to you."

Revivalist, be an agent of awakening. Preach the Gospel in season and out of season. Share your testimony with believers and unbelievers alike. Lay hands on the sick and watch them recover. Step out in risky faith. Be the salt and light. Burn and shine for Him.

— *Prayer* —

Father, in the name of Jesus, I want to be fully awake—and stay awake—to Your presence. I want to know Your perfect will in all things and release intercession that brings revival to the earth. Remind me to pray at all times and build myself up in my most holy faith for the task at hand.

DECEMBER 31

The Ultimate Goal of Revival

"That He might present her to Himself a glorious church, not having spot or wrinkle or any such thing, but that she should be holy and without blemish" (Ephesians 5:27).

Jesus is coming back for a glorious church. I see the foreshadow of the glorious church rising in the midst of world crises. I see the foreshadow of the glorious church awakening in the nations. I see the foreshadow of the glorious church making intercession.

Ephesians 5:26-27 tells us Jesus loved the church and gave Himself for her, that He might sanctify and cleanse her with the washing of water by the Word, that He might present her to Himself a glorious church, not having spot or wrinkle or any such thing, but that she should be holy and without blemish.

The glorious church is birthed in revival and matured in the awakening unto transformation. What does the glorious church look like?

The glorious church is a consecrated church. The glorious church consecrates herself, cooperating with ongoing sanctification that transforms each member from glory to glory. The consecrated church accepts her highest calling to be transformed into the image of Christ.

The glorious church is a unified church. The five-fold ministry we see right now is "until something." Ephesians 4:11 expounds upon this: "And He Himself gave some to be apostles, some prophets, some evangelists, and some pastors and teachers, for the equipping of the saints for the work of ministry, for the edifying of the body of Christ, till we all come to the unity of the faith…"

The glorious church is a triumphant church. Paul tells us in 2 Corinthians 2:14-15, "Now thanks be to God who always leads us in triumph in Christ, and through us diffuses the fragrance of His knowledge in every place. For we are to God the fragrance of Christ among those who are being saved and among those who are perishing."

The triumphant church is a church that has resisted the enemy's temptations to enter lukewarm Christianity. The triumphant church is a church that has maintained its first love to the end.

— Prayer —

Father, in the name of Jesus, would You help me get my eyes off the Bride and onto the Bridegroom when I get frustrated with the ways of the church? Help me set my mind on things above, and see the church through Your eyes of love so that I will labor in prayer for Your revival.

394

ABOUT JENNIFER LECLAIRE

Jennifer LeClaire is senior leader of Awakening House of Prayer in Fort Lauderdale, Florida, founder of the Ignite Network, and founder of the Awakening Prayer Hubs prayer movement. Jennifer formerly served as the first-ever female editor of *Charisma* magazine and is a prolific author of over 50 books. You can find Jennifer online at www.jenniferleclaire.org. Get equipped at School of the Spirit at www.schoolofthespirit.tv.

Visit her South Florida church at www.awakeninghouseofprayer.com.

JOIN THE PRAYER MOVEMENT

Awakening Prayer Hubs is a prayer movement with a heart to see souls saved, churches revived and nations awakened. We have hundreds of prayer hubs in nations all over the world. Our prayer hub leaders are equipped and resourced to succeed as prayer furnaces in their cities.

Launch a hub, join a hub, or sponsor a hub at www.awakeningprayerhubs.com.

GET EQUIPPED FOR THE CALL

At School of the Spirit, you'll find an in-depth selection of courses on prayer, spiritual warfare, deliverance and prophetic ministry, creative arts, Christian living and more. There's never been a better time to invest in yourself. Go deeper into the things of God with me and students from all over the world. Get equipped at www.3choolofthespirit.tv.

Printed in the USA
CPSIA information can be obtained
at www.ICGtesting.com
LVHW021308301223
767800LV00006B/104